Building Prosperous Knowledge Cities

This book is dedicated to the rapidly and strongly emerging Global Knowledge Based Development Community, and our beloved families

Building Prosperous Knowledge Cities

Policies, Plans and Metrics

Edited by

Tan Yigitcanlar

Queensland University of Technology, Australia

Kostas Metaxiotis

University of Piraeus, Greece

Francisco Javier Carrillo

Tecnologico de Monterrey, Mexico

Edward Elgar

Cheltenham, UK • Northampton, MA, USA

Published by
Edward Elgar Publishing Limited
The Lypiatts
15 Lansdown Road
Cheltenham
Glos GL50 2JA
UK

Edward Elgar Publishing, Inc.
William Pratt House
9 Dewey Court
Northampton
Massachusetts 01060
USA

A catalogue record for this book
is available from the British Library

Library of Congress Control Number: 2011932941

MIX
Paper from
responsible sources
FSC® C018575
FSC
www.fsc.org

ISBN 978 0 85793 603 5

Typeset by Servis Filmsetting Ltd, Stockport, Cheshire
Printed and bound by MPG Books Group, UK

Contents

PART III METRICS FOR BUILDING PROSPEROUS KNOWLEDGE CITIES

Contributors

Kristina Vaarst Andersen, Department of Innovation and Organizational Economics, Copenhagen Business School, Denmark

Björn T. Asheim, Department of Human Geography, University of Lund, Sweden

Bhishna Bajracharya, Institute of Sustainable Development and Architecture, Bond University, Australia

Francisco Javier Carrillo, Center for Knowledge Systems, Tecnologico de Monterrey, Mexico

Santiago Cavazos, Department of Information Technology Administration, Monterrey University of Technology, Mexico

Gülnur Çevikayak, Department of City and Regional Planning, Izmir Institute of Technology, Turkey

Anne Dornan, Knowledge Capital, Manchester, UK

Kostas Ergazakis, School of Electrical and Computer Engineering, National Technical University of Athens, Greece

Ana Cristina Fachinelli, Department of Graduate Programs in Business Administration, University of Caxias do Sul, Brazil

Ana María Fernández-Maldonado, Department of Urbanizm, Delft University of Technology, The Netherlands

Ricardo Emmanuel Flores, Center for Knowledge Systems, Monterrey University of Technology, Mexico

Peter Franz, Halle Institute for Economic Research, Germany

Blanca C. Garcia, Northern Borderlands Research College, Mexico

Cathy Garner, Knowledge Capital, Manchester, UK

Octavio González, Department of Information Technology Administration, Monterrey University of Technology, Mexico

Greg Hearn, Center for Creative Industries and Innovation, Queensland University of Technology, Australia

Caren Heidemann, Department of Urban Planning and Development, Municipality of Essen, Germany

Richard Hu, Faculty of Business and Government, University of Canberra, Australia

Joan K. Imukuka, Institute of Sustainable Development and Architecture, Bond University, Australia

Kevin Johnson, Geografia, Australia

Klaus R. Kunzmann, School of Planning, Technical University of Dortmund, Germany

Stine Laursen, London School of Economics and Political Science, UK

Alicia Leal, Industrial Engineering Department, Monterrey University of Technology, Mexico

Rainer Lisowski, Department of Urban Planning and Development, City of Oldenburg, Germany

Mark Lorenzen, Department of Innovation and Organizational Economics, Copenhagen Business School, Denmark

Janaína Macke, Department of Graduate Programs in Business Administration, University of Caxias do Sul, Brazil

América Martínez, Department of Information Technology Administration, Monterrey University of Technology, Mexico

Kirsten Martinus, Department of Urban and Regional Planning, Curtin University of Technology, Australia

Kostas Metaxiotis, Department of Informatics, University of Piraeus, Greece

Clas Meyer, Faculty of Business and Social Sciences, University of Applied Sciences, Osnabrück, Germany

Kevin O'Connor, Faculty of Architecture, Building and Planning, University of Melbourne, Australia

James A. Powell, Pro-Vice-Chancellor for Enterprise and Regional Affairs, Universities of Salford, UK

Glen Searle, School of Geography, Planning and Environmental Management, University of Queensland, Australia

Linda Too, Institute of Sustainable Development and Architecture, Bond University, Australia

Koray Velibeyoğlu, Department of City and Regional Planning, Izmir Institute of Technology, Turkey

Klaus Wermker, Department of Urban Development, University of Duisburg, Germany

Stefanie Wesselmann, Faculty of Business and Social Sciences, University of Applied Sciences at Osnabrück, Germany

Joris van Wezemael, Department of Geosciences, University of Fribourg, Switzerland

Rodolfo Wilhelmy, Department of Information Technology Administration, Monterrey University of Technology, Mexico

Tan Yigitcanlar, School of Urban Development, Queensland University of Technology, Australia

Foreword

Competing: important stimuli for knowledge cities to become prosperous

Peter Franz

KNOWLEDGE CITIES: ONLY BY CHANCE?

There is a common sense that amongst the cities that have decided to pursue a 'knowledge city' developmental strategy, those housing universities and research institutes dispose of an advantageous endowment for this strategy. There is a growing number of 'virtual universities', but as long as the vast majority of universities and research institutes locate within the jurisdictions of towns and cities, this potential advantage will continue to exist. On the other side it has to be stated that the sheer fact of science institutions existing in a city is not a sufficient condition for strategic 'knowledge cities' action. Activities like these are still a rare exception. The normal state of affairs is a 'living side by side' of a primarily locally oriented city administration and a science institution with a predominant global, or at least extra-regional, orientation. Since spatial transport costs for bits and bytes have shrunk to a negligible size, the next place to connect with may be a foreign university in the far distance, but where the fellow scholars are dealing with the same puzzles of the discipline. The more the scientific staffs are linked with the global scientific community, the more local rootedness remains isolated and neglected. In some countries, such as Germany, the publicly financed universities and research institutes – as corporations under public law - are even exempted from their duties as land tax payers. This means that the cities gain economically only indirectly by the expenditure of the staff and the students among local retailers and services, but only insofar as they reside within the city region.

An initial situation like this will raise the question of what events or forces may help to overcome this 'living side by side' without consequences for urban development. Sometimes an individual may walk on stage, driven by a special mission or conviction that universities should engage more in political or economic issues of the city region. Or a mayor, perhaps a graduate of the university in the town, builds up an idea that some university departments might hold knowledge valuable for the solution of pressing urban problems, and thus starts communication with scientists in those departments. If convictions like these come up with a sort of charismatic leadership this could be a recipe to overcome the suboptimal 'steady state' of institutional inertia in specific cases. Such processes take place by chance – they are based on a special constellation of local conditions, and elude systematic political intervention. Considering this unsatisfactory situation, a plea is made in the following sections for more profound scrutiny of the suitability of competitive procedures as a potential path to a more systematic transition to a 'knowledge cities' strategy.

POLITICAL INTERVENTION BY MEANS OF COMPETITIONS

Nowadays, after a financial crisis attributed partly to deregulation trends forced by exponents of neoliberal thinking, advocates of competitive procedures have to be prepared for harsh criticism, as their plea can be interpreted as an argument for increasing penetration of everyday life by elements of the economic sphere. The arguments to follow demonstrate that such reproaches of commodification and 'economic imperialism' are unfounded in the present case.

From the viewpoint of political science, competitive procedures present several promising features for flexible handling. In many modern societies the political system can be described as a multi-level system with (at least) national, regional and municipal dimensions. According to the 'from government to governance' debate a multitude of studies indicate the dwindling usefulness of traditional hierarchical measures for the attainment of complex political goals. A knowledge city development strategy can hardly be initiated by top-down command; it requires the voluntary involvement of a vast number of actors at different political levels. In contrast to that in launching competitions, the higher-level political actor replaces command with strategic 'management by objectives', places confidence in regional or urban self-organization, and in the ability of local actors to identify crucial local strengths. The act of publishing a call for tenders implies political framing through (1) the delimitation of the target group of competitors, (2) setting the standards for the desired deliverables from the competitors, and (3) setting incentives for the succeeding competitors. Simultaneously it is the initiator's task to point out a transparent and understandable evaluation procedure for the contributions of the competitors.

Beyond that, can interventions in the shape of competitions be brought into play, not only by political actors representing public government, but also by other actors such as NGOs, non-profit organizations, or regional development agencies? A precondition for such actors to apply this measure is their legitimacy, perceived by the public, to be active and to pursue political goals in the subject area in question. Last but not least, an organization's capability to endow their calls for tender with sufficient financial and/or reputational incentives has to be mentioned.

From the view of economics, competition is primarily conceived as a general mechanism that helps societies or economies find the way to an efficient organization of production and consumption. This theory of competition as a discovery procedure goes back to Hayek ([1968] 2002). To become effective, competition is in need of the constitutional environment of a free market society. This interpretation of competition as a continuous mechanism differs from the view of competition as a spatially and chronologically restricted (confined) measure.

Both views, however, agree with the function of competition as a mode to discover new and yet unknown potentials and solutions. This feature might be a reason for the relatively frequent application of competitions as a measure in innovation policy and in regional policy. As a rule, political interventions in this domain are based on the innovation systems approach (Lundvall 1992; Cooke 1998). According to this approach a region's innovativeness is dependent on the networking and cooperation of a variety of actors (amongst them firms, universities, chambers, technology transfer units, patent commercialization agencies). In this context competitions are expected to stimulate (a) intensified information flow and division of labour in existing networks, (b) the foundation of new industry or technology networks, or (c) new R&D bi- or multilateral cooperation between regional actors. Frequently these processes are summarized under the heading of 'cluster formation'. Systematic evaluations of competitions in the domain of innovation policy have shown an enhanced cooperation and communication between the participating regional key actors (Dohse 2000). In several cases the activities stimulated by the prospective incentives continued after terminated competition even on the side of the non-winners, and some submitted projects were realized without additional grants (Eickelpasch and Fritsch 2005). Results like these indicate that the measure of competitions is suited for the activation of endogenous potentials in regions with a relatively low level of innovative activities.

COMPETITIONS AS TRIGGERS FOR KNOWLEDGE CITIES STRATEGIES

With the general reflections from the section above in mind, we now can return to the topic of knowledge cities. The screening of science policy and urban development policy in diverse countries arrives at the conclusion (result) that already some competitions have been practised at the national and at the international level. There is a yearly nationwide 'City of Science' competition in Germany, held since 2005 (see Wesselmann et al. in this volume; Hohn and Meyer 2011), and a yearly worldwide 'Most Admired Knowledge City' (MAKCi Awards) competition organized by the World Capital Institute (WCI), a non-profit professional organization having organized also four 'Knowledge Cities World Summits' since 2007. Within the EU context a group of larger European cities with 123 full and 17 associated members called 'EUROCITIES' offers a yearly award for one of the member cities. The applications have to be submitted by local government authorities (http://www.eurocities.eu/main.php; accessed 10 February 2011).

These international and national competitions are complemented by calls for tenders with a local focus. Frequently they center around the development of a special science quarter, campus or district within the territory of a larger city. Similar to other urban development projects they involve the task of combining elements of architectural, public transport, social and economic planning to a concise development concept. An example of this type of competition is the 'International ideas competition' for a science city in Copenhagen, issued by the University of Copenhagen and the Danish University Property Agency in 2010 (http://campus.ku.dk/english/vidensbydel/ideas_competition/; accessed 10 February 2011). Silberberger et al. (2010) refer to the fact that these 'design competitions' force the competitors to compile pieces of knowledge from diverse subfields and to combine them in a practicable 'know-how' proposal. Thus the submitted proposals help to advance promising 'knowledge city' strategies, and even the discursive processes of the juries by 'selecting, rejecting, evaluating, critically considering possibilities, good or bad designs and future scenarios' (ibid., p. 293) can be conceived as contributions to this kind of knowledge creation.

Whereas competitions of the Copenhagen type strive primarily for development concepts from professional planners – similar to architectural competitions – other ones are launched as a trigger for the activation of actors from different local subsystems (economy, science, local politics, education), and so are more similar to competitions in innovation policy. Local actors, as yet un- or under-connected, are expected to develop commitment and to cooperate for the product – in most cases an outline for a local knowledge city strategy – to be submitted. As the following section shows, this desired networking effect becomes an especially important precondition for urban contexts with *several* universities and/or research institutes.

Networking serves as an opener for further add-on effects to take place. In the course of networking activities new synergies, undiscovered until now, may be realized. Continued networking helps to strengthen the identification of outstanding actors with their city and may lead to enduring constellations capable of quick collective response even in the post-competition phase and with regard to new problems. This 'activation effect' may occur in any cities taking part in the competition, and not only in the winner cities.

SCIENCE-SPECIFIC COMPETITIONS: COMPETING FOR EXCELLENCE

Based on the principle of science as a public good nearly all countries finance their (public) universities with budgetary resources. Besides this basic funding more and more countries have started since the 1990s to practice complementary modes of university financing. With this new strategy governments try to stimulate the universities to produce higher quality research and teaching. A common feature of these new modes of financing is their selective nature. Only those universities that pass a systematic evaluation (criterion: scientific achievement in the past) successfully (Gläser 2007), or present the best concepts for future academic activities, get the benefit of complementary grants. The usual arrangement for the latter mode of financing takes place in the form of competitions, e.g. initiatives for excellence. Examples for these are 'Brain Korea 21' (Moon and Kim 2001), the program 'Centers of Excellence' of the Australian Research Council (http://www.arc.gov.au/ncgp/ce/ce_default.htm; accessed 4 March 2011) or the recent 'Exzellenzinitiative' (Leibfried 2010) in Germany.

In Germany this new initiative mobilized 70 universities submitting 253 concepts for graduate schools, 283 concepts for (research) excellence clusters and 47 action plans for the future (Neidhardt 2010). A remarkable networking effect of the 'Exzellenzinitiative' was the – in Germany unusual up until that time – cooperation between universities and non-university research institutes who had to pool their resources in order to demonstrate a 'critical mass' in their plans for excellence clusters. Another effect was the partial adoption of this competition on the national level by the Land governments at the federal level. These Land-specific regulations oblige universities (full universities and universities of applied sciences) in the respective Land to compete for additional grants. In the case of Saxony-Anhalt, the framing agreement between the government and the universities stresses the cooperation with non-university research institutes and the cooperation with private firms in Saxony-Anhalt as important preconditions for eligibility (http://www.sachsen-anhalt.de/index.php?id=47926; accessed 4 March 2011).

WHAT ARE THE CONNECTING LINKS OF THESE INITIATIVES FOR EXCELLENCE TO KNOWLEDGE CITY STRATEGIES?

First, the publicity around the winning academic institutions and their rising reputation has a positive effect in the short run for the respective cities presenting themselves as locations for science. There is an additional long term effect if the winning universities and research institutes succeed in converting their additional funds into higher quality in research and teaching. These gains in reputation feed back to the city image as a renowned science location.

Second, in cities with a multitude of science institutions it cannot be assumed that their managers have at their disposal a precise conception and a common vision of the specific strengths and weaknesses of the local science system. In order to gain capability to coordinate action the representatives (or a legitimized committee) have to detect, to negotiate and to agree to a specific strength–weakness profile of their science location. This sounds easy, but may prove a difficult step, because the actors that are going to take stock of the local science institutions' profile (a) have to demonstrate a legitimate concern, and (b) must have the support of academia's vast majority with respect to the results presented. Sometimes it takes several attempts to reach this required legitimacy in a city (Franz 2009). The agreement on such a strength–weakness profile is also a prerequisite for related efforts in marketing the city as a science location.

Third, as far as excellence-oriented competitions involve criteria for science institutions to build up links with private firms of the regional economy, universities and research institutes are forced to focus their attention on at least parts of their environment. Science institutions have a choice of diverse linking channels suitable for their purposes: intensified technology transfer, intensified support of spin-offs, joint R&D ventures, common conception of a course of studies or extended vocational training, visiting stays of firm employees at research institutes and vice versa.

In choosing one or more of these activities the science institutions should also consider some structural features of the surrounding firms. An environment with predominating small-size firms and less absorptive capacity provides few arguments for choosing technology transfer and R&D cooperation as the most suitable measures.

NO DISADVANTAGES?

It seems to be a matter of argumentative fairness that a proponent for applying competitions in order to initiate knowledge city strategies, and laying stress on the advantages of such a procedure, should say some words about potential disadvantages. Apart from the general critical attitude towards competitions as a further penetration of everyday life with economic principles (commodification), already mentioned in the introductory section, the main criticism is that the installment of competitions distracts from optional changes in the regulatory framework (Dohse 2000; Franz 2008). This means, for example, that deregulatory steps for universities in national or federal university laws might lead to higher autonomy for the university managers to communicate and to form coalitions with local politicians and business leaders, in comparison to a competition that seeks to overcome the existing regulatory hurdles to cooperation with a high sum of prize money. Such hurdles may consist in the dependence of universities on departmental bureaucracy when the future use of certain real estate parcels of the university's property are negotiated with the city officials, or when the decision to establish a new course of studies in agreement with representatives of a certain industry first has to be approved by super ordinate authorities. As long as such regulatory hurdles exist the implementation of even the most advanced prize-winning concept bears the risk of failure, because it cannot escape from the task of tackling these hurdles in some way.

Finally, it should not be withheld that deregulatory efforts in university laws have increased in recent years, at least in the Western hemisphere. This may come from an international learning effect by comparing 'best practice' elsewhere, but also from the experience that more autonomous science institutions will become faster in realigning their quality profiles, and more responsible regional players.

From this perspective the increasing diffusion of knowledge city strategies serves as a push factor for more autonomy on the side of the science institutions. Competitions and contests have the potential to speed up this process, but they should not be conceived as a surrogate for required changes in the regulatory framework.

REFERENCES

Cooke, Phil (1998), 'Introduction: origins of the concept', in Hans-Jürgen Braczyk, Phil Cooke and Martin Heidenreich (eds), *Regional Innovation Systems: The Role of Governances in a Globalized World*, London: UCI Press, pp. 2–25.

Dohse, D. (2000), 'Technology policy and the regions – the case of the BioRegio Contest', *Research Policy*, **29** (9), 1111–1133.

Eickelpasch, A. and M. Fritsch (2005), 'Contests for cooperation – a new approach in German innovation policy', *Research Policy*, **34** (8), 1269–1282.

Franz, Peter (2008), 'From University Town to Knowledge City: strategies and regulatory hurdles in Germany', in Tan Yigitcanlar, Koray Velibeyoğlu and Scott Baum (eds), *Knowledge-Based Urban Development: Planning and Applications in the Information Era*, Hershey, PA: IGI Global, pp. 101–115.

Franz, Peter (2009), 'Knowledge City Berlin? Potenziale und risiken einer stadtentwicklungsstrategie mit dem fokus wissenschaft', in Ulf Mathiesen and Gerhard Mahnken (eds), *Das Wissen der Städte. Neue stadtregionale Entwicklungsdynamiken im Kontext von Wissen, Milieus und Governance*, Wiesbaden: VS Verlag für Sozialwissenschaften, pp. 95–110.

Gläser, Jochen (2007), 'The social orders of research evaluation systems', in Richard Whitley and Jochen Gläser (eds), *The Changing Governance of the Sciences: The Advent of Research Evaluation Systems*, Dordrecht: Springer, pp. 245–265.

Hayek, Friedrich A.V. ([1968] 2002), 'Competition as a discovery procedure', reprinted in *Quarterly Journal of Austrian Economics*, **5** (3), 9–23.

Hohn, Stephanie and Clas Meyer (2011), 'Key factors for the success of knowledge cities in Germany: findings of an empirical study, 2010, http://www.melbourneknowledgesummit.com/portals/14/proceedings/documents/16_Hohn.pdf, accessed 31 March 2011.

Leibfried, Stephan (ed.) (2010), *Die Exzellenzinitiative. Zwischenbilanz und Perspektiven*, Frankfurt and New York: Campus.

Lundvall, Bengt-Åke (ed.) (1992), *National Systems of Innovation: Towards a Theory of Innovation and Interactive Learning*, London: Pinter.

Moon, M. and S. Kim (2001), 'A case of Korean higher education reform: the Brain Korea 21 Projects', *Asia Pacific Education Review*, **2** (2), 96–105.

Neidhardt, Friedhelm (2010), 'Exzellenzinitiative – Einschätzungen und Nachfragen', in Stephan Leibfried (ed.), *Die Exzellenzinitiative. Zwischenbilanz und Perspektiven*, Frankfurt and New York: Campus, pp. 53–80.

Silberberger, J., J. van Wezemael, S. Paisiou and I. Strebel (2010), 'Spaces of knowledge creation: tracing "knowing in action" in jury-based decision-making processes in Switzerland', *International Journal of Knowledge-Based Development*, **1** (4), 287–302.

Preface

Introducing: knowledge-based development of prosperous knowledge cities

Tan Yigitcanlar, Kostas Metaxiotis and Francisco Javier Carrillo

BUILDING PROSPEROUS KNOWLEDGE CITIES

That this is the century of knowledge cities, is an insight many people have already experienced but many more have yet to realize (Carrillo, 2006; Yigitcanlar et al., 2008a). Once that insight takes place, the space of possibilities for urban development and for the upgrade of human experience, both leapfrog.

A critical and constructive adoption of the knowledge cities paradigm requires an understanding of the reach and depth of both urban life and knowledge-based experience in global futures. A recently released report by the McKinsey Global Institute (MGI, 2011) indicates the extent to which *urban economic history* (as the report calls it) is changing dramatically nowadays. According to this source, a mere 600 urban centers concentrating only a fifth of the world's population, generate more than half of global GDP. While stressing the emergence of cities as development engines, this fact might reinforce the received view that well-known megalopolises will continue to concentrate both population and production, and that today's major destinations around the world will consolidate tomorrow (Yigitcanlar et al., 2008b; Metaxiotis et al., 2010).

That is not necessarily the case. The McKinsey Report also shows that while in 2007, nearly half of global GDP came from 380 cities in developed regions, by 2025 one-third of these cities will no longer enter the top 600 and 135 new cities will make it to this list. To quote the report, 'over the next 15 years, the makeup of the group of top 600 cities will change as the center of gravity of the urban world moves south and, even more decisively, east' (MGI, 2011, p. 5). According to its forecasts, these 600 cities will in 2025 be home to 2.0 billion people (25 percent of total global) or 735 million households, and produce 64 trillion US dollars of GDP (nearly 60 percent of global GDP).

This quantitative perspective is further reinforced by a qualitative one: most of the labour force from these global urban centers are bound to be knowledge workers. This basically means that their value-addition activities will be based on the transformation of one form or another of *represented realities* (e.g., figures, as in financial analyses, images as in creative media, texts, as in e-mails) as opposed to industrial-era manual transformation of matter and energy. This also – and most critically – means that the daily life of the vast majority of these people will be subject to the value dynamics characteristic of knowledge-based production and knowledge-based cultures. For example, they will not necessarily have to 'go to' the office or the school to work and learn respectively; furthermore, working and schooling may not be separate activities any more. And most probably, by 2025 people will have a much better idea of what exactly these dynamics are than we have today, when we are only able to characterize most of our findings about knowledge-based value production as mere counterexamples to conventional economic wisdom.

Aware of these circumstances, an increasing number of urban governments and city managers are looking into knowledge-based urban development to prospect their cities' futures. Many of them are becoming increasingly at ease with concepts and tools such as collective intellectual capital and capital systems to assess their present status and plan their future development. Whether included or not in McKinsey's *City 600* list (MGI, 2011), any single city is taxed today with the challenge of understanding, mapping, valuing and sustainably developing the total capital – both tangible and knowledge-based– that will determine its viability.

Perhaps for some of these cities, a full understanding of their unique capital base will help them develop alternative strategies to those pursued by most current *City 600* prospects. Prosperity is no longer confined to accumulating material and financial assets. Knowledge-based prosperity is open to innovative ways of balancing the total capital base. Melbourne, recently distinguished as Most Admired Knowledge City – MAKCi (WCI, 2010), also made it to Frommer's '10 Best Cities for Walking' (Frommer, 2011), and was second in the Economist Intelligence Unit's Most Livable City ranking (EIU, 2011). Whatever its profile and corresponding strategy, every city counts increasingly on its knowledge capital. This ultimately means all cities face the challenge of developing as knowledge cities.

Nevertheless, actual models, tools and cases in the emerging field of knowledge-based development (KBD) are still scarce. This book aims at exemplifying policy-making, as well as planning and assessment practices in building knowledge cities from across the world. The emphasis on the diverse actions involved in knowledge-city building is indicative of the way intangible capital interplays with more traditional infrastructural and financial capital.

INTRODUCTION

The book is structured in three parts, each comprising a natural block of practices, and is rounded up with an Afterword. Part I looks at Knowledge Cities policies, Part II at Knowledge Cities planning and Part III at Knowledge Cities metrics issues. In the following paragraphs the contents of each part in turn will be summarized.

In this Preface, the three co-editors Yigitcanlar, Metaxiotis and Carrillo argue for the relevance of a knowledge-based development approach to cities by looking first at the leading role of cities in economic, social and cultural development and then at the primacy of intangible assets in the evolution of knowledge cities.

Peter Franz's Foreword looks at competition as a trigger for knowledge cities strategies. Franz looks at diverse city competition practices as healthy arenas where cities strive for excellence in becoming knowledge cities. He argues that these competitive perspectives are critical to sound policy-making insofar as strengths and weaknesses become evident and also argues that scientific competition may help obtain strategic focus and institutional collaboration. Nevertheless, he also looks at some potential risks of competition particularly with regard to potential distractions from regulatory innovations.

PART I: POLICIES FOR BUILDING PROSPEROUS KNOWLEDGE CITIES

Chapter 1 by Björn T. Asheim (Innovating: creativity, innovation and the role of cities in the globalizing knowledge economy) looks at cities as the new economic engines and as the cradles of creativity and innovation. In doing so, Asheim discusses Florida's well-known creative class approach, drawing a schematic line of argument for this perspective. He then moves on to characterize a knowledge-based development approach through a typology of k-bases and relates these to the creative class as innovation agents. From here, a fresh look at Regional Innovation Systems follows with reference to the urban context. On these grounds, a distinction (and later integration) between two modes of innovation is drawn depending on the knowledge base type and the extent to which it is market-driven. Asheim concludes by offering some insights into collaboration and social capital as an urban milieu for effective innovation.

In Chapter 2, Mark Lorenzen et al. (Creating: the creative class-based knowledge city models of Denmark) proceed to analyze the application of creative class-based approaches to Danish cities. To begin, the authors provide a description of the characteristics and geographical distribution of the creative class in Denmark, thus testing two of Florida's key theses: technology and tolerance. Next, they develop policy implications by differentiating four city models with reference to Denmark: Big, Proximate, Specialized and Quaint, each discussed and exemplified. Such analysis enables them to draw some specific policy conclusions for further development of Danish knowledge cities.

In Chapter 3 (Organizing: spontaneously developed urban technology precincts) Gülnur Çevikayak and Koray Velibeyoğlu look at knowledge precints (defined as new urban areas where knowledge is the driving force of the economic and urban development). The authors' goal is to clarify the potential of spontaneously developed urban technology precints, by looking at the spatial and organizational characteristics of Izmir in Turkey as a case study. Hence, the first part of the chapter covers the transformation process of technology precints. The second part involves examples of spontaneously developed urban technology precincts. Finally, the third part looks at the 'Izmir Technology Diamond' as a case study and its potential as a technology precint.

In Chapter 4 (Globalizing: what makes Australian information technology industry companies go global?), Glen Searle and Kevin O'Connor aim at researching firm-level factors associated with information technology (IT) exports from Australia. In doing so, they use data from a random stratified sample of IT firms in Sydney and Melbourne. Drawing from these data, they identify company attributes associated with differing levels of exports and also explore factors associated with Australia's global location that are perceived to disadvantage Australian IT producers. Overall, their work shows to what extent the profile of the export activity in the Australian IT industry is connected to the knowledge base of cities. They conclude that the long-term development of the IT industry in both Sydney and Melbourne will depend largely on the further evolution of these as knowledge cities.

Kirsten Martinus (Chapter 5: Attracting: the coffeeless urban café and the attraction of urban space) looks at how public space adjacent to key transport infrastructure can contribute to innovation systems and new economy efficiency. The author offers a review of the literature on two aspects: how urban form may contribute to knowledge productivity and the design characteristics of the urban systems required for innovation. These aspects are exemplified through field research examining human presence in and movement through a particular space outside a busy train station in Kobe, Japan. Martinus concludes by reaffirming earlier observations that attraction and retention of human capital is a critical function of urban space in knowledge cities.

In turn, Wesselmann et al. in Chapter 6 (Researching: key factors for the success of knowledge cities in Germany) deal with the following research question: Which strategic and operational measures do cities implement to try and raise their profile as a science city? In tackling this question, they carried out a study of the 'City of Science' annual competition in Germany. Following a typification and profile analysis of participant cities, they exemplify with a case-study of the North-Eastern German city of Oldenburg. Overall, they emphasize the positive effects from the competition, with best results shown by medium-sized cities wanting to be repositioned as knowledge cities.

To end Part I, Chapter 7 by González et al. (Participating: knowledge citizens' competences and knowledge city transformation), deals with a critical, yet often overlooked, element of knowledge cities: knowledge citizens. The authors identify a set of competences that will allow citizens to leverage the knowledge value of their city. They first look at existing literature, identifying existing competencies taxonomies, and related these to the Most Admired Knowledge City (MAKCi) framework. They go on to design a dedicated taxonomy and analytical framework. Finally, the authors specify implementation requirements and develop a tool for the assessment and development of knowledge citizens' competences.

PART II: PLANS FOR BUILDING PROSPEROUS KNOWLEDGE CITIES

After such a wide perspective of elements for knowledge cities' understanding, analyzing and policy-making, Part II takes us into the planning phase. To begin with, Cathy Garner and Anne Dornan offer Chapter 8 (Piloting: knowledge-based development policy and practice in building a vibrant ecosystem). In their chapter, they propose a view of cities as modern open networked innovation centers. Furthermore, they identify a series of key attributes of an innovation ecosystem. They also offer an ample characterization of urban innovation and refer it to the case of Manchester as a test-bed. They conclude that while such an innovation ecosystem approach can be the basis for sound knowledge-based development (KBD) policies, it poses special challenges for policy makers and practitioners in terms of leadership and entrepreneurship.

Chapter 9, by Kostas Metaxiotis and Kostas Ergazakis (Formulating: an integrated strategy for the development of knowledge cities) look at the challenge of building integrated knowledge city strategies. First they review and compare existing knowledge cities regarding the formulation of their strategies. Then they present a method aimed at containing an integrated strategy: KnowCis 2.0. This method is comprehensive of the major processes in policy management: diagnosis, strategy formulation, action plan, implementation and evaluation. Next, the authors exemplify the method with a case study of a Greek municipality. Finally, they assess the results of the case study and discuss the impact, constraints and lessons learnt of this experience. Overall, their work underlies the importance of systematic and comprehensive frameworks for knowledge cities planning, implementation and assessment.

In Chapter 10 (Designing: combining design and high-tech industries in the knowledge city of Eindhoven), Ana María Fernández-Maldonado approaches the case of this city in the Netherlands with a focus on ways to combine business- and people-oriented perspectives in practice. The chapter addresses the main assumptions of the business-oriented, the people-oriented, and the comprehensive perspectives of urban KBD. Next, it describe the problems of implementing comprehensive approaches. Then Eindhoven is presented as a case study. The author concludes that this city provides a good example of successful integration of technology and design on the one hand and of business-oriented and people-oriented perspectives on the other. Strong regional identity and organizational capabilities are credited as major KBD assets of this knowledge city.

Richard Hu with Chapter 11 (Clustering: concentration of the knowledge-based economy in Sydney) aims to make an empirical contribution to understanding the concentration of the knowledge-based economy in Central Sydney. The Location Quotient is used by the author to compare employment by industries in Central Sydney with Metropolitan Sydney in 1996–2006. According to Hu 'The results indicate which industries are concentrated in Central Sydney, which industries with concentration fall into the category of the knowledge-based economy, and how the concentration patterns have shifted temporally.' The author claims that a systematic measurement of employment in Central vs. Metropolitan Sydney may provide a holistic understanding of KBD concentration.

Chapter 12 by Ana Cristina Fachinelli and Janaína Macke (Connecting: community supported universities for knowledge city transformation) looks at the specific role of community supported universities or CSU (to be differentiated from community colleges) in social capital development and community transformation. The particulars of the case are the University of Caxias do Sul and the corresponding city of Caxias do Sul in Southern Brazil. Several core dimensions of social capital are pointed out as parameters of universities' impact upon the communities they belong to. The authors identify the CSU as a reference for the development of Caxias do Sul as an emerging knowledge city.

In Chapter 13 (Promoting: programs for and challenges of the knowledge-based small business), Joan Kay Imukuka et al. reconstruct the concept of small knowledge-based business by looking first at alternative definitions of small and medium sized enterprises (SMEs) and then at the characterization of small knowledge-based businesses (KBB). In assessing the potential role of KBBs, the authors identify a series of barriers that may impair KBD policies: sector width, knowledge workers' availability, access to risk capital, technical expertise, entrepreneurial orientation and managerial characteristics. They conclude that these barriers should be dealt with for the effective implementation of policies aimed at consolidating the role of small knowledge-based businesses.

Chapter 14 (Enterprising: academics, knowledge capital and towards PASCAL universities) by James A. Powell provides a refreshing look at the emerging redefinition of the terms of integration of universities into their communities' life and work. The author starts by carrying out a review of global best practices in closing the gap between academia and their communities. A state-of-the art framework is exemplified by the 'Universities of the Modern Renaissance' consortium, which in turn becomes the model for the PASCAL International Observatory, an attempt to reach further in co-creation and community empowerment. The chapter concludes with a description of PASCAL key characteristics and short examples of practices.

Closing Part II, Caren Heidemann et al. (Chapter 15, Transforming: turning knowledge cities into a knowledge region) sketches out a recent initiative in the Ruhr in Germany, to turn an old industrial region into a knowledge region. The focus of this project has been to change the regional economy from coal mining and steel production to knowledge development, as the Ruhr in Germany found itself in a comparably weak position to compete with other metropolitan city regions such as Munich, Stuttgart, or Berlin. They move on to present the CampusRuhr Initiative, as a unique strategic bottom-up process of spatial policy integration, involving major stakeholders of the regional knowledge society. The main goal of this initiative is a spatially and mentally integrated network of modern institutions in the former industrial region, as a condition for the region to become an integrated knowledge environment. Although these efforts are reportedly still in a preliminary phase, it is concluded that such an approach can prove useful in generating and sharing similar experiences across the region.

PART III: METRICS FOR BUILDING PROSPEROUS KNOWLEDGE CITIES

Part III (Metrics for Building Prosperous Knowledge Cities) moves now further into the application realm by looking at some of the aspects involved in comparing knowledge cities' dimensions for purposes of explaining, comparing, benchmarking or assessing knowledge city models, plans, policies and program implementations.

First, Kevin Johnson explores employment self-containment (ESC) ratio in Melbourne's Knowledge Economy region (Chapter 16: Commuting: the geography of Melbourne's knowledge economy). Johnson uses Australian Bureau of Statistics Census data to map a workforce's employment and residential distribution at the geographical scale of the Statistical Local Area. Investigating different permutations of the knowledge economy (KE) workforce allow the author to identify preferences for residential and work locations as well as opportunities for influencing job distribution and transport use. As the author concludes, 'The more we understand what creates these patterns; the better positioned we are to shape their evolution.' The chapter ends with a listing of the main distribution and commuting patterns of KE workers in Melbourne.

Chapter 17 by Francisco J. Carrillo and Ricardo E. Flores (Measuring: knowledge-based development metrics, evolution and perspectives) provides a state-of-the-art review on progress made in understanding and designing scientifically sound and practically viable KBD composite indicator systems. A discussion on current practices and methodological issues is presented next, based on the landmark European Union knowledge economy index (KEI) study. Finally, the authors discuss some general considerations on the evolution of KBD measurements and describe an emerging research agenda in different countries that tackles some major common issues thanks to an active collaboration program in the KBD community.

Next, Chapter 18 (Comparing: knowledge-based urban development of Vancouver, Melbourne, Manchester and Boston) by Tan Yigitcanlar, provides a comparison of several well-known KCs. It first provides an overview of KBD and the emergence of KCs, including some of its core processes. The author then introduces his urban KBD framework and proceeds with its application to comparing knowledge-based urban development characteristics of Boston, Vancouver, Melbourne and Manchester.

He then concludes by discussing KC transformations and the benefits of the assessment framework for evaluating KBD strategies.

Finally, Part III concludes with Chapter 19 by Alicia Leal and Blanca C. Garcia (Benchmarking: knowledge-based development metrics through the MAKCi exercise). This chapter reports on first results from applying statistical modelling to emerging Knowledge-City benchmarking methodologies. The main objective is to put forward the Generic Capitals System (GCS) taxonomy as a methodological tool to identify how tacit knowledge conversion generates quantitative intangible indicators by means of simulation and pattern modeling. Next, authors expand on such research work and collaboration, elicited by the GCS taxonomy in recent years, and the metrical implications it has triggered. Finally, Leal and Garcia introduce a practical application of the GCS through recent research on the construction of a MAKCi index, built on statistical probability.

AFTERWORD

The three sections in the book and the cumulative learning of all the chapters, lead to the Afterword (Chapter 20) by Joris van Wezemael (Concluding: directions for building prosperous knowledge cities). The author points out, while acknowledging the wealth of contributions in the volume, the remaining need to clarify the key concepts common to these: knowledge and development. In doing so, he claims that in order to deliver an original contribution to urban development, the specificities of knowledge-based urban development should be both recalled and developed. He concludes that, in striving for the ideal involved in this book's title, a deeper inquiry into knowledge and self-organization, an appreciation of the deliberative potential of knowledge and a careful handling of KBD with regard to place diversity will be required.

Hence, a full conceptual and applied cycle is covered through all of the chapters contributing to this volume. In gathering these contributions from the global KBD community we hope that readers may gain valuable insights into the new space of possibilities for urban development and for the upgrade of the overall human experience.

REFERENCES

Carrillo, F.J. (ed.) (2006), *Knowledge Cities: Approaches, Experiences, and Perspectives*, New York: Butterworth-Heinemann.

Economist Intelligence Unit (2011), 'A summary of the liveability ranking and overview', Economist Intelligence Unit, February.

Frommer, A. (2011), 'Frommer's 10 Best Cities for Walking Report 2011', http://www.frommers.com/slideshow/index.cfm?group=391&p=1. Retrieved 31 March 2011.

Metaxiotis, K., Carrillo, F.J. and Yigitcanlar, T. (eds) (2010), *Knowledge-based Development of Cities and Societies: An Integrated Multi-level Approach*, Hersey, PA: Information Science Reference.

MGI (McKinsey Global Institute) (2011), *Urban World: Mapping the Economic Power of Cities*, MGI, March 2011. Available at www.mckinsey.com/mgi

WCI (World Capital Institute) (2010), *MAKCi Awards Results 2010*, WCI, http://www.worldcapitalinstitute.org/content/wci-presents-2010-makci-awards-results. Retrieved 26 March 2011.

Yigitcanlar, T., Velibeyoğlu, K. and Baum, S. (eds) (2008a), *Knowledge-based Urban Development: Planning and Applications in the Information Era*, Hersey, PA: Information Science Reference.

Yigitcanlar, T., Velibeyoğlu, K. and Baum, S. (eds) (2008b), *Creative Urban Regions: Harnessing Urban Technologies to Support Knowledge City Initiatives*, Hersey, PA: Information Science Reference.

Acknowledgements

We would like to thank a number of individuals and organizations who have been as passionate as we have about writing and publishing this book and who supported the research, policy development, advocacy and project work on knowledge cities and knowledge-based development.

First, we wish to thank the World Capital Institute (www.worldcapitalinstitute.org), for bringing us together under its Executive Board and also making resources available for the preparation of this book.

Second, thanks go to our publishing team at Edward Elgar Publishing, who had the foresight to recognize the value and relevance of such a text, and who have been extremely supportive during the evolution of the book.

Lastly, we would like to thank sincerely our fellow authors and reviewers, who have contributed to this project by sharing their knowledge and giving freely and willingly of their extremely valuable and scarce time.

PART I

Policies for building prosperous knowledge cities

1. Innovating: creativity, innovation and the role of cities in the globalizing knowledge economy

Björn T. Asheim

INTRODUCTION: THE URBAN TURNAROUND

In the first decade of the 2000s strong evidence has been presented substantiating an argument for an urban turnaround taking place. While the discourse on industrial districts, clusters and new economic spaces dominated in the 1980s and 1990s (Piore and Sabel, 1984; Porter, 1990; Storper, 1997), in the 2000s focus has been directed towards cities as the node of new economic activities, new forms of collaboration and organization as well as the preferred location of the creative class (Florida, 2002; Storper and Venables, 2004; Asheim et al., 2007a).

The academic discussions during the first decade of the 2000s have been characterized by a growing number of researchers arguing that the future competitiveness of advanced, developed nations will be built on diversity and variety and not on specialization. This runs against a traditional cluster policy, which is based on the exploitation of specialized localization economies. Krugman (2010) concluded that his New Economic Geography approach was not any more relevant for analysing developed economies as they had moved towards diversity as their primary competitive strength. (However, it was still useful in the rapidly growing, emerging economies, especially China.) Boschma and his colleagues (Boschma and Frenken, 2010) have demonstrated that firms and regions basing their activities on related variety are the most innovative and competitive. Lundvall and colleagues (Lorenz and Lundvall, 2006) have maintained that firms combining the science technology innovation (STI) and doing, using and interacting (DUI) modes of innovations perform best, and Laursen and Salter (2006) have shown that firms sourcing broadly from both R&D and experience based knowledge are the most innovative. Lastly, Florida (2002), building on Jacobs's work (1969), argues that large city-regions demonstrating strong urbanization economies are the most innovative and competitive locations due to their openness, diversity and tolerance, which attract the highly educated 'Creative Class' favoured by high-tech and creative industries. Glaeser adds to this that 'cities make people smart' (Glaeser, 2010). These new observed tendencies cover developments of business climate (what is good for business) as well as people climate (what is good for people) (Florida, 2002).

CITIES AND THE CREATIVE CLASS[1]

Traditionally, the focus of urban as well as regional development has been on business climate, launching policy measures intending to attract new business to cities as well as to support the growth of existing industry. The attractiveness of cities based on an above-average level of human capital, the best research universities of a country, and their positions as infrastructural hubs (e.g. the main airport with the best international flight connections) has resulted in an industrial structure dominated by highly value added and/or research based industrial and service activities (e.g. KIBS – knowledge intensive business services).

Richard Florida's work, first presented in *The Rise of the Creative Class* (2002) expands the perspectives of the attractiveness of cities by arguing that people climate (factors that positively affect the location of people) is becoming increasingly important as a complement to the business climate (factors that positively affect the location of businesses) in fostering regional economic growth, and in some sectors of the knowledge economy, a people climate even constitutes the most important factor. What follows from this argument is that people, particularly those who work in the growing high-technology and creative industries, do not follow jobs; rather, jobs in these industries follow people. This point runs contrary to what has been common wisdom for years – that firms that create jobs have to be attracted through fiscal or structural (cluster and innovation) policies in order to promote regional growth and development (Asheim and Coenen, 2005; Asheim et al., 2006a). In contrast, Florida argued that in the knowledge economy, it is crucial to improve the people climate by creating and catering to diversity, openness, and tolerance in addition to more conventional factors of urban attractiveness, such as a rich cultural scene, interesting architecture, and well-developed recreational facilities.

Florida's points of view have gained broad interest around the world, including Europe, where his ideas and policy recommendations have become widespread (Florida and Tinagli, 2004). In the Nordic countries, the recognition that countries with a small population cannot produce enough talent and thus need to attract and retain talent from abroad made Florida's thesis of interest to policymakers on national and regional levels. The widespread acceptance of Florida's conclusions raises the issue of whether his thesis is valid when it is implemented in different economic, social, political, and cultural contexts from those in the United States (Asheim 2006, 2009). Florida's thesis was developed in a North American context, which represents a different variety of capitalism from that of Europe (a liberal versus a coordinated market economy) (Hall and Soskice, 2001; Asheim, 2009). Thus, Florida's tendency to make big claims and generalizations and to draw far-reaching conclusions, mainly on the basis of US statistical data on a high aggregate level, combined with narratives, needs to be theoretically and empirically qualified.

The basic reasoning of the creative class approach is that technology, talent, and tolerance are three crucial cornerstones that facilitate regional growth in the knowledge economy. The 3Ts are regarded as interconnected parameters that individually have a positive but limited influence on growth but that together have a significant synergetic effect. As Florida (2002, p. 249) put it, 'Each is a necessary but by itself insufficient condition: To attract creative people, generate innovation and stimulate economic growth, a place must have all three.'

Florida acknowledged the numerous different explanations of regional growth that can be found within the fields of regional economics and economic geography. Glaeser (1998) is especially credited for his human capital perspective, which argues that a high concentration of educated people propels regional growth. In contrast, the creative class thesis argues that not only educated people are necessary to promote regional growth; other parameters – a talented workforce and a base of economic activities – are equally important for regional growth in combination with a tolerant, open-minded, and diverse people climate. The addition of tolerance to well-known parameters of economic growth is perhaps the most innovative part of the creative class thesis in that a focus is placed on aspects that have to do with the inclusion and well-being of people. In sum, the creative class approach focuses on three related elements: a good people climate attracts and retains creative and talented people, who, in turn, fertilize the ground for a competitive business climate, and, finally, a good and competitive business climate brings about economic growth. Figure 1.1 presents a schematic form of the argument.

The presence of a tolerant environment offers diversity and quasi-anonymity, which are treasured by the creative class and provide space for people who do not fit into the common norms. This again increases the opportunities for innovative thinking and for the further development of new competitive knowledge.

The tolerance parameter covers a broad range of elements that influence

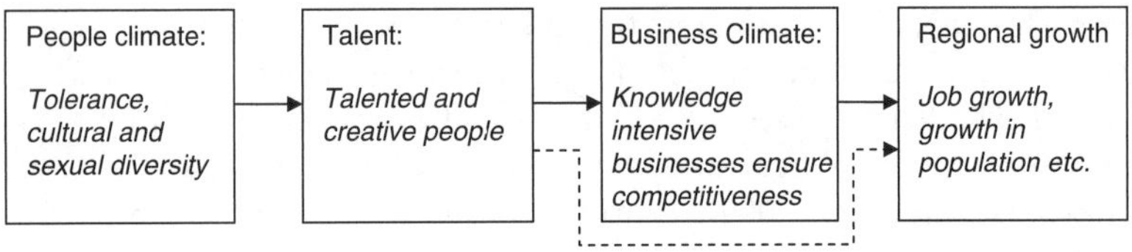

Figure 1.1 Schematic line of argument of the creative class approach

the milieu and atmosphere of a city. Most important, tolerance has to do with low entry barriers, such as openness toward newcomers and open-mindedness toward different cultures and different norms that may help regions compete for talent, with an assumption that open-mindedness makes it easier for newcomers and that people who deviate from the norms can be creative and innovative. Knowledge-intensive businesses move to regions with a high concentration of talents and creative workers.

Finally, one of Florida's achievements is to imprint the concept of a creative class on the minds of politicians and urban planners. Florida linked business policies with educational and cultural policies – thereby building a powerful coalition among three major areas in local, regional, and national politics. A people climate can be seen as a set of ingredients in a business climate, in that the presence of human capital and talent is essential for attracting and developing new high-technology industries, exploiting Jacobian urbanization economies (Jacobs, 1969), and consequently fostering the economic growth of cities.

THE DIFFERENTIATED KNOWLEDGE-BASE APPROACH

The creative class, as defined by Florida, in most developed OECD countries contains 30 per cent to 40 per cent of the employment and, in some regions, more than 45 per cent, covering a variety of occupations. I argue that the assumption that such a large creative class should have the same locational preferences for where they want to work and live is naive. Thus, I maintain that the specific knowledge bases of the industries in which members of the creative class work and which are reflected in their education and work experience will result in different trade-offs among jobs, occupations, lifestyles, and places of living and, consequently, between the relative importance of a people versus a business climate when making locational decisions, which, consequently, will make some groups of the creative class more attracted to large city regions than other groups.

The innovation process of firms differs substantially among various

Table 1.1 Differentiated knowledge bases: a typology

Analytical (science based)	Synthetic (engineering based)	Symbolic (art based)
Developing new knowledge about natural systems by applying scientific laws; *know why*	Applying or combining existing knowledge in new ways; *know how*	Creating meaning, desire, aesthetic qualities, affect, intangibles, symbols, images; *know who*
Scientific knowledge, models, deductive	Problem-solving, inductive, custom production	Creative process
Collaboration within and between research units	Interactive learning with customers and suppliers	Experimentation in studios, project teams
Strong codified knowledge content, highly abstract, universal	Partially codified knowledge, strong tacit component, more context-specific	Importance of interpretation, creativity, cultural knowledge, sign values, implies strong context specificity
Meaning relatively constant between places	Meaning varies substantially between places	Meaning highly variable between place, class and gender
Drug development	Mechanical engineering	Cultural production, design, brands

Source: Asheim and Gertler, 2005; Asheim et al., 2007a; Gertler, 2008.

industries and sectors whose innovation activities require specific 'knowledge bases', which depend on different types of talent in different modes and phases of the innovation processes (Asheim and Gertler, 2005; Asheim et al., 2007a). We use three knowledge bases – analytical, synthetic, and symbolic (Asheim, 2007; Asheim et al., 2007b) – because this typology encompasses and acknowledges the diversity of professional and occupational groups and competencies that are involved in the creation of various types of knowledge. These knowledge bases contain different mixes of tacit and codified knowledge, codification possibilities and limits, qualifications and skills required by organizations and institutions, and specific innovation challenges and pressures. Table 1.1 presents a summary of the characteristics of the three knowledge bases.

An analytical knowledge base refers to economic activities for which scientific knowledge that is based on formal models and codification is highly important, such as biotechnology and nanotechnology. University–industry links and respective networks are important and more frequently observed, and knowledge inputs and outputs are more often codified than in the other types. This does not imply that tacit knowledge is irrelevant, since both kinds of knowledge are always involved and needed in the process of knowledge creation and innovation (Nonaka et al., 2000; Johnson et al., 2002). Knowledge creation in the form of scientific discoveries and (generic) technological inventions is more important for this category of knowledge. Knowledge application takes the form of new products or processes, such as new firms and spin-off companies formed on the basis of radically new inventions or products.

A synthetic knowledge base refers to economic activities in which innovation takes place mainly through the application or novel combinations of existing knowledge, frequently observed today in plant engineering, specialized advanced industrial machinery, and building of advanced equipment for extractive industries. Synthetic knowledge is often formed in response to the need to solve specific problems through interactions between customers and suppliers, which implies that synthetic knowledge is more sensitive to distance than is analytical knowledge (Moodysson et al., 2008). Research and development (R&D) is, in general, less important than in the analytical knowledge base. University–industry links are, however, relevant, but they are clearly more in the field of applied R&D than in basic research. Tacit knowledge is more important than for analytical knowledge, particularly because knowledge often results from learning by doing, using, and interacting (Lorenz and Lundvall, 2006). Compared to analytical knowledge, more concrete know-how, craft, and practical skills are required in the creation and diffusion of knowledge. These skills are often acquired in professional and polytechnic schools or in on-the-job training. Overall, this type of knowledge leads to incremental innovation, dominated by the modification of existing products and processes.

Symbolic knowledge is applied in the creation of meaning and desire, as well as in the aesthetic attributes of products, producing designs, images, and symbols, and in the economic use of such forms of cultural artifacts. The increasing significance of symbolic knowledge is evidenced by the dynamic development of cultural production, such as media (filmmaking, publishing, and music), advertising, design, brands, and fashion (Scott, 1997, 2007). A crucial share of work is dedicated to the 'creation' of new ideas and images. As a well-known Italian designer noted, the market for design is about people's dreams, and increasingly people are buying objects with intellectual and spiritual nourishment in mind (Brussels Airlines, 2009). Competition thus increasingly shifts from the 'use-value' of (tangible) products to the 'sign-value' of (intangible) brands (Lash and Urry, 1994, p. 122). In cultural production, the input is aesthetic, rather than cognitive, in quality, and as a result, the knowledge required is often narrowly tied to a deep understanding of the habits and norms and 'everyday culture' of specific social groups. Because of the cultural embeddedness of interpretations, symbolic knowledge is characterized by a distinctive tacit component and is usually highly context specific. The process of socialization (rather than of formal education) is important not only for gaining 'know-how,' but also for acquiring 'know-who,' that is, knowledge of potential collaborators with complementary specialization through informal, interpersonal (face-to-face) interaction in the professional community (Asheim et al., 2007a; Christopherson, 2002).

The three knowledge bases are intended as ideal types,[2] with most activities in practice comprised of more than one knowledge base. The degree to which certain knowledge bases dominate, however, varies and is contingent on the characteristics of the firms and industries as well as different types of activities (e.g., research and production).

When Florida discussed economic activity attracting and/or being attractive to the creative class, he was referring to new and emerging high-technology and creative industries drawing on analytical and symbolic knowledge bases respectively. However, more traditional industries that are engineering based and draw on a synthetic knowledge base also employ talent from the creative class. Thus, the strong preferences for a people climate that Florida linked to talent employed in the new and emerging industries do not necessarily apply to people who work in more traditional industries. We argue that an engineer who works in an industry that makes packaging machines or automotives based on a synthetic knowledge base will not necessarily share identical preferences for living in a large city-region with an artist, a film director, or a creative designer in an advertising agency (based on a symbolic knowledge base) or a researcher in a biotechnology firm (based on an analytical knowledge base).

Past economic structures have different influences on the three types of knowledge bases. Synthetic knowledge is closely linked to institutions and organizations that constitute the regions' economic structure and, thus, regions that are more dependent on synthetic knowledge will display a more path-dependent regional development. Florida's reference to Pittsburgh illustrates this point. Analytical and symbolic knowledge bases are, in contrast, less sensitive to established economic structures and more attracted to diversity. Consequently, they stand out as being less dependent on the historical trajectories of a certain place and more responsive to new development.

Innovations in industries that are based on symbolic knowledge are about 'artistry' (Storper, 2009) and will often result from 'selective forms of cross-fertilization among cognate domains of activity, as among fashion, design, the arts and media' (Storper and Scott, 2009, p. 163). Fast fashion or high fashion 'learns from an alternative circuit of cities, the arts, and the "street"' (Storper, 2009, p. 14), which emphasizes that symbolic knowledge is highly context specific. To exploit such information and turn it into useful knowledge for innovation, one has to 'be there,' enjoy being there, and participate in the relevant activities, which is necessary for understanding the cultural specific, the 'unique' images, symbols, sign values, and multicultural milieu constituting the basis for the competitiveness of cultural products in a globalizing economy. In the case of cultural industries, diverse and urban 'sites and spaces are particularly important, since they are the arenas in which taste is negotiated and constructed. For highly aestheticized, subjective, symbolic, and experiential products, the negotiation of taste is central to the creation and adherence of value' (Power, 2009). New York and Toronto are excellent examples of such diverse and highly urbanized environments. Preferences for urban living among people who perform activities with a symbolic knowledge base that are found in the media, advertising, and design have been well documented by, for example, Gertler and Vinodrai (2004) and Grabher (2001). Generally, the postulated presence of a new subjectivism in postcapitalist societies, which is expressed by a stronger need and opportunities for self-realization in work life and leisure time (Thrift, 2005), represents arguments for the attractiveness of the people climate of large city-regions to certain parts of the creative class working in industries that are based on the symbolic and (at least to some extent) analytical knowledge bases.

Members of the creative class working in analytical based occupations, such as world-renowned scientists, often require a well-equipped laboratory and highly qualified colleagues at leading universities, public research institutes and/or corporate R&D units. Such organizations are usually located in large city-regions. Moreover, scientists may prefer larger city-regions, since they can more easily function as nodes in global research communities. Evidence already exists on how the development of (temporary) network organizations between an industry and a university as the new career track for scientists makes large city-regions more attractive because they offer a larger potential labor market for scientists (Lam, 2007). This means that the business climate is the most important; however, all things being equal, the people climate may well be the final decisive factor. It would be reasonable to think, for example, that Copenhagen would have problems attracting and retaining foreign talents, while Stockholm would not. The obvious explanation in such a case would be the more tolerant, open, and multicultural environment in Stockholm, since Sweden still has the most liberal immigration laws in Europe, which makes adaptation and immigration faster and easier, while Denmark has introduced the most restrictive laws in Europe in the past 10 years.

REGIONAL INNOVATION SYSTEMS

Innovation systems are both selection environments and sources of new variety creation. The innovation systems approach, developed in the late 1980s, places innovation at the centre of economic growth. It advocates continuous upgrading of productive capabilities and an active role of government (Lundvall, 2008) in shaping selection processes and stimulating creativity. It represents a shift from a linear view on innovation, mainly understood as conventional science and technology policies, to a policy approach that views innovation as an interactive process in which many different social actors take part (Lundvall, 2008). Therefore it is also the first policy approach emphasizing that a systematic long term relationship between key stakeholders (university, industry and government/ public sector) can play a strategic role in the promotion of innovation and competitiveness.

The innovation system approach was developed in the beginning of the 1980s in the context of an OECD project on 'Science, Technology and Competitiveness'. The ambition was to develop a more dynamic perspective on innovation and learning in the promotion of economic growth with an active role of government (Lundvall, 2008). This view represented a non-price competitiveness national policy or a high road strategy of innovation-based competition, which later was also proposed by Porter (Porter, 1990).

Regional Innovation Systems (RIS) constitutes a strategic instrument in the implementation of urban and regional innovation policies (Asheim et al., 2006b; Asheim et al., forthcoming). RIS is most commonly defined as consisting of two subsystems and their reciprocal interaction as well as relations to non-regional agency and organizations. These two subsystems are the *knowledge exploration and diffusing* subsystem consisting of universities, public and private research institutes, corporate R&D divisions, technology transfer organizations etc., and the *knowledge exploitation* subsystem constituted by regional clusters of industries interacting with the knowledge exploration subsystem.

However, in addition to this narrow definition of a RIS, it can be defined in a broad way. A RIS broadly defined includes the wider setting of organizations and institutions affecting and supporting learning and innovation in a region, where all types of higher educational institutions (and not only universities) are included. This type of system is less systemic than the narrowly defined types of innovation systems. Firms mainly base their innovation activity on interactive, localized learning processes stimulated by geographical, social and cultural/institutional proximity, without much direct contact with knowledge exploring organizations but mostly benefiting from them through their training of skilled people (Asheim and Gertler, 2005).

From a policy perspective an important difference exists between a narrow approach to innovation system analysis, focusing only on organizations and institutions created for the explicit purpose of promoting innovations (i.e. traditional science and technology policy), and a broad approach that maintains that other public policies, affecting firms' and nations' innovative performances and competitiveness, also need to be taken into account. This includes for instance education and labor market policies as well as institutional, cultural and social factors (Edquist, 2005; Lundvall, 2008).

RIS narrowly defined is a R&D based system which seeks to exploit the outcome of research from universities and public and private research institutes. This mode of innovation can be characterized as the S(cience) T(echnology)I(nnovation) mode of innovation based on the use of codified scientific knowledge, which is a science push/supply driven high-tech strategy able to produce radical innovations (Berg Jensen et al., 2007). According to Lundvall (2008), the STI mode of innovation could broadly be associated with the analytical knowledge base.

However, I would maintain that the STI mode is not only limited to an analytical knowledge base, but must also include synthetic and symbolic knowledge bases. In the case of synthetic knowledge and STI, this can be illustrated by reference to applied research undertaken at (technical) universities, which clearly must be part of the STI mode, but mainly operates on the basis of synthetic (engineering) knowledge (drawing on basic research at science departments of universities creating new analytical knowledge). An important distinction in this case is made between application development and technology development. Application development means solving concrete problems in connection with building the specific equipment for customers. This is carried out drawing on internal engineering competence as well as in interaction with suppliers and customers, and is, thus, an example of the D(oing), U(sing) and I(nteracting) mode of innovation. Technology development means development of more general platform technologies, which represents the technological basic competence for carrying out application development. While the application development is only made in-house or in user-producer relationships, technological development takes place in cooperation with (technical) universities as applied research projects, and represents, thus, the STI mode of innovation.

The DUI mode of innovation is a user (market or demand) driven model based more on competence building and organizational innovations and producing mostly incremental innovations. The DUI mode of innovation is characterized by its focus on harnessing experience-based knowledge and continuously as well as pragmatically recombining knowledge from various internal and external sources. Thus, the DUI mode would mostly resemble the synthetic (and symbolic) knowledge bases. Consequently, it involves numerous actor groups in flexible forms of organizations and networks, and generates knowledge which may be highly tacit and specialized to its context of development and application and, thus, path dependent. Other higher education institutions (HEIs) than universities (i.e. the applied universities) are important suppliers of skills and competences for carrying out innovation within this mode.

However, the DUI mode is on the other hand not limited to industries based on synthetic or symbolic knowledge, as also dominantly analytical based industries (e.g. pharmaceutical and biotech industries) make use of synthetic knowledge in specific phases of their innovation processes (Laursen and Salter, 2004; Moodysson et al., 2008).

Concerning the case of the symbolic knowledge base an increased importance of a STI mode of innovation can be substantiated partly by the new tendency of changing design education, from being artisan based to being placed at universities and other HEIs with (to a certain degree) research based teaching, and partly by the steadily increasing research in game software and new media at HEIs (universities and polytechnics). In some countries, e.g. in Denmark, this research is located at new, specialized universities (e.g. the IT university in Copenhagen). The case of DUI in co-existence with analytic knowledge based industries is indicated by the importance ascribed to non-science system information sources (i.e. synthetic knowledge) by research-intensive companies operating in industries dominated by analytic knowledge bases (Laursen and Salter, 2004). This broadening of what constitutes the STI mode of innovation shows that also activities based on synthetic and symbolic knowledge bases need to undertake new knowledge creation and innovation in accordance with the STI mode, and, thus, need systemic relations with universities or other types of R&D institutes (e.g. in a regional innovation system context).

The degree to which certain knowledge bases dominate, however, varies and is contingent on the characteristics of firms and industries and between different types of activities (e.g. research and manufacturing). According to Laestadius (2007) this approach avoids classifying some types of knowledge as more advanced, complex, and sophisticated than other knowledge, or considering science based (analytical) knowledge, characterizing the STI mode of innovation, as more important for innovation and competitiveness of firms, industries and regions than engineering based (synthetic) knowledge or artistic based (symbolic) knowledge, which is the dominating knowledge input in the DUI mode of innovation. This also emphasizes the importance of the complementary role different HEIs in a region can play in the provision of this complex mix of skills and competences. While universities are the prime producer of analytical knowledge, other HEIs such as polytechnics are important suppliers of synthetic and symbolic knowledge. The two modes of innovation will be differently manifested with regard to RIS and clusters. The narrowly defined RIS corresponds to the STI mode of innovation, while the more broadly defined RIS would more easily accommodate the DUI mode (Lundvall, 2008).

Even in large cities (e.g. in Berlin) the majority of the SMEs can clearly be categorized as belonging to traditional industries. This relates to the two modes of innovation, as the knowledge based industries (SMEs and large) innovate based on the STI mode of innovation, and have well developed contacts with the universities and research institutes. The traditional industries (SMEs and large) on the other hand, which innovate following a DUI mode of innovation, to a certain degree lack similar good contacts with R&D milieus at the applied universities (Asheim et al., 2003), due to the professors' lack of time to devote themselves to research (basic and applied), and also generally have little support to develop the DUI mode of innovation as such.

However, the universities of applied sciences tend to be more open and better equipped to get involved with regional partners from industry, the health sector or welfare services. The main reason for this is that their fields of study and research (engineering based on synthetic knowledge as well as social work, business administration, and health services) are dominantly application oriented and are closer, and thus more immediately relevant and adaptable to the needs of industry and public institutions than what is found at the universities and basic research institutes. However, universities of applied science have, as already mentioned, far fewer resources available for research due to the high amount of teaching.

The training of highly skilled workers and the provision of necessary intermediate technical skills and competence within these more applied areas of education and research are of significant importance for the future employees of these sectors when engaging in user–producer interactive learning and promoting incremental innovations in their work situation. These kinds of skills and competencies are of key importance for improving the performance of the DUI mode of innovation to obtain a better platform for the integration with the STI mode of innovation where universities play the leading role in the knowledge exploration subsystem as described above.

This distinction between the two modes of innovation is helpful in order to avoid a too one-sided focus on promoting science-based innovation of high-tech firms at the expense of the role of learning and experience-based, user-driven innovation. However, it also indicates the limits of such innovation strategies in a longer term perspective and, thus, emphasizes the need for firms in traditional manufacturing sectors and services more generally to link up with sources of codified knowledge in distributed knowledge networks (Berg Jensen et al., 2007).

COMBINING THE DUI AND STI MODES OF INNOVATION

Innovations occur through new combinations of existing knowledge, skills and resources. As evolutionary theory suggests (Metcalfe, 1998), the broader and more diverse the knowledge bases, the larger the scope for innovation (Asheim and Gertler, 2005). New research confirms that combining the two modes of innovation seems to be most efficient with regard to improving economic performance and competitiveness, i.e. firms that have used the STI mode intensively may benefit from paying more attention to the DUI mode and vice versa (Berg Jensen et al., 2007). The ability of firms to search and combine knowledge from different sources seems to be more strongly associated with innovativeness than either interfacing predominantly with customers or suppliers applying a DUI mode of innovation, or with research system actors in STI oriented processes (Laursen and Salter, 2006). SMEs, for example, changing technological trajectory by supplementing their informal knowledge, characterized by a high tacit component (i.e. the DUI mode of innovation), with competence arising from more systematic research and development (i.e. the STI mode of innovation) can avoid being locked in a price squeezing, low road competition from low cost countries. In order to do this they will need to raise their absorptive capacity through hiring skilled people graduating from HEIs (often supported by mobility schemes). In the long run, it will be problematic for most firms to rely exclusively on informal localized learning, and they must, thus, also gain access to wider pools of both scientific and engineering knowledge on a regional, national and global scale (Asheim et al., 2003). However, the DUI-based type of innovations will still remain the key to the competitive advantage of most traditional SMEs, as strong tacit, context specific knowledge components, found in, for example, engineering knowledge dominating the DUI mode, is difficult to copy by other firms in different contexts (i.e., they will not become ubiquitous). This will be the basis for sustaining these firms' and regions' competitive advantage also in the long run (Porter, 1998).

In combining these two modes, the issues of cognitive distance, organizational forms and absorptive capacity become crucial (Nooteboom, 2000; Cohen and Levinthal, 1990). The process of absorbing ideas and knowledge has been conceptualized as involving several stages of interfacing and social processing, which are tightly interwoven with organizational forms. If the cognitive distances and the differences in processes of knowledge acquisition, assimilation and transformation between the two modes of innovation are perceived by key actors to be too wide, it will not be possible to combine them and to view them as complementary instead of incompatible alternatives. There will be a lack of absorptive capacity within firms and regional clusters to acknowledge and appreciate the potential gains of the other mode of innovation as well as to access and acquire the necessary competence to combine the two modes of innovation. This broad based innovation policy needs both narrowly and broadly defined innovation systems to be implemented in order to promote innovation and competitiveness.

In all except possibly a few very large economies, the most important source of variety in the knowledge bases will be found abroad. The ability of entrepreneurs and firms of a country to tap into global networks of knowledge and use it productively (open innovation) will in many cases be more important than the creation of new knowledge at home. Thus, the international dimension of globally distributed knowledge networks (open innovation) has increased dramatically in importance over the last decade. This means that it is more than ever vital for policy relevant research to understand how the international context interacts with nation- and sector-specific conditions in affecting competitiveness and economic growth. Arguably, an efficient knowledge economy is based on innovation systems with a high degree of openness and diversity, not only concerning knowledge strictly defined, but also with respect to tolerance towards the cultural, religious and ethnic characteristics of the carriers (e.g. entrepreneurs and researchers) of that knowledge (Fagerberg and Srholec, 2008; Florida 2002).

CONNECTIVITY IN REGIONAL INNOVATION SYSTEMS

As touched upon above, large city or metropolitan regions usually have the best and largest universities in a country, which play an important strategic role as the key node in the knowledge exploration subsystem of regional innovation systems (RIS). However, the general impression is still dominated by the characteristics of a fragmented, metropolitan RIS (Tödtling and Trippl, 2005). The structural characteristics of fragmented metropolitan regions could be summarized as follows:

1. Metropolitan regions are normally regarded as centres of innovation with the presence of R&D organizations and universities, business services, and headquarters of international firms. As a consequence, R&D activities are usually above average. However, some metropolitan regions are lacking dynamic clusters of innovative firms due to the problem of fragmentation, i.e. the lack of innovative networks and interaction between universities–firms as well as among local companies. Such regions display an industrial structure characterized by so called 'unrelated variety', i.e. by having a diversity of sectors which do not complement each other, and, thus, do not produce knowledge spillovers. This may represent an important innovation barrier in such regions, resulting in the development of new technologies and the formation of new firms often being below expectations.
2. Normally metropolitan regions have an above-average educational level; especially with respect to higher education, they have the largest national universities, and a well-developed network of other HEIs. In addition, they also house R&D institutes and departments of the large national and international companies. Thus, the challenge of the HEIs in a fragmented metropolitan region is more about increasing the impact of the presence of education and research than about increasing the number of students and amount of research, i.e. the main problem is the weak connectivity in the RIS.

One reason for this is partly that universities in metropolitan regions traditionally have focused on their national and in some cases also international roles, and ignored the role they can play in promoting regional development. Due to the increased focus on the third task this has slowly been changed, and more and more we see that these universities no longer see any conflict between taking on their regional responsibility and keeping their national and international ambitions. This change in attitude is of strategic importance for achieving a well-functioning RIS in these regions. Another problem has been a lack of trust and social capital among the main actors of the RIS. Universities not interested in their regional task combined with either national multinational companies or foreign multinationals and a rather low regional commitment have not produced enough social capital and trust, which are of paramount importance to achieve a high degree of connectivity in RIS. Thus, the spatial proximity found between actors in the RIS in metropolitan regions has not been matched with a similar social and institutional proximity, which is characteristic of smaller regions such as the industrial districts of the Third Italy (a region of Italy including Tuscany, Umbria, Marche, Emilia-Romagna, Veneto, Friuli, and Trentino-Alto Adige/Südtirol) (Asheim, 2000; Boschma, 2005). The changes in attitude described above together with increased globalization pressures have increased the awareness of the benefits of exploiting the local knowledge infrastructures more intensively, and of not only relying on corporate as well as national and international R&D resources. The industrial structure in these regions is generally more R&D intensive than in other types of regions, thus the benefits of exploiting the knowledge exploration subsystem of the RIS can really pay off in increased competitiveness and innovativeness. Finally, these regions with a rich endowment of knowledge, research, competence and skills should exploit the possibilities of building on the ideas of related variety and diversify into new but related industries. Also with regard to skills provision and attraction new research has shown that the hiring of workers with related skills and competencies has a stronger impact on firms' performance than the recruiting of workers with unrelated skills (Boschma and Frenken, 2010). These insights should also be reflected in the educational programs of the HEIs in the region. In fragmented metropolitan regions the impact of universities taking on a more developmental role, and contributing proactively to building and strengthening the RIS, could be considerable, and would play a major role in improving innovativeness and competitiveness in these regions. However, in taking up this challenge universities have to be supported by public government and industry in a well-functioning private–public initiated triple-helix collaboration.

The increased interest in and importance of the third task of universities could be described as a change from mainly taking on 'generative' to more and more engaging in 'developmental' roles Gunasekara (2006). Generative roles refer primarily to the provision of limited, discrete knowledge outputs such as scientific and technological information, equipment and instrumentation, skills or human capital, networks of scientific and technological capabilities and prototypes for new products and processes, in response to business or public sector demands (Benneworth et al., 2009).

In taking on developmental roles universities in contrast constructively interact with broader regional governance structures shaping the development of regional institutional and social capacities (Gunasekara, 2006) and, thus, more directly promote regional economic development. Universities typically become involved in strengthening as well as creating new systemic connections within RIS, hopefully resulting in positive, long-lasting impacts on regional economic growth (Benneworth et al., 2009).

CONCLUSION: COLLABORATION AND SOCIAL CAPITAL

The tendency of large cities having fragmented regional innovation systems points to the need of improved collaboration and cooperation at both system and actor levels. In a globalizing knowledge economy, understanding innovation as interactive learning implies that co-operation is necessary to make firms and regions competitive. Building social capital is a key strategy in promoting such cooperation – within firms, within networks of firms and within regions among relevant stakeholders. Social capital can arise both from civicness and from organizational and institutional innovation. But, while the latter can be built, the former can only be built on.

This raises the general question of the role of social capital in economic development. Florida argues that social capital is not conducive to promoting an innovative economy and that it has a strangling effect on creativity and innovation. Instead of seeking places that offer social control, people of the creative class are attracted by places (often large cities) that offer cultural diversity and quasi-anonymity – that leave space for individuality. Florida argues that social capital, as defined by Putnam (1993), is exclusive in the sense that social interaction is based on communities of likeness. The problem with Putnam's social capital, according to Florida, is that its exclusive nature eliminates diversity and hence limits space for innovative thought. Simultaneously, the exclusive nature of strong ties makes it difficult for outsiders, for example, migrants, to enter social circles, and thus lowers the degree of mobility.

This view goes against earlier insights that linked innovative performance to social capital. Putnam's (1993) work is cited in many of these studies to argue that social capital, understood as networks and connections, trust, common norms and rules, and so forth, is crucial for creating learning environments and transforming knowledge into product or process innovations (e.g., Asheim, 2000; Maskell and Malmberg, 1999). According to this strand of literature, innovation, understood as interactive learning, will have better odds when a high level of social capital is present. Evidence from the Nordic countries, for example, shows that social capital can be a powerful driver of innovation and economic growth.

Florida's reference to Putnam's work suggests an understanding of social capital as bonding, that is, rooted in civicness. However, social capital can also be considered as 'bridging,' as a result of organizational and institutional innovation at the societal level (e.g., labor market regulation and legislation in the Nordic countries).

The presence of social capital in the form of a strong tradition of cooperation adds to the high level of human capital in the workforce in the Nordic countries in a synergistic way, and represents an international competitive advantage. This organized way of bringing society inside the firm by internalizing labor market institutions of cooperation and regulation in intra-firm learning organizations, based on broad participation, is an alternative way of achieving an integration (or 'fusion') of economy and society (Piore and Sabel, 1984) compared to the industrial district model, in which the firm is embedded in the spatial structures of social relations of the externally surrounding community. These contrasting models of integration and contextualization of the firm also reflect the alternative interpretations of social capital mentioned above, i.e. as rooted in the 'civicness' of communities as found in industrial districts (where social capital represents 'bonding') or through formal organizations at the system level of societies, as is the case in the Nordic countries (where social capital implies 'bridging'). The latter represents not only cooperation but also planned collective action among groups of actors (e.g. firms, trade unions, authorities) (Sabel, 1992).

NOTES

1. The following two sections are based on published work carried out with Högni Kalsö Hansen (Asheim and Hansen, 2009).
2. Ideal types are a mode of conceptual abstraction in which the empirical input constituting the ideal types exists in reality, while the ideal types as such do not.

REFERENCES

Asheim, B.T. (2000), 'Industrial districts', in G. Clark, M. Feldman and M. Gertler (eds), *The Oxford Handbook of Economic Geography*, Oxford: Oxford University Press, pp. 413–431.

Asheim, B.T. (2006), 'Economic geography as (regional) contexts', in S. Bagchi-Sen and H. Lawton Smith (eds), *Past, Present and Future of Economic Geography*, London: Routledge, pp. 173–185.

Asheim, B.T. (2007), 'Differentiated knowledge bases and varieties of regional innovation systems', *Innovation – The European Journal of Social Science Research*, **20**(3), 223–241.

Asheim, B.T. (2009), 'Guest editorial: introduction to the creative class in European city regions, *Economic Geography*, **85**(4), 355–362.

Asheim, B.T. and Coenen, L. (2005), 'Knowledge bases and regional innovation systems: comparing Nordic clusters', *Research Policy*, **34**, 1173–1190.

Asheim, B.T. and Gertler, M. (2005), 'The geography of innovation: regional innovation systems', in J. Fagerberg, D. Mowery and R. Nelson (eds), *The Oxford Handbook of Innovation*, Oxford: Oxford University Press, pp. 291–317.

Asheim, B.T. and Kalsø Hansen, H. (2009), 'Knowledge bases, talents and contexts: on the usefulness of the creative class approach in Sweden', *Economic Geography*, **85**(4), 425–442.

Asheim, B.T. et al. (eds.) (2003), *Regional Innovation Policy for Small-Medium Enterprises*, Cheltenham, UK and Northampton, MA, USA: Edward Elgar.

Asheim, B., Cooke, P. and Martin, R. (eds) (2006a), *Clusters and Regional Development: Critical Reflections and Explorations*, London: Routledge.

Asheim, B.T. et al. (2006b), *Constructing Regional Advantage: Principles – Perspectives – Policies*, Final report from DG Research Expert Group on 'Constructing Regional Advantage', DG Research, European Commission, Brussels.

Asheim, B.T., Coenen, L. and Vang, J. (2007a), 'Face-to-face, buzz and knowledge bases: socio-spatial implications for learning, innovation and innovation policy', *Environment & Planning C*, **25**(5), 655–670.

Asheim, B.T., Coenen, L., Moodysson, J. and Vang, J. (2007b), 'Constructing knowledge-based regional advantage: implications for regional innovation policy', *International Journal of Entrepreneurship and Innovation Management*, **7**(2/3/4/5), 140–155.

Asheim, B.T., Boschma, R. and Cooke, P. (forthcoming), 'Constructing regional advantage: platform policies based on related variety and differentiated knowledge bases', *Regional Studies*.

Benneworth, P., Coenen, L., Moodysson, J. and Asheim, B.T. (2009), 'Exploring the multiple roles of Lund University in strengthening the Scania regional innovation system: towards institutional learning?', *European Planning Studies*, **17**(11), 1645–1664.

Berg Jensen, M. et al. (2007), 'Forms of knowledge and modes of innovation', *Research Policy*, **36**, 680–693.

Boschma, R. (2005), 'Proximity and innovation: a critical assessment', *Regional Studies*, **39**, 61–74.

Boschma, R. and Frenken, K. (2010), 'Technological relatedness and regional branching', in H. Bathelt, M.P. Feldman and D.F. Koegler (eds), *Dynamic Geographies of Knowledge Creation and Innovation*, London and New York: Routledge (in press).

Brussels Airlines (2009), 'Industrial revolutions', *There! European Network In-Flight Magazine*, February, 70–72. Available online: http://btheremag.com/2009/02/01/industrial-revolutions

Christopherson, S. (2002), 'Why do national labour market practices continue to diverge in the global economy? The "missing link" of investment rules', *Economic Geography*, **78**, 1–20.

Cohen, W.M. and Levinthal, D.A. (1990), 'Absorptive capacity: a new perspective on learning and innovation', *Administrative Science Quarterly*, **35**(1), 128–152.

Edquist, C. (2005), 'Systems of innovation: perspectives and challenges', in J. Fagerberg, D. Mowery and R. Nelson (eds), *The Oxford Handbook of Innovation*, Oxford: Oxford University Press, pp. 181–208

Fagerberg, J. and Srholec, M. (2008), 'National innovation systems, capabilities and economic development', *Research Policy*, **37**(9), 1417–1435.

Florida, R. (2002), *The Rise of the Creative Class . . . And How It's Transforming Work, Leisure, Community, and Everyday Life*, New York: Perseus Books.

Florida, R. and Tinagli, I. (2004), *Europe in the Creative Age*, Report, Carnegie Mellon Software Industry Center, Pittsburgh, Penn.

Gertler, M. (2008), 'Buzz without being there? Communities of practice in context', in A. Amin and J. Roberts (eds), *Community, Economic Creativity and Organization*, Oxford: Oxford University Press, pp. 203–226.
Gertler, M. and Vinodrai, T. (2004), 'Designing the economy: a profile of Ontario's design workforce', Report prepared for the Design Industry Advisory Committee, University of Toronto, Toronto.
Glaeser, E. (1998), 'Are cities dying?', *Journal of Economic Perspectives*, **12**, 139–60.
Glaeser, E. (2010), Key note lecture. Association of American Geographers' Annual Conference, Washington DC, April.
Grabher, G. (2001), 'Ecologies of creativity: the village, the group, and the heterarchic organization of the British advertising industry', *Environment and Planning A*, **33**, 351–74.
Gunasekara, C. (2006), 'Reframing the role of universities in the development of regional innovation systems', *Journal of Technology Transfer*, **31**(1), 101–111.
Hall, P. and Soskice, D. (eds) (2001), *Varieties of Capitalism: The Institutional Foundations of Comparative Advantage,* Oxford: Oxford University Press.
Jacobs, J. (1969), *The Economy of Cities*, New York: Random House.
Johnson, B. et al. (2002), 'Why all this fuss about codified and tacit knowledge?', *Industrial and Corporate Change*, **11**, 245–62.
Krugman, P. (2010), Key note lecture. Association of American Geographers' Annual Conference, Washington DC, April.
Laestadius, S. (2007), 'Vinnväxtprogrammets teoretiska fundament', in S. Laestadius et al. (eds), *Regional växtkraft i en global ekonomi. Det svenska Vinnväxtprogrammet*, Stockholm: Santerus Academic Press, pp. 27–56.
Lam, A. (2007), 'Knowledge networks and career: academic scientists in industrial-university links', *Journal of Management Studies*, **44**, 993–1016.
Lash, S. and Urry, J. (1994), *Economies of Signs & Space*, London: Sage.
Laursen, K. and Salter, A. (2004), 'Searching high and low: what types of firms use universities as sources of knowledge?', *Research Policy*, **33**, 1201–1215.
Laursen, K. and Salter, A. (2006), 'Open for innovation: the role of openness in explaining innovation performance among UK manufacturing firms', *Strategic Management Journal*, **27**, 131–150.
Lorenz, E. and Lundvall, B.-Å. (eds) (2006), *How Europe's Economies Learn: Coordinating Competing Models*, Oxford: Oxford University Press.
Lundvall, B.-Å. (2008), 'National innovation systems – analytical concept and development tool', *Industry & Innovation*, **14**(1), 95–119.
Maskell, P. and Malmberg, A. (1999), 'The competitiveness of firms and regions: ubiquification and the importance of localized learning', *European Planning Studies*, **6**, 9–25.
Metcalfe, J.S. (1998), *Evolutionary Economics and Creative Destruction*, London: Routledge.
Moodysson, J., Coenen, L. and Asheim, B.T. (2008), 'Explaining spatial patterns of innovation: analytical and synthetic modes of knowledge creation in the Medicon Valley life science cluster, *Environment & Planning A*, **40**(5), 1040–1056.
Nonaka, I. et al. (2000), 'SECI, Ba and Leadership: a Unified Model of Dynamic Knowledge Creation', *Long Range Planning*, **33**, 5–34.
Nooteboom, B. (2000), *Learning and Innovation in Organizations and Economies*, Oxford University Press, Oxford.

Piore, M. and C. Sabel (1984), *The Second Industrial Divide: Possibilities for Prosperity*, New York: Basic Books.
Porter, M. (1990), *The Competitive Advantage of Nations,* London: Macmillan.
Porter, M. (1998), 'Clusters and the new economics of competition', *Harvard Business Review*, November–December, 77–90.
Power, D. (2009), 'Review of Elizabeth Currid's "The Warhol Economy: How Fashion, Art, and Music Drive New York City"', *Economic Geography*, **85**, 101–102.
Putnam, R. (1993), *Making Democracy Work*, Princeton, NJ: Princeton University Press.
Sabel, C. (1992), 'Studied trust: building new forms of co-operation in a volatile economy', in F. Pyke and W. Sengenberger (eds), *Industrial Districts and Local Economic Regeneration*, Geneva, International Institute for Labour Studies, pp. 215–250.
Scott, A.J. (1997), 'The cultural economy of cities', *International Journal of Urban and Regional Research*, 2, 323–339.
Scott, A.J. (2007), 'Capitalism and urbanization in a new key? The cognitive-cultural dimension', *Social Forces*, **85**, 4.
Storper, M. (1997), *The Regional World. Territorial Development in a Global Economy*, New York and London: The Guilford Press.
Storper, M. (2009), 'Regional context and global trade', Roepke lecture in economic geography, *Economic Geography*, **85**, 1–21.
Storper, M. and Scott, A.J. (2009), 'Rethinking human capital, creativity and urban growth', *Journal of Economic Geography*, **9**, 147–67.
Storper, M. and Venables A.J. (2004), 'Buzz: face-to-face contact and the urban economy', *Journal of Economic Geography*, **4**, 351–370.
Thrift, N. (2005), *Knowing Capitalism: Theory, Culture and Society*, London: Sage.
Tödtling, F. and Trippl, M. (2005), 'One size fits all? Towards a differentiated regional innovation policy approach', *Research Policy*, **34**(8), 1203–1219.

2. Creating: the creative-class based knowledge city models of Denmark

Mark Lorenzen, Kristina Vaarst Andersen and Stine Laursen

INTRODUCTION

Any policy aimed at improving a city's knowledge infrastructure must aim to boost the city's attractiveness to knowledge workers. Much incumbent research has focused on the attractiveness of urban amenities (Roback, 1982; Glaeser et al., 2001; Lloyd and Clark, 2001; Shapiro, 2006). However, the work by Richard Florida and associates (Florida, 2002a; 2002b; 2002c; 2005a; 2005b; 2008) constitutes a different perspective which has made a notable impact in both the policy and scholarly worlds (e.g. Gertler et al., 2002; Montgomery, 2005; Boyle, 2006; Andersen and Lorenzen, 2005, 2009; Raush and Negry, 2006; Weick and Martin, 2006; Lorenzen and Andersen, 2009; Andersen et al., 2010). Simplified, Florida argues that in a globalized economy where knowledge constitutes competitive advantage, it is possible to analytically identify a type of knowledge workers who are particularly important, because they are engaged technically, socially, and/or artistically with creativity in their job. This *creative class* within the labor force has particular preferences for amenities such as high-quality housing, work empowerment, and specialized consumption. While the creative class shares these preferences with highly educated labor, Florida is able to demonstrate empirically that the US creative class has a more unique trait: it prefers to locate in cities with particularly high levels of cultural services, ethnic diversity, and tolerance towards non-mainstream lifestyles. Florida further claims that as a result of this preference-driven pattern of location of the creative class, diverse and ethnically and culturally rich cities prosper economically, as innovation-intensive firms pursue them into these cities. Malanga (2004), Glaeser (2005), Peck (2005), and Scott (2006) are examples of criticisms of Florida's argument and empirical designs.

Most incumbent research on the creative class is based on North American data. The policy lessons hitherto drawn from this research have, understandably, on the one hand, ignored the potential huge problems in transferring city policies to countries of other sizes and institutions, and, on the other hand, glossed over differences between different city types in each country. This chapter seeks to help to remedy these shortcomings, by studying the creative class in a small European welfare economy: Denmark. With a population of only 5.5 million, short geographical distances, a well-developed infrastructure, and a universal welfare state, Denmark offers an empirical setting that well complements the North American research. The chapter hence seeks to develop some policy lessons for cities in small, open welfare economies, and its main point is that very *different* city strategies all have potential for attracting knowledge workers.

The chapter falls into four sections. The next section briefly describes the characteristics and geographical distribution of the Danish creative class, and tests the applicability to Denmark of Richard Florida's two central propositions. These are what we may call the 'technology thesis' (=the creative class creates prosperous knowledge cities) and the 'tolerance thesis' (=soft city qualities attract the creative class). The third section develops policy insights by pointing to four different Danish city models for attracting the creative class. The fourth section is the conclusion.

THE DANISH CREATIVE CLASS

Florida (2002b, 2002c) defines the creative class as consisting of three types of knowledge workers:

- *Bohemians* with job functions that entail artistic forms of creativity (e.g. artists, designers, and writers),
- The *creative core* with job functions that entail mostly technical creativity (e.g. researchers, engineers, and doctors), and
- *Creative professionals* with job functions that entail creativity in a generic and managerial sense (e.g. managers, finance people, and lawyers).

The creative core has the highest skill levels and accounts for most of the innovation created by the creative class. However, even if the bohemians are relatively few and account for only a modest part of the creative class's contribution to economic growth, according to Florida, this has the most specialized preferences and is pioneering the preferences of the creative class in general. Aspects of the preferences of the bohemians disseminate to the rest of the creative class, stimulating its 'bourgeoisie-bohemian' – or, affectionately, 'bobo' (Brooks, 2001) – ethos.

Combining labor market statistics with qualitative interviews, we analyzed the composition and location of the creative class in Denmark, and we also investigated what attracts these knowledge workers to different Danish cities. In the following, we shall present our results. For a description of the method, see the chapter's Appendix.

The Composition of the Danish Creative Class

The creative class constituted 25 per cent of the Danish labor force in 2004, but as this figure does not include people who freelance or are self-employed, the creative class may realistically comprise a third of the Danish workforce. The creative professionals are the largest group, constituting approximately 2/3, with the creative core making up roughly 1/3 and bohemians being a very small group of a few per cent. Not surprisingly, the creative class has high average education levels: 44 per cent has completed a higher education of three or more years, as compared to 22 per cent for the population in general.

It is also worth noting the cultural consumption patterns of the Danish creative class. While Richard Florida suggested that the creative class in North America was attracted to cities with generally high cultural opportunities, his work did not analyse in much detail what kind of opportunities. This analysis has been made in the Danish context (Andersen and Lorenzen, 2009; Bille, 2010). The result of the analysis is that the Danish creative class consumes culture differently than the rest of the labor force. It is more culturally active, attends more pop and rock concerts, and visits art exhibitions and art museums, city landscapes and cultural sites more often. In short, the creative class is a major consumer of urban cultural activities that tends to be consumed in an individual and flexible manner.

The Geography of the Danish Creative Class

In Richard Florida's North American findings, the larger the population of a city, the larger its attractiveness to the creative class (Florida 2002a, 2002c). A survey of European cities has confirmed this size dynamics. Cities below a certain population size have too small labor markets and markets for services to attract the creative class (Lorenzen and Andersen, 2009).

This size effect could, with some variation, be traced in Denmark. Copenhagen is the only Danish city with a population of more than a million, and Aarhus, the second largest city, has a population of a mere 300 000. Nevertheless, we found that the Danish creative class did agglomerate in these two national centers, measured both by absolute figures and share of the labor market. Below Aarhus, the size effect seemed to taper off. The third largest Danish city, Odense, did not attract the third largest share of the creative class, and many larger provincial cities had low shares of the creative class, even if several of these cities had good infrastructures and universities. Surprisingly, a range of smaller cities attracted higher shares of the creative class than their population size would suggest. Some of these were small cities in relative proximity of Copenhagen and Aarhus, but others were located far away from the national centers.

The Technology Thesis: Does the Danish Creative Class Create Prosperous Knowledge Cities?

Richard Florida proposes that the creative class boosts city prosperity because creative knowledge workers start and attract high-technology and high-growth companies (Florida, 2002c). In order to test this 'technology thesis', we measured the economic impact of the creative class on Danish cities by correlating the presence of the creative class with different statistical indicators – one of prosperity, one of the technology intensity of local industry, and one of the activity level of local industry (for the definition of indicators, see the Appendix). We found that in 2004, cities' presence of the creative class correlated strongly ($p=0.537$ at significance level 0.01) with prosperity, and moderately ($p=0.315$) with technological intensity. However, the correlation between cities' presence of the creative class and industrial activity was very weak ($p=0.043$).

This result with only partial support for the technology thesis reflects a measurement problem for which earlier empirical work on the North American creative class has also been criticized. While we may reasonably assume that the creative class, being mobile and career-seeking, is attracted to prosperous, high-tech cities with highly active industries offering ample employment opportunities, Richard Florida suggests that the creative class also reinforces, or may even kick off, growth. But a statistical correlation between the presence of the creative class and various indicators of prosperity, technology, and industrial activity cannot elucidate the causalities at play (Malanga, 2004): does the creative class create prosperity and technology, or is it merely attracted to cities that are already prosperous and high-tech? Having rich statistical data at our disposal, we addressed this problem by using time series. We correlated cities' presence of the creative class in the year 1996 with how the other statistical indicators developed in the subsequent eight-year period. This statistical exercise provided strong support for the technology thesis. We found that Danish cities' creative class in 1996 correlated strongly ($p=0.624$) with prosperity growth in the period 1996–2004, moderately (p=0.293) with technological intensity growth, and moderately (p=0.243) with industrial activity growth. Hence, the cities that have managed to attract a strong presence of the creative class are more likely to experience subsequent start-ups of new companies, many of them in high-tech industries, and a general rise in income levels.

Our qualitative interviews lent insights into the causalities at play. The interviewed managers of Danish knowledge-intensive companies pointed out that given outsourcing of routine work, the ability of these companies to attract knowledge workers is increasingly central to competitiveness, and at the time of the interviews, all managers reported that their companies regularly had to decline orders because they were unable to hire the necessary workers. Such problems were prominent particularly for technically creative workers and for workers with a cross-disciplinary skill set, such as engineers with project management experience, artistic creatives with a financial expertise, or creative professionals with specialized technical skills. By far, shortages of creatives were most severe in cities with small shares of the creative class. One interviewed manager mentioned that in order to avoid losing creatives, his company had shifted its R&D department away from such a city.

The Tolerance Thesis: Do Soft City Qualities Attract the Danish Creative Class?

A second important element in Richard Florida's theory is the 'tolerance thesis': the creative class is attracted by soft city qualities, such as (primarily cultural) service offer (that is, service sector business and employment opportunities) and tolerance to diverse (foreign, as well as bourgeoisie-bohemian) life styles (Florida, 2002c). In order to test this thesis, we correlated two indicators of Danish cities' service offer and three indicators of their tolerance with the development of their creative class. These correlations were all significant (at the 0.01 level), but none of them was strong. Concerning service offer, we found that cities' cultural opportunities and public generic service levels, both in 1996, correlated weakly with their growth in the creative class in the subsequent period 1996–2004 (p=0.037 and 0.099, respectively). Concerning tolerance, cities' presence of foreign nationals, as well as of the social inclusion of non-Western immigrants, also in 1996, correlated weakly with their subsequent growth in the creative class (p=0.129 and 0.102), while the correlation between cities' share of bohemians in the labor force and subsequent growth in the creative class was moderate (p=0.316) (in the latter correlation, we of course excluded bohemians from the creative class).

Although these correlations were weak, the high significance of these relationships lent moderate support for the tolerance thesis for Denmark, although it is noteworthy that cultural opportunities seemed to matter so little for Danish cities' ability to attract creatives. Our qualitative interviews with members of the Danish creative class allowed us to explain the statistical finding that cultural opportunities and tolerance are not always the dominant attractors of the Danish creative class. The statements of the interviewees suggested that soft attractors were always balanced with hard ones. One example was housing prices. Since particularly younger creatives were unwilling to compromise on the quality of housing, but at the same time were unable to afford the expensive and desirable properties in the major cities, they increasingly needed to locate elsewhere. Living in the countryside meant longer commuting to work, but this was often offset by locating close to family, which often offered to babysit for young career-oriented couples. A second example was job opportunities: career options remained a key variable for the choice of location. While the major cities generally offered better opportunities, a handful of smaller cities that had developed world-class, specialized high-tech firms, offered competitive, even better, career options for particular creative job functions, typically engineers.

Concerning soft factors, interviews suggested that cultural opportunities did matter to the location decisions of the creative class, but not always those opportunities that can be measured statistically. Interviewees highlighted the ambiance of a city as vital, particularly beautiful cityscapes, authentic architecture, intimate squares, greenery, and proximity to the sea. A sense of social inclusion was also often stressed as very attractive, and several other interviewees said that their preferred cultural activities, in addition to larger events such as concerts and plays, encompassed local community activities. One interviewee mentioned Singapore as an example of a city that, if he should move abroad, would be too 'hardcore' to live in. The stated reason was what he felt would be lack of civic participation and inclusion and sense of community, and a too highly paced lifestyle. The pace of life, and having free time for family and leisure, were stressed by several of the interviewed creatives. Many pointed to Copenhagen as a work environment with an unattractive work/life balance, particularly for those employed in the larger companies. The greater distances between amenities and services in the major cities were mentioned as unattractive. For example, parents among our interviewees emphasized that not just the abundance but also the quality of public generic services such as education and child care was important, and short transport times were a key factor in this respect.

KNOWLEDGE CITY MODELS: THE BIG, THE PROXIMATE, THE SPECIALIZED, AND THE QUAINT

Denmark is a small country with rich national statistics, and this allowed us to analyze the geographical distribution of the creative class in more depth than was possible for earlier research on North America. Most notably, we were able to look closely at differences in the ways different Danish cities attract the creative class. In the sections above, we confirmed the Danish version of a general trend: the creative class is attracted to the opportunities offered in larger cities – in Denmark particularly Copenhagen and Aarhus. However, we were also able to identify factors that attract the creative class to other and smaller cities, such as cheaper housing, higher-quality and more accessible generic public services, specialized job offers and more attractive work/life balance, as well as cultural opportunities that are hard to measure statistically, such as authenticity, greenery and a sense of community. Consequently, Aarhus and Copenhagen, while remaining firmly in place as the first and second most popular choice for the creative class, do not have a monopoly on attracting knowledge workers.

In this section, we seek to synthesize these insights into stylized models of knowledge cities that, in fundamentally different ways, are able to attract the creative class. We discuss four such knowledge city models:

1. *The Big* The national hubs, competing (globally) on attracting the creative class on account of their size and diversity. In Denmark, the only two knowledge cities corresponding to this model are Copenhagen and Aarhus.
2. *The Proximate* Satellite cities and commuter towns around the major cities, offering lower living costs in combination with access to the major cities' specialized service offers and occasionally their labor markets. In Denmark, examples of knowledge cities corresponding to this model are Roskilde, Randers, Værløse, and Skanderborg.
3. *The Specialized* Medium-sized cities with industrial cluster(s) offering specialized career options outside the major cities' catchment area. In Denmark, examples of knowledge cities corresponding to this model are Sønderborg and Aalborg.
4. *The Quaint* Cities with peculiar qualities of place, such as natural beauty, authentic architecture, or a thriving local community. In Denmark, examples of knowledge cities corresponding to this model are Svendborg and Fanø.

In the following, we shall discuss these knowledge city models in greater detail, and touch upon some of their policy challenges.

The Big City Model

Cities with populations of more than 500 000 are well connected to global infrastructures and transportation systems, and as they often sport a whole gamut of different industrial clusters and knowledge institutions (e.g. universities), they are simultaneously specialized and diverse (Lorenzen and Frederiksen, 2008). This means that they are in a 'size game' when attracting the creative class. In major cities, the number of jobs, specialized services and cultural opportunities does not merely grow proportionally with population numbers, it grows exponentially, in a self-reinforcing manner (Lorenzen and Andersen, 2009). Because the Big Cities hence possess more of the city qualities the creative class looks for, they also have a disproportionate share of the creative class.

This attractiveness, however, is constantly in danger of eroding through congestion. Big Cities may struggle with issues of overpopulation, traffic jams, pollution, and pressure on public generic services such as daycare, elder care and health care. Furthermore, the global competition for creatives between similar metropolises is growing. This combination of issues constitutes a policy challenge: Big Cities need to play the 'size game' without becoming too congested. Across North America and Western Europe, large-scale public investments in infrastructure and environmental improvements are now routinely part of policies to attract the global creative class. However epic in scope, these policies often fail to also address equally important yet less conspicuous issues in retaining the creative class in Big Cities. Public generic services, such as health care, childcare, and elder care, are issues where Big Cities often fall behind.

In Denmark, the only two cities that play the 'size game' are Copenhagen and Aarhus, and with their unique size and offer of specialized services and jobs, these two cities assert a particular pull on the Danish creative class. Copenhagen and Aarhus are also the only Danish cities big enough to compete globally for international investments as well as the global creative class – the majority of which lives in Copenhagen. When compared to its European neighbors such as London, Paris and Hamburg, Copenhagen is surprisingly competitive, despite its comparatively modest size and cultural homogeneity. The lack of ethnic diversity is offset by the city's other qualities, such as good transport infrastructure, good housing, and attractive design and architecture. However, without continuous investments in avoiding congestion, architectural uniformity, and excessive gentrification, Copenhagen's attractiveness to the creative class may be eroded. Our study of the Danish creative class suggested that already today, the risk of congestion and the erosion of generic public services compared to provincial towns adversely affect the attractiveness of Copenhagen and Aarhus to some members of the Danish creative class.

The Proximate City Model

Our study of the Danish creative class indicated that small cities, even those with few jobs or evident city qualities, may attract high shares of the creative class if they are geographically near Big Cities. A smaller city's limited diversity and specialized services may be offset by it being within the Big City's catchment area. Such a Proximate City may offer jobs and a (limited) range of generic public services, relying on the proximate Big City for more specialized services. This is the case for some provincial towns that lie near national hubs, such as Newark near New York or Luton near London. Other Proximate Cities are pure commuter towns relying on Big Cities for both specialized services and jobs. While depending on Big Cities, Proximate Cities compete directly with these for creative class residents. Their attractiveness stems from a combination of easy accessibility to the Big City and lower house prices and cheaper or better public generic services targeting commuters, such as schools and daycare institutions.

As the attractiveness of Proximate Cities hinges upon competitive prices and quality of housing and generic services, the greatest political challenges of such cities are, naturally, price hikes and erosion of service provision. The inflow of high-income creative workers to such cities may boost property prices, and it may tempt policymakers to increase tax levels and prices of generic public services. However, as Proximate Cities possess no unique city qualities of their own, erosion of their price and generic services advantage would make them very vulnerable to losing creatives to newer commuter towns elsewhere.

In the Danish Copenhagen and Aarhus regions, only the part of the creative class with high purchasing power (the creative core, such as doctors and scientists), or those with low expectations of living standards (the bohemians, such as artists) live in Copenhagen or Aarhus cities proper, while the rest of the creative class tends to cluster in small provincial towns (such as Roskilde or Randers) or commuter towns (such as Værløse and Skanderborg) around the Big City in the center of the region. In the Copenhagen region, the affluent creatives congregate in the exclusive northern suburbs, while the lower-paid creatives are more likely to live in southern suburbs. Even if the quality of housing in these areas is not comparable, they both sport green spaces, forests and the seaside, as well as good daycare and schools.

The Specialized City Model

In Denmark as well as elsewhere, specialized economic activity in the guise of industrial clusters plays an increasing role for economic growth (Martin and Sunley, 2003). Many such clusters, particularly those dependent upon international investments, leading universities, or artistically creative workers, are located in Big Cities, but others continue to grow in provincial towns or 'new industrial spaces' (Scott, 1988). As clusters offer employment opportunities in highly specialized fields, they exert a pull on some types of creative workers. Consequently, a number of relatively small cities that are not near any Big City, but sport an industrial cluster, are able to develop high shares of the creative class.

The policy challenge for such Specialized Cities is twofold. First, an industrial cluster's job offer is highly specialized, and that means that it attracts only certain types of creatives – for example, particular specialties of engineers who are single and in early stages of their career and hence willing to compromise on lifestyle preferences for a period of time. With the progression of their career, and their establishing a family, however, many such creatives leave Specialized Cities in order to move to Big Cities. The policy challenge for Specialized Cities is hence to be able to retain the creative class longer, for example by offering jobs for spouses. Second, while industrial clusters experience periods of intensive growth, specialization is also risky. Many clusters experience economic lock-in and decline (Martin and Sunley, 2006). Consequently, a policy challenge for Specialized Cities is also to avoid over-specialization of industrial activity, and promote flexibility and transformation, for example, through investing in new fields of technology and education.

In Denmark, examples of Specialized Cities are Sønderborg, specialized in mechatronics, and Aalborg, with a dominant ICT cluster. After decades of specialized growth, both these Danish cities face notable policy challenges. Sønderborg has problems retaining its mechanical engineers due to the lack of local cultural opportunities and employment opportunities for spouses, and Aalborg is in a difficult process of de-locking its local industry from its narrow specialization as the world markets for ICT shift.

The Quaint City Model

A fourth city type has, without being Big, Proximate, or Specialized, managed to attract high shares of the Danish creative class. Cities such as Svendborg and Fanø are members of an exclusive club of small Danish cities enjoying natural beauty in combination with a particular history mirrored authentically in their contemporary urban landscapes. Artists and bohemians have flocked to such Quaint Cities for many decades, infusing them with active local communities and arts scenes. Today, with the growing bourgeoisie-bohemian lifestyle of the creative class, many creatives are willing to sacrifice the specialized service and job offers in Big, Proximate, or Specialized cities for an authentic and beauty- and community-oriented lifestyle in a Quaint City. As their purchasing power grows and their jobs get increasingly digitized, many creatives are able to import the specialized services they seek, and work wholly or partly from home, making a life in Quaint, but remote, cities less inconvenient.

The main policy challenge for the Quaint Cities is to strike the right balance between quaintness and convenience. These cities' authenticity, beauty, and strong local sense of community are often due to their remote location, their small size, and their slow pace of change. Living in such a city means limited opportunities for shopping and, for those who are not self-employed or have digitized jobs, arduous long commutes to work. Consequently, policymakers in such cities often see it as necessary to infuse them with Big City-type shopping and entertainment offers and to improve their accessibility. However, if implemented without respect for beauty and authenticity, such policies tend to destroy small cities' attractiveness, without making them able to compete with Big or Proximate Cities on service offer and accessibility. The landscape in Denmark, as in so many other countries, is increasingly dotted with shopping malls, amusement parks, highways, and bridges to the benefit of one-day tourists and transit traffic, but to the detriment of those local communities these infrastructures were meant to boost.

CONCLUSION

In this chapter, we applied Richard Florida's theory of the creative class to the context of a small, culturally and geographically homogenous, welfare economy: Denmark. On the one hand, we found that even if this context is hugely different from the North American one where the creative class was first studied, the general trends proposed by Richard Florida can also be recognized in Denmark. Knowledge workers, in the guise of the creative class, are important in creating, or at least reinforcing, prosperous knowledge cities. In turn, these knowledge workers are attracted to soft city qualities, such as diverse service and cultural offers and tolerance of foreign and bourgeoisie-bohemian lifestyles. Therefore, the Danish knowledge workers agglomerate, like the North American ones, in the major cities, the national hubs. However, on the other hand, the small size of Denmark means that there are only two major cities, and we were able to find a gamut of other and smaller knowledge cities that are either in symbiotic relationships to major cities or have their own independent models of attracting knowledge workers.

This more complex picture of knowledge cities we are able to paint in our Danish study is highly influenced by the well-functioning Danish transportation system and the Danish welfare state, where families typically have two wage earners and where a relaxed work/life balance is appreciated. For many knowledge workers, it is feasible to live in proximity to, rather than in, major cities, and for some, it is feasible to opt out of the congestion and high-paced work life in major cities altogether. The four creative class-based knowledge city models of Denmark we have pointed to in this chapter demonstrate that knowledge workers balance hard factors such as job opportunities and living costs with soft factors such as service offer, cultural opportunities, tolerance and lifestyles. Hence, our study demonstrated that investing in cultural opportunities is not the magic bullet that many policymakers believe it to be. For some cities, such investments may be a good knowledge city policy, increasing its attractiveness to creatives. However for other cities, different investments should take higher priority.

Throughout the last decade, the research on the creative class has led to a flood of public policies. Across the world, cities compete to attract knowledge workers. However, such policies are often one-dimensional and inspired almost exclusively by the research on the North American creative class. Failing to take differences between cities, and between national contexts, into account, policymakers aim at implementing policies that are remarkably similar. In effect, these policies pit provincial towns against major cities, and seem to suggest that such different cities should compete on the same qualities. Our study of the Danish creative class presented in this chapter suggests that different policies should be developed for different knowledge cities. In Denmark alone, we have demonstrated four distinct, and all successful, models of attracting knowledge workers. In other national contexts, there may be more, and policymakers would do well to investigate before applying policies. One size does not fit all.

REFERENCES

Andersen, K.V. and M. Lorenzen (2005), *The Geography of the Danish Creative Class: A Mapping and Analysis*, Copenhagen: imagine.

Andersen, K.V. and M. Lorenzen (2009), *Den Danske Kreative Klasse: Hvem er den, hvordan ser den ud, hvor bor den – og hvad betyder det?*, Aarhus: Klim.

Andersen, K.V., H.K. Hansen, A. Isaksen and M. Raunio (2010), 'Nordic city regions in the creative class debate: putting the creative class thesis to a test', *Industry and Innovation*, **17** (2), 215–240.

Bille, T. (2010), 'Cool, funky and creative? The creative class and preferences for leisure and culture', *International Journal of Cultural Policy*, **16** (4), 466–496.

Boyle, M. (2006), 'Culture in the rise of tiger economies: Scottish expatriates in Dublin and the "creative class" thesis', *International Journal of Urban and Regional Research*, **30** (2), 403–26.

Brooks, D. (2001), *Bobos in Paradise: The New Upper Class and How They Got There*, New York: Simon and Schuster.

Florida, R. (2002a), 'The economic geography of talent', *Annals of the Association of American Geographers*, **92** (4), 743–755.

Florida, R. (2002b), 'Bohemia and economic geography', *Journal of Economic Geography*, **2**, 55–71.

Florida, R. (2002c), *The Rise of the Creative Class: And How It Is Transforming Work, Leisure, Community and Everyday Life*, New York: Basic Books.

Florida, R. (2005a), *Cities and the Creative Class*, London: Routledge.

Florida, R. (2005b), *The Flight of the Creative Class: The New Global Competition for Talent*, New York: HarperCollins.

Florida, R. (2008), *Who's Your City? How the Creative Economy is Making Where to Live the Most Important Decision of Your Life*, New York: Basic Books.

Gertler, M.S., R. Florida, G. Gates and T. Vinodrai (2002), *Competing on Creativity: Placing Ontario's Cities in North American Context*, Toronto: Ontario Ministry of Enterprise, Opportunity and Innovation and the Institute for Competitiveness and Prosperity.

Glaeser E.L. (2005), 'Review of Richard Florida's "The Rise of the Creative Class"', *Regional Science and Urban Economics*, **35**, 593–596.

Glaeser, E.L., J. Kolko and A. Saiz (2001), 'Consumer city', *Journal of Economic Geography*, **1**, 27–50.

Lorenzen, M. and K.V. Andersen (2009), 'Centrality and creativity: does Richard Florida's creative class offer new insights into urban hierarchy?', *Economic Geography*, **85** (4), 363–390.

Lorenzen, M. and L. Frederiksen (2008), 'Why do cultural industries cluster? Localization, urbanization, products and projects', in P. Cooke and R. Lazzeretti (eds), *Creative Cities, Cultural Clusters, and Local Economic Development*, Cheltenham, UK and Northampton, MA, USA: Edward Elgar, pp. 155–179.

Lloyd, R. and T.N. Clark (2001), 'The city as an entertainment machine', in K.F. Gotham (ed.), *Research in Urban Sociology 6, Critical Perspectives on Urban Redevelopment*, Oxford: Elsevier, pp. 357–378.

Malanga, S. (2004), 'The curse of the creative class', *City Journal*, Winter, 36–45.

Martin, R. and P. Sunley (2003) 'Deconstructing clusters: chaotic concept or policy panacea?', *Journal of Economic Geography*, **3** (1), 5–35.

Martin, R. and P. Sunley (2006) 'Path dependence and regional economic evolution', *Journal of Economic Geography*, **6**, 395–437.

Montgomery, J. (2005), 'Beware "the creative class": creativity and wealth creation revisited', *Local Economy*, **20** (4), 337–343.

Peck, J. (2005), 'Struggling with the creative class', *International Journal of Urban and Rural Research*, **29** (4), 740–770.

Raush, S. and C. Negrey (2006), 'Does the creative engine run? A consideration of the effect of creative class on economic strength and growth', *Journal of Urban Affairs*, **28** (5), 473–489.

Roback, J. (1982), 'Wages, rents, and the quality of life', *Journal of Political Economy,* **90** (6), 1257–1278.
Scott, A.J. (1988), *New Industrial Spaces: Flexible Production Organization and Regional Development in North America and Western Europe*, London: Pion.
Scott, A.J. (2006), 'Creative cities: conceptual issues and policy questions', *Journal of Urban Affairs*, **29**, 1–17.
Shapiro, J.M. (2006), 'Smart cities: quality of life, productivity, and the growth effects of human capital', *Review of Economics and Statistics*, **88** (2), 324–335.
Weick, C.W. and J.D. Martin (2006), 'Full-time and part-time independent inventors: rising with the creative class', *International Journal of Entrepreneurship and Innovation,* **7**, 5–12.

APPENDIX: THE METHOD

The creative class was approximated using register data: Statistics Denmark's labor market database. The geographical analytical unit chosen for 'city' was municipalities. Our econometric exercise used the following indicators (based on Florida, 2002c):

- *Population* = Number of all inhabitants (residents) in a city.
- *Presence of creative class* = The share in a city of the employed residents occupied within creative professions, defined as the ISCO codes 245 (Journalism, art, and writing), 3131 (Work with sound, light and pictures related to photography, film and theatre), 347 (Work within art, entertainment, and sports), 521 (Modeling), 211 (Work within physics, chemistry, astronomy, meteorology, geology, and geophysics), 212 (Work within mathematics and statistics), 213 (IT planning and development), 214 (Architecture and engineering), 221 (Work within biological natural science), 222 (Work within medicine, odontology, veterinary science and pharmaceutics), 231 (University and college teaching), 232 (High school teaching), 233 (Elementary school teaching), 234 (Specialty teaching), 235 (Other work related to education), 243 (Work related to information and distribution of culture), 244 (Work within social science, humanities and high level social work), 247 (Work related to administration of the law within the public sector), 1 (High level management), 223 (Midwives and high level nursing), 241 (Work related to the organization and economy of business), 242 (Work within law), 31 (Technical work in non-biological areas), 32 (Technical work in biological areas), 341 (High level sale and marketing), 342 (Business services), 343 (Administrative work), 345 (Work related to police investigation), and 346 (Work related to social guidance and care).

- The creative class is further divided into three subgroups:

    - *The creative core* = Employed occupied within specific (technical or educational) creative professions defined as the ISCO codes 211, 212, 213, 214, 221, 222, 231, 232, 233, 234, 235, 243, 244, and 247.
    - *The creative professionals* = Employed occupied within specific (generic or managerial) creative professions defined as the ISCO codes 1, 223, 241, 242, 31, 32, 341, 342, 343, 345, and 346.
    - *Bohemians* = Employed occupied within specific (artistic) creative professions defined as the ISCO codes 245, 3131, 347, and 521.

- *Prosperity* = The share of inhabitants in a city with incomes above the national Danish mean.
- *Cultural opportunity index:* The number of employees in a city working in industries with NACE 553 (Restaurants and related activities), NACE 554 (Bars, night clubs, cafés and related activities), NACE 921 (Film and video), NACE 922 (Television and radio), NACE 923 (other entertainment), NACE 925 (Libraries, archives, museums and other cultural activities), NACE 926 (Sports).
- *Technology intensity of industry* = The share of the employees in a city working within hi-tech industries, defined as the NACE codes 244 (Manufacture of pharmaceuticals, medicinal chemicals and botanical products), 300 (Manufacture of office machinery and computers), 321 (Manufacture of electronic valves and tubes and other electronic components), 322 (Manufacture of television and radio transmitters and apparatus for line telephony and line telegraphy), 323 (Manufacture of television and radio receivers, sound or video recording or reproducing apparatus and associated goods), 331 (Manufacture of medical and surgical equipment and orthopedic appliances), 332 (Manufacture of instruments and appliances for measuring, checking, testing, navigating and other purposes, except industrial process control equipment), 333 (Manufacture of industrial process control equipment), 334 (Manufacture of optical instruments and photographic equipment), 335 (Manufacture of watches and clocks), 341 (Manufacture of motor vehicles), 342 (Manufacture of bodies (coachwork) for motor vehicles; manufacture of trailers and semi-trailers), 343 (Manufacture of parts and accessories for motor vehicles and their engines), 353 (Manufacture of aircraft and spacecraft), 642 (Telecommunications), 721 (Hardware consul-

tancy), 722 (Software consultancy and supply), 723 (Data processing), 724 (Data base activities), 725 (Maintenance and repair of office, accounting and computing machinery), 726 (Other computer related activities), 731 (Research and experimental development on natural sciences and engineering), 732 (Research and experimental development on social sciences and humanities), 742 (Architectural and engineering activities and related technical consultancy), 743 (Technical testing and analysis), and 921 (Motion picture and video activities).

- *Activity level of industry* = Number of employers (private + public businesses and organizations) in a city per 1000 inhabitants.
- *Public generic service level* = Number of employees in a city working as public teachers, health workers, and social workers (defined as NACE codes 80 and 85) per 1000 inhabitants.
- *Presence of foreign nationals* = Share of the population in a city born outside Denmark.
- *Social inclusion of non-Western immigrants* = A city's employment rate of immigrants born outside Scandinavia, the EU, USA, Canada, Australia and New Zealand.

As a supplement to register data, we carried out a total of 92 qualitative interviews in nine cities:

- The national and regional centers (Copenhagen, Aarhus, Odense and Aalborg)
- Cities with a large share of the creative class compared to the size of their populations (Svendborg, Sønderborg, Ærø, and Fanø)
- One city with a small share of the creative class compared to the size of its population (Esbjerg).

The interviews were done on-site, used a semi-structured interview protocol and were subsequently transcribed/summarized. In the interviews, we asked politicians, public servants, and local business managers of knowledge-intensive companies about the economic and political impact of the creative class. Furthermore, group interviews with members of the creative class explored their location preferences and lifestyle choices.

3. Organizing: spontaneously developed urban technology precincts

Gülnur Çevikayak and Koray Velibeyoğlu

INTRODUCTION

In recent years, cities have begun to compete with each other mainly based on their level of knowledge production, innovation, creativity and learning, and they have started to become more dynamic, complex, diverse, open and intangible (Finquelievich, 2002). Improving the knowledge-intensive business and service sector is an important issue for knowledge cities to develop their economic base.

At the heart of the new innovation environment, *technology precincts* are faced with innovative processes to deliver today's needs. The traditional concept of 'technology precinct' starts to be changed in terms of new urban precincts where knowledge is the driving force of the economic and urban development (Seitinger, 2004; Tidd, 2003).

The pioneer force of knowledge-based urban development is knowledge-intensive business and service sectors, such that knowledge has become the fourth factor of production beside land, labour and capital. Commercializing new knowledge causes increase in the knowledge-based business and service sectors and awareness of the centrality to the urban context of sustained face-to-face contact, and especially quality of life in the vibrant, dynamic city (Corey and Wilson, 2006). This process brings knowledge-based innovative environments that contain new technology development areas with new contents. In this chapter, those new technology developments that locate in the inner city are named urban technology precincts (UTPs).

UTPs can appear in two ways. The first way is the renovation and rebuilding of old or abandoned industrial grey or brown fields into new technology-based, vibrant areas with a strong identity and brand. The second way is a self organizing process that occurs by accumulation of information and communication technology (ICT) based services in a particular urban area.

These spontaneously developed areas have unique opportunities to create local urban technology precincts for entrepreneurships. They exist in small accumulated ICT-based areas which could develop a strong identity and brand as well-known UTPs with the help of small-scale interventions within small budgets.

The aim of this chapter is to clarify the potential of spontaneously developed urban technology precincts by researching their spatial and organizational characteristics, using a case study from Izmir, Turkey. In this context the chapter has three parts. The first involves the transformation process of technology precincts, and the second part examines spontaneously developed urban technology precinct examples and their characteristics. The last part is the case study: Çankaya in Izmir, which is known as the 'Izmir Technology Diamond'. It is accepted as an emerging inner city technology precinct waiting for development by local authorities. It has the potential to be a powerful source of local economic development, and to supply cultural and social prestige to Izmir.

URBAN TECHNOLOGY PRECINCTS

Over the years, conventionally defined scientific and technology parks have taken different roles: they have acted as regional development organizations, provided innovation support and added value services for their tenants, and run real estate businesses (Graham, 1999). However, due to changing urban and especially economic trends, they have had to temporize and face evolutionary processes. In the literature, technology development areas' starting point is accepted as the idea of concentrating companies in one single area, with the first industrial park/district, the Central Manufacturing District in Chicago, created in 1905 (Castells, 1994; Seitinger, 2004; Annerstedt, 2006). The idea continues with science parks, which first appeared in 1950 with Menlo Park and Stanford Science Park in Chicago.

Conventional technology development areas have been classified under various names as technopoles/technopolises, research parks, business parks, and technology centres, but the generic umbrella has been accepted as 'science park' (Vanhoudt 2006; Seitinger, 2004; Pages and Condom, 2008). Science parks tend to provide the opportunity for a degree of institutional co-operation between university and industry, besides being producers of high-technology products and services. In relation to the changes in urban and economic structure, technology developments are classified in three generations (Annerstedt and Haselmayer, 2006) (see Figure 3.1):

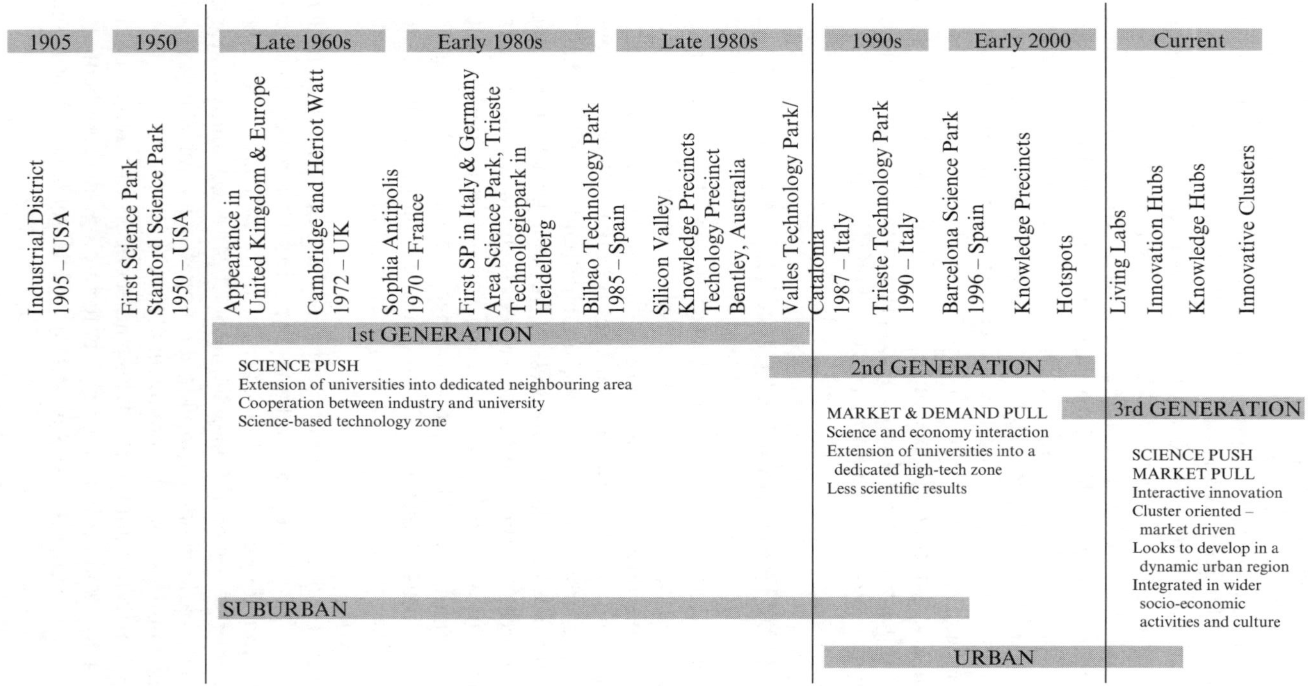

Sources: Vanhoudt, 2006; Pages and Condom, 2008; European Commission Report, 2007.

Figure 3.1 Evolution of technology precincts

- *1st generation* Science Push (1960s): Science-based technology zone
- *2nd generation* Market and Demand Pull (1980s): Science and economy interaction
- *3rd generation* Interactive Innovation (Current)

The first generation has been perceived as science push, and the second one as *market and demand pull.* Today, the third generation is based on *interactive local flows* located in a vibrant urban community consisting of science–industry–government relations and local, regional and even global innovation activities.

The buzz concepts of 'creativity and innovation' are the seedbeds for the current technology developments (van Winden and van den Berg, 2004). Knowledge transfer gives way to knowledge exchange, and knowledge becomes a competitive and commercial issue for cities. Development of creative, knowledge-based and technology-intensive services and sectors within certain precincts of the inner city generate important aspects of the spatiality of the knowledge economy (Hutton, 2004). These new innovative precincts are shaped by the integration of culture (liveliness) and urban development (diversity) by the increasing significance of technology in value-added production, and by the competitive advantage of the inner city for creative and innovative sectors.

The current trend of UTP is to integrate functions of technology, industry, service and business sectors and culture by combining living, working, learning and playing entities. Urban technology precincts have emerged as a principal policy issue in connection with city development and are under pressure from competing city-regions due to economic globalization.

Locating in a vibrant environment is important because of the need to supply talented, highly skilled workers with desirable quality of life in an integrated living, working and playing area. These processes might involve technology areas in related developments and issues such as accessibility of public services to high-tech businesses, management of clustering of competencies, real-estate asset values and the quality of the environment and place branding and marketing.

New innovative environments combine technology, including computer graphics and imaging, software design, multimedia industries and graphic design industries that have been deeply influenced by technological development; culture, represented by creative human capital and design functions; and place, more specifically the innovative milieu of the inner city (Hutton, 2004).

Hutton (2004, p. 93) labels these new innovative precincts as 'new industry clusters within the inner city' and composes a typology for them according

Table 3.1 Requirements of third generation technology development areas

Business requirements	Attracting the right people Interaction and communication Accessibility, openness and convenience Flexibility – functional, financial & physical Image – identity/differentiation
Spatial requirements	Diversity of accommodation Concentration of functions and people (intensification) Dispersal – supporting people wherever they work Identity / sense of place
Requirements of 'knowledge workers'	Increasing mobility of workforce Increasing focus on quality of life Greater provision of leisure and amenity

Source: Tidd, 2003.

to their specialized production in the inner city and their to space–place relation. He distinguishes stages of development in the evolution of the inner city's knowledge economy and identifies in at least a preliminary way the distinctive spatiality of new production formations in the metropolitan core. He develops a provisional typology of inner city new innovative sites and spaces, including Extensive Production Districts, Induced Compact New Industry Clusters, 'Signifying' Knowledge Economy Precincts, Spontaneous New Industry Clusters, and 'Incipient' New Industry Districts and Sites. According to his research, the emergence of these new territorial forms of industrial activity, differentiated internally by scale considerations, industrial mix, and functional specialization, among other factors, represents the reorganization of urban space to meet changing market demands and ascendant forms of intermediate services production.

New innovative technology development areas can be named under various types according to their geographical scale, functional capacity, clustering environment and also their emerging process (Table 3.1).

There are new terms, such as living labs, technology hotspots, i-hubs, knowledge precincts, knowledge corridor and (the most comprehensive) knowledge city (Figure 3.2). They are the interdependent and interrelated scales of knowledge/creativity. These scales have soft edges. Connections across all scales are part of the overall knowledge assets in a city. The living labs are the smallest part of urban technology precincts. They work as a laboratory that consists of ICT-based technologies. These labs can be

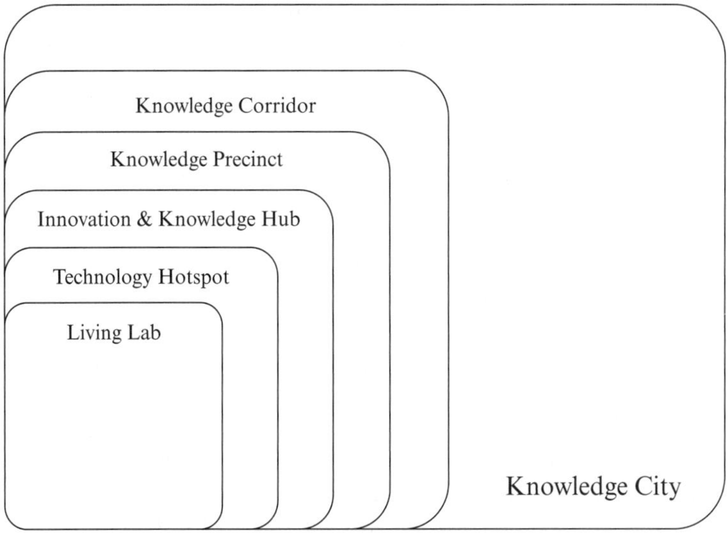

Figure 3.2 Scale of new technology precincts

in a single building or a flat. Technology hotspots seem similar to living labs. However, hotspots can occupy any place in the inner city. They can be recognized by their knowledge identity. They emerge spontaneously in a part of the city with an accumulation of ICT-based firms and also business and service sectors. Sometimes a technology hotspot area can consist of streets that include many ICT-based firms. When we go to the upper scales, the land area they cover and the functions they include can change. For example, knowledge precincts are seen as developer engines of growth and of creative urban regions (see Aw and Koh, 2005). A knowledge precinct promotes and manages the flow of knowledge and technology amongst universities, research and development (R&D) institutions, companies and markets, as well as facilitating the creation and growth of innovation-based companies through incubation and spin-off processes, and providing other value-added services such as high quality space (including living and recreation areas) and facilities (Yigitcanlar et al., 2008). The knowledge city is on the highest scale of data. It can consist of all those urban technology precinct examples.

In summary: third generation areas tend to promote a wide variety of interactions and have the appearance of mixed-use environments, blurring the boundaries between physical, digital, economic, social and cultural spaces. The most recognizable difference between the conventional and the contemporary technology development areas appears in business and service sectors due to provision of accessibility, flexibility, seamless connectivity, and integrated functions in a work–live–play–learn and place identity.

SPONTANEOUSLY DEVELOPED URBAN TECHNOLOGY PRECINCTS

The chapter examines two spontaneously developed urban technology precincts (SDUTP) Silicon Alley, New York and SoFo, Stockholm. These examples were evaluated by adopting the research of INTELI (Cunha and Selada, 2007), which is used as an analysis tool to understand the main characteristics of new urban technology precincts.

The INTELI Project (Cunha and Selada, 2007) was conducted under two main questions: (1) how science, technology, innovation and creativity can be placed at the service of urban policy and redevelopment, and (2) what are the best practices that should underlie the definition of urban policies as regards the design and planning of new innovative environments. It examines new innovative knowledge-intensive areas around the world, with methodology establishing a set of dimensions of analysis. Therefore, worldwide examples are reviewed according to seven dimensions: Governance; Clustering Environment; Cultural Environment; Built Environment; Talent and Social Environment; Natural Environment; and Connectivity (see Figure. 3.3).

International Best Practice: Silicon Alley and SoFo

Two well-known worldwide best practice examples are chosen, considering their success, popularity and branding in terms of knowledge-based development. Situated in the context of New York's development as a global city, Silicon Alley is the first example, including advanced producer services and the dramatic growth of ICTs in an increasingly transnational economy. Silicon Alley is a very popular area in terms of being an industry cluster of about a thousand new media firms since the early 1990s. The second example is known as SoFo (South of Folkungagatan), a design district in Stockholm established in 2002 within a neighbourhood that was previously residential (Koskinen, 2009). Today, the area has become the hub of fashion in Stockholm.

Both Silicon Alley and SoFo have dense concentrations not only of ICT but also of media, design, and art. These areas both provide a frame, focus, and leadership, as well as a pool of resources for creating, running, and maintaining design as a core element in the district's identity

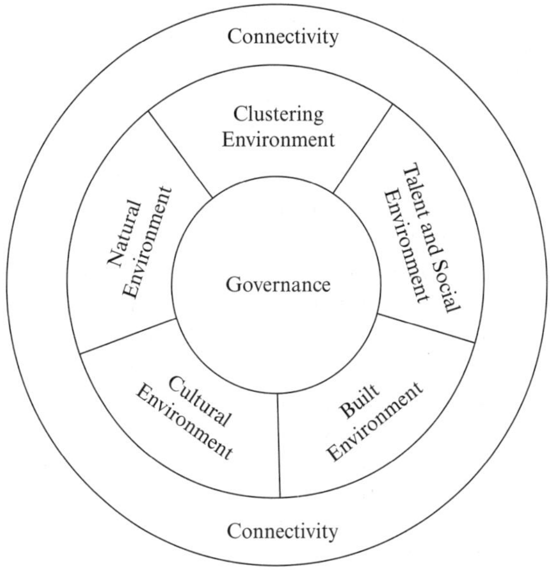

Source: Cunha and Selada, 2007.

Figure 3.3 Dimensions of analysis of INTELI

(Koskinen, 2009, 13). One of the emerging common properties of these areas is the quality of creative work relations in contemporary business services and knowledge-intensive service networks, mediated by advanced ICT infrastructure. Both Silicon Alley and SoFo are success stories for spontaneously developed urban technology precincts.

Silicon Alley is a media- and ICT-based cluster which originally referred to the cluster of such companies extending from the Flatiron District down to SoHo and TriBeCa along the Broadway corridor, but as the location of these companies spread out, it became a general term referring to the dot.com industry in New York City as a whole. Table 3.3 shows the characteristics of these examples according to seven distinctive dimensions.

The typical location pattern of Silicon Alley within Manhattan can be characterized as a concentration within urban centres or even specific streets, building complexes or buildings, facilitated by a low need for office space and the location preferences of the creative key personnel (Fuchs, 2000, p. 564). This shows the persistence of agglomeration effects, as the concentration of multimedia production attracts even more firms and staff. Concentration in particular streets still gives identity to Silicon Alley.

The name of Stockholm's SoFo emerged as a pun on New York's SoHo and is an invention of local entrepreneurs who have attempted to re-brand the area as a centre of creative and innovative fashion and retailing since 2003. SoFo is a mixed-used environment and like Silicon Alley it is home to many of Stockholm's other creative industries, including advertising agencies, media companies and publishers. Although compact, SoFo also offers a wide selection of restaurants, bars, coffee shops, and art galleries.

Design is a real phenomenon for the area. It creates design-based identities such as logos, event nights, and identity-based shops. Stockholm Design District SoFo organizes activities, websites, and shopping maps, to attract certain types of customers and businesses; pushing development in an increasingly more artistic and design-oriented direction.

When we scrutinize both examples in terms of the dimensions mentioned above, the main point is creating compact mixed-use environments, consisting of all that is needed for work–live–play–learn. The best practice cases suggest that SDUTPs develop through infiltration of corporations and firms in the inner city. At the beginning, the market economy dictates firms' location in the most suitable areas in the central business district (CBD), but after that they start to transform their environment positively. The result is that over time these environments emerge as vibrant areas with a distinct identity through interaction with the existing local context.

The necessity of being closer to knowledge-based business and service sectors brings an intersection of multiple usages and creates a mixed-use environment. When we examine SDUTP examples in terms of design, existing social, cultural and natural amenities shape their emergence or disappearance. Therefore, any interventions to the environment should be careful and small in scale.

Physical interventions should be limited to small touches such as restoration of historical buildings, streetscape, and colour of buildings, besides adding new advertisement tools such as kiosks and signboards. These implementations can be done with the help of local government, private entrepreneurships and existing universities' support. In SDUTPs, interaction among the different environments – residential, business, finance, media, recreational, social and cultural – stimulates the dynamics of the area. As we compare our worldwide examples (Table 3.2), best practice points to the presence of good knowledge infrastructures in cooperation with companies of creative or soft industries (Indergaard, 2004).

On the one hand, a culture of entrepreneurship is important. Besides the presence of knowledge and creative workers, the environment tends to be diverse, multicultural and vibrant, with the presence of foreign talents. Congregation of small–medium entrepreneurships constitutes spontaneously-developed urban technology precincts. In this context,

Table 3.2 Spontaneously developed urban technology precincts: assessment of international best practice

	Silicon Alley/New York	SoFo/Stockholm
Typology	Compact Knowledge Economy Cluster	Incipient New Innovative Precinct
Governance	• Corporations and interfirms • Bottom-Up Approach • Market-Centered System	• Local Entrepreneurs • Bottom-Up Approach • Market-Centered System
Clustering environment	• Existing Local Context • Clustering Areas: On-line (Internet, or world wide web) and CD-ROM products and services and also publishing, broadcasting and advertising	• Existing restaurants and local context • Clustering areas: fashion and retail, advertising agencies, media companies and publishers
Connectivity	• "Intranet" development • Integrated with the region	• Transport connections • Near to local social and recreational social places
Talent and social environment	• Qualified multimedia, business, finance and service sector	• Qualified designers, publishers, retail owners and also artists
Built Environment	• Live and work together • Closely associated with service and business sector • Diverse and strong complex community	• Mixed-use environment • Includes other social and recreational local places • Distinct character
Cultural Environment	• Cultural blend and diversity of ethnic traditions, viewpoints and value systems	• Design-based identities • Cultural activities
Natural Environment	• Not enough information	• Not enough information

knowledge-intensive firms come together at the place of interaction of liveliness, diversity, mix-use environments, quality of life, flexibility and adaptability.

On the other hand, identity of place is the other most important key for urban technology precincts. At this point, after their emergence process and at the time for their improvement, government or private investors should admit their role in this scene. For instance, governmental policies such as land use zoning decisions or promotion policies can be developed.

Table 3.3 General characteristics of SDUTPs

Governance	Connectivity	Clustering environment	Built environment	Talent & social environment	Cultural environment	Natural environment
• Market-centered system • Bottom-up approach	• Locating at central business district • Walkable distances • Virtual connectivity	• Knowledge and creative intensive sectors	• Infiltration based • Mixed-use (working-living-learning-playing) environment • Interactive environments • Proximity to business and service sectors	• Qualified human resources • Knowledge and creative workers • Diverse and multicultural environment • Social networks	• Existing cultural blend • Distinctiveness and unique identity ('genius loci') • Cultural and entertainment facilities • Vibrant and inspiring life	• Developing potential Assets • Creating environmental quality

Source: Cunha and Selada (2007).

As a source of local economic development, and as a matter of the political and social prestige of cities, the potential of spontaneously developed urban technology precincts, as well as planned ones, cannot be ignored from the SDUTP examples and literature review, the general characteristics can be summarized as in Table 3.2.

IZMIR TECHNOLOGY DIAMOND: AN EMERGING SDUTP

According to the socio-economic development study in the Izmir Development Agency Development Plan 2009–2013, and Alkin et al.'s (2007) 'City Competitiveness Index', Izmir is the third biggest city of Turkey. It is the centre of the Aegean Region, and has natural, cultural and also knowledge assets besides high institutional structure, information and communication infrastructure and strong access networks.

Izmir is affected by the knowledge economy in terms of its local economic development. Today, many public authorities, NGOs and SMEs struggle to develop ICTs to enhance local economic development and urban human resources. Izmir Development Agency's (2008) report asserts that firms that are connected with each other, or compatible services which locate at the same place, should be investigated and clustered to cause awareness of each other and supply suitable arenas to study together. In this context, Çankaya, Konak District is selected as the focus of the case study because of its local reputation as home to software development, computer hardware services, graphic and media firms. The identified existing knowledge-intensive service and business in Çankaya shows the IT capacity of the area. According to research results, 72 knowledge-intensive firms have been identified around Çankaya.

This ICT-based cluster is bounded by main vehicular access roads that give a diamond shape to the area (Figure 3.4). Moreover, it is observed that some areas have a technology hotspot character, for example around Şair Eşref Boulevard and 1362 Street through individual office buildings.

The research area was examined according to the base reference of INTELI (Cunha and Selada, 2007), and scrutinized in terms of seven dimensions (Table 3.3). Each of these seven dimensions refers to a state of existing characteristics and represents the case area's potential as SDUTP and hotspot. They also show the urban pattern, existing functions and sectors, and identity of the area besides creating, disseminating and using knowledge and creativity for economic growth.

In the process of assessment, we used qualitative research techniques

Figure 3.4 Izmir Technology Diamond and hotspot areas (Google Earth)

Table 3.4 Valuation framework of knowledge intensive firms

Category	Evaluation criteria	Value
Creative supplier	Knowledge generators	3
Technical service	Knowledge users	2
Distributors	Knowledge disseminators	1
Total		6

such as observations, checklist, and interviews. Additionally, to obtain quantitative data we utilized archival data from the Turkish Statistical Institute, NGOs and professional associations.

In order to evaluate the knowledge capacity of the firms, a valuation framework was prepared illustrating the three main categories as Creative Suppliers, Technical Service, and Distributors (Table 3.4).

The Creative Suppliers category, valued as 3, reflects knowledge generation by way of software-based firms that work on software systems and generate software databases of their own, and graphic design, media and web design, and advertisement based firms. The second category is defined as technical services or supporters and is valued as 2. The last category contains distributors and is valued by the lowest score, 1.

According to the results of this evaluation framework, most of the creative supplier firms are on Şair Eşref Boulevard and 1362 Street. It was seen that Şair Eşref Boulevard was the best example for the study, with its hotspot character of including many ICT-based SMEs. On the other hand, Izmir Technology Diamond has SDUTP character, covering all work, live and play concepts besides having a unique identity.

The case area was analysed according to the establishment of the set of dimensions shown in Figure 3.5. Under Governance, the aim is to clarify coordination of actors – public and private – involved in the management of the innovation habitats. Connectivity includes physical accessibility, such as transport networks, as well as digital infrastructures and flows for sustainable connectivity. Clustering Environment covers the business climate and knowledge infrastructure of the area, and the interactions between universities and other research institutions and companies. In terms of Talent and Social Environment, the level of qualifications, mobility and diversity of the workers in the community are defined. Physical dimensions of the area, land use decisions, existing architecture, and public spaces are clarified by Built Environment research. Finally, Cultural Environment shows us the cultural and entertainment amenities of the area, while Natural Environment determines existing environmental quality.

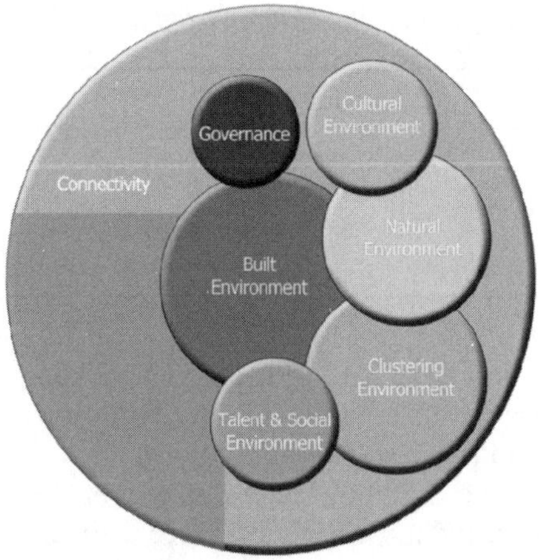

Note: The size of bubbles defines dimensions from the weakest (smallest) to strongest.

Figure 3.5 Dimension synthesis of the case area

Results of the Survey

According to the key themes, Izmir Technology Diamond is well connected, and the built environment is the most valuable dimension for the area. Moreover Clustering Environment shows an accumulation of knowledge-intensive firms in the area. Additionally Cultural and Natural environments have similar potentials. The weakest dimensions are Governance and Talent and Social Environment (Figure 3.5).

In this respect, if we compare results of Izmir Technology Diamond with key foundations of SDUTPs, three main headings are obtained. The first one is *missing and non existing* properties of the area that should be handled and implemented to sustain the success of the area. The second one is *existing properties* of the area that can be improved. These existing values form Izmir Technology Diamond's initial local potentials for having technology precinct character. The third point refers to properties that exist in the area but *need improvement*. This means that by small interventions, these properties can be turned to potential for the area.

The accumulation process of knowledge-intensive sectors depends on main knowledge assets. Thus, rather than requiring big investments for creating new knowledge-intensive areas, the case study area needs its potential to be restated and advertised to local authorities and also to local residents, to sustain experience of place.

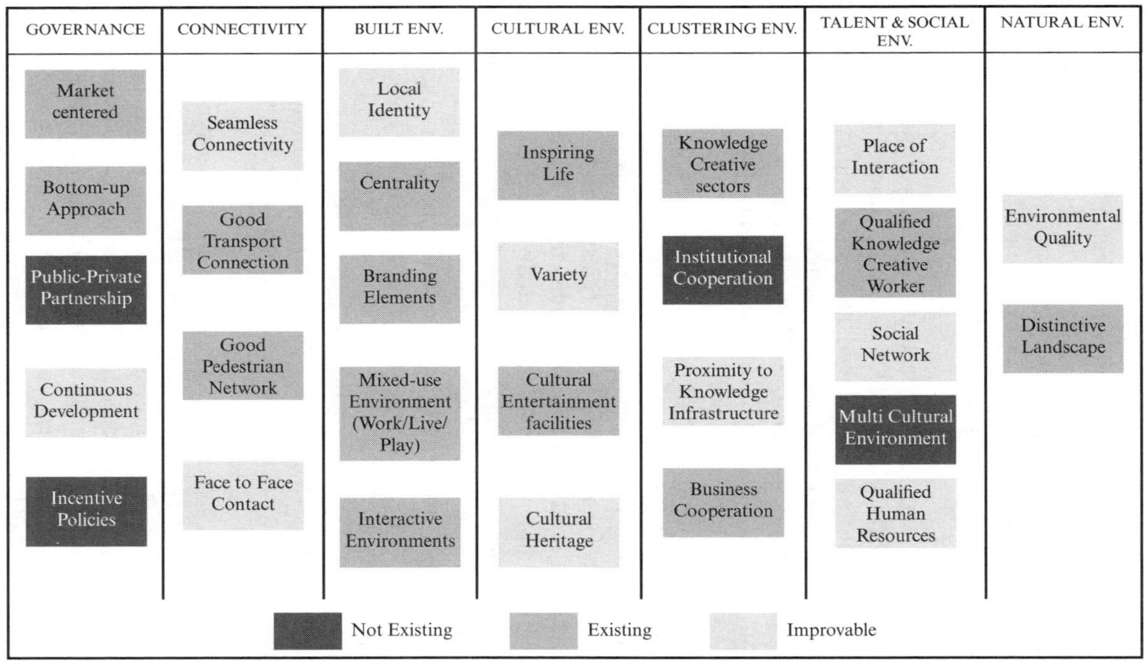

Figure 3.6 *Foundations of SDUTPs: indications of Izmir Technology Diamond*

In Turkey, SMEs consist of three main groups (by structure that hosts annual and annual net sales):

(a) Micro-size business: less than 10 employees, or businesses with financial balance not exceeding 1 million Turkish Lira.
(b) Small business: less than 50 employees, or businesses with financial balance sheet not exceeding 5 million Turkish Lira.
(c) Medium-size business: less than 250 employees or businesses with financial balance sheet of not more than 25 million Turkish Lira.

The mechanism of state support depends on turnover, portion of shares and financial statement (Kong, 2009). However, knowledge- and creative-intensive service sectors are not named under small and medium entrepreneurships in Turkey, which causes insufficient funds and credits for them. They struggle to stand on their own. This might block the continuity of development in the area. As in Silicon Alley, Izmir Technology Diamond should be supported by local authorities with encouraging policies such as tax reductions and sustaining IT infrastructure, land policies, private-public partnerships and so on.

Being at the middle of the main transportation axis sustains ease of access to the area. Good pedestrian and transportation networks are an important value for SDUTPs. Izmir Technology Diamond is well connected but could improve seamless connectivity, which is the main feature for knowledge-based developments. The speed and IT infrastructure of the area should be redesigned and improved. In the area, face-to-face contact is still important in addition to virtual access. The main problem for the Izmir Technology Diamond is advertisement for SMEs to create recognition of the area.

Proximity, clustering and premium access to different infrastructures, services, and amenities strengthen the concept of centrality. The integration of interactive environments with technology districts is a core necessity.

The study area is a mixed-use environment of fashion, media and commerce – CBDs trigger the ability for sustaining the best practice concept of work–live–play–learn. In terms of design issues, local identity and branding elements should be handled with a view to establishing an identity. The starting point can be the area's historical heritage, especially in terms of listed building restorations, with the aim of creative- and knowledge-based social and cultural centres such as the historic Atlas Hotel and the Turkish State Liquor and Tobacco Monopoly building. The existing historic fire station, which has been adapted for re-use for urban archives, can be integrated by knowledge- and creative-based entities. Culture Park hosts international fairs that create unique opportunities for branding of the area. This idea can be developed and improved by organizing software and IT fairs.

Cultural environment can be enriched by creativity-based amenities. In the study area, entertainment and cultural facilities are limited but the surrounding facilities make up for this. Moreover, inspiring surroundings are another reason for choice of location for firms. Izmir Technology Diamond integrates natural and cultural facilities near to the area. On one hand, the innovation environment of the area can be classified as knowledge commercialization because knowledge and creative sectors use the area for producing and marketing their own designs. Accumulation of knowledge-intensive firms, distributors and technical services provides a compact and unified structure in the inner city, and is beneficial as an innovation centre for the city and as a focal point for institutional relationships.

On the other hand, there are some firms that locate at Izmir Technology Diamond only for marketing, and their creativity department is in the techno park area of Izmir Institute of Technology. Although SDUTPs have direct relationships with institutions and universities, the relocation of related firms from inner city to suburban techno park areas will result in diminishing importance and visibility. For instance, according to our survey study, knowledge-intensive firms choose to locate on the upper floors of office buildings, which can be interpreted as: not willing to be disturbed; reject having a retailer identity and shop front; and (as in Silicon Alley) low rent. Regeneration should not move them to ground floors, or these firms that have accumulated may decide to move to a separate zone created especially for them.

CONCLUSION

This study asserts that spontaneously developed urban technology precincts want to locate at the centre of the core, inner city, to supply diversity and vibrancy, and create their identity. Therefore the most important point is, while these spontaneously developed areas are being improved, their main character should be protected. These areas can be thought of as instant generations, and causing faults in their spontaneous life may cause death of their potential.

Izmir Technology Diamond is a simple example of a spontaneously developed urban technology precinct. It has many existing physical, social, cultural and technological amenities waiting for improvement to sustain social and economic development for Izmir with its unique character. Its location at the middle of the city centre and its integration of living, working and playing facilities, besides good connectivity, might make its transformation easy.

Existing knowledge and creative workers are invisible to the local citizens and authorities. The aim should be to push other knowledge workers to the area to sustain its prestige. This depends on branding, marketing and advertisement. But sometimes an avalanche effect can be negative for these types of technology areas. Because of the rising interest in the area, an increase in real estate values causes existing knowledge capacity to escape to other places, instead of pushing knowledge workers in. With this regard, the main point is to sustain place quality and integration of the seven analysis dimensions supporting knowledge-based urban development and the character of spontaneously developed urban technology precincts. This chapter has explored the characteristics of spontaneously developed inner city technology precincts. In this context, the important first step was achieved by investigating SDUTPs in line with worldwide examples to introduce specifications, techniques and qualities. Within achieved qualities and components from the evaluation of global practices, this element served to analyse and assess suitable cities and regions to designate the opportunities and potentials of those areas for a technology-based development.

This chapter mainly focused on ICT-based business and service sectors. However, new knowledge intensive ICT-based sectors are exemplified by software design, internet design and services, computer graphics and imaging and multimedia industries. So, research into clarifying spatial and organizational characteristics should be done for other services. Their organizational characteristics may differ. Furthermore, the study struggles to define potentials of self-organizing systems and their characteristics; therefore, in our future research, the policy making processes for those systems will be further scrutinized.

REFERENCES

Alkin, K., Bulu, M. and Kaya, H. (2007), 'City competitiveness index: an approach to measure the competitiveness level of cities in Turkey', *Istanbul Ticaret Üniversitesi Sosyal Bilimler Dergisi*, **6** (11), 221–235.

Annerstedt, J. (2006), 'Science parks and high-tech clustering', in *International Handbook on Industrial Policy*, Cheltenham, UK and Northampton, MA, USA: Edward Elgar.

Annerstedt, J. and Haselmayer, S. (2006), 'Third generation living labs: the quest for user-centered mobile services', *eChallenges Proceedings.*

Aw, A. and Koh, C. (2005), 'One-North Initiative: where ideas grow', in Waikeen

Ng and Judith Ryser (eds), *Making Spaces for the Creative Economy*, Singapore: ISOCARP.

Castells, M. and Hall, P. (1994), *Technopoles of the World: The Making of 21st Century Industrial Complexes*, London: Routledge.

Corey, K. and Wilson, M. (2006), *Urban and Regional Technology Planning: Planning Practice in the Global Knowledge Economy*, New York: Routledge.

Cunha, I.V. and Selada, C. (2007), 'Creative urban regeneration: the case of innovation hubs', 24–25, *3rd IET International Conference on Intelligent Environments Conference Paper*, INTELI, http://www.inteli.pt/uploads/documentos/documento_1220959067_7946.pdf, accessed October 2008.

European Commission Report (2007), 'Regional research intensive clusters and science parks', prepared by an independent expert group (Chairman Christian Saublens) Eurada, Brussels, Belgium.

Finquelievich, S. (2002), 'Cities and science and technology parks innovation environments as a new urban hierarchy', Conference Paper, XIX IASP World Conference on Science & Technology Parks, 3–6 September, http://www.links.org.ar., accessed 5 February 2009.

Fuchs, G. (2000), 'The role of geography in the information economy: the case of multimedia', Jahrgang, Heft 4.

Graham S. (1999), *Planning Cyber-Cities? Integrating Telecommunications into Urban Planning*, University of Newcastle, UK.

Hutton, T. (2004), 'The new economy of the inner city', *Cities*, **21** (2), 89–108.

Indergaard, M. (2004), *Silicon Alley: The Rise and Fall of a New Media District*, New York: Routledge.

Izmir Development Agency (2008), 'Izmir Development Plan for 2009–2013'.

Kong, L. (2009), 'Making sustainable creative/cultural space in Shanghai and Singapore', *Geographical Review,* **99** (1), 1–22

Koskinen, I. (2009), 'Design districts', *Massachusetts Institute of Technology,* Vol. 25–4.

Pages Llach, J. and Vila Condom, P. (2008), 'Science and technology parks: creating new environments favourable to innovation', *Paradigmes*, Issue no.0, May, www.gencat.cat/diue/doc/doc_25819940_3.pdf.

Seitinger S. (2004), 'Spaces of innovation: 21st century technopoles', Submitted to the Department of Urban Studies and Planning in partial fulfilment of the requirements for the degree of Master in City Planning in MIT.

Tidd, P. (2003), 'Ports and cities in the 21st century', ECOPorts Conference, Barcelona.

Van Winden, W. and Van den Berg, L. (2004), 'Cities in the knowledge economy: new governance challenges', European Institute for Comparative Urban Research, Discussion Paper, http://www.mie.ro/urbactII/urbact/projects/strike/Executive_summary.pdf, accessed on 21 May 2009

Vanhoudt, P. (2006), 'Too much of a good thing', *European Investment Bank Research.*

Yigitcanlar, T., Velibeyoglu, K. and Martinez-Fernandez, C. (2008), 'Rising knowledge cities: the role of urban knowledge precincts', *Journal of Knowledge Management*, **12** (5), 8–20.

4. Globalizing: what makes Australian information technology industry companies go global?

Glen Searle and Kevin O'Connor

INTRODUCTION

Although Australia has a significant information technology (IT) industry sector, there is still a large trade deficit in IT goods and services. Information, communication and technology exports in 2008–2009 were less than exports in 1999–2000. There is a strong policy imperative to use the existing IT industry base to generate greater exports and become a more significant player in the global IT industry. At present, however, there is inadequate data relating to factors impeding or assisting exports on which to base such policy. In particular, the role of Australia's position in global chains of IT production, and of Australia's peripheral global location, is poorly understood. This chapter is an initial attempt to explore firm-level factors associated with IT exports from Australia. It uses data from a random stratified sample of IT firms in Sydney and Melbourne to identify company attributes associated with differing levels of exports. It also uses data from this sample to explore factors associated with Australia's global location that are perceived to disadvantage Australian IT producers.

SERVICE INDUSTRIES AND EXPORTS

One important characteristic of knowledge based urban development is the development of knowledge intensive service activities. The local impact of these activities is likely to be greater if they become export activities, just as in an earlier era manufacturing firms in metropolitan economies brought growth and wealth to urban areas by exporting to distant markets. The export of services has been a steadily expanding activity, but its association with the urban location of firms is a more complex matter.

This chapter attempts to explore that complexity as it is expressed in the Australian IT sector.

Services as an Export Activity

Decisions by firms to export and start globalizing have been understood to be part of a straightforward set of stages as reviewed by Bell (1995), deriving from some foundation research carried out on exporting firms by Johanson and Wiedersheim-Paul (1975) and expressed for multinational firms by Dunning (1993). That analysis has suggested that firms go through stages in their approach to export activity. In the beginning they develop a skill or productive capacity in a home market, which they then export directly. Here one can see the local knowledge base as the foundation for the export function. In a second stage firms invest in production facilities in selected foreign markets; here they are transferring the knowledge base from their home city to other markets. Finally, firms engage in the geographically complicated global production networks that are common in many industries. Here the home based knowledge of the firm can be expressed in the management and organization skills to ensure the mobility and co-ordination of component movement and final production.

How might that model work for services? Zou and Stan (1998) showed that early thinking on this issue spanned a wide array of approaches. Further work has exposed two critical perspectives. The first is that exporting at each stage actually requires the use of services, often drawn from a home base. Daniels (2000) has highlighted this aspect in research by exploring the question whether services are exported like a commodity, or whether their real function is 'servicing [manufacturing/commodity] exports'? This distinction has important implications for the way that the knowledge base of a city, expressed though its service sector, is felt in local development. If services are exported like commodities, local firms need to create facilities in new markets which will hopefully generate income and profits that will be returned to the home base. Alternatively, a significant role for services can be the facilitation of physical exports (raw materials or manufactured goods) via finance, marketing, government liaison, transport and logistics functions, for example: what Balabanis (2005) has recently labelled 'export intermediaries'. In turn, the exporting firm is likely to look to its current bank, advertising agent, and transport service suppliers to support its international expansion. In this situation, the home knowledge base will be expanded and enriched via its exposure to the global activities of the manufacturers, as the service firms 'service exports' (Pain and Van Welsum 2004). In addition, there are often significant regulatory and cultural limits on the supply of services in foreign markets, which encourages exporters to obtain services from their home city. Banking regulations, for example, limit overseas banks from operating without first gaining a licence; the same can be said for legal firms. For these activities it is possible to be involved in a foreign market on behalf of a client, but it may be more difficult to actually establish a presence in such a market. O'Connor and Daniels (2001) illustrated that outcome by showing that the concentration in service trade is actually between countries with highly developed service sectors. So rather than supplying a market where a product is missing, service exports are most developed in markets where service functions are already sophisticated. This paradox emerges from the way that services are linked to production and need a well developed skill base (and regulatory structures) to operate.

A second important dimension is that services can be exported yet still made within the supplying country. In research on this topic, these activities have been labelled 'domestically located service exports' (Roberts 1999). Education, tourism and health services provide the best examples. To obtain these exports clients need to come into a country. So the expansion of the knowledge base of a metropolitan region can be the foundation for service exports without going through the basic model of export activity outlined above. Hence knowledge based service sector development can have a strong export orientation while at the same time directly adding to the economic functions and activity within the home base city. O'Connor and Daniels (2001) showed that in Australia in 1998 the concentration on these activities was greater than in other countries. In contrast business service exports were less significant.

These general perspectives show that the rapid expansion of service exports may have unexpected associations with the local production facilities and through that, the knowledge base of a city. In this way, the urban knowledge base becomes a globalizing force. Due to their special features, the way that service exports influence a city will be very different to what we have seen as manufacturers became exporters. This may have some special relevance in Australia where the manufacturing sector is not as large as it was in the past (although its export exposure is still significant in some sectors).

IT as an Export Activity

The implications of the interpretations of service activity may need to be re-interpreted for the IT industry in the rapidly changing digital world. Roberts (1999: 85) identified this activity as 'wired' exports, noting at the time that improvements in telecommunications will probably increase this activity especially as 'ICTs become more integrated into the process of service provision' (Roberts 1999: 81). The rapid expansion in computer based outsourced activities from countries such as India and elsewhere illustrates that expectation (Javalgi et al. 2004; Parthasarathy 2004; Saxenian 2006).

Significantly, Roberts (1999) found computer services firms were three times more likely to use the 'wired export' approach than all business service firms in her sample. Bell (1995) explored export activity by small computer software firms. He notes entry barriers are low and the size of the enterprise is not critical. He observes:

> Small software developers with only a handful of staff can develop excellent packages which have great export potential. High-value, low-volume offerings make physical distribution easy [while] transmission of software via electronic means can be an added advantage. [Also] intra-industry relationships with hardware manufacturers and integrated systems developers impact on the export strategies of small software firms. (Bell 1995: 74)

IT as an Export Activity in Australia

From this overview it is apparent that when we consider IT exports from Australia we have a number of dimensions to explore. First, computer services can now be moved easily across the globe. That would suggest that an advanced country like Australia could be a significant actor in this sector. Second, if the home based market is the foundation of development, and firms then reach out to the global market, might the small scale of the Australian market act as a limitation on the development of exporting forms? Alternatively, are there some special features in the Australian market (such as the services supplied to the mining industry or to specialized agriculture, or maybe to some other innovative areas such as solar energy and medical research) that provide a 'niche' skill that can then be exported? Third, the IT industry is dominated by a small number of large companies. That could have two consequences for IT exporting firms in Australia. Firstly, the link to the global operators could provide conduits for local firms (which may in the long run be absorbed into the large firm). Looked at in this way, the link to the larger firm can overcome the problems and difficulties of entering overseas markets for small Australian firms. Secondly, however, the sheer scale of the global firm could limit the Australian firm to the Australian market alone and make it impossible to enter global markets because the local firm's product would lack a profile overseas. Finally, there is the issue of the intensity of competition in this sector, and whether Australia provides the public support and capacity for its firms to compete with nations in the Asia Pacific region such as Taiwan, Singapore, India and increasingly China.

Hence the capacity for the Australian IT sector to be involved in export activity, and through that to enrich and enhance the knowledge base of Australian cities, is an open question. It deserves research attention to explore and address any special features that might shape the outcome, and so contribute to the understanding of the sector in general, while also providing a clearer base for the articulation of policy designed to assist firms in the sector.

FIRM SAMPLING METHODOLOGY

To engage with these issues and understand the nature of Australia's role in the IT industry's globalization, the chapter analyses the characteristics of a sample of IT industry firms in Sydney and Melbourne. Data for this analysis was obtained from a telephone questionnaire that was administered to a random stratified sample of IT industry firms in the two cities. The sample target was 50 firms in each of IT industry sectors of software production, computer systems/services and technical support, and internet and multimedia. The target was 20 firms in each of the sectors of data preparation, computer hardware, internet service providers, and computer peripherals. The sample was skewed toward large firms, using data from the *Kompass* directory, to ensure a more even coverage of total industry employment. *Yellow Pages* company listings were used in addition to *Kompass* listings as the latter directory gave less comprehensive coverage of the industry, especially of smaller firms. However, as no employment data was available for companies listed in the *Yellow Pages*, all such companies were included in the sample of firms with less than 50 employees. Where a firm in the *Yellow Pages* sample was found in the interview to have more than 50 employees, it was counted as one of the sample in the appropriate (larger) size category.

The number of firms actually interviewed is shown below in Table 4.1. The overall number of firms sampled was less than targeted, due to lower than expected response rates. The number of software production firms sampled was more than targeted, because a number of firms classified in *Kompass* or the *Yellow Pages* as computer service providers were found to be principally software producers when interviewed. Nearly all of the internet service providers listed in the two directories were found to be resellers – and therefore excluded – rather than originator providers, thus accounting for the few firms interviewed

Table 4.1 Level of exports by IT industry type

Exports as % of total sales	Software production	Internet & multimedia production	Hardware production	Computer services	Peripherals production	Internet service providers
50 & above	5	2	1		3	–
5 to 49	21	10	2	1	2	–
0 to 4	36	30	5	11	11	5

in this category. The same was true to a lesser extent in the case of hardware producers.

IT EXPORTS AND COMPANY CHARACTERISTICS

IT Industry Type

The IT industry sector contains a variety of production types. Some of these could be expected to have greater possibilities for export than others. Table 4.1 sets out the survey findings on the association between level of exports of each firm and their IT industry branch.

Table 4.1 confirms the small exposure to exports by Australian IT firms. Very few in the sample exported more than 50 per cent of their total sales value. Even in the next level used here (5–49 per cent) export exposure is low, with only one group prominent. Industry type influences the level of exports. Software producers had the highest rate of exporting, with 42 per cent of sampled firms exporting 5 per cent or more of their production (measured by sales value). Computer services and ISP companies had virtually no firms exporting 5 per cent or more of production. Much software can be used across a range of applications, and so is not as contextually-dependent as computer services, for example. The latter derive their main revenue from problem-solving for specific workplaces, and the resulting service is not one that can be exported easily. ISP companies are restricted to intra-national markets in part because they operate in the context of nationally based telecommunication regulations and associated telecommunication providers. Most multimedia production is carried out on a project-by-project basis, restricting the scope for cross-firm applications, although Table 4.1 suggests that the skills involved can be applied to overseas clients in many cases.

Company Type and Size

A central issue concerning IT exports relates to the role of multinational corporations (MNCs). These can be seen as the core components of the global IT sector, operating throughout the world and drawing on sub-contractors for specialist supplies and services. Around these companies a cluster of smaller IT companies operates, most of them servicing local markets, but many serving as sub-contractors to multinationals or exporting niche products themselves. IT exports are thus hypothesized to be generated by a combination of multinational production platforms and specialist small national firms. Multinationals in countries that are not production platforms would be expected to be importers rather than exporters of IT goods and services. The survey therefore obtained data on the involvement of multinationals in IT exports from Australia. It also obtained data on company size, to test (inter alia) the hypothesis that larger local companies might have sufficient levels of skills and innovation to engage in export activity. Table 4.2 sets out the resulting data on how multinational status and firm size are related to export levels.

The data in Table 4.2 show that the greatest exposure to exports is actually in the hands of small Australian companies. Eleven of the 12 firms exporting more than 50 per cent of their production were Australian firms. However, among the most numerous small firms only seven out of a total of sixteen have the high level exposure. The MNC influence is very small, even if Australian based. This exposes a significant influence upon IT export activity in Australia. The idea that MNCs might utilize a local base and begin export industry (developed from the experience of manufacturing) is obviously not relevant to the IT industry. The 16 foreign MNCs interviewed had some – mostly minor – role as Australian export

Table 4.2 Level of exports by IT company type and size[a]

Exports as % of total sales	Australian non-MNC less than 50 employees	Australian non-MNC 50 or more employees	Australian MNC less than 50 employees	Australian MNC 50 or more employees	Foreign MNC less than 50 employees	Foreign MNC 50 or more employees
50 & above	7	1	1	2	–	1
5 to 49	23	1	1	3	2	3
0 to 4	86	6	–	–	4	6

Note: [a]Size denoted by number of employees at establishment of interviewee.

Table 4.3 Level of exports by level of innovation in last 3 years

Exports as % of total sales	None	New products	New routines/ processes
50 & above	4	5	2
5 to 49	12	21	2
0 to 4	41	38	10

platforms. Most, however, operated just as importers of IT goods or services into Australia. It is possible that foreign ownership is a limiting factor on IT exports from Australia as these companies seem to serve separate regional markets and do not encourage movement of services between their regional operations.

Level of Innovation

A high level of innovation might be expected to be associated with a greater propensity to export. Greater innovation levels increase the likelihood that new products capable of being exported will be produced. Table 4.3 sets out survey data on levels of innovation, measured by new products or routines/processes introduced in the last three years, and their relationship with export levels. While the table shows there is a positive relationship between the introduction of new products and whether firms export more than 5 per cent of their production, it is not statistically significant (χ square 2-tailed P value = 0.18). It is possible that a more exact measure of innovation would produce a more significant relationship. There is no relationship between the introduction of new routines or processes and the level of exports.

Sources of Knowledge

The type and extent of knowledge accessed by firms can be hypothesized to influence levels of exports. In this regard, there is an extensive debate about the relative roles in IT production of tacit knowledge based on face-to-face communication, and 'global pipeline' knowledge gained by linking into global production chains. The survey asked respondents to list their various sources of knowledge. The results are shown in relation to levels of exports in Table 4.4.

Overall there is little correlation with the different types of knowledge and the level of exports. Some types of knowledge have a more positive association with exports than others, however. The most significant of

Table 4.4 Level of exports by sources of knowledge[a]

	Exports as % of total sales		
	50 & above	5 to 49	0 to 4
Suppliers	7	24	64
Customers	9	34	82
Similar firms & peers	3	15	30
Professional forums, conferences, fairs	6	29	56
Books, journals	4	19	46
Own R&D	8	27	68
Consultants	3	12	29
New employees	2	12	32
Ex employees	–	2	13
Internet	5	12	51
Universities, research agencies	4	9	19

Note: [a]Totals include every source listed for each firm.

these are universities and research agencies (in nearly all cases universities were the knowledge source in this category). This accords with conventional wisdom about the relationship between university research and strong high tech clusters. By contrast, neither consultant knowledge nor 'own R&D' had a particularly positive association with exports. Knowledge from similar firms and peers had a moderately positive association with exports. This tends to validate the hypothesized role of tacit knowledge, though other strong potential sources of tacit knowledge such as suppliers and customers did not show a distinctive influence on exports. Most firms drew on a number of sources of knowledge, suggesting that richness of knowledge was seen as vital to staying competitive.

Types of Sales

The hypothesized role of global chains of production in the IT sector suggests that MNC contracts will be vital for firms to participate in exporting along these chains. More generally, sales via contracts might decrease the risks of exporting, as opposed to sales on open export markets. Table 4.5 shows data from the survey on the main types of sales of respondent firms, and compares this with export levels. The importance of MNC contracts for exports is clearly shown. Of the nine respondent firms with such contracts, all but one exported 5 per cent or more of their total production. The eight such firms could thus be considered as part of global production chains. Nevertheless, these firms were a clear minority of all

Table 4.5 Level of exports by main type of sales[a]

Exports as % of total sales	Open market/ distributors	MNC contracts	Non-MNC contracts/govern-ment contracts	Unspecified type of contracts
50 & above	4	2	1	4
5 to 49	15	6	10	5
0 to 4	35	1	17	18

Note: [a]Includes all types mentioned where main type not identified.

respondent firms with exports above 5 per cent. Global production chains thus explain only a small part of Australian IT exports. Table 4.5 indicates that other categories of sales are not particularly associated with export activity.

Inter-firm Collaboration

Different forms of inter-firm collaboration could be expected to assist firms in exporting their production. Participation in global production chains, for example, requires collaboration of various kinds. Table 4.6 shows the main type of inter-firm collaboration used by each respondent firm, and compares this with export levels. Firms with no collaboration are seen to be much less likely to export more than 5 per cent than firms engaged in some type of collaboration. Firms engaged in reseller/vendor agreements are the most likely to be exporting. Such agreements greatly reduce the risks of exporting. Partnerships and alliances also produce an increased likelihood of exporting. These both generate either more assured export markets to partners, or else enable firms to join with partners to engage in more complex forms of production or draw on specialist knowledge to make exports more competitive.

Table 4.6 Level of exports by main type of inter-firm collaboration[a]

Exports as % of total sales	Zero collabora-tion	Reseller/ vendor agreement	Partner-ship	Sub-contracting	Project cooperation/ collaboration	Alliance	Joint venture
50 & above	2	2	–	3	1	–	3
5 to 49	5	7	4	15	4	6	2
0 to 4	36	3	4	39	12	6	8

Note: [a]Includes all types mentioned where main type not identified.

Perceived Disadvantages of Australia's Location

A major research issue for the analysis of Australian IT exports concerns the role of Australia's location in relation to the global IT sector, and of disadvantages that might arise from this location. A working hypothesis might be that the peripheral position of Australia has negative effects that hinder IT exports. To explore this, the survey questioned firms about the level of disadvantage they felt arose from Australia's location in the global IT sector (Table 4.7).

Perceptions about how disadvantageous they considered Australia's global location to be indicate that most IT-exporting firms perceive some disadvantage, although only two firms exporting over 5 per cent of their production saw their location as highly disadvantageous. Less obviously, a quarter of firms exporting less than 5 per cent of their production also saw Australia's location as a disadvantage to varying extents.

Comments from exporting firms indicated that Australia's global location was particularly disadvantageous for making sales. This involved making telephone calls outside normal Australian working hours (with one firm saying that overseas clients were a 'communications nightmare'), or the necessity of travelling to see clients in person. The US market was especially cited as one where face to face communication with clients was necessary. This could involve a journey of 24 hours to some locations. One firm with a major overseas client said that the client needed 'local hand holding', while another firm said there was a stigma attached to Australian firms by overseas clients. Firms selling to Asia-Pacific Economic Cooperation (APEC) countries did not report similar difficulties from Australia's location, presumably because of the closeness of their time zones.

A number of non-exporting firms also reported disadvantages associated with Australia's location. Phone calls outside normal hours could

Table 4.7 Level of exports by perceived disadvantage of Australia's location in global IT sector[a]

Exports as % of total sales	1 (no disadvantage)	2	3	4	5 (high disadvantage)
50 & above	3	2	3	2	–
5 to 49	12	6	10	5	2
0 to 4	71	7	14	1	2

Note: [a]Includes all types mentioned where main type not identified.

also be necessary for software or hardware support, particularly to US multinational offices. One firm reported time problems in getting current hardware from overseas. Similarly, firms drawing on overseas supplies or sub-contractors outside the Asia-Pacific area reported disadvantages associated with the need to make phone calls well into the night. Conversely, a foreign multinational said that software developers in India were willing to get up in the middle of the night to discuss work issues. An animation firm saw Australia's location as an advantage, because time differences meant they could work on projects while their North American partners were resting, and vice versa, using internet file exchanges.

SYDNEY VERSUS MELBOURNE

The chapter now briefly explores the possible influence of the different economic bases of Sydney and Melbourne on IT exports and thus IT industry-related globalization in each city. Of the 11 sample IT firms exporting 50 per cent or more of their production, eight are located in Sydney and three in Melbourne. This reflects the larger size of Sydney's IT industry, in turn related to Sydney's bigger national commercial role. Three of the Sydney firms listed banking and finance as a main client industry, while none of the Melbourne firms did. This suggests that Sydney's role as Australia's main financial centre has produced specialized skills and/or a specialized client base that has aided IT exports. Four of the Sydney firms, but no Melbourne firms, listed mining/oil and gas as a main client industry. This is at odds with Melbourne's more dominant role as a location for major mining companies, but it does reflect a legacy of medium-sized mining production and exploration companies in Sydney (cf. Daly, 1984). It also accords with one study that noted Perth has been losing mining industry services to better networked and resourced firms in both Sydney and Melbourne (Spiller Gibbons Swan Pty Ltd and National Institute for Economic and Industry Research, 2000). Two of the three Melbourne firms had major client industries that were connected to specialized aspects of Melbourne's economy. One animation firm listed gaming publishers as the main client industry, corresponding to Melbourne's bigger animated games industry which has been a policy priority of the state government. Another produced road-related hardware and software for governments and consultants, which perhaps reflects the concentration of road research expertise in Melbourne, especially in the Australian Road Research Bureau. Thus the economic base of the respective cities can be seen as having some influence on the type of IT exports from each city and the nature of their engagement with the global IT industry.

CONCLUSION

The research reported above has established a profile of the export activity in the Australian IT industry. It shows that the small local firm is strongly represented. These results suggest that the current context reflects local firms that have developed a product in response to local demand, and then taken it to an export market, rather than an alternative where major international corporations utilize a national base for production and subsequently export. The latter has been an important stage in the evolution in the fortunes of the IT industry in some nations. One question created by the research is why Australia has not attracted this form of major corporation sponsorship and development.

A second question is: what have been the characteristics of the Australian market that have stimulated the IT product development for export? An answer to this question will require understanding of the circumstances of each firm. The work on Melbourne and Sydney suggests that some of the major sectors of the economy have been key stimulants to service activity, some of which in turn has been exported. As some Australian firms have a global role and global scale in these activities, it is possible that IT needs have created special requirements which have been addressed by local firms and have then been developed for use in these sectors on the global market. Alternatively, the exports could be part of new and different industries that have emerged from innovative thinking in activities that are not exported, perhaps in an activity like health services. Further detailed research work will be needed to expose this perspective in detail.

Recognizing the differences that would be exposed by exploring these questions will create some clarity for policy. Should Australia be providing more support for small firms to export services developed to serve its leading industries, or should it be encouraging more innovation in all activity? Secondly, should Australia be looking at ways to attract major corporations to develop IT products in Australia and so export, or should it be assisting the small home based firms? Articulating answers to these questions will depend on extensions to the work outlined in the current chapter.

Finally the results show the subtle ways that important service activity is connected to the knowledge base of cities. A range of city based factors (suppliers, customers and universities) played a part in the development of products. In addition the concentration of particular industrial sectors in Australia's two major cities is acknowledged as an influence on IT export activity. These two forces emanate from the knowledge base of these cities and show that the long term development of the IT industry, including the extent to which it becomes further globalized, will be deeply implicated with the evolution of the knowledge base of its host cities.

ACKNOWLEDGEMENT

The research for this chapter was funded by an Australian Research Council Discovery grant.

REFERENCES

Balabanis, G. (2005), 'Determinants of export intermediaries' service-mix configurations', *International Marketing Review*, **22**(4), 436–459.

Bell, J. (1995), 'The internationalization of small computer software firms: a further challenge to "stage" theories', *European Journal of Marketing*, **29**(8), 60–75.

Daly, M.T. (1984), 'The revolution in international capital markets: urban growth and Australian cities', *Environment and Planning A,* **16**(8), 1003–1020.

Daniels, P.W. (2000), 'Export of services or servicing exports?', *Geografiska Annaler: Series B, Human Geography,* **82B**(1), 1–15.

Dunning, J.H. (1993), *Trade, Location of Economic Activity and the Multinational Enterprise: A Search for an Eclectic Approach*, London: Unwin Hyman.

Javalgi, R.G., C.L. Martin and P.R. Todd (2004), 'The export of e-services in the age of technology transformation: challenges and implications for international service providers', *Journal of Services Marketing*, **18**(7), 560–573.

Johanson, J. and P.F. Wiedersheim-Paul (1975), 'The internationalization of the firm – four Swedish case studies', *Journal of Management Studies*, **12**(3), 305–22.

O'Connor, K. and P. Daniels (2001), 'The geography of international trade in services: Australia and the APEC region', *Environment and Planning A*, **33**(2), 281–296.

Pain, N. and D. van Welsum (2004), 'International production relocation and exports of services', http://scholar.google.com.au/scholar?start=10&q=Export+of+services+&hl=en&as_sdt=2000, accessed 26 August 2010.

Parthasarathy, B. (2004), 'India's Silicon Valley or Silicon Valley's India? Socially embedding the computer software industry in Bangalore', *International Journal of Urban and Regional Research,* **28**(3), 664–685.

Roberts, J. (1999), 'The internationalisation of business service firms: a stages approach', *Service Industries Journal,* **19**(4), 68–88.

Saxenian, A.L. (2006), *The New Argonauts: Regional Advantage in a Global Economy*, Cambridge, MA: Harvard University Press.

Spiller Gibbons Swan Pty Ltd and National Institute for Economic and Industry Research (2000), 'South West urban system economic study – future Perth', Unpublished report prepared for the Western Australian Planning Commission, Perth: WAPC.

Zou, S. and S. Stan (1998), 'The determinants of export performance: a review of the empirical literature between 1987 and 1997', *International Marketing Review*, **15**(5), 333–356.

5. Attracting: the coffeeless urban café and the attraction of urban space

Kirsten Martinus

INTRODUCTION

Large cars and extensive highways often signify success for industrializing cities. In contrast, attracting talented human capital and intimate urban space are symbolic of the new economy. Castells (2000) argued that contemporary urban planning is:

> based on knowledge, organized around networks, and partly made up of flows, the informational city is not a form but a process, a process characterized by the structural domination of the space of flows. (p. 429)

Indeed, many see *flows* and *accessibility* (Bertolini and Dijst, 2003) or *knowledge nodes* and *linkages* (van Winden and van den Berg, 2004) as more suitable in urban planning than traditional *zones* and *proximity*. The organic globally competitive knowledge city facilitates innovation by attracting human capital and enabling connectivity and accessibility on all levels (virtual, physical, global, local) in open urban systems.

Bertolini and Dijst (2003) suggested this could be generated in highly accessible mobility environments (train stations, airports and so on) being physical spaces able to anchor human interaction in the borderless new economy and sensitive to the physical mobility needs of individuals and organizations (Bertolini et al., 2008). Leveraging a point-to-point mass transport function, such environments are platforms to layer human socio-economic activity (such as recreation, work, learning) potentially connecting local actors to the wider global system.

This chapter asserts that the attraction of public space adjacent to key transport infrastructure can contribute to innovation systems and, as such, economic efficiency in the new economy. The next section reviews literature on how urban form may contribute to knowledge productivity and the complex urban systems required for innovation. The following section presents research examining human attraction, presence in and movement through a particular space outside of a busy train station in Kobe, Japan. It concludes that the street-side café buzz and excitement of the space is capable of enhancing 'the knowledge productivity of local inputs by facilitating human spatial movement and providing opportunities for knowledge spillovers' (Martinus, 2010: 733).

THE URBAN FRAMEWORK OF INNOVATION

Human attraction in the local milieu has become crucial to the process of innovation. Howells (2002) suggested that innovation itself was geographically concentrated. Other research has observed that regional innovation systems are unique. They are the product of distinctly different dynamics and flows of information and knowledge through a network of actors (Lambooy, 2005; Simmie, 2002). The efficacy of actor collaboration in facilitating knowledge creation and organization varies between countries, and even between regions of the same country. These local variations not only impact on competitive advantage, but make it difficult to formulate effective policies and strategies to support innovation. Van Winden and van den Berg (2004) suggested categorizing knowledge cities according to labour market size, level of cultural diversity and integration into the global economy. They stated that each had very different dynamics and systems contributing to the foundation and organization of knowledge activities. They concluded that adopting policy sensitive to local conditions would better address knowledge economy issues, such as increasing social exclusion.

The process of knowledge creation itself does not generate innovation, but rather it is the diffusion and useful application of knowledge by various actors (Lambooy, 2005). Lambooy (2002) proposed that three interrelated environments act as selection mechanisms for the innovative success of a particular region – spatial, market and institutional. The local spatial environment is seen to 'influence accessibility, the availability of information and the possibility of organization based on personal contacts. (It) provides a kind of selection mechanism which may or may not provide conditions favourable to meet the new requirements of change' (p. 1029).

Urban space, therefore, can be seen as a new economy resource. It can provide a platform for human attraction, knowledge exchange and social networks with positive multiplier effects reaching beyond cities or districts of innovation. Indeed, Gospodini (2002) noted that urban development had a positive influence 'on the economic development of all classes and groups of cities within the European global urban system' (p. 69).

The following sections examine regional and local innovation, as well as the significance and function of facilitators, transfer mechanisms and flows.

INNOVATION IN THE URBAN ENVIRONMENT

Cooke (2001) suggested that regional innovative systems are best represented by an interactive network model of different actors from education, government and firms. However, research remains unclear as to how local spatial mechanisms work together to influence the innovation process, making the implementation of policies to promote this difficult.

Population density and industrial clustering (geographical concentration) are often seen as central, facilitating the spread of tacit knowledge, access to quality networks and the matching of relevant economic actors or useful input and outputs. Carlino et al. (2007) argued that they create strong externalities for innovation through knowledge spillovers, and Lambooy (2005) that they allow the formation of interconnected complimentary firm networks which generate synergies conducive to innovation. However, Simmie (2002) noted that the knowledge spillover hypothesis did not adequately explain regional imbalances in innovation. He suggested that first-class and globally competitive cities of innovation need sufficient local–global links of different knowledge types and sources to ensure continued learning throughout the innovation process. Lambooy (2002) concurred observing that the breadth of knowledge and strategic economic relations required are often external to the region. Malecki (2002) also found that networks are of greatest importance to cities of innovation, with hard networks (teleco, transport infrastructure and so on) supporting soft networks of public and private sectors and their interactions.

Others have found that nurturing cultural and environmental factors attracts high-value human capital (soft infrastructure), as well as creating urban spaces of improved life quality and diverse interaction. Such environments are conducive to innovation (Edvinsson, 2006; Florida and Tinagli, 2004). Martinus (2010) advocated the importance of both hard and soft components as inadequate hard infrastructure (including hard networks) constrained soft infrastructure (and networks) performance: 'cities have a maximum innovative capacity for a fixed level of infrastructure (capital asset) after which increasing inputs (such as skilled labour, creativity) will cause decreasing returns to scale for innovation' (p. 732). That is, increasing soft infrastructure (and network) components in environments with low levels of hard infrastructure is economically inefficient for the production of innovation and knowledge.

Knowledge based urban development (KBUD) literature also supports a dual soft and hard infrastructure approach. Based on Carillo (2002), KBUD broadly describes any 21st century new milieu environments, such as knowledge precincts, science parks, technopoles, high-tech zones and creative cities (Yigitcanlar et al., 2008). Each piece of research adds to the debate on the importance of developing regions specifically for knowledge and innovation. However, knowledge facilitators are largely focused on soft socio-economic infrastructure (policy development, education, human capital, creativity, ICT, industry and so on). There is limited analysis of the hard infrastructure mechanisms facilitating innovation. For example, KBUD research-to-date does not explain how urban development can leverage daily knowledge opportunities through human flows or the local–global construct of physical human-scale spaces.

The range of research considering innovative capacity and how to best support it, highlights the variation and complexity of social, economic and spatial factors. These extend beyond any one element, such that each of the above contributes to an understanding of regional transfer mechanisms and flows. Martinus (2010) proposed five classifications of hard and soft infrastructure (connectivity; education and skills; business and industrial networks; creativity and culture; and diversity) important for innovation and knowledge development 'based on human qualities associated with innovative activity' (p. 734). This approach is consistent with innovation as a by-product of human thought, creativity and endeavour. Indeed, much literature on innovation focuses on enhancing soft infrastructure aspects of the local–global environment. The possibility that urban space can attract and strengthen local social capital (Hanna et al., 2009; Martinus, 2010) and support innovation presents an interesting paradigm for the regional innovation system.

The Contribution of Local Space

Beriatos and Gospodini (2004) saw modern cities as eclectic landscapes of heritage-rich and cutting-edge innovative architecture reflecting opposing spheres: 'tradition with rather local spatial reference, and. . .of innovation having more universal or global spatial references' (p. 187). Gospodini (2006) found urban life increasingly centred on leisure and culture, and modern cities characterized by new economy production clusters (such as knowledge-intensive, financial, cultural services) dispersed throughout the inner city and outer-metro strategic areas rather than in the CBD. He suggested these clusters were 'sifting/expanding the spatial core and altering the city's spatial organization and structure' (p. 314) providing critical socio-economic infrastructure capable of driving new economy production and redefining urban consumption patterns. He saw this infrastructure as offering local identity, environmental amenities and opportunities for social interaction and knowledge exchange.

Indeed, new economy wealth and global competitiveness is no longer just a function of technology, business and institutional environment, but includes measures of coherent city planning, amenity levels, infrastructure and quality of life (Sim et al., 2003). Gospodini (2002) observed that cities of minimal natural resources were particularly reliant on urban design such that '*avant-garde* design of urban space combined with large scale interventions appeared to control the city's future' (p. 69). This is linked to the capacity of urban space to attract people; connecting them to each other, as well as to work, life and leisure possibilities.

Leisure and non-work opportunities are now as important to competitive advantage as industrial structure. Social, leisure, entertainment and culture aspects of the city are connected to economic competitiveness (Beriatos and Gospodini, 2004; Gospodini, 2006; Hall, 2000; Hannigan, 2003), with more liveable and pleasant cities better equipped to attract high-value knowledge workers (Carlino and Saiz, 2008; Clark, 2004; Florida and Tinagli, 2004). Clark (2004) observed that cities are being viewed as life-style playgrounds by citizens who act like tourists demanding more aesthetic urban considerations. He noted this is driving a new breed of policies centred on 'enhancing a distinct urban life style and neighbourhood amenities' (p. 512). This is just as relevant to local neighbourhoods as it is to the Central Business District (CBD) in the context of knowledge creation, and suggests a role for local urban space in supporting wider new economy objectives.

Some contend that spaces hold the vital force of cities, such that the 'ordinary and extraordinary activities of public spaces constantly evade the "tightness" of design and control and produce spaces that are "loose"' (Huxley, 2007). If 'loose' spaces indiscriminately allow people to move in and out freely, spaces of greater 'looseness' are likely to be more appealing to a broad spectrum of humanity. Optimizing human movement and interaction will allow spaces to foster environments supportive of local innovation and knowledge-based activities (Martinus, 2010), and enable diversity in human perspectives across the whole knowledge exchange process and lifecycle (Edvinsson, 2006). Urban space is a potential knowledge resource for cities of innovation.

The largely unpredictable nature of human movement and interaction makes the construction of such spaces difficult, but incorporating richness in human activity and experience is likely to attract and retain human diversity. For example, Gehl (2007) contended that, within certain limits, designing space according to three dominate outdoor activity types (necessity, optional and social) could influence how long people stayed in, the number of people attracted to, and activities which developed around the space. Jacobs (1961) espoused the importance of urban vitality generated through mixed land-use and activities. Banerjee (2007) argued urban space design should support socio-cultural activities to encourage human interaction and public life, where private spaces (coffee shops, bookstores) were just as relevant to public life as public spaces. Oldenburg (2007) thought a balanced life required a daily injection of work, domestic and social experiences, and that growing family and work demands had generated the need for a more social and stimulating 'third place' with qualities inherent in the accessibility and neutrality of urban space (public or private).

Despite implicit links, little is known of how urban space might support our increasingly global and high-tech lifestyles or contribute to national innovation systems and knowledge productivity. Spaces which do so will probably be sympathetic to modern needs, including increasing work/life/leisure pressures of globalization. This is likely to mean transposing human movement and life onto urban space itself.

For example, consider how urban space might alleviate feelings of time and space compression arising from the large socio-economic structural shifts occurring as 'space becomes virtual and global transactions occur in *real time*' (Walker, 2009: 487). We now live in a contradictory world where personalized instant global access means we do not need to leave our computers, but yet national productivity rests on human interaction, stimulation and creativity. Cities must connect people across otherwise disparate worlds (local to global; virtual to physical) through the capacity of human-scale and vibrant local urban space to satisfy individual time/space needs.

The idea of 'space' being compressed is strongly influenced by global happenings. Social space and human relations are increasingly difficult to define by territorial boundaries, places or distances, local events (Betancourth, 2002; Legge, 2005). The local urban framework is no longer about who resides there, but its relevance to the outside world. Hard infrastructure (teleco, transport) is viewed as central in facilitating the local–global flow of soft elements (human capital, data). It has become almost inconceivable that highly innovative places are not hard wired into the global community through the Internet and transport network to leverage physical and virtual flows of data and knowledge.

The compression of 'time' has blurred the lines of what is work and what is not (Scholarios and Marks, 2004), with ever-increasing time-saving devices only adding to feelings of time deprivation (Walker, 2009). Given rapid globalization, advancing technologies and growing access to information, it seems unlikely these pressures will ease. Indeed, human response has been to do more rather than less. Activities are streamlined and time is more efficiently planned. Gospodini (2006) noted that '*multi-tasking* itself can be considered as characteristic of the human interactions that underpins new media production activities' (p. 316). Key public space can facilitate this by employing city and urban design high in daily time-saving elements and incorporating a multitude of uses. Such spaces will better reflect and support new economy workers, and therefore the innovation process itself.

In their analysis of learning and knowledge generation, Amin and Roberts (2008) contended that the 'intersection between network space, corporate space and regional space define the geography of knowledge, with each spatial axis (office, building, region internet connectivity, space of mobility and flow, virtual space and network architecture) contributing something specific to the knowledge process' (p. 366). They added an interesting dimension to the importance of capturing the energy of increasingly trans-territorial networks in a specific point of time and space. Dvir and Pasher (2004) suggested that innovation ecology models should be applied to knowledge cities, as innovation is based upon creating conversations. Certain urban structures (museums, libraries, cafés, industrial parks) provide the 'building blocks' for conversations driving creativity and innovation.

Dvir et al. (2006) added that any properly designed space has potential to be vibrant and drive innovation. This chapter contends that the function of some spaces makes them more appropriate than others. More specifically, urban space adjacent to key public infrastructure is a prime location to mass a region's vitality. For example, train stations are key infrastructure drawing people through a transport function. This can be leveraged by concentrating other infrastructure, amenities and services around it to provide a convenient hub of daily business and living activities.

Not doing so around train stations, as local entry points for regional and global knowledge, signifies a wasted opportunity to concentrate urban vibrancy, human connectivity and interaction. Such a scenario is economically inefficient for innovative cities. The following section presents the results of a survey outside a train station in Kobe, Japan with an environment supportive of local innovation and knowledge-based activities.

NO COFFEE AT THIS URBAN CAFÉ

Martinus (2010) asserted that future economic sustainability requires planning to consider urban forms' contribution to innovation and knowledge-based activities. Central to this is the notion that space can attract people and concentrate a city's vital force to become a seedbed for innovative activities. It is likely that some spaces will be more adept at doing this than others.

This section presents the results of a survey assessing why a specific space adjacent to a Japanese train station has fostered an extraordinary capacity to attract and retain people. The space appeared to be a subcultural magnet for the whole community. Vibrancy and human interaction in the space resembled a busy urban café in which longer and more frequent visits increased the likelihood of serendipitous meetings. This chapter proposes that attraction and retention of human capital is a critical function of urban space in cities of innovation.

Site Selection and Survey Methodology

The survey site was selected as the most vibrant location outside of a train station in a mid-size city with a natural capacity for knowledge development and innovation. Innovation was assessed using globally recognized patent statistics (OECD and WIPO), and natural innovative capacity was evaluated as the speed at which the city adapted to knowledge creation after an initial knowledge economy policy shift (see Martinus, 2011).

OECD (2009) ranked Japan's global innovation as second to USA, and WIPO (2008) as number one. OECD found Kinki Region (containing Kobe, Osaka) to be the third (in absolute values) most highly innovative region in the world after Kanto (containing Tokyo) and California, USA (Usai, 2008). Therefore, Kinki was the most appropriate study region; its mid-size city of Kobe was selected for the following reasons.

Kobe sustained severe economic and urban infrastructure damage during the 1995 Great Hanshin Earthquake, with 32% of Greater Kobe and more than 50% of the CBD destroyed (Olshansky et al., 2005). Consistent with national knowledge economy objectives and as a means of rebuilding the devastated city, Kobe officials recognized that the large number of established drug companies and universities could transform the city into a centre of advanced medical research and excellence (Kruger, 2002). Technology parks (super computers, biotech) were also developed under this vision and to confirm Kobe as a global hub of information and knowledge exchange. Kobe amazingly regained 75–90% of its former capacity by 1999 (Olshansky et al., 2005). In 2004, Kobe joined UNESCO's Creative Cities Network as City of Design (City of Kobe, 2009a); and in 2009, it was ranked 37th in the world for innovation (Tokyo is 9th, Sydney 22nd and Melbourne 20th) (2thinknow, 2009).

Sannomiya station sits at the heart of Kobe's over 1.5 million people (City of Kobe, 2009b), and is at the convergence of Hankyu, JR, Hanshin,

Portliner and Subway lines. Each terminal has several busy exits of people walking through, waiting for friends or alternative transport (bus, car and so on). As such, each exit presented a possible site to conduct the survey (Figure 5.1).

Given the importance of attracting and retaining human capital, a site was chosen where people appeared most relaxed and willing to spend time. This was observed as a site outside of Hankyu Sannomiya station (Figure 5.2), famously nicknamed for its three stone-paved bumps: The Humps (by foreigners), Oppai Yama (or O-Yama by younger people, meaning Breast Mountain Park) and Sankaku Koen (by older people, meaning Triangle Park).

With metal benches and scattered stone seats (Figure 5.3), this grey cobble paved site is central to a variety of retail, banking, education, business and financial services, 24-hour minimarts, bookstores, eateries (fast food, cafés, restaurants), entertainment (karaoke, bars) and tourism activities. It attracts a cross-section of the community: elderly, high school and university students, foreigners (working and tourists), musicians, street entertainers, trendy youth, businesspersons, mothers with children and homeless.

A total of 80 people sitting or standing at the site completed a survey in either English or Japanese depending on language competency. This avoided language difficulties as the researcher was an accredited Japanese–English interpreter. The survey aimed to establish prior and intended movement of participants, as well as reasons for being in, feelings associated with, and the likelihood of meeting an acquaintance at the site. People passing through or waiting on the fringe of the site for transport were not asked to participate. The survey was conducted over one week, in the evening (4–8pm) and daytime (10am–2:30pm) on weekdays (Monday–Thursday) and at the weekend (Friday–Sunday). 20 people were asked in each of the four time slots to capture the widest possible range of answers, with evening and daytime representing peak and non-peak travel periods respectively.

Observations and Survey Results

The site was lively and interesting, attracting all age groups: 30% of participants were 16–25 years, 31% were 26–35, 12.5% were 36–45, 11.5% were 46–55 and 15% were over 55. 16% of participants were non-Japanese (foreigners) from countries including the USA, Australia, New Zealand, Colombo, Samoa, Indonesia and Ghana.

People volumes during non-peak weekday (6pm to 9pm at any given time) were lower than in the other three periods. High turnover and volume

Figure 5.1 Train station entrances around Sannomiya station

Figure 5.2 Hankyu Sannomiya station and survey site (grey dot)

Figure 5.3 Survey site taken from various angles

during weekday and weekend peak and non-peak periods made data collection easy with people more willing to participate and provide personal information after watching others interacting with the researcher. Several people noted that doing the survey 'killed time' and 'added interest to their life' and represented why they were at the site – 'it (the site) always has different things going on, like a foreigner doing a PhD survey' (translation of Japanese answers). Foreign participants were particularly eager to engage with the researcher.

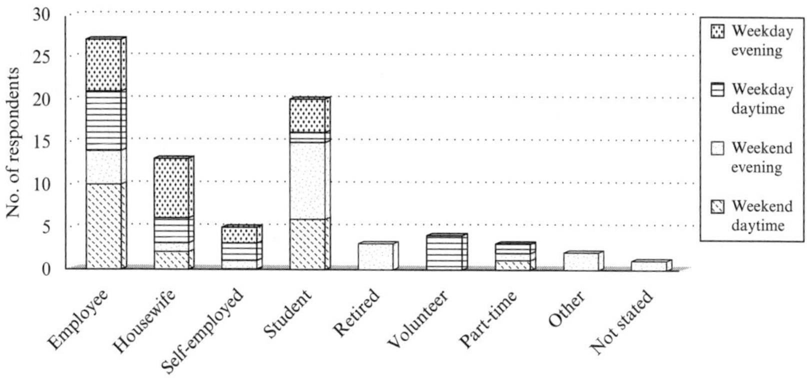

Figure 5.4 Survey response to 'What is your current occupation?'

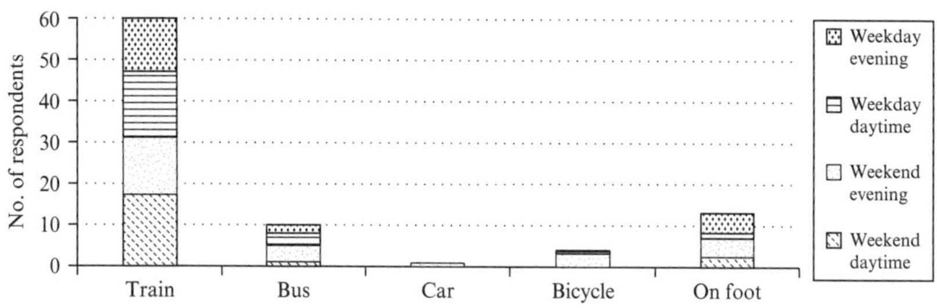

Figure 5.5 Survey response to 'How did you get here?'

Most participants were either employees (34%) or students (25%), which is consistent with the sites' proximity to the central business district (CBD) and several universities. 16% classified themselves as housewives ranging from 20+ year old mothers to 70+ year olds. 6% were self-employed, 5% were volunteers (all women), 4% were retirees (males only, same age women ticked housewife), and 4% had part-time jobs (all women). Employees and self-employed were higher during the day, while housewives preferred weekday evenings and students anytime during weekends (Figure 5.4). In general, the range of people and occupations added to the interest and vibrancy of the site.

High public transport and pedestrian usage reflected the site's position outside a train station and pedestrian-orientation (Figures 5.5 and 5.6). 75% travelled by train to the site and 40% intended to for their next activity; 16% travelled to and 55% left the site on foot. 12.5% reached the survey site by bus, while only 2.5% intended to use it to their next destination. Only one person used a car (1.25%) and four people (5%) used a bike

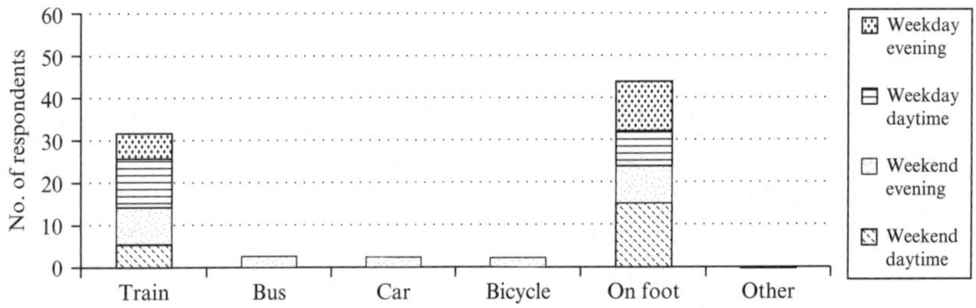

Figure 5.6 Survey response to 'How will you travel to your next activity?'

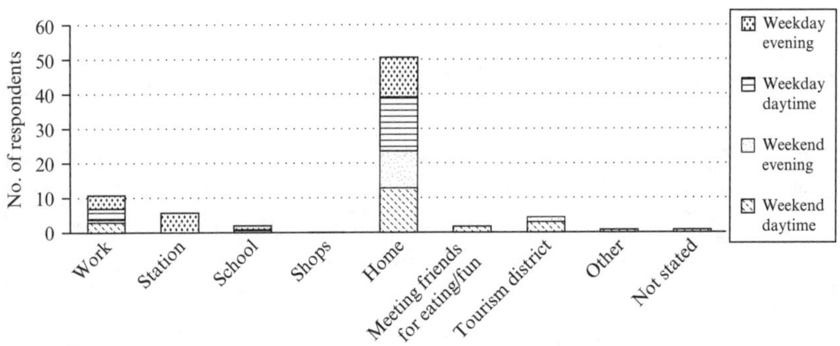

Figure 5.7 Survey response to 'Where did you come from?'

to reach the site, while four people intended to use car (2.5%) and bike (2.5%) to their next activity.

Pedestrians standing at and walking through the site created an ever-changing organic landscape, adding vibrancy and a unique human narrative. During non-peak periods, there were between two and eleven different groups of people gathered waiting for friends; this increased to between five and twenty during the weekend and peak periods. Weekend groups included large organized groups. For example, a group of 25 Mormons from different countries met for a monthly one-hour meeting at the site before separating for individual missionary work in Kobe and surrounds. In another example, the site was a regular meeting point for Kobe City walks organized by a Kansai walking club of approximately 100 members.

The majority of participants (64%) reported coming from home. This percentage was lower in the evening (55%–60%) than during the day (65-75%). Among other participants, 14%, 8% and 6% reported coming respectively from work, the station or the nearby tourism precinct (Figure 5.7). Of those coming from the station, most were in the evening (6%).

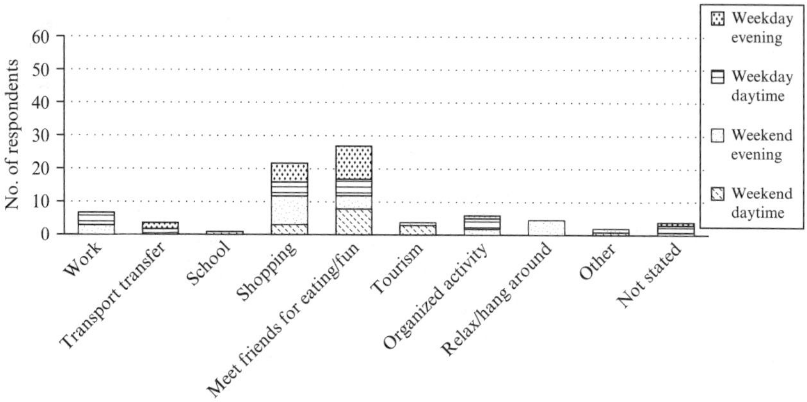

Figure 5.8 Survey response to 'Why did you come here?'

These results and observations of pedestrian movement largely reflected commuting flows, with the majority heading away from the station (mostly north-west towards Kitanozaka and north towards Flower Road) in the morning and towards the station from these directions in the early evening. Commuting flows were less evident from 6:30pm with many walking towards the trendy restaurants and vibrant night entertainment of Kitanozaka.

The importance of entertainment in the city was reflected in the high number of people meeting friends for entertainment (33%) or shopping (27%), particularly in the evening (35% and 37% respectively) (Figure 5.8). During the day (weekend and weekday), most people were attracted for entertainment with friends (32%), shopping (17%), work (17%) or an organized activity (12%). 54% intended to go to some form of leisure activity (Figure 5.9), such as 'meet friends for eating/fun' (30%), 'shops' (14%) 'organized activity' (6%) and 'tourism' (4%), while16% were going home, 14% to work and 12% did not state their intended destination. Figure 5.10 is a breakdown of intended destinations, indicating that more went to work weekday daytime (and home in the evenings) and met friends for leisure in the other three time periods.

These responses along with observed high pedestrian volumes indicate site density and vibrancy but not human interaction or connectivity. Indeed, some research has found that greater density is not an indicator of human interaction and community network strength, suggesting that it may adversely affect social capital formation (Glaeser and Gottlieb 2006; Glaeser et al. 2001). To evaluate the survey sites' capacity to attract people and provide a platform for human interaction and connectivity,

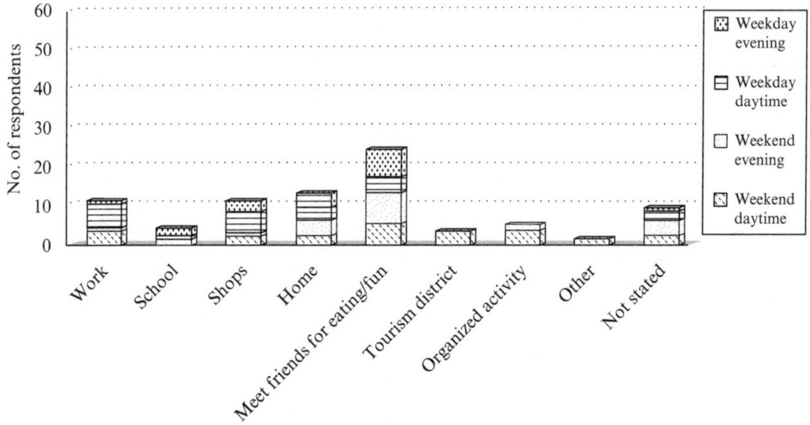

Figure 5.9 Survey response to 'Where are you going immediately after this?' (by destination)

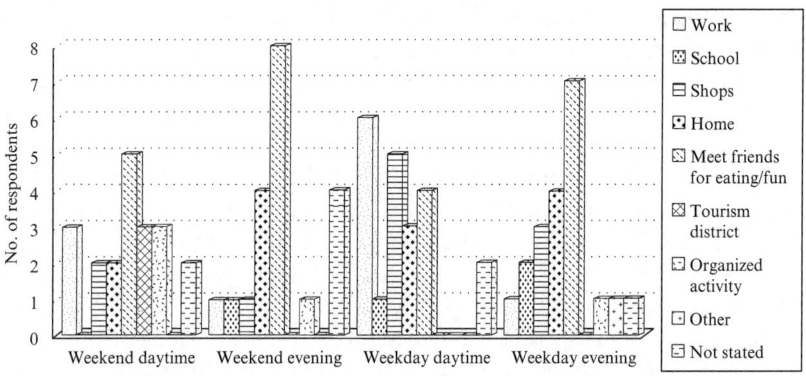

Figure 5.10 Survey response to 'Where are you going immediately after this?' (by location)

participants were asked how often they came to the site and the likelihood of meeting an acquaintance unexpectedly.

The site's general high attraction was highlighted by 80% reporting coming often, comprising 15% coming every day, 17.5% twice a week, 12.5% once a week, 17.5% once every two weeks and 17.5% once a month. Only 15% came less than once a month, and 5% noted it was their first visit. Visit frequency was positively correlated with the likelihood of an unexpected meeting (Figure 5.11); that is, the more frequently

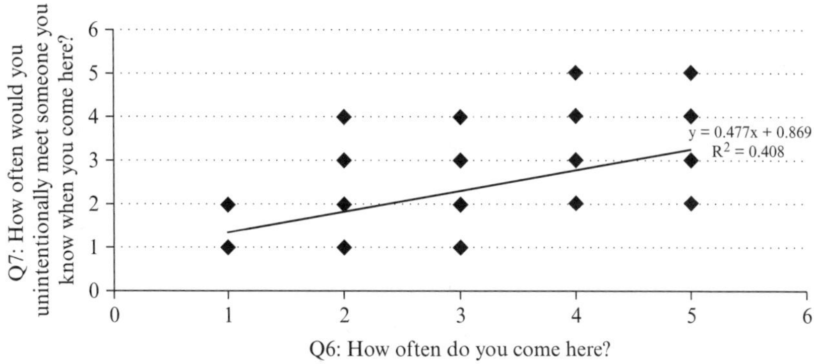

Figure 5.11 Correlation between visit frequency and unexpected meetings

someone visited the site, the more likely they were to bump into a friend serendipitously. As such, the site appeared likely to support human interaction and connectivity strengthening local networks, and therefore social capital.

An example of this was in the instant bond which formed when a group of students from the researcher's Western Australian (Curtin University) sister university (University of Hyogo) was approached. All knew her University of Hyogo research counterparts and some had studied English at Curtin University.

Human connectivity of a space relates to its capacity to attract and retain people, which is partly reflected in how people react to and interact with the space. When asked about the atmosphere of the place, 77% reported positive feelings, 9% negative and 14% were either indifferent or did not state feelings (Figure 5.12). Most (38%) enjoyed passive interaction with the lively and fun atmosphere of the space, including people-watching (with comments of 'noisy with lots of different people', 'lots of youth', 'love it') and enjoying live bands. 15% found it aesthetically pleasing (comments: 'international and interesting', 'lots of foreigners', 'big city feel', 'lots of tall buildings', 'sophisticated and trendy'), 15% found it relaxing, 9% central for meeting friends, and 6% convenient to other activities in the city (comments referring to amenities, such as 'lots of bookstores', 'can eat out', 'shopping').

Most negative comments noted the increase in unsocial behaviour in the evening (8%), 5% cited idle youth and 3% that it was not pretty or relaxing (comments: 'undesirables [homeless, men looking for a date] may approach'). Only one person (1%) took offense to the art in the space, noting that naked statues are morally inappropriate in a public

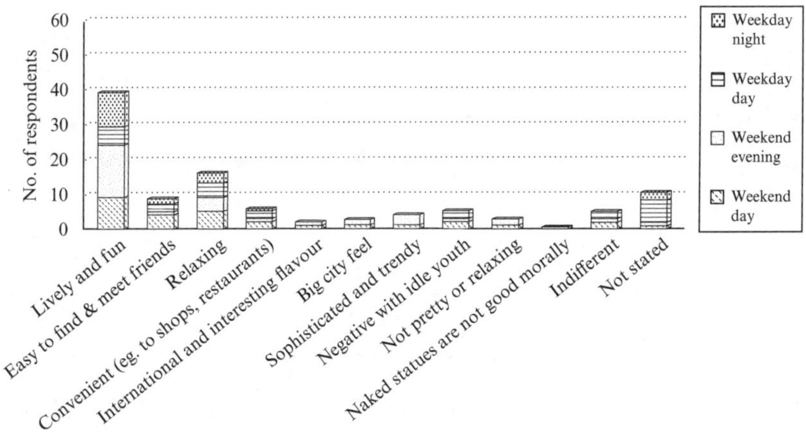

Figure 5.12 *Survey response to 'What sort of atmosphere do you think this place has?'*

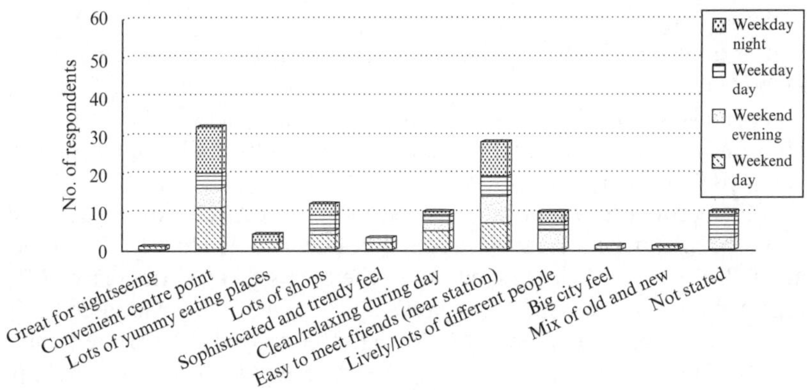

Figure 5.13 *Survey response to 'What are the strengths of this place?'*

place and against Mormon beliefs. This raised an interesting point on the attractiveness of the space. The Mormon missionary who made this comment was part of the 25–30 informally gathered Mormons, who despite mutual consent that the statues were offensive, made no comment regarding moving monthly meetings to another location. It was concluded that the benefits (and attractiveness) of the space for the Mormons outweighed negative aspects.

Figures 5.13 and 5.14 illustrate perceived strengths and weaknesses,

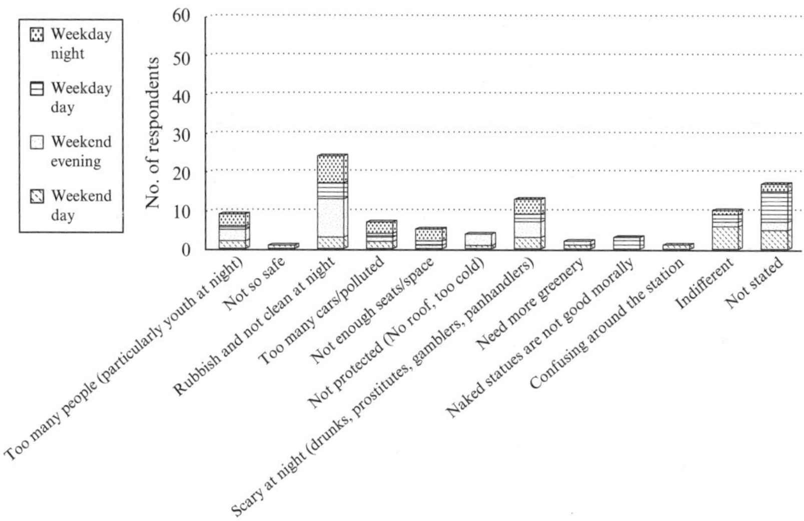

Figure 5.14 *Survey response to 'What are the weaknesses of this place?'*

and an overall positive reaction to the space by respondents, with 112 comments relating to positive and 96 to negative aspects.

Most noted the convenience of the space being within walking distance of many Kobe destinations (28%) and an easy meeting point as 'everyone knows this place' and 'it is close to the train station' (25%). As one respondent noted 'it is easy to find people as it is not too big and there are not too many people. It doesn't feel like a passageway or like you are in the way. It doesn't have too many exits unlike inside the train stations where there are too many people flowing through and exits everywhere'.

14% commented on its convenience to specific activities, such as access to shops (11%), restaurants and other eateries (3%) and sightseeing (1%). 12% felt its strengths lay in aesthetic elements, such as cleanliness and sunshine (10%), sophisticated and trendy (3%), mix of traditional and modern (1%) and having a big city feel (1%). 10% noted its vibrancy and capacity to attract people, including 'people watching' (comments: 'lively, so don't get bored', 'lots of youth so fun', 'lots of different people', 'lots of foreigners'). Site observations supported this; many appeared not to be waiting for anyone but passively enjoying space (some even leaving briefly to buy a drink and return). Others were observed sitting for long intervals several times during study periods; two reported regularly spending over six hours 'hanging around' the space because 'it always had something interesting happening'.

Most negative feedback related to night increase in rubbish (25%) and anti-social behaviour/feelings of insecurity (24%, comments: 'too many people', 'not so safe', 'scary at night', 'pachinko players [gamblers]', 'undesirable people', 'panhandlers', 'dangerous and scary at night', 'noisy at night', 'too many drunks', 'mizushobai' [referring to night activities and nightclubs toting for business, bars and escort services]). 9% noted a lack of basic conveniences (seats, protection from the elements), and 7% did not like the numbers of cars driving around the space and associated pollution. 3% (Mormons) thought the statues were morally offensive, particularly to children and women. However, as observed above, these negative feelings were not enough to keep respondents away from the space.

CONCLUSION

This chapter suggests that urban space adjacent to key public infrastructure, such as train stations, can contribute to economic efficiency in a knowledge economy. Leveraging urban form to optimize human attraction, interaction, vibrancy and connectivity is likely to strengthen regional innovative flows. Successful, attractive, interactive, vibrant and connected spaces accumulated on national or regional levels can consolidate innovation systems and increase knowledge productivity.

The survey of a public space outside Hanku Sannomiya station, Kobe, Japan, found lack of aesthetic appeal had little bearing on its above-average capacity to attract and retain local and global populations. To some extent, this represented its borderless appeal and capacity to facilitate human capital, knowledge and information flows. There are two points to be drawn from this. Firstly, the diversity in surrounding infrastructure and amenities supported vibrancy by encouraging human diversity and movement. Secondly, human diversity and movement in the space created an organic non-discriminatory milieu capable of supporting and building local social capital.

In addition, there was a high correlation between the number of times the space was frequented and the likelihood of an unplanned meeting. This produces a fluid and unplanned environment of human connections generating a network of ad hoc personal and business relations supplementing other more formal avenues. The spontaneity of this is likely to enhance creativity and connectivity, supporting greater efficiency in the innovation and knowledge development process.

The space has nurtured an atmosphere of humanity and culture reminiscent of a busy streetside café. Its vibrant and socially inclusive environment adds to local identity and social amenity, which, in turn, contributes to the knowledge economy priorities of better human attraction, interaction, vibrancy, movement and connectivity. The diversity of people attracted demonstrated a capacity to cluster knowledge, offer opportunities for interaction, strengthen local social capital and enhance knowledge exchange. The space likely contributes to Kobe's regional innovation system. Perhaps, it is by leveraging and consolidating human aspects that urban space provides knowledge infrastructure, increasing new economy sustainability and efficiency.

REFERENCES

2thinknow (2009), 'Innovative cities index 2009 city rankings', http://www.innovation-cities.com/reference/index/innovation-cities-index-2009/, accessed 20 February 2010.

Amin, A. and J. Roberts (2008), 'Knowing in action: beyond communities of practice', *Research Policy,* **37**, 353–369.

Banerjee, Tridib (2007), 'The future of public space: beyond invented streets and reinvented spaces', in Mathew Carmon and Steve Tiesdell (eds), *Urban Design Reader*, Oxford, UK: Architectural Press, pp. 153–162.

Beriatos, E. and A. Gospodini (2004), '"Glocalising" urban landscapes: Athens and the 2004 Olympics', *Cities,* **21**(3), 187–202.

Bertolini, L. and M. Dijst (2003), 'Mobility environments and network cities', *Journal of Urban Design,* **8**(1), 27–43.

Bertolini, L., F. le Clercq and T. Straatemeier (2008), 'Urban transportation planning in transition', *Transport Policy,* **15**(2), 69–72.

Betancourth, C. (2002), 'Living on (multipli)cities of times: the case of the Ranstad-Holland', *GaWC Research Bulletin,* **85**.

Carlino, Gerald and Albert Saiz (2008), 'City beautiful', *Working Title No.08-22*. Philadelphia, US: Federal Reserve Bank of Philadelphia.

Carlino, G., S. Chatterjee and R. Hunt (2007), 'Urban density and the rate of invention', *Journal of Urban Economics,* **61**(3), 389–419.

Carrillo, F. (2002), 'Capital systems: implications for a global knowledge agenda', *Journal of Knowledge Management,* **6**(4), 379–399.

Castells, Manuel (2000), *The Rise of the Network Society, The Information Age: Economy, Society and Culture* (2 edn), vol. 1, Oxford, UK: Blackwell.

City of Kobe (2009a) 'Kobe: UNESCO city of design', http://unesdoc.unesco.org/images/0018/001840/184066E.pdf, accessed 30 August 2010.

City of Kobe (2009b) 'Population', http://www.city.kobe.lg.jp/foreign/english/information/information_03.html, accessed 30 August 2010.

Clark, Terry (ed.) (2004), *The City as an Entertainment Machine*, London, UK: Emerald Group.

Cooke, P. (2001), 'From technopoles to regional innovation systems: the evolution of localised technology development policy', *Canadian Journal of Regional Science,* **24**.

Dvir, R. and E. Pasher (2004), 'Innovation engines for knowledge cities: an innovation ecology perspective', *Journal of Knowledge Management,* **8**(5), 16–27.

Dvir, R., Y. Schwartzberg, H. Avni, C. Webb and F. Lettice (2006), 'The future center as an urban innovation engine', *Journal of Knowledge Management,* **10**(5), 110.

Edvinsson, L. (2006), 'Aspects on the city as a knowledge tool', *Journal of Knowledge Management,* **10**(5), 6–13.

Florida, Richard and Irene Tinagli (2004), *Europe in the Creative Age*, Pittsburgh, US: Carnegie Mellon Software Industry Center.

Gehl, Jan (2007), 'Three types of outdoor activities', in Mathew Carmon and Steve Tiesdell (eds), *Urban Design Reader*, Oxford, UK: Architectural Press, pp. 143–146.

Glaeser, E. and J. Gottlieb (2006), 'Urban resurgence and the consumer city', Discussion paper No. 2109, Cambridge, MA: Harvard University.

Glaeser, E., J. Kolko and A. Saiz (2001), 'Consumer city', *Journal of Economic Geography*, **1**(1), 27–50

Gospodini, A. (2002), 'European cities in competition and the new "uses" of urban design', *Journal of Urban Design,* **7**(1), 59–73.

Gospodini, A. (2006), 'Portraying, classifying and understanding the emerging landscapes in the post-industrial city', *Cities,* **23**(5), 311–330.

Hall, P. (2000), 'Creative cities and economic development', *Urban Studies,* **37**(4), 639–650.

Hanna, K., A. Dale and C. Ling (2009), 'Social capital and quality of place: reflections on growth and change in a small town', *The International Journal of Justice and Sustainability,* **14**(1), 31–44.

Hannigan, J. (2003), 'Symposium on branding, the entertainment economy and urban place building: introduction', *International Journal of Urban and Regional Research,* **27**(2), 352–360.

Howells, J. (2002), 'Tacit knowledge, innovation and economic geography', *Urban Studies,* **39**(5/6), 871–884.

Huxley, M. (2007), 'Book review: loose space: possibility and diversity in urban life', *Urban Studies,* **44**(12), 2495–2496.

Jacobs, Jane (1961), *The Death and Life of Great American Cities*, New York, US: Random House.

Kruger, D. (2002), 'Bridging the science and business gap', *Far Eastern Economic Review,* **165**(25), 32–35.

Lambooy, J. (2002), 'Knowledge and urban economic development: an evolutionary perspective', *Urban Studies,* **39**(5/6), 1019–1035.

Lambooy, J. (2005), 'Innovation and knowledge: theory and regional policy', *European Planning Studies,* **13**(8), 1137–1152.

Legge, Karen (2005), *Human Resource Management: Rhetoric and Realities,* Basingstoke, UK: Palgrave/Macmillan.

Malecki, E. (2002), 'Hard and soft networks for urban competitiveness', *Urban Studies,* **39**(5), 929–945.

Martinus, K. (2010), 'Planning for production efficiency in knowledge-based developments', *Journal of Knowledge Management,* **14**(5), 726–743.

Martinus, K. (2011), 'City infrastructure supporting innovation', *Journal of International Knowledge-Based Organizations* (forthcoming).

OECD (2009), *OECD Science, Technology and Industry Scoreboard 2009*, Paris: OECD.

Oldenburg, Ray (2007), 'The character of third spaces', in Mathew Carmon and Steve Tiesdell (eds), *Urban Design Reader*, Oxford, UK: Architectural Press, pp. 163–169.
Olshansky, R., I. Kobayashi and K. Ohnishi (2005), 'The Kobe earthquake: ten years later', *Planning,* **71**(9), 36.
Scholarios, D. and A. Marks (2004), 'Work-life balance and the software worker', *Human Resource Management Journal,* **14**(2), 54–75.
Sim, L., S. Ong, A. Agarwal, A. Parsa and R. Keivani (2003), 'Singapore's competitiveness as a global city: development strategy, institutions and business environment', *Cities,* **20**(2), 115–127.
Simmie, J. (2002), 'Knowledge spillovers and reasons for the concentration of innovative SMEs', *Urban Studies,* **39**(5/6), 885–902.
Usai, S. (2008), 'The geography of inventive activities in OECD regions', STI Working Paper 2008/3, Paris: OECD.
van Winden, Willem and Leo van den Berg (2004), 'Cities in the knowledge economy: new governance challenges', The Netherlands: European Institute for Comparative Urban Research.
Walker, J. (2009), 'Time as the fourth dimension in the globalization of higher education', *Journal of Higher Education,* **80**(5), 483–509.
WIPO (2008), 'World patent report: a statistical review', WIPO Publication No. 931 (E), Switzerland: World Intellectual Property Organization.
Yigitcanlar, Tan, Koray Velibeyoglu and Scott Baum (eds) (2008), *Knowledge-based Urban Development: Planning and Applications in the Information Era*, Hershey, US: Information Science Reference.

6. Researching: key factors for the success of knowledge cities in Germany

Stefanie Wesselmann, Clas Meyer and Rainer Lisowski

INTRODUCTION

Knowledge, research and creativity have become the main preconditions for innovation in cities and regions. Intellectual capital is recognized by local governments and firms as one of the vital sources of competition in urban and economic development within a knowledge-based economy. A worldwide competition for talent, universities/research institutes and innovative enterprises can be observed. Having a science city profile is essential for this contest. Knowledge-based urban development has gained popularity as a powerful strategy for sustainable economic, social and urban growth, and for the post-industrial development of city-regions.

The Stifterverband, the business community's innovation agency for the German science system, representing 3000 companies, business associations and individuals, tries to support this process of modernization through the competition 'City of Science' among German cities (www.stifterverband.de).

The winning city is entitled to call itself the 'City of Science' for one year, a title that earns considerable media coverage in the country and encourages local knowledge stakeholders to co-operate. From 2005 until 2009, 46 German cities have participated in the contest.

As attorney of the Stifterverband and on the basis of a complete inventory count (N=46 in 2009), the authors analysed in a research programme the sustainable effects of the competition on the participating cities, 'winners' as well as 'losers'. The scientific study indicates which positive synergies could be found in the cities and which knowledge-based strategies have been set up in the urban spaces. Compared with other studies in this field, it is founded on a large empirical base.

The case study describes in detail positive and negative effects on the urban development of Oldenburg, the 'city of science 2009'.

RESEARCH OBJECTIVES

The focus of the study was not to analyze the potential factors of academic location (e.g. the number of academic and research institutions, students or patents), as commonly occurs in the current rankings. The central research question was: Which strategic and operational measures do cities implement to try and raise their profile as a science city?

In particular the following aspects were studied:

- Does the city have a strategic plan in which it establishes science and research as an important factor in the location profile?
- Is the science based location strategy secured by town council decisions?
- Does the city administration provide special contact persons for scientific topics or even scientific offices?
- What events have been implemented to make scientific issues visible for the inhabitants and as an external image factor? What innovative formats have emerged and how diverse were these?
- Of what quality are the network relationships between science, city, economy and culture?
- Are these networks established long term and characterized by regular meetings of the relevant actors?
- Did taking part in the contest have a positive impact on the cities, in particular with respect to the networks between partners in science, business, culture, administration and politics?

WHAT IS THE TITLE 'CITY OF SCIENCE' AWARDED FOR?

Since the competitive programme was launched in 2005, six cities have won the title (Bremen/Bremerhaven (2005), Dresden (2006), Braunschweig (2007), Jena (2008), Oldenburg (2009) and Mainz (2010) (Figure 6.1).

Following a list of criteria, cities are encouraged to participate in the annual contest. The criteria include a wide range of different activities and formats, which are addressed to many different audiences. The concepts from the scientific field should be as imaginative and interdisciplinary as possible. Of even greater importance is the role of local co-operation

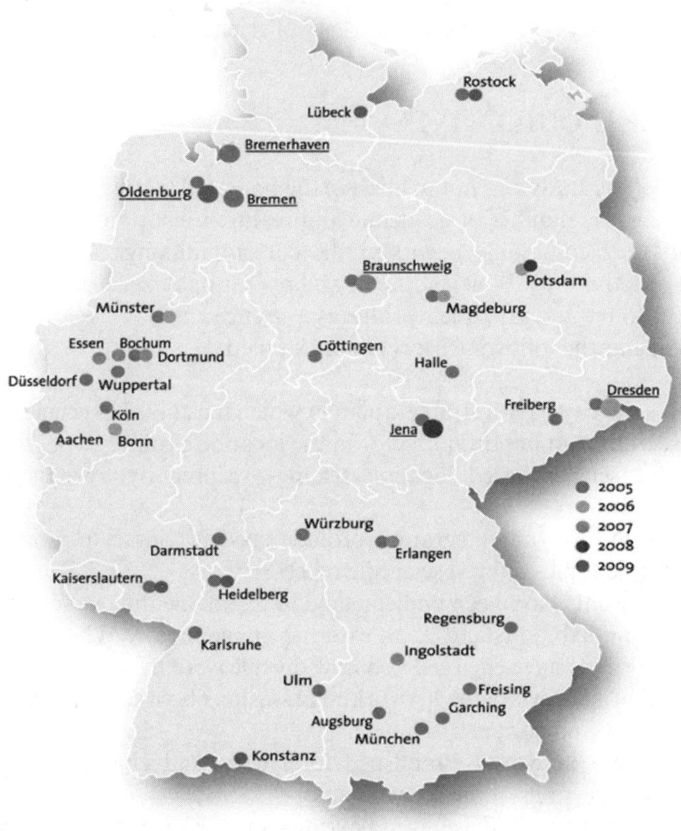

Figure 6.1 Participating cities in the evaluation process

between science, industry and the city, which is traditionally characterized by stability and sustainability.

To attain the 'city of science' title, the following criteria have been established by this body:

- An active role of communities in the network formation;
- Dialogue-orientation and a wide range of different activities and formats
- Originality of approaches;
- Interdisciplinary approaches;
- Cooperation between universities and other partners;
- Cooperation between science and industry;

- Cooperation of science with art and culture;
- Sustained effects of urban activities;
- Importance of science for urban development.

METHODOLOGY

The scientific study of the University of Applied Sciences in Osnabrück and the Stifterverband took place from the 1 January 2009 to 1 May 2010 and consists of a multilevel empirical research concept, including qualitative and quantitative approaches. The study was based on an extensive analysis of documents and websites (secondary research). The applications were particularly evaluated with regards to network structures, institutional arrangements, innovative forms of scientific communication, political back-up programs and strategic concepts. Relevant stakeholders out of ten cities were questioned in face-to-face interviews. These were people who had coordinated the application process or had accompanied it actively, namely mayors, city marketing managers, cultural heads of department, managers of big economic enterprises, employees of city administrations, project managers, press and communication experts, leaders of science and research facilities.

On the basis of these expert interviews, the questionnaire was designed for the complete inventory count of all participating cities until 2009 (N=46). The rate of return was 76 per cent (n=35).

SELECTED FINDINGS OF THE EMPIRICAL STUDY

The research is the first-ever evaluation of the 'City of Science' competition and provides valid information about the different strategic approaches in becoming a knowledge city in Germany. The study provides statistical data about different clusters of knowledge cities in general, as well as background information on specific examples, for instance Oldenburg.

The contest offers the cities involved the chance to recognize their scientific potential and provides an optimal start for their strategic location positioning. It was remarkable to observe that the city administrations could find their specific role in the local networks and concentrated more strongly upon presentation and coordination processes. The establishment of branch-covering networks and new communication and interaction processes intensifies the dialogue with the general public.

For example, the evaluation reveals the following results:

- For 85 per cent of the cities analyzed, the application for the contest had a positive impact on the networking process. Despite not winning the title, the cities still benefited from a large variety of synergies.
- In 72 per cent of the cities, new contacts/cooperation between scientific institutions and city government developed through the competition. In 11 cities (34 per cent) commercial enterprises and scientific institutions emerged to establish new collaborative relationships. In 11 cities, the cooperation between science and culture increased.
- 46 per cent of the local authorities were able to involve stakeholders in the application process with whom they had not been in contact before. New forms of cooperation were established with museums, schools, non-school venues, hospitals, cultural institutions, associations, companies, but also with dedicated individuals. These persons have planned a whole series of events and carried them out independently.
- In 61 per cent of the cities, public administrations acted as moderators, coordinators and central contact points for all partners involved. In many cases, the mayors themselves used personal contacts and various cooperation partners and corporate sponsors to support their application concepts. In these cities special committees were often found, steering system groups or working groups which were settled directly with the political guidance of the city.

CLUSTER ANALYSIS

This study demonstrates that in the majority of cities the process of applying has motivated previously isolated disciplines and areas to work more closely together. The policy-makers and residents of many cities have become aware of the role of science as an engine for urban development and structural change. New knowledge-based strategies, formats of science communication and networks now exist in the cities. A new enlightenment for science and research has been established with long-lasting effects on the minds of numerous citizens.

The hypothesis could be confirmed, that the contest is some kind of catalyst for location profiling through science and research. But this is not equally true for each city. The leverage effect of the contest was very unevenly distributed.

A cluster analysis divided the sample into three groups: 'outriders' (n=5, 14 per cent), 'profiteers' (n=17, 49 per cent) and 'latecomers' (n=13, 37 per cent) (Figure 6.2, Table 6.1).

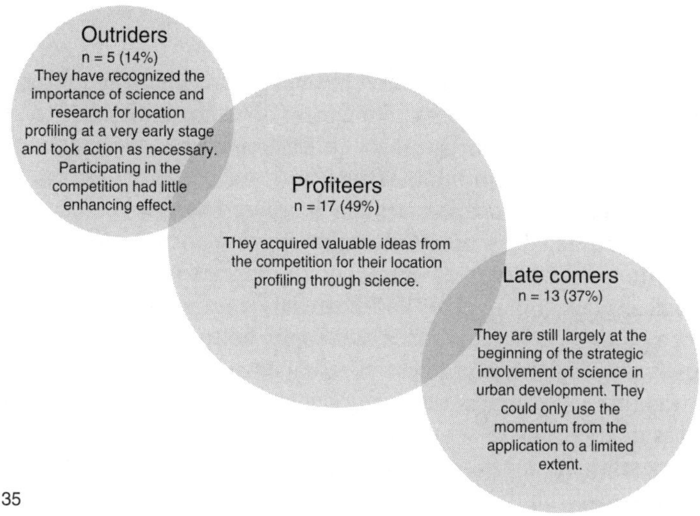

Figure 6.2 Cluster analysis

Table 6.1 Criteria of typification

Proposed typification	Outriders	Profiteers	Late comers
	n=5 (14%)	n=17 (49%)	n=13 (37%)
Prominence of science and research for the city	Already essential before the competition	Invigorated by the competition	Identified very late
Formal decisions of municipal parliament	Existent	Changes in the master plan for city development	No / overall less positive trends of development
Strategic plan of action	Existent	Existent	No approach visible
Dedicated contact person	Already Existent before the competition	Changes in organization and team	None and also no changes
Established networks	Well established	Process of optimization	Weakly existent
Specific types of scientific communication	Multifarious	Established and developed by the competition	Only few types are established

Note: n=35

The 'Outriders'

In these cities, science and research have played a determining role in location profiling for many years. The group does not limit itself to classical university towns, which use their colleges and the surrounding science facilities for location communication.

The science-based location strategy is secured by town council decisions and is underpinned by many activities relevant for location. Changes in the location draft were not necessary any more within these cities, since strategically developing plans had existed for a long time. Moreover, cross-sector networks between science, economy, culture and city management were already set up regardless of competitive participation. Similarly, this was true for contacts regarding scientific interests with the respective city administrations. They organized science marketing, maintained the network relations and co-operated in the development of scientific formats. The synergies from the application process were smaller in this group.

In the analysis of these cities the following criteria were taken:

- Science and research has already been the central theme for location communication, independent of the competition. The competition had no reinforcing effect, because the best approach had already been established.
- Science was and is now being used as a key driver for the development of the site. Formal decisions ensured the strategic profile.
- The city disposed and still disposes of a strategic development plan which guarantees sustainability and future orientation.
- The city government has already established strong participation among competition coordinators and contacts for science in the city administration.
- The network structures between politics, science, economy and culture existed before participation in the competition and were optimally structured, so that innovations were not necessary.
- The city operates effective scientific communication. Many styles from the application system have been successfully implemented and permanently anchored.

The 'Profiteers'

The second category includes participant cities that have recognized knowledge as a future engine, but they have not yet fulfilled all the criteria. The most important characteristic feature is that the participation in the competition has unfolded the biggest leverage effect in this group. Scientific subjects had their place in strategic city development before the participation in the competition. However, during the course of the application a clear step forward is recognizable. The same is true for the network structures. These were expanded in the course of the application and the collaboration was intensified. Central for the classification was, among other things, that these cities have recognized their weaknesses and their potential to optimize. They have used the competitive impulse actively.

To earn the classification of 'competition profiteers' at least five of the following six characteristics had to be found. In doubtful cases, further positive development trends and activities were included in the assessment process.

- Science and research played an important role before the competition. Afterwards, the application process increased the awareness of these issues significantly, or the competition was classified as an initial function for the dynamics of knowledge development.
- Science had already adapted itself strategically in the location, shaping what town council decisions would guarantee / or the competition has caused changes in the location shaping draft.
- Provided that before the competition no scientific contacts were set up, personnel, organizational or institutional changes or restructuring were carried out as a result of the competition.
- Existing weak network structures were achieved by the competitive participation and have changed qualitatively and quantitatively since then.
- The city had a strategic development plan.
- Many of the original event ideas from the application system have been implemented even without the city winning the title, and some of these formats have become sustainable.

The 'Latecomers'

The cities of this cluster are still in the planning phase, which concerns the strategic integration of science in urban development. The presence of universities of excellence or a good reputation as a science city was not sufficient in the context of this analysis for a classification in the first two clusters. The interest of research was not focused on the potential factors, but rather on the strategic basis of a knowledge-based urban development. Participation in the competition had no lasting effect in these cities. The classification of the 'latecomers' was especially based on the first two clusters and their criteria. In cases of doubt, the existing strengths and potentials were considered and compared with new developments.

For the classification, the following seven features were relevant. At least six had to be met:

- The strategic profile of the science is being treated as a casual theme, and there is no apparent competitive effect on the profile to be determined.
- Contact persons for scientific topics are not available, and no personnel or organizational changes have been made.
- The networks of the application process will only be used for irregular or occasional collaborations which were established only for the application and then disbanded.
- Strategic development plans on science and research do not exist.
- Ideas and formats from the application processes have not been carried out at all or only to a slight extent. Permanently established events do not occur.
- Notable network effects, new forms of institutions or partners were not apparent.
- Positive trends were difficult to detect and the city had little drive.

The 'latecomers' are primarily small towns with up to 200 000 inhabitants, like the 'outriders'. The 'profiteers' will be more likely in the medium-sized cities in which up to 500 000 inhabitants reside. There were a total of six candidates from big cities with over 500 000 inhabitants.

THE CASE STUDY OF 'ÜBERMORGENSTADT OLDENBURG': LESSONS LEARNED FROM THE 'CITY OF SCIENCE 2009'

This case study presents a typical 'profiteer' of the competition. Oldenburg, a city in northwest Germany with about 160 000 inhabitants was awarded the title 'City of Science 2009'. After an unsuccessful application in 2005, this was the city's second attempt to attain the award. The newly elected mayor Gerd Schwandner (a former professor himself) created a staff unit 'scientific affairs' to prepare for the 2009 nomination campaign. The creation of this staff unit – reporting directly to the mayor – might have been the tipping point for a new strategy of repositioning the entire city.

Pin your hopes on bottom up-participation . . .

Why was the second bid successful, while the first one failed? After losing the nomination in 2005 one conclusion was quite clear: If the city wanted to apply again – and this time successfully – it would have to reshape its strategy. The jury back then criticized the fact that not enough effort had been made to involve the citizens. Responding to this, two modules of participation were designed. First, opinion leaders from the fields of science, business, media and culture were invited to collaborate for the application. In the summer of 2007 thirteen so-called 'idea factories' ('Ideenschmieden') were organized. Each one took place at a special location such as disused electric power transformation station or a tropical orangery in the botanic garden. The aim was to establish a creative environment for the exchange of ideas. Ten to twelve participants were invited. The mixture of those invited was crucial – they came from different branches of society and ranged from young to mature and established. The result was amazing. More than 100 project proposals were developed.

The second module addressed the entire population of the city. Each 'ordinary citizen' had the opportunity to submit his or her proposal – through a newly created webpage, via postcards, by attending presentations during a special event in the summer of 2007, or by walking into the campaign office and proposing ideas to the staff unit members.

. . .but do not forget top down-processes!

Bottom-up participation was important, and it was successful due to two reasons: (1) it created an atmosphere of interest and stakeholdership, as those who took part in the campaign could easily be convinced to participate in the actual 'city of science' programme after Oldenburg had won the title; and (2) the bottom up process created a multitude of good ideas. In this way the project was creative.

Despite its creativeness and positive atmosphere there was something a bottom-up process could not generate: a coherent strategy for the campaign, the application and – on an even broader scale – a strategy for the city as a whole. Bottom up-processes create 'broadness' – but it is top down-processes that produce 'spikiness'.

Therefore we intended to create a counter flow model in order to balance creativity and strategy. A strategic core of very few persons was responsible for strategy. While the bottom-up models created projects and ideas, the steering committee decided which 'narrative' should be portrayed in the 'City of Science' campaign. It was this group that decided to focus on Florida's (2002) '3 Ts' (talents, technology, tolerance) and on the made-up word 'Übermorgenstadt' (meaning 'day-after-tomorrow city'.) This expression has a positive connotation in German and served as a slogan for the project.

Substance of Style

It was only afterwards that one key factor for success became obvious: the new design, originally created for the application campaign. This design was so successful that it not only replaced the city's corporate design after 2009 but also earned two internationally respected awards in 2010 (IF-Design-Award and red dot award). Most of us think about science in equations and statistics, and things that cannot be measured seem to be obscure. Nevertheless we gained the impression that Virginia Postrel, a *New York Times* journalist, may have hit the mark, when she wrote a few years ago about the 'substance of style'.

In the case of Oldenburg positive feedback and comments on the new corporate design were impressive. This encouraged the administration to abolish the old corporate design (although it had been created only five years earlier) and implement the new one, based on the new 'Übermorgenstadt' line. Local and regional businesses were particularly interested in a new 'brand' and co-financed the further development and transition of the 'City of Science' ideas into the general city marketing scheme.

Further Gains

The year as 'City of Science 2009' was expensive for the city and its partners in science and business. More than 1.5 million Euros were spent officially (probably 3.0 million is a more accurate estimate, counting in unofficial sponsorship for additional projects such as 'medicine of tomorrow') by industry and commerce for some projects; more than 400 events and projects were organized; several dozen groups, institutions and, businesses were involved; and countless overtime hours were accumulated. Was it worth the effort? We would say yes. The events gave a boost to tourism with an additional 40000 overnight stays (which have resulted in an estimated gross value-added of about 4 million Euro), not to mention the improved image. But the most important benefit of all may only be felt in the future. It is immaterial and not easy to seize (and hopefully will not be abandoned by electoral change in offices), but the 'spirit' of the City of Science idea has given inspiration to a city that otherwise had neither a focus nor a plan for its future development.

To give just one example, urban planning in Germany is often a question of designing a preparatory land-use plan (Flächennutzungsplan). The more than 15 year old plan will now be supplemented by STEP 2025 – short for Stadtentwicklungsplan (City Development Plan). The core idea of STEP is Übermorgenstadt and how to transform the city into a 'true' City of Science. Three city quarters for further development have been identified: Science Quarter (the two traditional campuses), White Campus (the future campus of the University Medical Center), and the Creative Quarter (where several museums, socio-cultural theatres etc. can be found). Oldenburg's urban planning intends to design a strategy to foster the development of these core quarters to transform the character of the city. The resulting projects will be dovetailed with city marketing and programmes of the Economic Development Department.

Further Steps

Smart House: Additionally the municipality and its partners from business and science will highlight a project called the 'Smart House'. At one of the most visible places in Oldenburg – facing the baroque castle – a decrepit 16th-century house will be extensively restored and improved, and furthermore enlarged and fused with a modern 21st century building designed by the German architects Behnisch Architekten. The idea is twofold.

The first idea is, to develop a platform for communication between science and 'ordinary' people. We know that science events (such as the Edinburgh Science Festival) foster PUSH (public understanding of science and humanities); the intention of the 'Smart House' is to do the same on an everyday basis.

The second idea is to generate a showcase and focal point for all the City of Science efforts. The Smart House will represent regional strongholds in research areas such as sustainable energy, information technology and demographic change. The building's modern, crystal-like façade and powerful sustainable energy generation will supply CO_2-free energy for the modern as well as the ancient part of the building. (One can only imagine the innumerable obstacles in transforming a 400-year-old house into a zero emission building.)

Talents campaign: Some European cities have demonstrated how talent can be recruited. Barcelona's 'Talencia' initiative and Groningen's 'city of talent' campaign are two interesting projects that should be analyzed by anyone who deals with science and city. Medium sized cities, in particular, can learn much from the Dutch provincial capital with its 190000 inhabitants. By working together on a policy platform, all important social powers have been integrated to foster development in two crucial areas: energy and health care. Groningen's 'city of talent' campaign benefited from the work done over the previous ten years. Oldenburg will try to follow the successful path of its Dutch twin city.

If we regard Oldenburg as a case study for the entire City of Science programme, one outcome should be stressed (although it might be the most difficult one to measure). A project like City of Science can change the attitude of an entire population towards a certain issue. Oldenburg's scientific institutions are quite young. The university will celebrate its 40th anniversary in 2014 (the same year that the Rijksuniversiteit Groningen will celebrate being 400 years old). The impact of science on transforming the economic, social and cultural appearance of the city has been enormous, especially over the last 15 years. Paradoxically this fact is not well known outside the local and regional scientific community. Large event-related projects like Übermorgenstadt can help to create awareness of the importance of science for a knowledge-based economy simply by creating a 'spirit' for science.

CONCLUSION

The challenge for each city is to secure positive income from the application; the title-winners in particular want this in order to develop a City of Science into a 'science city'. Oldenburg is a good example of this development.

It is not only Oldenburg that can be evaluated as a success, however: 85 per cent of the recorded cities in the census (n = 35) revealed positive effects from the competition. These include the creation and establishment of long term performance networks as well as innovative forms of scientific communication. Despite not having won the title, 38 per cent of cities carried out most of the events originally planned for their application. Some of these events have been so successful that they have become an integral part of the city's events calendar. The joint implementation of events is classified as an important factor in network training.

The importance of science in location positioning in 55 per cent of cities has increased; in 42 per cent of cases the urban profiling concept is being reorganized from the science perspective. With the recruitment of research institutions or high potentials in cities, new sectors of high importance for the local research system have been added. This shift of emphasis in economic development and city marketing is attributed partly to partaking in the competition.

The cluster analysis shows nearly half of cities (49 per cent, n=17) as 'competition profiteers'. These have clearly recognized the importance of science and research for location profiling and have strategically anchored this topic. Even without a title win, these cities have benefited from the competition in many different ways.

The other half, which is divided into two groups, has hardly benefited from the competition at all. A small minority of 14 per cent (n=5) are among the 'outriders' who have distinguished themselves for years through research and science. They gained a negligible advantage by joining in the competition. The larger proportion of 37 per cent (n=13), the 'late comers', do not seriously drive the strategic integration of science into urban development. In this group there are a disproportionate number of smaller cities.

It is striking that the 'profiteers' are mainly medium-sized cities that want to be repositioned as a knowledge city. This result could imply that more consideration should be given to the different sizes of the cities. Small cities, for instance, should be supported differently from medium or large ones.

Critical to the sustained effect of the City of Science competition is the support of local politics. In some cities there are increasing signs that council members prefer to keep their distance from knowledge economy issues. These sceptical if not negative signals from councils are expected to continue particularly during times of tight budgets.

REFERENCES

Carrillo, Francisco Javier (2006), *Knowledge Cities: Approaches, Experiences and Perspectives*, Butterworth-Heinemann.

Cars, Göran, Patsy Healey, Ali Madanipour and Claudio de Magalhaes (2002), *Urban Governance, Institutional Capacity and Social Milieu*, Aldershot, Burlington USA, Singapore, New York: Ashgate.

Florida, Richard L. (2002), *The Rise of the Creative Class: And How It's Transforming Work, Leisure, Community and Everyday Life*, New York: Basic Books.

Hohn, Stefanie, Clas Meyer and Matthias Schmidt (2009), Standortentwicklung durch Wissensnetze. Auswirkungen der Wissensgesellschaft auf kommunale Netzwerkbildungsprozesse zwischen Wissenschaft, Wirtschaft, Kultur und Stadtverwaltung, in Neues Verwaltungsmanagement – Verwaltung modernizieren, Ressourcen nutzen, Abläufe optimieren, Handbuch, Stuttgart: Raabe Verlag, pp. 1–19.

Hohn, Stefanie, Clas Meyer and Rainer Lisowski Wissenschaftsstädte im Vergleich. Ergebnisse der empirischen Untersuchung des Wettbewerbs 'Stadt der Wissenschaft', in Neues Verwaltungsmanagement – Verwaltung modernizieren, Ressourcen nutzen, Abläufe optimieren, Handbuch, Raabe Verlag, pp. 1–21.

Matthiesen, Ulf (2004), *Stadtregion und Wissen: Analysen und Plädoyers für eine wissensbasierte Stadtpolitik*, Wiesbaden: Verlag VS.

Matthiesen, Ulf (2005), 'Knowledge spaces – pleading for a knowledge turn into a socio-spatial research', Working Paper, Institut für Regionalentwicklung und Strukturplanung, Erkner.

Mayntz, Renate, Friedhelm Neidhard, Peter Weingart and Ulrich Wengenroth (2008), Wissensproduktion und Wissenstransfer – Wissen im Spannungsfeld von Wissenschaft, Politik und Öffentlichkeit, transcript Verlag Bielefeld.
Yigitcanlar, T. (2009), 'Planning for knowledge-based urban development: global perspectives', *Journal of Knowledge Management*, **13** (5), 228–242.

7. Participating: knowledge citizens' competences and knowledge city transformation

Octavio González, Rodolfo Wilhelmy, Santiago Cavazos and América Martínez

INTRODUCTION

Knowledge is presently more valuable than ever. Ergazakis et al. (2006) explain that although 'knowledge has been the critical source of progress since the origins of the human kind on earth, what is new and rapidly evolving nowadays, is the explicit and purposeful management of knowledge as a strategic resource'. The need for sustainable development and the creation of value in all the areas of a city have been the principal reasons to look at the concepts of knowledge, and knowledge-based development, as factors of balance and sustainable high quality of life. For Chatzkel (2004) 'the knowledge factor differentiates a region'. He suggests that 'physical and financial resources still are important, but knowledge and actionable knowledge specifically, is the most powerful factor of production'.

The Knowledge Cities official website (Knowledge Cities, 2010) suggests that a '[Knowledge City] (KC) is one that searches for the creation of value in all its areas', meaning that the economic benefit or the increase in production is not the principal goal of this kind of city, as is the appreciation and capitalization of the total value produced by human activity. That is because, as Carrillo (2010) explains, the total value produced by human activity includes different forms of knowledge capital.

As long as a knowledge city searches for the capitalization of the total value produced by human activity, a knowledge city is as valuable as its human capital. Buendía et al. (2005) say that 'there is an undoubted relation between the citizen and the city where he/she evolves; both are constituted and outlined mutually in a dynamic manner'. For these authors, 'there is a strong relation between the development of a city and its human capital'. In fact, Goldberg et al. (2006) suggest citizens are the key towards defining a knowledge city.

Citizen participation is widely recognized as a factor of social change. As a result of that, there are research papers (Irvin and Stansbury, 2004; Adamson, 2010; Hughes, 2011; Nour, 2011) focused on how citizen participation can influence the government's decisions and the community's development. Nevertheless, these papers revolve around the premise that society should participate in specific areas. In this investigation, the objective is not to study the social characteristics that enable social participation; instead, this chapter analyzes the citizens' competences required to enable social participation.

This work concerns the citizens, rather than society, because the daily decisions (consumption, relationships, distribution of time) made by them affect their community. Furthermore, they create a culture that persists over time. For this reason, identifying the citizen competences that promote participation of each individual based on information and knowledge, will contribute to a sustainable knowledge-based development. Subsequently, this research is more focused on how citizens can improve their cities by participating daily with specific actions, rather than organizing society to improve specific areas.

Following such trends, Martínez (2006) has developed her research focusing on the competence profile of the knowledge citizen, based on the value categories that are relevant to the knowledge cities context, and which constitute the reference and the background that the present chapter draws from. She observes that there have been advances on the instrumentation line in the competence profile of the knowledge citizen, through the design of digital systems that make it possible to approach citizenship allowing self-evaluation and self-management in the learning process, as well as developing citizen competences (Martinez and Pacheco, 2010, 2011).

This chapter identifies a set of competences that will allow citizens to leverage the knowledge value of their city. The MAKCi framework is used to explain how citizens impact the said value. This framework was chosen based on its wide adoption and the fact that it encompasses the city's value elements in their entirety.

METHODOLOGY

The research was conducted in three stages (see Figure 7.1), the first being a review of taxonomies. This allowed the identification of patterns in their structure and implementation. This first stage began with a thorough

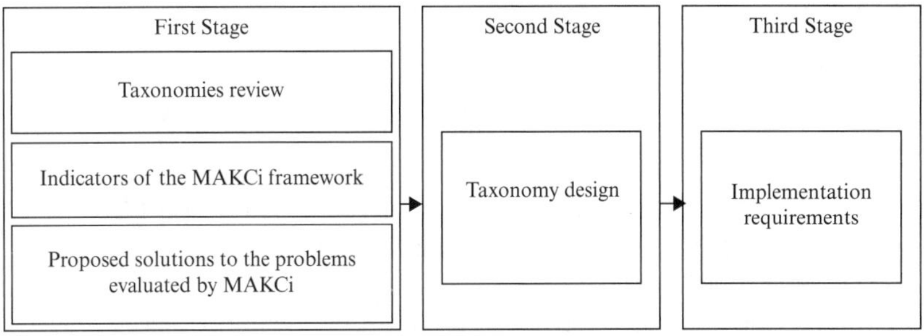

Figure 7.1 Stages in the design of the research

review of the Most Admired Knowledge City (MAKCi) Awards framework (see http://www.worldcapitalinstitute.org/makciplatform). The goal was to choose indicators that demonstrate a direct relation with their variation as caused by citizens' actions. Problems that cause a sub-optimal performance in the indicators were then identified. The next step in this stage was to propose solutions, a step which included another round of research to locate proposed citizen actions that attack the specific problems identified previously.

The second stage involved functional analysis of the compiled research, which yielded a taxonomy of 30 citizen competences. This taxonomy design was based on the theory researched during the first stage and was focused on promoting active participation of each individual citizen. These competences were arranged with the specific capital they leverage, along with their specific indicators that demonstrate a citizen's development of the competence.

The third stage consisted in finding the best way to measure, evaluate and develop the said competences. This was achieved by comparing taxonomy implementations reviewed in stage one.

DEVELOPMENT

Taxonomies Review

A taxonomy is a classification system whose objective is to group objects based on similar characteristics (structure, colour, behaviour, etc.). The taxonomies found in the first stage are described briefly from Box 7.1 to Box 7.7.

BOX 7.1 BECTA

Name: Becta
Reference: http://about.becta.org.uk/ ("Becta", 2010)
Purpose: Becta leads the national drive to inspire and lead the effective and innovative use of technology throughout learning.
Target: Teachers and students.
Instrument: It uses information and communication technology; basically web tools.

BOX 7.2 CITIZEN'S BRIEFCASE

Name: Citizen's briefcase
Reference: http://maletinciudadano.org/ ("Maletín Ciudadano", 2010)
Purpose: A site that allows a person to learn the essential civic competences and their strengths and weaknesses as a citizen, suggesting a guideline to increase the knowledge, skills, attitudes and civic values.
Target: Citizens.
Instrument: A dynamic website in permanent construction.

BOX 7.3 GLOW

Name: Glow
Reference: http://www.ltscotland.org.uk/glowscotland/index.asp ("Glow", 2010)
Purpose: To enhance the quality of learning and teaching in the classroom by fully supporting the delivery of curriculum for excellence. The purpose of curriculum for excellence is encapsulated in the four capacities – to enable each child or young person to be a successful learner, confident individual, a responsible citizen and an effective contributor.
Target: Teachers, students, parents, school managers, school administrators and local authorities.
Instrument: A national directory, forums, video, audio, mail, messenger and chat.

BOX 7.4 INSTRUCTOR COMPETENCES ASSESSMENT INSTRUMENT

Name: Instructor Competences Assessment Instrument
Reference: http://www.pro-net2000.org/CM/content_files/70.pdf ("Instructor Competences Assessment Instrument", 2010)
Purpose: Designed to help programs verify and validate staff and use that information for program improvement and professional development planning.
Target: Adult educators.
Instruments: Interviews, questionnaires, observations, portfolios, journals and lesson plans.

BOX 7.5 MANAGEMENT COMPETENCES ASSESSMENT INSTRUMENT

Name: Management Competencies Assessment Instrument
Reference: www.pro-net2000.org/CM/content_files/71.pdf ("Management Competences Assessment Instrument", 2010)
Purpose: To identify and increase the competences that all managers should acquire to be effective in their professional development.
Target: Managers.
Instrument: Performance evaluations, administrative reports and administrative portfolios.

MAKCi Framework

The Most Admired Knowledge City (MAKCi) Awards are given once a year at the Knowledge Cities World Summit. These awards are 'an international expert consulting process established to identify and recognize those communities around the world who are successfully engaging in formal and systematic knowledge-based development processes under the flag of Knowledge Cities' (WCI, 2007). The MAKCi Framework includes eight knowledge capital dimensions and combines the MAKE Awards methodology with the WCI Generic Capitals System (GCS) taxonomy (WCI, 2010). This framework 'is a knowledge-economy model that involves an assessment of the value base on which

BOX 7.6 PERSONAL COMPETENCE MANAGER

Name: TEN Competence
Reference: http://www.tencompetence.org/web/guest ("TEN Competence", 2010)
Purpose: Support individuals, groups and organizations in Europe in the life-long development of their abilities by developing and promoting the most suitable technical and organizational infrastructure, making use of open-source, standards-based sustainable and innovative technologies.
Target: Individuals, groups and organizations.
Instrument: The PCM (Personal Competence Manager) is a website where users have access to tools to organize the participation and creation of programs for the development of competences, focusing on the context of social networks.

BOX 7.7 THE NATIONAL EDUCATION NETWORK

Name: The National Education Network
Reference: http://www.nen.gov.uk/ ("National Education Network", 2010)
Purpose: The National Educational Network is a dedicated, educationally focused resource for teaching and learning without constraints of time or location. Harnessing unique expertise, it enables a safe, secure, collaborative and creative learning experience for pupils, teachers and parents. This harnesses the power of broadband technology to deliver unique content and services, enabling users to share learning resources at every level, to deliver a personalized learning experience.
Target: Students, teachers and parents.
Instrument: Website with didactic resources such as games, animations and videos.

the future development of a city is made possible through a recombination or trading of existing capitals, both traditional and knowledge-based' (Garcia, 2008). The eight knowledge capital categories of the framework are:

1. Identity capital
2. Intelligence capital
3. Financial capital
4. Relational capital
5. Human individual capital
6. Human collective capital
7. Instrumental-material capital and
8. Instrumental-intangible capital

Each of the city's value elements can be classified in one of these dimensions. Specifications and goals for each capital are explained in the next section, to ease further understanding of the relevance of each competence proposed.

Proposals and Taxonomy

The taxonomy suggested should be read through four levels. The first level, called 'capital', corresponds with the capital of the MAKCi framework to be leveraged. The second level, called 'area', indicates the aspect in which the citizen should become competent so as to leverage the specific capital. The third level is the actual 'competence' to develop, and the fourth level points out the indicators that will demonstrate if the citizen has developed those competences (Figure 7.2). The logic for the functional analysis is one proposed by MINEDUC-DIVESUP (2003).

Identity capital

According to García (2007) the 'Identity [is] the capability to create and evolve a distinctive and well-positioned urban personality'. The city's reputation is represented by how well positioned this urban personality is, so, if the reputation is improved, the identity metrics will increase.

One way to improve the city's reputation is to organize festivals and events. Bu (2009) notices that 'sports events are tools for elevating the image and appeal of a city'. He exemplifies this with the cases of Barcelona, Rotterdam, Turin and China. Sports events are not the only events important to increase the city's promotion. Kavaratzis and Ashworth (2007) explain that 'cultural events and festivals play a very important role in marketing [. . .] because they are "big moments of visibility" through which the city can attract significant international attention at one time'. Another way to leverage identity is to maintain the city's traditions. Culinary objects, as mentioned by Palmié (2009), have the power to explain significant aspects of the collective identities of their original creators and consumers.

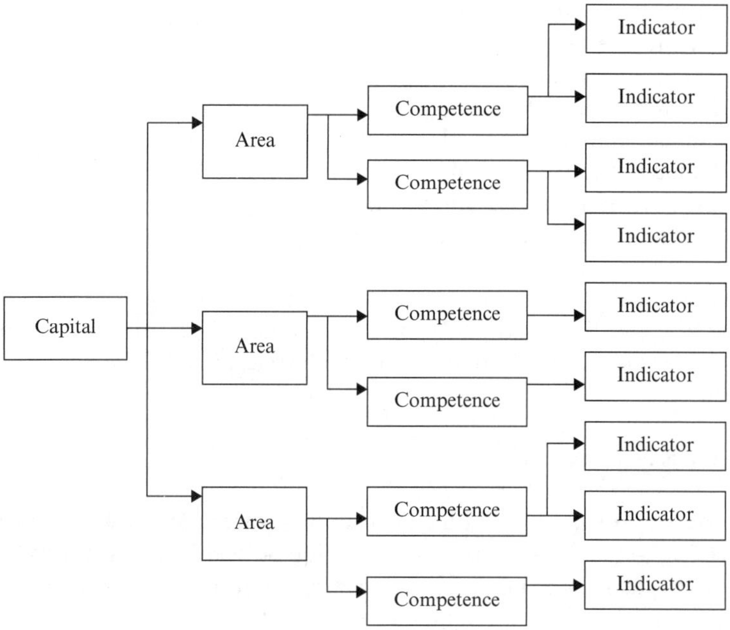

Figure 7.2 Levels in the functional analysis

Drawing from these authors, two competence areas that empower citizens to leverage their city's identity were devised: 'active participation in festivals and events' and 'culinary tradition' (Table 7.1).

Intelligence capital

According to García (2007) 'Intelligence [is the] capability to identify/ foresee and adequately respond to significant agents and events'. In order for the city to identify/ foresee an opportunity or a threat, it should be able to read the context, the environment and clearly understand the consequences of its actions. This is the reason the citizens should have precise information from reliable sources to be able to generate an opinion by themselves and create strong public opinion. Citizens can achieve this by practicing 'lifelong learning', and developing competences to leverage the city's intelligence.

Longworth and Davies (1996) explain that 'Lifelong learning is the development of human potential through a continuously supportive process which stimulates and empowers individuals to acquire all the knowledge, values, skills and understanding they will require throughout their lifetimes with confidence, creativity and enjoyment in all roles, circumstances and environments.'

Table 7.1 Identity capital

Area	Competence	Indicator
Active participation in festivals and events	Values the region's festivals and events	The citizen identifies the region's most important events The citizen specifies all implications that the regional festivals and events have on the city
	Active participation in region's festivals and events	The citizen has participated in the planning of a regional festival or event The citizen has participated in the organization of a regional festival or event The citizen has participated in the coordination of a festival or event The citizen has functioned as staff in a regional festival or event. The citizen has attended at least one regional festival or event
Culinary tradition	Knows the importance of the city's culinary traditions	The citizen identifies the benefits of maintaining the city's culinary traditions The citizen can explain the impact of the city's culinary traditions in the development of the city
	Learns and promotes the city's culinary traditions	The citizen can prepare the city's culinary traditions The citizen has taught how to prepare the city's culinary traditions to others

Work invested in developing the lifelong learning process of citizens will pay off by increasing the city's intelligence. Developing individual competences in order to generate a strong and focused individual opinion will leverage a strong and focused public opinion as well (Table 7.2).

Financial capital

According to García (2007), financial capital is the 'capability to generate and sustain a healthy monetary base'. The easiest way a citizen can leverage financial capital is taking care of his/her individual health. As Arreola-Ornelas et al. (2003) point out:

> Health plays a very important role in dismissing poverty, because healthier individuals are more productive, and a productive individual reflects in better

Table 7.2 Intelligence capital

Area	Competence	Indicator
Lifelong learning	Information self-management	The citizen identifies the most important sources of information in his or her context The citizen clearly identifies the benefits of having up to date information
	Continuous acquisition of new competences	The citizen identifies the opportunities for personal growth produced by the acquisition of new competences The citizen identifies new competences applicable to his/her context and environment The citizen is able to design a complete program to acquire new competences and to prove he/she has the self-control to implement it
	Professional and social contexts	The citizen has continuous interaction with colleagues The citizen continuously verifies the most relevant sources of information for his/her professional context The citizen identifies the social implications of the most important political events in the week The citizen continuously verifies the most relevant sources of information for his/her social context
	Application of knowledge in different contexts	The citizen has participated in projects of different professional areas The citizen has participated in projects of different social areas

wages; at the same time a healthy individual can compete in equal conditions to others. So, health puts the individual in equity of circumstances, and that improves their wages, but also the economic growth.

Another point to focus on is the social inequity encouraged by discrimination and social divides. Kliksberg (2006) explains that 'A wide number of researchers indicate that inequity acts like a powerful brake on the [financial] development [of a city]' and explains some consequences in the national and international levels. A citizen can increase the financial capital of the city in two ways: paying attention to the city's 'public space', and being tolerant towards cultural diversity (Table 7.3).

Relational capital

García (2007) defines relational capital as the 'capability to develop quality interactions with all significant internal and external agents'. One way to increase this capital's measurement could be the promotion of tolerance. Shatz (2004) says tolerance is the base for security in a social environment, as well as an important concept for democratic life. 'The social and economic inequity based on gender, can injure the global performance in a lot and different areas, affecting demographic, medical, economic and social variables', as pointed out by Sen (2000).

Drawing from these authors, the research proposes that 'tolerance for diversity', 'social cohesion' and 'gender equity' increase the relational capital dimension of a city (Table 7.4).

Human individual capital

According to García (2007), human individual capital possesses a 'capability to create conditions for the full biological and psychological development of residents'. Borja (1998) remarks that 'in the public space the diversity is expressed, the interchange is produced and tolerance is learned. The quality, the propagation and the accessibility of public space will define, in a big part, the citizenship development'. Borja (1998) explains the public space as the social collective space, public and multifunctional, characterized by accessibility and evaluated by the intensity and quality of the social relations that it promotes between groups, behaviors and cultures. This author proposes that a 'city that functions exclusively by private cars and with specialized and closed centers (administrative centers, shopping centers, etc.) does not facilitate the development of the citizens, instead promoting division, individualism and exclusion'.

In that sense, the citizen's competences that should be developed to increase the human individual capital are presented in Table 7.5.

Human collective capital

According to García (2007), human collective capital is the 'capability to enhance the goal achievement potential of its constituent communities'. The first step towards reaching a city's goals is to define them, so, there should be a social organization and citizen participation for planning, developing and improving each goal.

Velásquez and González (2003) explain that citizen participation

Table 7.3 Financial capital

Area	Competence	Indicator
Health care	Health and quality of living	The citizen points out how and why his/her purchasing power increases when his/her health improves
		The citizen points out how and why eating habits, sports habits and hygiene habits increase health
	Indexes of health	The citizen identifies the purpose of the body mass index (BMI)
		The citizen identifies the purpose of the waist-hip ratio (WHR)
	Utilization of the index of health	The citizen proves that he/she can calculate own BMI
		The citizen proves that he/she can calculate own WHR
	Hygiene habits	The citizen identifies oral hygiene habits
		The citizen identifies body hygiene habits
	Active participation in health care	The citizen applies knowledge about hygiene habits
		The citizen exercises 5 days a week
		The citizen maintains a healthy diet
Attention to and proliferation of the public space	Understanding the public space	The citizen identifies the difference between public space and private space from a social perspective and not from a legal perspective
		The citizen understands the concept 'Collective Act'
	Development of public space	The citizen identifies the social benefits of promotion and development of the public space
		The citizen identifies the individual advantage of promoting and developing the public space
	Promotion of public space	The citizen participates in collective acts, either cultural or commercial
		The citizen uses alternative means of transportation
		The citizen acquires products / services in a variety of places
Tolerance of diversity	Religious diversity	The citizen tolerates different religions
	Racial diversity	The citizen treats people of different races equally
	Sexual diversity	The citizen treats people of different sexual preferences equally

Table 7.4 Relational capital

Area	Competence	Indicator
Tolerance of diversity	Religious diversity	The citizen treats people with religious beliefs different to theirs in an equal fashion
	Racial diversity	The citizen treats people from a race different to theirs in an equal fashion
	Sexual diversity	The citizen treats people with sexual preferences different to theirs in an equal fashion
Social cohesion	Integration in the community	The citizen participates in neighborhood activities
Gender equity	Gender equity	The citizen treats people of the opposite sex in an equal fashion

Table 7.5 Human individual capital

Area	Competence	Indicator
Attention and proliferation of the public space	Understanding the public space	The citizen identifies the difference between public space and private space from a social perspective and not by a legal perspective The citizen understands the concept 'Collective Act'
	Development of public space	The citizen identifies the social advantage of public space promotion and development The citizen identifies the advantage of promotion and development of public space
	Promotion of public space	The citizen participates in collective acts, either cultural or commercial The citizen utilizes alternative means of transportation The citizen acquires products / services in a variety of places

'improves the efficiency and effectiveness of the public management as long as it can conciliate intentions and construct consensus, by decreasing the environment barriers, and reaching results with the acceptance of the interested'. For these reasons, Table 7.6 proposes the citizen's participation to leverage the city's human collective capital.

Table 7.6 Human collective capital

Area	Competence	Indicator
Citizen participation	Uses of alternative media to express ideas	The citizen uses the web to express ideas in social networks The citizen uses the web to organize peaceful mobilizations
	Support to the community	The citizen continuously donates money The citizen continuously donates time and effort to social projects
	Voting	The citizen has voted in the last three public elections

Table 7.7 Instrumental-material capital

Area	Competence	Indicator
Transparency	Reproach corruption	The citizen identifies acts of corruption The citizen understands the impact of corruption in the community
	Transparent actions	The citizen has denounced corruption acts when witnessed The citizen has not offered or accepted bribes in any situation
Ecological footprint	Environmental commitment	The citizen understands the ecological impact of his/her actions The citizen is aware of sustainable forms of energy and opts to use them frequently The citizen practices and understands the benefits of recycling

Instrumental-material capital

García (2007) defines instrumental-material capital as the 'capability to take advantage of location and to build and renew a world-class physical infrastructure'. Accordingly, taking care of the investment on sustainability will leverage the instrumental-material capital. Mancl et al. (1999) propose three areas of knowledge to improve the city's sustainability: environmental literacy, ecological energetics (sun, water, wind) and materials cycling that involve understanding the accumulation of resources in the natural cycles (Table 7.7).

Table 7.8 Instrumental-intangible capital

Area	Competence	Indicator
Academic skills	Education and self-development	The citizen identifies the benefits of improving his/her education
Creative skills	Cultural practice	The citizen practices a form of art
Entrepreneurship	Entrepreneurial attitude	The citizen participates in environmental initiatives The citizen identifies areas of improvement for the environment and takes action

Corruption adversely affects the government budget by decreasing funding in infrastructure and affecting the perception of foreign investors due to the lack of clear and strict laws. Mauro (1997) says:

> Corruption may also bring about loss of tax revenue when it takes the form of tax evasion or the improper use of discretionary tax exemptions. [. . .] By affecting tax collection or the level of public expenditure, corruption may have adverse budgetary consequences. [. . .] The allocation of public procurement contracts through a corrupt system may lead to inferior public infrastructure and services.

Instrumental-intangible capital

García (2007) specifies that instrumental-intangible capital is the 'capability to transfer knowledge and foster innovation in all major areas of city life'. Ducker (1993) explains that innovation is the specific tool of entrepreneurs; it is the means by which they exploit change as an opportunity for a different business or a different service.

Ducker (1993) suggests that innovation depends on entrepreneurship, but innovation is also about research, so 'scientific and technology education', 'art and culture', and 'entrepreneurship' will leverage the instrumental-intangible capital (Table 7.8).

IMPLEMENTATION REQUIREMENTS

The taxonomy review phase revealed instruments to evaluate and develop competences mostly consisting of media centric elements, such as games, animations, videos, chat, etc. Most of these types of tools can be incorporated in a dynamic website. Furthermore, websites are a good means of

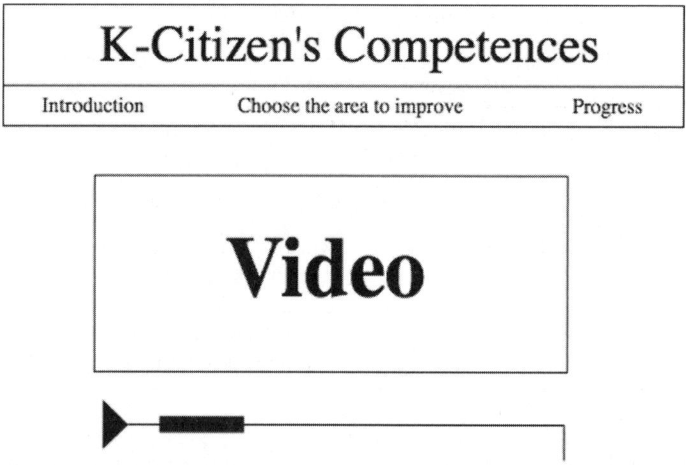

Figure 7.3 'Introduction' screen

achieving a wide availability among potential users and their use can be proliferated quickly with the help of social networks. Websites also allow the tools to be used individually or in group form, as well as in public or private institutions. These reasons support the choice of a website as a means to implement and distribute the tools to develop and evaluate citizen competences. The website should operate free of cost, so as to attract more users. It should also be easy to use and configure.

A proposal for such a website is presented in Figure 7.3. Three main sections include an introduction, a section for the specific areas to improve and a progress section. The introduction section will feature a video to highlight the use of the tool itself, as well as the benefits of developing one's competences.

The second section (Figure 7.4) presents the user with areas to develop in no particular order. The tool does not force the users to develop all areas, it should rather allow users to choose areas of their preference and/or interest. Each area presents the user with a set of questions that enable their current evaluation in each specific area of interest. Answers to these questions should be time stamped, so as to enable a future analysis of data once the user is re-evaluated with the questions in a future time. An important aspect is that users are only presented with the areas and competences to be developed, along with their questions, but not with the actual indicators. This is important so as not to overwhelm users with technical information unnecessary for their growth. Indicators concern only those administrating and deploying the tool.

The third section (Figure 7.5) showcases personal statistics and tailored

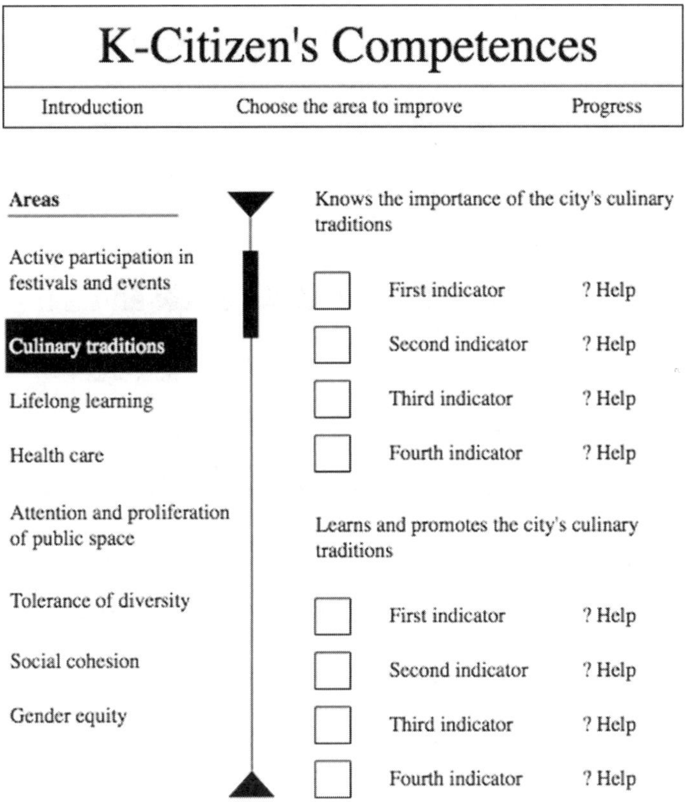

Figure 7.4 Screen to select area of improvement

recommendations to each user. A chat mechanism is also present, to allow the exchange of ideas, opinions and questions between users.

CONCLUSION

This research enabled the design of 30 competences along with a tool for their evaluation and continuous development. The research reported in this chapter suggests concrete actions for citizens to improve themselves and their cities, as well as indicating that each citizen has the absolute capacity of evaluating and developing their own competences.

The next step to be taken is to deploy the website proposed previously in the form of a case study. A significant study, for instance, is to evaluate a group of teenagers, between 13 and 18 years old, on a monthly basis. After

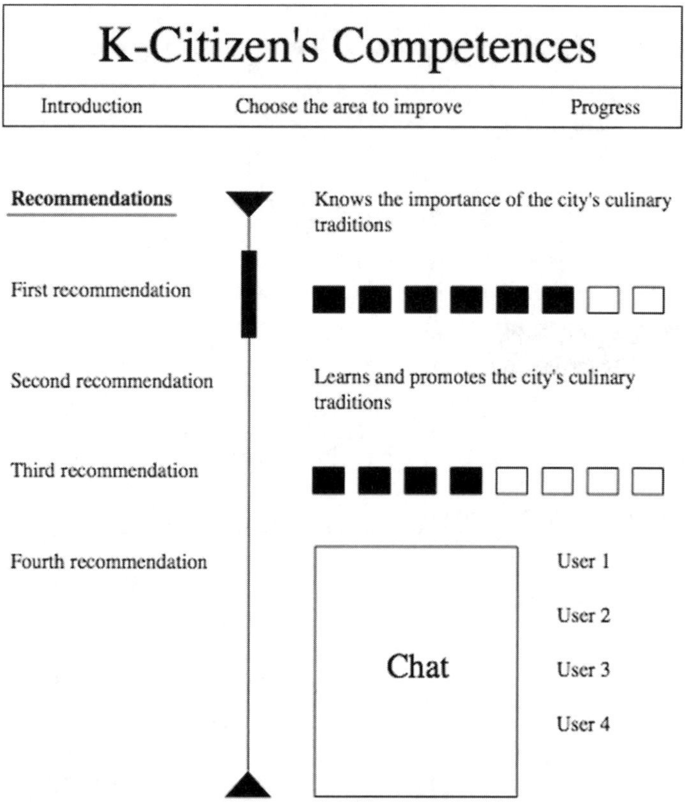

Figure 7.5 Screen to track progress

a sufficient amount of time (perhaps six months), the results could be compared to prove that the development of competences actually promoted positive changes in their community.

REFERENCES

Adamson, D. (2010), 'Community empowerment', *International Journal of Sociology and Social Policy*, **30** (3/4), 114–126.

Arreola-Ornelas, Héctor, Juan Garduño-Espinosa, Herman Soto Molina, Victor Granados García and Evangelina Martínez Rodríguez (2003), 'Los efectos de la salud sobre el crecimiento económico: Hallazgos microeconómicos y macroeconómicos', in Onofre Muñoz, Luis Durán, Juan Garduño and Hermán Soto (eds), *Economía de la salud*, Distrito Federal, México: Instituto Mexicano del Seguro Social, pp. 33–47.

Becta (2010), about.becta.org.uk, accessed 25 July 2010.
Borja, J. (1998), 'Ciudadanía y espacio público', *Urbanitats*, **1** (7).
Bu, T. (2009), 'Beijing Olympics: a new brand of China', *Asian Social Science*, **5** (3), 84–90.
Buendía, A., A. Martínez and S.D. Martínez (2005), 'Competencias del ciudadano en la ciudad de conocimiento', in Mujica Alazne (ed.), *Conocimiento para el desarrollo,* San Sebastian, España: Universidad de Deusto, pp 215–236.
Carrillo, Franciso J. (2010), 'Knowledge-based value generation', in Kostas Metaxiotis, Francisco J. Carrillo and Tan Yigitcanlar (eds), *Knowledge-Based Development for Cities and Societies Integrated Multi-Level Approaches*, Hershey, US: IGI Global.
Chatzkel, J. (2004), 'Greater Phoenix as a knowledge capital', *Journal of Knowledge Management,* **8** (5), 61–72.
Ducker, Peter F. (1993), *Innovation and Entrepreneurship*, New York, US: HarperBusiness.
Ergazakis, K., K. Metaxiotis, J. Psarras and D. Askounis (2006), 'A unified methodological approach for the development of knowledge cities', *Journal of Knowledge Management,* **10** (5), 65–78.
García, B.C. (2007), 'Working and learning in a knowledge city: a multilevel development framework for knowledge workers', *Journal of Knowledge Management*, **11** (5), 18–30.
García, B.C. (2008), 'Global KBD community developments: the MAKCi experience', *Journal of Knowledge Management*, **12** (5), 91–106.
Glow (2010), www.ltscotland.org.uk/glowscotland/index.asp, accessed 25 July 2010.
Goldberg, M., E. Pasher and M. Levin-Sagi (2006), 'Citizen participation in decision-making processes: knowledge sharing in knowledge cities', *Journal of Knowledge Management,* **10** (5), 92–98.
Hughes, M. (2011), 'The challenges of informed citizen participation in change', *Transforming Government: People, Process and Policy*, **5** (1), 68–80
Instructor Competencies Assessment Instrument (2010), www.pro-net2000.org/CM/content_files/70.pdf, accessed 25 July 2010.
Irvin, R.A. and J. Stansbury (2004), 'Citizen participation in decision making: is it worth the effort?', *Public Administration Review*, **64** (1), 55–65
Kavaratzis, M. and G.J. Ashworth (2007), 'Partners in coffeeshops, canals and commerce: marketing the city of Amsterdam', *Cities*, **24** (1), 16–25.
Kliksberg, B. (2006), 'La Discriminación de la Mujer en el Mundo Globalizado y en América Latina', *Formación Gerencial*, **5** (1), 11–58.
Knowledge Cities (2010), www.knowledgecities.com/glossaries/kcity.html, accessed 25 July 2010.
Longworth, N. and W.K. Davies (1996), *Lifelong Learning: New Visions, New Implications, New Roles for Industry, Government, Education and the Community in the 21st Century*, London, UK: Kogan Page.
Maletín Ciudadano (2010), maletinciudadano.org, accessed 25 July 2010.
Management Competencies Assessment Instrument (2010), www.pro-net2000.org/CM/content_files/71.pdf, accessed 25 July 2010.
Mancl, K., C. Kathleen and M. Morrone (1999), 'Environmental literacy of Ohio adults', *Ohio Journal of Science*, **99** (3), 57–61.
Martínez, América (2006), 'Knowledge citizens: a competence profile', in Javier

Carrillo (ed.), *Knowledge Cities Approaches, Experiences, and Perspectives*, Burlington, US: Elsevier, pp. 233–244.

Martínez, A. and M. Pacheco (2010), 'Desarrollo de un prototipo para promover las competencias ciudadanas', in *Symposium conocimiento e innovación: Las redes para la transformación*, Symposium conducted at the meeting of Comunidad Iberoamericana de Sistemas de Conocimiento, Guayaquil, Ecuador.

Martínez, A. and M. Pacheco (2011), 'Capital humano en las ciudades de conocimiento: Desarrollo de competencias ciudadanas', in *Symposium 41º Congreso de investigación y desarrollo: ciencia para el desarrollo*, Symposium conducted at ITESM, Monterrey, Mexico.

Mauro, Paolo (1997), 'The effects of corruption on growth, investment and government expenditure: a cross-country analysis', in Kimberly A. Elliott (ed.), *Corruption and the Global Economy*, Washington, US: Institute for International Economics, pp. 87–116.

MINEDUC-DIVESUP (2003) 'Identificación de competencias laborales a través del Análisis Funcional', www.chilecalifica.cl/prc/n-0-complab1.pdf, accessed 25 July 2010.

National Education Network (2010), www.nen.gov.uk, accessed 25 July 2010.

Nour, A.M. (2011), 'Challenges and advantages of community participation as an approach for sustainable urban development in Egypt', **4** (1), 79–91.

Palmié, S. (2009), 'Intangible cultural property, semiotic ideology, and the vagaries of ethnoculinary recognition', *African Arts,* **42** (4), 54–61.

Sen, Amartya (2000), '¿Qué impacto puede tener la ética?', participar.org/documentos/Etica_Sen.pdf, accessed 25 July 2010.

Shatz, M. (2004), 'Social tolerance and social civility: key elements for transitioning democratic countries', in Symposium towards democratic pluralism: challenges for social development in the 21st Century, conducted at the meeting of Inter-University Consortium for International Social Development, Mumbai, India.

TEN Competence (2010), www.tencompetence.org/web/guest, accessed 25 July 2010.

Velásquez, F. and E. González (2003), *¿Qué ha pasado con la participación ciudadana en Colombia?,* Bogota, Colombia: Fundación Corona.

WCI (World Capital Institute) (2007), 'The Most Admired Knowledge City (MAKCi) Full Report', World Capital Institute & Teleos, http://www.worldcapitalinstitute.org/makci/history accessed 25 July 2010.

WCI (World Capital Institute) (2010), 'The Most Admired Knowledge City (MAKCi) Full Report', World Capital Institute & Teleos, http://www.worldcapitalinstitute.org/makci/history accessed 1 April 2010.

PART II

Plans for building prosperous knowledge cities

8. Piloting: knowledge-based development policy and practice in building a vibrant ecosystem

Cathy Garner and Anne Dornan

INTRODUCTION

Innovative places are poles of attraction in the knowledge-based economy. Some places have a greater capacity to create or absorb ideas than others. While Thomas Friedman (2005) declared that 'The world is flat' the truth is that despite global connectivity and globalized economies, innovative capability clusters in those places which have an openness to new ideas and the capacity to exploit them.

This clustering is associated with the level of *absorptive capacity* in any innovation ecosystem. Absorptive capacity depends on many factors, including the willingness of the leadership in the system to be open to new ideas, new people and new ways of working. Moreover, the authors argue that the very nature of modern open networked innovation requires a system-based approach and now needs novel interventions by government or public agencies, further emphasizing the need for an open attitude to new thinking. Traditional approaches to innovation interventions have relied on top-down, output driven performance management in which pre-determined outcomes are specified to secure investment. Modern place-based innovation is created 'bottom-up' as an outcome of collective entrepreneurship and thus the conditions for this to thrive need to drive support and intervention mechanisms. This chapter sets out to describe the new requirements for innovation and how pilot interventions can be developed under the right conditions to increase the absorptive capacity of an innovation ecosystem.

BACKGROUND

Knowledge-based economies require new approaches to economic development. While the ability to create new knowledge has served development since the dawn of time, there are a number of significant changes, described by David and Foray (2001) as transformational, that characterize a modern 21st century knowledge economy.

First, the pace at which knowledge is being created, accumulated and at which it also depreciates has increased dramatically – creating the need for new organizations or communities consisting of networks of individuals. These networks produce and circulate new knowledge across organizational boundaries, creating a fertile environment for innovation. Their cross-organizational focus makes them a challenge for conventional supply-side economic development interventions.

Second, the relative importance of intangibles which rely on human capital rather than purely natural resources or physical capital is a feature of advanced knowledge economies and societies. Knowledge workers are mobile workers and the need to attract, retain and release the creativity of this human capital in any place goes beyond its physical environment and building form, although each may be necessary if not sufficient to attract and retain talent.

Third, innovation is increasing in both pace and range of sources as it becomes a currency of productivity and competitive advantage in the connected globalized economy. Whilst propinquity may be important for the first two transformational characteristics, it is increasingly likely that innovation value chains will extend globally and therefore the ease of connectivity to other innovation hubs becomes a critical asset for places.

These transformational factors which now drive economic growth together with the underlying ubiquitous presence of the internet and its digital connectivity are leading to a re-calibration of economic development approaches and a focus on innovation in modern knowledge-based economies. As a recent study by the Washington Economic Development Commission (2009) has pointed out, this implies that efforts need to become more substantially people-focused, providing an attractive and supportive infrastructure to attract and retain agile entrepreneurs and their businesses. Collaborating to compete and building partnerships locally and globally become vital to success. Relationships become important as pre-cursors to transactions.

In many places innovation policy has lagged behind this rapidly changing face of innovation practice and the lack of understanding amongst policy makers can be seen to put a brake on the ability of places to realize their potential to become vibrant innovation hubs in the global knowledge-based economy.

MODERN OPEN NETWORKED INNOVATION

Innovation is a valued objective of knowledge-based economic development and yet too often it is neither clearly defined nor clearly understood as a process which requires not only ideation and creativity but a reduction to practice and absorption into general use. Innovation is not an end in itself but should be a servant of other objectives – such as new products and processes for business growth or societal benefit. There is a tendency to confuse creativity and innovation.

Landry and Bianchini (1995) set out the difference between creativity and innovation thus: 'Creativity is a divergent thought process that generates ideas, and is non-evaluative; whereas innovation is a convergent process concerned with the selection and implementation of ideas' (p. 4). While undoubtedly creativity is a necessary condition for innovation, it is not sufficient in itself. If innovation is what is vital to economic growth and the solving of global social problems, then we also need to factor in the skills of evaluation – including feasibility, cost-effectiveness and adoptability.

Innovation is iterative. It drives and is driven by the market or users, thriving in a continuous feedback loop between innovation and the uses of innovation. Innovation can be defined broadly – as 'a change that creates a new dimension of performance' (Drucker, 1985). It is not merely a new idea – but the practical application of that idea through a new product, a new process, a new organizational operation, a new marketing approach or a new service.

Innovation only exists when the new idea is used and/or applied. It can be radical and disruptive, destroying old ways of doing and working and creating obsolescence; or it can be incremental and additive – building on existing knowledge, products and services. Innovation is not universally beneficial.

Innovation is no longer the preserve of R&D and university laboratories or manufacturing businesses, but can come from the creative industries, the public sector and consumers themselves. While mainstream university research in science and technology remains important for long term inventive capacity, it is also now recognized that innovations which deliver both new market products and processes may also come from business processes, marketing and enabling technologies (ibid.). Studies of the success of iconic areas such as Silicon Valley and other technology 'hotspots' in the USA, have begun to demonstrate that many other factors beyond patenting and licensing have also played their part (Saxenian, 1994). A 'linear, technology transfer or technology push' model from universities to business has been shown to be a narrow interpretation of the actual processes which generate success (Lester, 2005).

Open innovation is driving a new paradigm of cross-sectoral, cross-industry and international collaborative efforts in which relational capital is the glue and in which certain individuals and organizations can play crucial 'bridging' roles. Supported and fuelled by the ubiquitous availability of digital connectivity, innovation has become distributed and diffuse, requiring very different approaches to policy and practical support mechanisms. Not only are innovations being sourced globally but customers may be anywhere across the world. At the same time, customers are demanding a degree of personalization of products and services that are challenging outdated business to business models and supply chains.

Digital connectivity has exploded not only the supply chains for business but also the customer base (Anderson, 2006). It may seem paradoxical that at the same time 'place' has become increasingly important in support of globally distributed innovation activity. However, underpinning these new models are the networks of people and organizations (David and Foray, 2001) which by necessity need to interact and exchange knowledge. As innovation in a knowledge-based economy requires effective communication across organizational boundaries and the ability to exchange and absorb tacit knowledge, then personal contact 'in a place' delivers outcomes which cannot happen at 'distance'.

THE CHALLENGE FOR INNOVATION POLICY

Metcalfe (2007) suggests that the design of innovation policy must no longer be seen in the context of equilibrium economics where a traditional market-failure approach is central to the design of policy interventions. Likewise Hutton and Schneider (2008) propose that to support innovation it needs to be recognized that the totality and subtlety of elements that generate innovation-driven growth are not captured by the narrow assumptions of market theory. Hutton and Schneider (2008) make the case that in advanced knowledge economies which rely on innovation to stimulate productivity, market failure is the norm rather than the exception.

To be appropriate, innovation policy has to recognize that:

- Economies evolve because knowledge evolves and innovations are the vehicles that bring new knowledge into use;
- Changes in knowledge are not external to the economic system but are embedded within it;
- Science and markets are both knowledge transmission systems.

In this context it is argued that an innovation systems approach is now the most appropriate lens for policy design to support increased levels of innovation. However, while an innovation ecology is the basis for a system, it is not a system in itself until subsets of the actors are connected with the intention to promote innovation and the purpose of the connections is to combine multiple sources of knowledge through the flow of information (Metcalfe, 2007).

As part of this understanding, it needs to be recognized that knowledge is essentially a personal attribute. This implies that knowledge exists in a distributed system and it changes in a manner dependent on the connections between the multiple actors. The generation and diffusion of innovation is therefore dependent on the effective working of the system. To intervene therefore relies on the identification of system failures. Common failures that need attention through policy and practical interventions include:

- Knowledgeable actors being missing from the system, such as design agencies, for example;
- Connections being absent which disrupt the flow of knowledge across sectors or for example between universities and firms;
- System boundaries may be drawn in the wrong place and access to vital knowledge, competencies or components of the innovation value chain may be out of reach.

A system-based approach to innovation requires incentives and interventions that are different from those which classical equilibrium economic (market) theorists would propose. If innovation is a key wealth creator, Hutton and Schneider propose that too much emphasis on competition, fast outcomes and commercialization drivers could well undermine innovation. Likewise overly zealous monopoly and protection policies (such as intellectual property rights) can have the same destructive effect. Policymakers need to aim for what they term 'goldilocks' markets that permit both creative destruction and sufficient rent to reward risk-taking (Hulton and Schneides, 2008, p. 28).

If innovation systems rely on person to person exchange of knowledge and reciprocity, then the issue of trust becomes important. Recent research is beginning to discover the importance of a collaborative and trust-based approach to the effective operation of markets and indeed the development of successful innovation ecosystems.[1]

Reciprocity and trust-based networks underpin the development of vibrant innovation ecosystems. Elinor Ostrom's[2] work challenges the basis of the Tragedy of the Commons – a construction of neoclassical economics that proposes that naked self-interest will destroy the public good through over-use. Ostrom (2009) has proposed that markets can organize production and consumption efficiently, but only when supported and nurtured by networks and communities. Through her work Ostrom proposed a new architecture of governance – what she called 'polycentric governance'. This mirrors the conditions needed for a thriving innovation ecosystem – horizontal sharing of leadership outside the organization and distributed leadership – where multiple actors work in their own individualistic way towards a common goal. This reflects the approach put forward by Benneworth (2007) in his examination of leadership for innovation.

Whilst an innovation systems approach is beginning to gain credence with policymakers, its implementation has been primarily at a national level. However, there is nothing inherently national in these characteristics. Indeed if anything, it is more likely that an innovation systems approach will work most effectively at an identifiable community level where communities of interest and shared values and objectives can be readily identifiable.

Contributors to a study of national innovation systems (Lundvall, 1992) proposed that innovation happens when 'interactive learning' between users and producers occurs. Geographic and cultural proximity was seen to encourage interactive learning and therefore innovation. Whilst an innovation systems approach is beginning to gain credence with policymakers, Andersen and Rossi (2010) argue that policy formulation for this approach is not yet mature. An innovation systems approach to innovation (NESTA, 2006, 2007) is a far cry from the well-tried policy interventions such as technology and science parks, incubators supporting university–industry technology transfer or raising local venture funds. An ecology approach is however challenging for policy makers. Stimulating the vibrancy of an ecology requires not only an understanding of the innovation assets in a place but also the form of interventions across diverse policy areas including education and skills, business support and changes in the culture of attitude to risk.

Innovation in a knowledge-based economy is an emergent process based on the gradual introduction of interactions that link previously unconnected agents, knowledge and goods in order to produce a relationship of interdependence. Networks are a powerful tool to make such connections. In such developed economies, the approach to stimulating innovation should be seen as a sequence of events in which new ideas are developed and implemented by people who engage in relationships with others and make the adjustments needed to achieve desired outcomes within an institutional and organizational context.

Reflecting on the characteristics distilled from innovation systems theory, it becomes clear that a number of key attributes of the system should be encouraged, including connecting the necessary ingredients for a local ecology. In piloting such an approach it is necessary to recognize that although public agencies and/or governmental initiatives can facilitate such an approach, it is unlikely that these will succeed 'on demand'.

Three key areas identified are described here:

- Leadership that can operate beyond the boundaries of the leader's organization – working in a horizontal and dispersed fashion and a style which is permissive of emerging innovation;
- Connecting institutions and people, to enable:
  - Person to person knowledge exchange;
  - The building of a community of innovators which leverages reciprocity, trust and mutual self-interest;
- A process for interactive learning by the community (learning by doing).

A CITY TEST-BED: MANCHESTER, UK

Manchester is and always has been an innovative place, a place where people have new ideas that are taken up and, in some cases, have changed the world. Manchester is the perfect place for an innovation ambition on the city-region scale.

Many of the building blocks (the ingredients that form the ecology) are already in place – international connectivity, good and fast-improving digital infrastructure, world class universities, great civic leadership and ambition, a vibrant third sector, and a bed-rock of great homegrown businesses coupled with national and international names attracted by talented people and the quality of the transformed regional centre. These are the necessary but not sufficient conditions for innovation to thrive.

The rationale for a focus on innovation in Manchester

Innovation is identified as one of five key drivers of productivity, alongside investment, skills, enterprise and competition. The contribution made by innovation to economic growth is significant: improvements in productivity resulting from innovation, technological catch-up and restructuring have been estimated to account for between a third and a half of the average business sector's Gross Domestic Product (GDP) growth over the past two decades (Scarpetta et al. 2000). NESTA (2009) showed that half of the growth in the UK economy between 2002 and 2008 could be attributed to 6 per cent of the companies – those that were the most innovative. This 'vital 6 per cent' (NESTA, 2009) showed twice the growth in jobs as non-innovating companies and demonstrated almost two times the level of sales growth.

The Manchester Independent Economic Review (MIER, 2009) stated that, 'Innovation is absolutely central to economic growth and prosperity in the long term. Cities and regions with a higher proportion of innovative businesses and individuals are those which prosper and whose inhabitants thrive' (p. 4).

Manchester therefore adopted innovation into its knowledge-based economic development strategy.

Testing the Innovation Systems Approach

During 2007, the city, led by the Manchester: Knowledge Capital partnership geared up to create a programme which aimed to:

- Achieve a step-change in the capacity for innovation in Manchester;
- Strengthen the innovation system across the city-region;
- Create a unique demonstration programme which could act as an exemplar for other UK and global players – a test-bed for interactive learning.

NESTA, the Northwest Regional Development Agency, Manchester City Council, Manchester: Knowledge Capital and the Commission for the New Economy worked together to pump-prime innovation activity across Manchester via the Manchester Innovation Investment Fund.

From 2006 NESTA was driving forward the thinking on understanding the nature and role of innovation and producing leading-edge research. Manchester had an ambition to undertake both a major research-based review and to seed entrepreneurial innovation. Based on the Manchester Science City Prospectus in 2005, the experience of stimulating the innovation ecosystem and supporting Innovation Partnerships with the private sector had been a major challenge due to lack of any dedicated funding.[3] This combination of factors and alignment of ambition and objectives led to the agreement to create the Manchester Innovation Investment Fund to support the test-bed.

The experience in Manchester reflects the general findings of studies across the European Union (Reid, 2009) that set out the policy challenges in introducing an ecosystem approach. Reid characterizes the position of such innovation policy as 'a misunderstood concept in terms of policy design and delivery, squeezed between a powerful "research lobby" and more classic economic or industrial development policies'. This uneasy positioning means that resistance to the novelty of the approach needs to be overcome and accepted by those more comfortable in a traditional paradigm of the linear R&D model or sectoral based interventions if the approach is to succeed.

Arnold (2004) depicts four systemic failures which need to be addressed:

- Capability failures (firm deficits, such as the lack of absorptive capacity);
- Institutional failures (barriers in universities, performance gaps in other agencies);
- Network failures (problems in the linkages between innovation actors or path dependency barriers from industrial structures; too rigid competition or monopolies);
- Framework failures (restrictive practices and background conditions such as the lack of consumer demand or negative attitudes to risk).

To tackle each of these in a system wide approach is not only daunting but potentially prohibitive in terms of public investment and lead-in time. A pragmatic approach to the most significant barriers to enable step-wise progress and improvement was seen to be the only practical approach. Through interactive workshops and team-based approaches the major weaknesses in the Manchester innovation ecosystem were identified and addressed, although given the nature of the UK policy environment and the use of public investment, some restrictions were inevitably met. Primarily the Manchester Innovation Investment Fund addressed institutional and network failures, as capability and framework failures were the focus of other initiatives and the legitimacy lay with other agencies.

Taking the understanding from the theoretical underpinning and combining this with practical local knowledge five themes were established early in the programme:

- To increase the understanding of innovation amongst policy makers and leaders;
- To inspire stakeholders to engage with the innovation agenda;
- To embed innovation in ongoing initiatives;
- To accelerate ideas through to investment and
- To build a community of innovators.

Van de Ven et al. (2008) drew on 17 years of research to describe the temporal characteristics of an Innovation Journey, showing how and why innovations emerge, develop, grow or terminate. Their insights shone a light on the need to appreciate the sequencing of events over time. From their research a road map of how an innovation journey unfolds was described. Manchester's journey was purposeful and based on substantial knowledge of what works. It was nonetheless 'innovating innovation'. The partners did not have a recipe book, a roadmap or any experienced guide who had taken an identical challenge with a city-region of 2.8M people. The focus was unashamedly seeking to address the perceived network failures whilst encouraging others to address identified specific barriers in other system characteristics. This, the partners believed, could achieve the greatest impact with relatively limited resources. Details of the most critical aspects of the Manchester journey are described below. Each was critical to the development of a more vibrant innovation ecosystem. These aspects were leadership, network development, and interactive learning.

Leading the journey

The leaders in this partnership were critical to charting Manchester's course and remain vital to the city's final destination. During the timing of the Manchester Innovation Investment Fund, the leaders had the courage, the foresight and the tenacity to step in when needed, to step back when appropriate, and to encourage, guide and sometimes chide when necessary. They invested their time, their funds, their power and their personal brands – to secure the best possible outcomes. Without that leadership, the journey would have been impossible. NESTA's own research on *Leading Innovation (*Benneworth, 2007) describes the journey in the transformation of an 'ordinary' region into one driven by innovation as being led by a coalition of actors. While this approach appears a simple process, Benneworth notes that the transition from one stage to another is often not straightforward and that a key aspect lies in having the right leadership for the right phase/stage of the journey. The aspiration of an innovation-driven region is to achieve the status of a 'jamming supergroup'. Such a region would be one that can hold the big names together effectively and coalesce into a community with multiple and competing visions for innovation policy, alongside great depth in innovation capacity – a place like Silicon Valley.

The challenge remains to ensure that the energy from the process does not dissipate as was observed through the MIRP studies (Van de Ven et al., 2008); there is also a risk that innovation stops completely when some aspects are implemented or when resources run out.

Manchester and its partners need to be mindful of this danger, especially at the current time when severe resource constraints are being imposed. The establishment of the Manchester Innovation Group, which crosses city-region boundaries and which straddles the convergent and divergent cycles of innovation, has already adapted the approach to embed innovation in the formal governance structures of the city-region. Creating a change in culture and enabling collective entrepreneurship to flourish through support to a limited number of interventions for only a short period cannot be the ideal scenario for cities which seek to command long-term success and recognition in the globally competitive economy.

Leadership is vital. Studies elsewhere have shown that a city's social networks can have a huge impact on the likely fortunes of that city. Leadbeater (2009) sets out a dramatic comparison of the fortunes of two industrial towns in the Rust Belt of the USA. Two quite comparable 'steel towns', Youngstown in Ohio and Allentown in Pennsylvania both faced serious decline due to global competition. Allentown has used its social capital and the outward looking approach of its business networks to release a surge of entrepreneurialism which has connected to opportunities and delivered a thriving revival. Youngstown, on the other hand, drew in on itself, rewarded a cadre of insiders, and rejected thinking and new ideas from outside, where upon its sectarian problems only became more acute. This is truly a tale of two cities – and one which not only demonstrates the role of leadership in enabling innovation to thrive but also the power of business and entrepreneurial networks.

Building a community of innovators: the Innovation Manchester Network

With the examples of Allentown and Youngstown firmly in mind, the Innovation Manchester initiative was developed to initiate and support networks among diverse actors in the innovation system and enable them to develop and deliver disruptive new solutions to the innovation challenges they themselves regarded as most serious and urgent. The network has ensured that businesses and higher education institutions were not only advisors on strategy, but an integral part of the solution.

The Innovation Manchester network was supported to grow through the careful use of social media. The social media strategy was something that was developed and adopted in real time. The web's free tools were used to raise awareness of Innovation Manchester and have now been expanded to a range of engagement approaches which have developed conversations with and between members of the community via the Innovation Manchester LinkedIn group.

The LinkedIn group is used as a mechanism for finding new 'unusual suspects' to bring into the Innovation Manchester core network and to support the development of the latest Innovation Manchester programme

(Innovation Boardroom). A first 'mini-boardroom' has sprung up spontaneously from the group discussions. The use of social media tools has enabled the original network to expand and yet to keep linked to the original participants, and a social network analysis has helped to demonstrate the changes in the composition of the network and its internal connections and deficits.

Innovation pilot projects and demonstrators: interactive learning

Innovation systems are not an end in themselves but are a means to economic development and social improvement; therefore, rather importantly, Manchester has used the network and the work of the Manchester Innovation Investment Fund to drive forward its economic progress, through innovative programmes which have furnished solutions to local problems or challenges.

In total, the innovation Manchester programme has supported the development of over 25 interventions, each of which has been separately evaluated and tested. Further work is proceeding to record and encapsulate the findings and lessons from these projects and a selection of them have been recorded in a NESTA publication – 'Driving Innovation in Cities: Learning from Greater Manchester' (NESTA, 2010). A snapshot of just three is given here.

Manchester Masters

The Manchester Masters, developed and managed by the public relations company Tangerine, was designed to inspire businesses to turn a negative trend around. This highly selective programme gives top graduates exposure to a broad range of marketing career opportunities in Greater Manchester. Successful candidates receive paid placements in local creative marketing and media companies over the span of an academic year, giving them the kind of broad work experience that they would normally only find in the graduate trainee programmes of a major corporation and making them aware of the quality jobs available on their doorstep.

This programme was designed to address the specific problem that Manchester was routinely losing its most talented creative students to London, whilst the creative companies in Manchester were unable to compete with the internships of their larger rivals – by working together the small companies demonstrated the maxim of 'collaborate to compete'.

Manchester: Integrating Medicine and Innovative Technology

While the Manchester Masters programme might be characterized as demand-led innovation. Manchester: Integrating Medicine and Innovative Technology (MIMIT) drives demand for innovation by building lasting relationships between clinicians, scientists, engineers and industry that can help identify emergent technology and pull it to market to address urgent, unmet clinical needs. A collaboration between the University of Manchester and Greater Manchester NHS and Primary Care Trusts, and in partnership with the world-leading Centre for Integration of Medicine and Innovative Technology at the Massachusetts Institute of Technology, this aims to capitalize on existing, underexploited strengths in medical technology in the Manchester City Region and to significantly increase the output of commercialized medical technology innovations from Manchester City Region.

MIMIT supports a large team of 'site miners' – specialist clinicians and research scientists – to identify unmet clinical needs and promising technologies, and to build productive relationships between them. Short-term impacts are already impressive.

The programme was in effect a franchise from a successful programme in the USA – Manchester being the first place in Europe to test and adapt the model for a different system. The programme was an excellent demonstration of the openness of Manchester to good ideas wherever they are to be found, and the absorptive capacity of the innovation system in the city.

Manchester Fablab

A third approach was to focus on helping innovators benefit from knowledge shared by others while encouraging them to share their own knowledge in return, increasing the value of the innovation commons for all. In Manchester, this approach was exemplified by Fablabs. Fablabs are Fabrication Laboratories: community workshops that provide the space, tools, materials and skilled staff for anyone to make pretty much anything. They offer a space, tools and advice to help individuals to unlock their capacity to create and invent.

At first glance, Fablabs look like a traditional physical infrastructure investment. But their novelty comes in the way they change the incentives for innovators to share their intellectual property with others. Businesses and inventors can pay to use the facilities to make proprietary prototypes, but they are open to anyone who wants to tap into their powers of invention for free if they share the fruits of their labours with the public. Manchester's Fablab opened in March 2010, joining a network of more than 30 Fablabs around the world, from Boston to Afghanistan.

This programme was a shining exemplar of what Ostrom has written about in innovation systems – the complete antithesis of the Tragedy of the Commons.

These three examples demonstrated that through a 'learning by doing' approach, the Innovation Manchester programme was able to extend its reach to a far wider community of innovators. The project leaders themselves became intermediaries in the system and demonstrated the 'power law' of networks. The Innovation Manchester programme has gained considerable momentum especially through its engaged intermediaries, and it is hoped that the effect on the innovation system will be self-sustaining.

CONCLUSION

Many of the lessons from the case studies set out here are not about the 'what' of the process but about the 'how'. Engaging mutual self-interest and creating a vibrant community of innovators and a networked cadre of leaders outside of those tasked with metropolitan governance is not susceptible to a command and control type mechanism or a top-down planned intervention – it is about empowering people to innovate; unleashing the power of networks; connecting the flows of knowledge to purposeful outcomes and moving away from an approach which gathers ingredients of the system. It is about entrepreneurial interactive learning.

In the 'science' of knowledge-based economic development the ingredients are now well documented. However, ingredients can be combined into many recipes and those who are engaged in the process bring their own individual approach to that combination. It is important to have the underlying ingredients but also to know the authentic competencies in a place, and to understand the assets and opportunities and challenges which exist in the marketplace. What is clear is that the recipe for Manchester in the UK or for Allentown, Pennsylvania will be different and will require a tailored approach to local circumstances. Cloned economic development strategies fail in the knowledge-based economy – in which, by definition, it is the unique combination of creativity and innovation that powers success.

An innovation ecosystem approach meets the needs of the 21st century knowledge-based economy – but poses challenges for policy makers and practitioners as traditional investment and interventions do not release the collective entrepreneurship which characterizes places that succeed. By drawing on theory, determining the critical areas of system failure, and constructing a programme to address the most important failures, places can support the development of a more vibrant ecosystem. Manchester and its partners instigated a bold series of interventions which have had impacts far beyond the project investments and have given a model on which others can draw. The ultimate success of this approach will be judged by whether the networks are self-sustaining and over time demonstrate increased collective entrepreneurship. The co-incidence of the global recession and its associated financial shocks will provide a major test for the resilience of the initiative.

NOTES

1. It has long been recognized that the venture capitalists of Silicon Valley prefer to invest locally – where they can get to know the individuals of the management team and build a trust-based approach to innovation. Culture and organizational landscapes are critical to the shaping of the innovation system. Saxenian (1994), documents this well in her comparison of the fortunes of Silicon Valley in comparison to Boston Route 128.
2. Elinor Ostrom was awarded the Nobel Prize for Economics in 2009.
3. No additional funding was accorded to the Manchester city-region under the Science City initiative.

REFERENCES

Andersen, B. and F. Rossi (2010), 'The flow of knowledge from the research base into use', SABIP working paper, www.ipo.gov.uk .
Anderson, C. (2006), *The Long Tail*, London: Random House.
Arnold, E. (2004), 'Evaluating research and innovation policy: a systems world needs systems evaluations', *Research Evaluation*, **13** (1), pp. 3–17.
Benneworth, P. (2007), *Leading Innovation*, London: NESTA.
David, P.A. and D. Foray (2001), 'An introduction to the economy of the knowledge society', Department of Economics, Discussion Paper Series, 84, Oxford: University of Oxford.
Drucker, P.F. (1985), *Innovation and Entrepreneurship*, UK: Butterworth.
Friedman, T.L. (2005), *The World is Flat: A Brief History of the Twenty-First Century,* New York: Farrar, Strauss and Giroux.
Hutton, W. and P. Schneider (2008), *The Failure of Market Failure*, Provocation, **8**, London: NESTA.
Landry, C. and F. Bianchini (1995), *The Creative City*, London: DEMOS.
Leadbeater, C. (2009), *Original Modern: Manchester's Journey to Innovation and Growth*, London: NESTA.
Lester, R. (2005), 'Universities, innovation and the competitiveness of local economies', Working Paper 05-010, Boston: MIT.
Lundvall, B.A. (1992), *National Systems of Innovation: Towards a Theory of Innovation and Interactive Learning*, London: Pinter.
Manchester Independent Economic Review (MIER) (2009), *Innovation, Trade and Connectivity Report,* www.manchester-review.org.uk, p. 4.
Metcalfe, S. (2007), 'Innovation systems, innovation policy and restless capitalism', in F. Malerba and S. Brusoni (eds), *Perspectives on Innovation*, UK: Cambridge University Press, pp. 441–454.
NESTA (2006), *The Innovation Gap*, London: NESTA.
NESTA (2007), *Innovation in UK Cities*, London: NESTA.
NESTA (2009), *The Vital 6 per cent*, London: NESTA.

NESTA (2010), *Driving Innovation in Cities: Learning from Greater Manchester*, London: NESTA.
Ostrom, E. (2009), 'Notes on complexity, communication and trust', Nobel Prize Lecture, Stockholm, 8th December.
Reid, A. (2009), 'Systems failures and innovation policy: do national policies reflect differentiated challenges in the EU27?', Paper presented to the 6 Countries Programme workshop on New Economic Ground for Innovation Policy, Bilbao, 14 September.
Saxenian, A. (1994), *Regional Advantage*, USA: Harvard University Press.
Scarpetta, S., A. Bassanini, D. Pilat and P. Schreyer (2000), 'Economic growth in the OECD area: recent trends at the aggregate and sectoral level', Economics Department Working Paper, 248, Paris: OECD.
Van de Ven, A.H., D.E. Polley, R. Garud and S.Venkataraman (2008), *The Innovation Journey,* Oxford: Oxford University Press.
Washington Economic Development Commission (2009), www.wedc.wa.gov.

9. Formulating: an integrated strategy for the development of knowledge cities

Kostas Metaxiotis and Kostas Ergazakis

INTRODUCTION

The Knowledge City concept has been substantially developed during the last years, thanks to the research work accomplished by many researchers and practitioners in the field of knowledge-based development (KBD). This research offers invaluable insights, views, concept definitions, frameworks, methodologies for developing Knowledge Cities (KC), capital systems, taxonomies, assessment techniques and so on, all related to the theme of KC. On the other side, many cities around the world are developing as KC and their approaches also constitute valuable sources of information and knowledge in relation to the theme of KC. Though still a rather young field of research, the KC concept has been well developed. However, as this mainly regards our theoretical understanding, the concept still needs development in terms of practicability (Henn et al., 2009).

Many international economic organizations such as the Organisation for Economic Co-operation and Development (OECD), World Bank (WB), European Commission (EC) and Asia-Pacific Co-operation (APEC) have provided some practical directions to build the knowledge economy in developed and developing countries (World Bank, 1999; OECD, 2001; APEC, 2000; European Commission, 2000). However, no viable framework to develop integrated KC development strategies exists (Dang and Umemoto, 2009).

The concept of KC is particularly broad and refers to many aspects of everyday life in a city. In this respect, the term 'integrated KC strategy', refers to a strategy that: is knowledge-based; takes into account the wide nature and the variety of issues related to the KC concept; and tries to incorporate these issues into the strategic interventions that are selected as well as to the particular actions and projects implemented so as to realize this strategy.

In addition, despite the fact that many cities globally are now considered as successful KC, only very few of them, such as Barcelona, Melbourne and Montréal, have managed to formulate integrated strategic approaches. The initiatives and approaches of the rest of the KC are rather ad hoc and not based on structured and specific methodologies. Despite the tremendous transformation potential of KC, local authorities in the EU and worldwide seem to be unable to formulated integrated KC development strategies (i.e. comprehensive local authority lead plans that outline the goals, stakeholders, process, budget, and monitoring mechanisms so as to make a city's knowledge future a reality) to tackle the knowledge divide, minimize social exclusion and improve the knowledge intensity in their regions. This is the major finding deriving from the review of approaches followed by cities so as to develop their KC development strategies, presented in this chapter.

However, creating values for citizens and businesses and providing modern knowledge-based services to modern citizens in the knowledge world, should be the major goals of sound KC development strategies and not goals of ad hoc and uncoordinated local authorities' initiatives and efforts.

In this chapter, the authors, after identifying the problem and recognizing the importance of integrated KC development strategies for the benefit of citizens, propose and describe an innovative and applicable methodology. This methodology further enhances an existing methodology for the formulation of KC development strategies (KnowCis) so as to strengthen local authorities' capacity to formulate citizen-centered knowledge cities strategies.

The chapter is structured as follows: the next section presents the need for formulation of integrated KC development strategies, by reviewing and comparing approaches of existing KC regarding the formulation of their strategies. In the third section, the proposed methodology is presented. The fourth section provides information about the successful pilot application of this methodology in a Greek municipality. Finally, the fifth section discusses limitations of the current approach as well as the main future research challenges.

THE NEED FOR FORMULATION OF KC DEVELOPMENT STRATEGIES

From the review of existing KC cases, it can be concluded that each city's approach for the formulation of KC development strategies is different. This is also the conclusion of another comparison study of KC (Martínez, 2006).

Only in a few cases (such as in Barcelona, Melbourne and Montréal) have integrated KC development strategies been formulated, taking into consideration at a satisfactory degree the complex and multi-dimensional true nature of the KC concept and using specific methodologies. In addition, in these cases, specific decision support tools and assessment models have also been adopted (for example, use of indicators). In the majority of other cases, the KC strategy cannot be considered as integrated. These cities were only based on ad hoc solutions and methods in order to define and formulate their strategies, without using structured and integrated methodologies. Such ad hoc solutions were:

- Consultations with local authorities' executives
- Deliberation with stakeholders
- Services provided by consulting companies
- Co-operation with important organizations within the city premises
- Use of international best practices.

Of course, these methods offer their own advantages, but they should be used in the framework of a specific and well-defined methodology and in combination with scientific methods and decision support tools, so as to offer their full potential.

Table 9.1 presents a synthesis of cities' approaches regarding the formulation of their KC development strategies. The second column refers to the methods used by the city so as to formulate its KC strategy, while in the third column there are some important comments.

More details on the above-mentioned cities' approaches are presented by Ergazakis et al., 2006a, 2009 and 2010. It should be noted at this point that, in general, the following factors (depicted in Figure 9.1) are important and affect the process of formulating development strategies for any city.

Moreover, as proposed by many researchers in the literature (Carrillo, 2006; Ergazakis et al., 2004, 2007; Palacios and Galvan, 2006), a successful KC should take into consideration many different aspects of social, economic and cultural life in the city, in order to achieve desired strategic objectives in the context of the knowledge economy. Consequently, the procedure is multi-parameter and particularly complex.

The benefits in economic growth, productivity, competitiveness, social inclusion, and sustainable development that the power of the KC concept could create, are nowadays increasingly demanding high policy initiatives to increase the adoption of KBD approaches and tackle the knowledge divide. In 2010, creating values for citizens and businesses as well as providing modern services to modern citizens in the knowledge world, should be major goals of sound and integrated KC development strategies, and not goals of ad hoc and uncoordinated local authorities' initiatives and efforts.

Table 9.1 City approaches for the formulation of KC development strategies

City	Methods for strategy formulation	Comments
1. Barcelona	Indicators, consultations, Barcelona Observatory mechanism, deliberations	• Barcelona's approach can be considered among the most integrated. During the process of formulating its KC strategy, a series of indicators have been constructed and their definition and comparison with indicators of other cities have facilitated the decision making process • Many decisions were the result of consultations with a great volume of citizens and other important actors and stakeholders • The Barcelona Observatory is a mechanism of continuous monitoring and benchmarking of city's position as a KC, in comparison with other cities (30 European cities and 60 cities from around the world) • Barcelona Observatory provides up-to-date information on key aspects of the city, so as to be used for decision-making. A series of indicators in various sectors (Knowledge Society, Business, Tourism and Culture, Quality of Life, Labour Market and Training) are recorded and updated
2. Stockholm	Consultations	• The decision making process for strategy formulation is mainly based on consultations and discussions with the business community, universities and various organizations • Stockholm is focused on the development of sectors with knowledge intensity such as biotechnology, where the city is among the leading regions in Europe
3. Montréal	Indicators, consulting services, inter-active tools, consultations, deliberations	• The Scientific Committee for the Knowledge City was the responsible actor for providing consulting services to the city's local administration for the formulation of the KC strategy, in 2003 (Montréal Knowledge City Advisory Committee, 2003)

Table 9.1 (continued)

City	Methods for strategy formulation	Comments
		• In 2005, after the announcement of the Programme 'Imaginer➤Réaliser Montréal 2025', the city has established a Group of Strategic Interventions and Tactics (GIST 2025) • This extensive programme (Montréal, 2010) is much more than a simple vision for the future. The main characteristic of this plan lies in the collective commitment of partner organizations, to use the KC concept as a foundation on which to build Montréal • Some of the means used for the strategy formulation are indicators, advanced interactive tools such as a 3D maquette, which allows executives to plan more effectively and in an integrated way, to measure more efficiently the results of the projects as well as enabling citizens to participate in the planning process
4. Munich	Political priorities	• Munich's approach regarding its development as a KC is not based on a comprehensive and integrated strategy, but only on some indicative political priorities and related initiatives (Streit, 2005; Munich, 2005) • City targets have not been described with clarity in a specific strategic plan and there is not an actor or stakeholder to undertake the promotion of the KC concept
5. Dublin	Consulting services, international best practices	• The decision for the KC strategy have been initially based on a series of consultations among local administration, local organizations for development and the Irish government • Recently the city's trade chamber has undertaken to provide consulting services in relation to the KC strategy

Table 9.1 (continued)

City	Methods for strategy formulation	Comments
		• A specific ten-point plan has been issued (Dublin Chamber of Commerce, 2008), outlining some practical recommendations in various target areas, based on international experience and best practices, for the establishment of Dublin as a KC region. However, there is no integrated strategic planning
6. Delft	Co-operation among various organizations	• There are various enterprises and institutions involved in the process of developing the city as a KC and defining the respective strategic priorities • These actors are: TU Delft (University of Technology), two HBO (Higher Vocational Education) establishments, the TNO (Netherlands Organization for Applied Scientific Research), Delft Municipality, Chamber of Commerce in Haaglanden, three Delft enterprise networks and VNO-NCWWest (The Confederation of Netherlands Industry and Employers) • There is a specific institution, called Delft Knowledge City (Delft, 2010) which focuses on bringing the projects and products that the city delivers, into the spotlight
7. Eindhoven	Consultations, deliberations	• The decisions regarding the strategic priorities for the KC development, have been the result of co-operation and consultations among the local administration, the private sector, social stakeholders and public organizations
8. Melbourne	Indicators, consultation	• The city of Melbourne is distinguished for its integrated strategic planning in relation to its development objectives (City of Melbourne, 2005; Yigitcanlar et al., 2008) • There is a specific Office of Knowledge Capital (OKC, 2010) which sets the specific priorities in co-operation with local

Table 9.1 (continued)

City	Methods for strategy formulation	Comments
		authorities. It designs projects and initiatives for the development of the city as KC, using well-defined indicators as the main method • The main strategic objectives are to develop and promote Melbourne locally, nationally and globally to achieve recognition as 'Australia's Knowledge Capital' and a 'Global University City', to facilitate collaboration across and between the university sector with governments, industries and communities and to form links with similar 'knowledge cities' to enable mutually beneficial interactions
9. Bilbao	Consultations, deliberations	• The strategy for the KC is mainly formulated through consultations and deliberations among important local authorities, important public organizations, companies, universities, etc. • The main result is the definition of a specific set of strategic priorities
10. Manchester	Consultations, deliberations	• 'Manchester: Knowledge Capital' is a strategic partnership driving innovation and economic transformation across the Manchester city-region • Through a partnership of all ten Greater Manchester authorities, four universities, the strategic health authority, other key public agencies and leading businesses, 'Manchester Knowledge Capital' is working to secure substantial and sustainable development of the city as a KC • 'Manchester: Knowledge Capital' has a small executive team, taking the lead on implementing the various programmes of activity

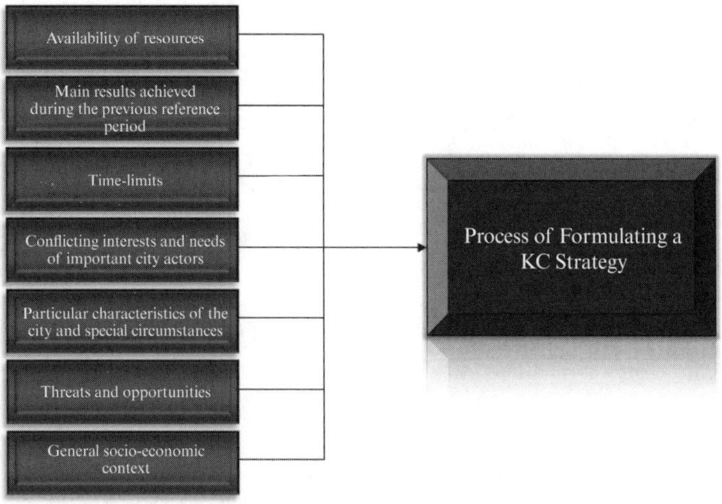

Figure 9.1 Factors affecting formulation of KC strategy

Although many cities have been developing as KC, only very few of them have managed to formulate integrated KC development strategies. A KC strategy relates to an ecosystem where citizens and communities, local and central government, and small and large enterprises (the three agents) take advantage of the city's infrastructures, skills and content (the three enablers) to enhance knowledge intensity in the region and, thus, increase social and economic welfare.

It is a comprehensive local administration lead plan that outlines the goals, stakeholders, process, interventions, projects, budget and monitoring mechanisms to make a region's knowledge future a reality. An integrated KC strategy is necessary to identify the knowledge ecosystem and infrastructure market failures that are limiting KBD, in order to identify enablers' accelerators that can quickly move the region exponentially to the knowledge future. So, how to build an integrated KC strategy? This is the crucial question. It is understood that the formulation of a successful strategy should be done in a very systematic way.

THE KNOWCIS 2.0 METHODOLOGY

The KnowCis (Knowledge Cities) methodology was developed in 2005–2007, and is the outcome of a multi-annual research on the fields of Knowledge Management (KM), Knowledge-Based Development (KBD) and KCs. This methodology has as its main purpose to assist and support local authorities in the process of developing their cities as KC. The first priority of the methodology is the setting up of a committee (Knowledge City Committee – KCC) which is co-responsible, along with the city's local government, for the consultation and co-ordination of the whole effort, from its very beginning. KnowCis consists of five main phases and takes into account nine different dimensions:

- *Phase 1*: *Diagnosis*. Before any attempt to outline a strategy, the KCC proceeds to a thorough diagnosis of the current city's status as a KC, based on studies, opinion polls and qualitative evaluations.
- *Phase 2*: *Formulation of strategy*. The diagnosis of the previous phase is important for the formulation of strategy that will be adopted. This strategy considers nine dimensions comprising sets of strategic interventions (goals). The specific characteristics, particularities, strengths and weaknesses of the city determine which interventions are needed as well as the priority of each one.
- *Phase 3: Creation of detailed action plan*. This phase is devoted to the creation of a detailed action plan for realizing the defined strategy. The action plan comprises specific projects to be implemented as well as interventions to specific processes that need improvement. Obviously, the appropriate financing must have been assured.
- *Phase 4: Implementation*. The KCC, the agencies and stakeholders participating in it, the local government, and other public or private organizations are implementing the defined actions. In this way, each stakeholder remains committed and contributes to the effort.
- *Phase 5: Measurement/Evaluation*. It is indispensable to measure the progress of the whole effort and evaluate the performance of the city as a KC, based on indicators and the consultation of evaluation experts.

Horizontal aspects are also considered, i.e. the open and equal participation of all citizens and stakeholders, the political and societal leadership/commitment and the KM procedures related to the effort. Phase 2 of the methodology (formulation of KC strategy) is critical for the success of the whole effort. It incorporates nine different dimensions and twenty five strategic interventions (goals), which are related to many of the aspects of social, economic and cultural life in a city.

In this way, phase 2 is supported by a decision support model which provides the following features:

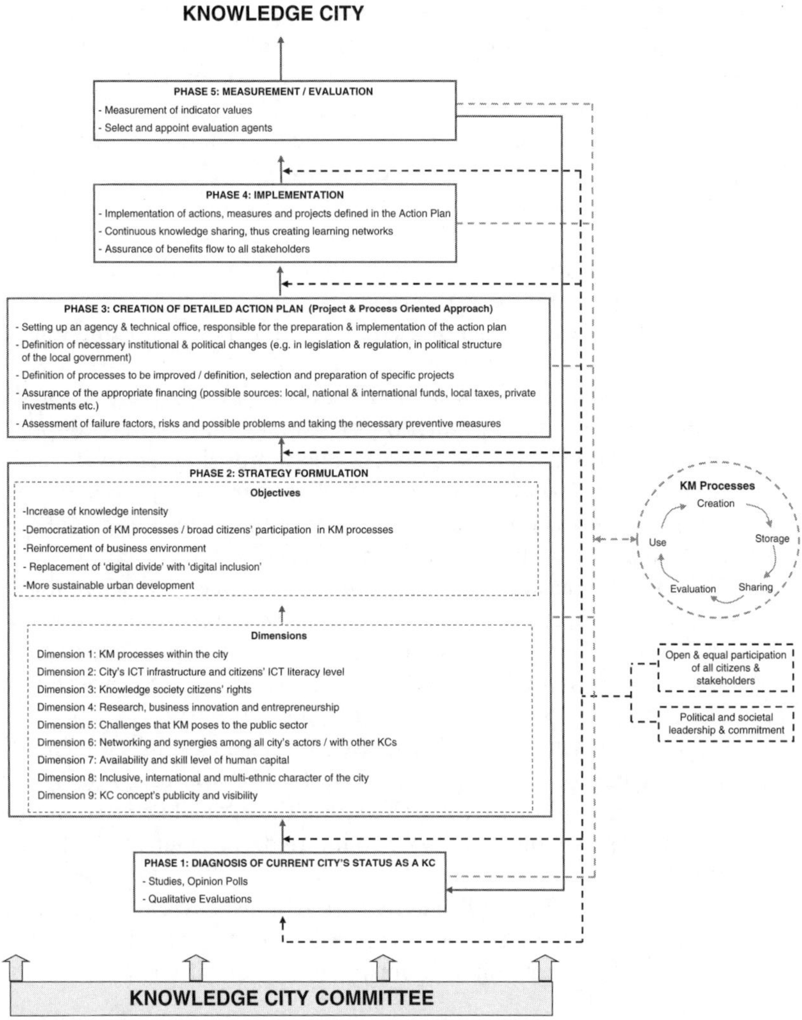

Source: Adapted from Ergazakis et al., 2007.

Figure 9.2 The KnowCis methodology

- Identification of appropriate strategic interventions (goals)
- Modeling of the city's current status as a KC via the development of related indicators
- Assessment of strategic interventions' necessity based on the indicators' values and through the benchmarking of other successful KCs cases

- Selection of the most appropriate form for each proposed intervention, based on its efficiency during the last reference period
- Prioritization of the proposed interventions (goals), based on a multi-criteria approach.

For further details on KnowCis methodology see Ergazakis et al., 2006b, 2007.

The proposed KnowCis 2.0 methodology includes the KnowCis plus some new features, specifically concerning Phase 3: Creation of Detailed Action Plan. These new features help local authorities to design integrated citizen-centric groups of actions. These groups of actions are called 'strings of actions'. Each string of actions comprises more than one action and has a common goal which refers to the real, daily life of citizens and enterprises.

As mentioned above, the main outcome of the KnowCis was the selection and prioritization of interventions (goals), according to the city's specific characteristics and needs. The new features added in KnowCis 2.0 concern phase 3, and aim to further assist local authorities to design specific strings of citizen-centric actions, so as to realize these strategic interventions (goals).

The main steps for the application of these new features included in KnowCis 2.0, are the following (also depicted in Figure 9.3):

1. A two-dimension table/matrix is designed
2. The rows of the table constitute the KC Dimension, in which all strategic interventions and goals of the KC are recorded, as these derive and result from the application of the KnowCis methodology.
3. The columns of the table constitute the Human Dimension of the strategy, and record all main issues related to real, daily life of citizens and enterprises.
4. A string of interconnected actions is developed for each of these main issues related to real, daily life of citizens and enterprises. Each string comprises groups of actions with a common goal, and is designed by cutting down the goals and directions of the strategy (i.e. rows of the table). The actions do not necessarily depend on each other temporally or financially, but all of them contribute to the same goal.
5. The effectiveness of each string is monitored by the local authority or the Knowledge City Committee, on the basis of specific metrics.

In Figure 9.3, Dimension N refers to any of the identified nine dimensions of the KnowCis methodology. A box (in column) indicates that a group of actions is designed, serving the goal in the specific row. In a column, all the

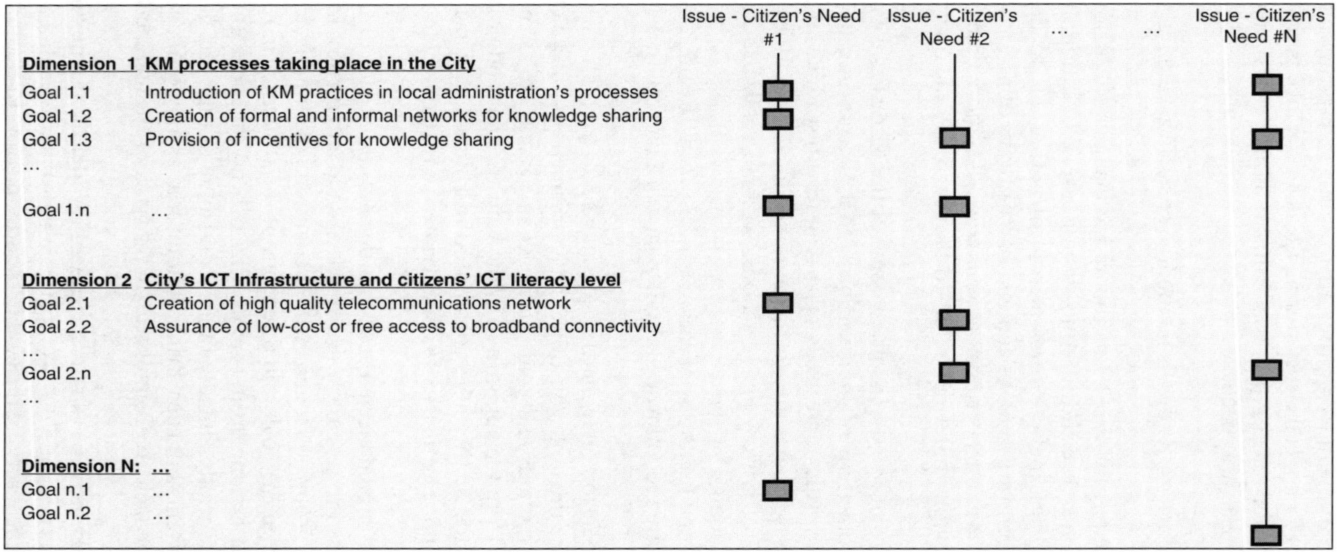

Figure 9.3 The main steps for the application of KnowCis 2.0 Methodology

actions (boxes) are connected with a vertical line. This indicates that these actions belong to a specific string.

Our methodology proposes ten strings of actions; these strings have been unequivocally defined after careful consideration of all important dimensions of citizens' and businesses' life. The ten strings are not overlapped and constitute the Human Dimension of a KC Strategy (Table 9.2).

In Figure 9.4 we present an example of String #1: Access to Knowledge, with a group of indicative actions. At the left side, all the possible dimensions and interventions of KnowCis methodology appear. At the right side, there are some indicative actions, all related to String #1: Access to Knowledge. Boxes indicate that the action(s) at the right side of the box contribute to the attainment of the goal at the left side of the box.

PILOT APPLICATION OF KNOWCIS 2.0 METHODOLOGY

The municipality of Maroussi is located in the northern suburbs of Athens. About 80 000 inhabitants live in the municipality and its area is 16.2 square kilometers. In economic terms, it is one of the most important municipalities in Greece. It is a centre of financial and cultural development. The city's infrastructure is well developed and a series of quality services are offered to the citizens. Some of the most important municipality assets are:

- In its premises lies the main complex in which the majority of the Olympic Games 2004 activities took place, such as the opening and closing ceremonies and a series of important field sports. This was a major event for the local region. Due to the Olympic Games, many of its infrastructures have been significantly improved. In addition, the region gained publicity and reputation outside the country, something that created new ways for co-operation with other cities. Citizens have realized that the co-operation and the synergy for a common goal can lead to amazing results.
- Maroussi is the heart of modern economic life in Athens, since it hosts the offices of numerous innovative and hi-tech enterprises. There are more than 1800 medium-sized and big companies based in the city.
- Maroussi is one of the largest commercial centers in Greece, with many stores and shopping malls.
- The municipality offers to its residents, through a series of innovative life-long learning initiatives, the possibility to acquire a high

Table 9.2 The ten proposed strings of actions

String	Actions
1: Access to knowledge	Relates to digital access to more explicit and tacit knowledge, beyond the formal educational process. It does not concern only pupils and/or students but also employees, business executives and professionals, anyone who produces, manages, uses or seeks tacit and/or explicit knowledge, in a digital way. Actions that enhance the management of knowledge in a more efficient and effective way, that ameliorate access to and availability of knowledge, support knowledge producers to share it, etc, can be included in this string
2: Support of work and employment	Related to the process of finding employment and to the facilitation of professional life citizens. It includes actions that facilitate the search for employment, the virtual access to the place of employment, the provision of advanced services to employees, professionals and knowledge workers, the provision of new employment opportunities from businesses by using new ICTs, and so on
3: Support of business innovation and entrepreneurship	Related to the support of innovation and entrepreneurship. It includes actions that support citizens to turn new and innovative ideas into new businesses, that facilitate the start-up of new enterprises as well as actions that are focused to business and help them to innovate, to better communicate among each other (B2B services), actions that support interoperability, and so on
4: Support of quality of life	Includes actions that target the provision of better health services to citizens, that contribute to entertainment, culture, sport, tourism, that ameliorate transportation and any other activity improving the quality of citizen's life, saving time and facilitating
5: Support of social and economic inclusion	Mainly concerns the inclusion of non-privileged or disadvantaged social groups and citizens who have a limited level of participation in the new knowledge era. It includes actions to strengthen and enhance citizens' participation in local activities and events, and, thus, contributes to the achievement of social cohesion

Table 9.2 (continued)

String	Actions
6: Interaction of citizens with the local administration	Focuses on the interaction of citizens with the local administration, with the aim to render it more easy, efficient and effective. It includes actions that aim to ameliorate and enhance e-government services, actions that strengthen the e-participation of citizens in decision making processes and policy formulation procedures, etc
7: Protection of the natural environment	Includes actions that aim to protect natural environment more effectively, through the use of new means. Indicatively: electronic surveillance and prevention of catastrophes (GIS), use of ICTs for energy saving and monitoring of energy efficiency, actions for civil protection, etc
8: Support of extroversion	Includes actions that aim to strengthen business development outside traditional local markets and beyond regional and national borders, while enhancing networking and communication with other cities and nations
9: Support of consumers	Concerns the strengthening of consumers so that they are able to electronically buy cheaper and better products, and receive up-to-date information regarding current prices. In parallel, this string includes actions concerning e-commerce for businesses and actions for NGOs and public bodies which, with the use of ICTs, can contribute to the better and more comprehensive provision of information and consumer protection
10: Knowledge region	Specialized actions that focus on the special characteristics of the region, and have as their main target to take advantage, exploit and promote the region's competitive advantages as well as to contribute to the better management of knowledge in the region.

level of skills and knowledge so as to remain competitive in the contemporary environment. The local government aims to continuously improve the municipality's infrastructure so as to attract businesses and offer a higher quality of life.

		S#1 - Access to knowledge ⇩ Integrated Intervention
Dimension 1	**KM processes taking place in the City**	
Goal 1.1	Introduction of KM practices in local administration's processes	• Introduction and use of KM systems and methods in the everyday operation of local administration • Creation of City's Forum in the metropolitan web-page • Creation of Info Centre addressed to young people for the provision of knowledge in various themes (ICTs, education, free time, professional training, etc)
Goal 1.2	Creation of formal and informal networks for knowledge sharing	• Operation of a structure for the provision of knowledge to citizens regarding city's offered services, collection of citizens' complaints about specific problems, etc • Better knowledge flow from universities and research institutes to the business sector through the creation of a specific structure
Goal 1.3	Provision of incentives for knowledge sharing	
Goal 1.4	Reinforcement of public libraries' network	• Reinforcement of the network of public libraries, through the introduction of innovative services (e.g. content digitalization with online indexing)
Dimension 2	**City's ICT Infrastructure and citizens' ICT literacy level**	
Goal 2.1	Creation of high quality telecommunications network	
Goal 2.2	Assurance of low-cost or free access to broadband connectivity	• Free Wi-Fi access for all citizens
Goal 2.3	Improvement of ICT use in schools, houses and businesses	• Introduction to schools of courses related to the use of ICTs • Promotion of the use of open-source software
Goal 2.4	Creation / improvement of metropolitan web-site	
Dimension 3	**Knowledge society citizens' rights**	
Goal 3.1	Definition and reassurance of knowledge society rights (accessibility, information, education and training, participation) for all citizens	
Goal 3.2	Creation of necessary conditions so that citizens make use of these rights	• Creation of public spaces with internet access for all citizens, in central spots in the city (City Hall, Library, etc.)

Dimension 4	**Research, business innovation and entrepreneurship**	
Goal 4.1	Improvement of city's economic performance in knowledge-intensive sectors	• Financing of development of thematic portals for e-learning delivery
Goal 4.2	Provision of incentives to companies for innovation	
Goal 4.3	Support of entrepreneurship and promotion of new and innovative ideas	• Development of Virtual Learning Centres (Start-ups)
Goal 4.4	Support of research / efficient promotion of research results throughout the city's knowledge agents	• Financing of Chambers for development of sectoral portals for training of employees • Development of training platforms for new entrepreneurs
Dimension 5	**Challenges that KM poses to the public sector**	
Goal 5.1	Continuous review of the international environment, for the latest developments concerning the services that KCs offer	• Development of thematic portal where knowledge will be available regarding other Knowledge Cities approaches, offered services, best practices, encountered difficulties, etc
Goal 5.2	Adaptation and integration of best practices to the policies, processes and services offered by the city	
Dimension 6	**Networking and synergies among all city's actors / with other KCs**	
Goal 6.1	Reinforcement of networking and interactions among all knowledge actors in the city	• Creation of a special Knowledge City Committee, which will be responsible for enhancing networking and interactions of knowledge actors, formulating KC strategy, establishing links with other KCs etc
Goal 6.2	Establishment of links and partnerships with other KCs	
Dimension 7	**Availability and skill level of human capital**	
Goal 7.1	Attraction and retention of high-level human capital	• Creation of web-site addressed to people recently moved to the city
Goal 7.2	Improvement of existing human capital's skill level	• Universities: Financing of on-line courses with VoD + e-learning content + digital journals • eLearning space for citizens of remote areas • eLearning for soldiers / citizens fulfilling military obligations • Digitalization of education material in laboratories, private educational centres, institutes, etc.
Dimension 8	**Inclusive, international and multi-ethnic character of the city**	
Goal 8.1	Improvement of immigrants' and minorities' living conditions	• Creation of public centres offering education services and vocational training to immigrants and minorities
Goal 8.2	Enhancement and reinforcement of the cultural, recreational and sporting activities taking place in the city and therefore of the city's visitors	• Initiatives for the better promotion of cultural, entertainment and athletic activities taking place in the city
Goal 8.3	Reinforcement of all the social groups' participation and e-participation in the public affairs	

Figure 9.4 Indicative example of String #1: Access to Knowledge

Finally, the municipality hosts various cultural, athletic, recreational and entertaining activities and events, something that creates a really vibrant atmosphere and enhances its multi-ethnic character.

Research staff of the Management and Decision Support Systems Laboratory (where the KnowCis and KnowCis 2.0 methodologies have been developed) had preliminary meetings with representatives of the municipality's local authority, in order to investigate potential ways of co-operation. It was decided that a period of familiarization with the concept and the KnowCis methodology was necessary. In this respect, in the subsequent period, a series of informative and educational actions and activities have taken place: presentations, interviews, workshops, meetings and informal discussions. The agenda incorporated: Principles of Knowledge Management (KM) and its importance, not only for organizations, but also for urban regions; Basic issues of KBD strategies and their advantages for urban regions; Needs that should be fulfilled by contemporary KBD strategies; The concept of the KC; Characteristics and advantages of KCs; Presentation of other cities' initiatives to be developed as KCs (case studies); KnowCis and KnowCis 2.0 methodologies.

The main result of this 'training' was that the representatives of the municipality were very enthusiastic about the concept of KC and its potential advantages, if it could be translated into a coherent and well-defined strategy. The question was whether Maroussi has the necessary potential to undertake such an initiative. The answer was positive and this was confirmed by the analytical assessment of its main assets. These are the main reasons for which Maroussi has been selected for the application of KnowCis and KnowCis 2.0 methodologies.

At the first phase, in a pilot project, the KnowCis methodology has been applied with success in this Greek municipality. Please refer to Ergazakis et al. 2006c, 2008 for more details regarding the steps followed and main results achieved. The most important result of the pilot application was the selection and prioritization of 23 strategic interventions (goals) for the development of the municipality as a KC.

During the second phase, the KnowCis 2.0 has been applied, also as a pilot. The purpose was to support the local authority of the municipality to select and formulate specific actions for achieving their strategic goals, as these have been identified and prioritized during the first phase. In total, more than 60 actions have been identified, for the ten strings of the KnowCis 2.0.

Figure 9.5 presents the group of actions to be implemented by the municipality, in relation to String #1: Access to Knowledge. It should be noted that the goals' ranking, as presented in Table 9.2 and in the subsequent analysis, does not follow a numerical order. It is based on goal

		S#1 - Access to knowledge → Integrated Intervention
Goal 2.2	Assurance of low-cost or free access to broadband connectivity	• Development of WiFi and WiMax network
Goal 4.1	Improvement of city's economic performance in knowledge-intensive sectors	
Goal 4.3	Support of entrepreneurship and promotion of new and innovative Ideas	• Development of virtual business Incubators
Goal 2.4	Creation / improvement of metropolitan web-site	• Full reconstruction of metropolitan web-site
Goal 1.1	Introduction of KM practices in local administration's processes	
Goal 1.2	Creation of formal and informal networks for knowledge sharing	• Creation of City's Forum in the metropolitan web-page • Reinforcement of Info-Centre addressed to young people • Reinforcement of Citizens' Desk Office
Goal 7.1	Attraction and retention of high-level human capital	• Creation of section in municipality's web-site addressed to people recently moved to the city
Goal 8.2	Enhancement and reinforcement of the cultural, recreational and sporting activities taking place in the city and therefore of the city's visitors	• Initiatives for the better promotion of cultural, entertainment and athletic activities taking place in the city
Goal 6.1	Reinforcement of networking and interactions among all knowledge actors in the city	
Goal 1.3	Provision of incentives for knowledge sharing	• Better Knowledge flow from/to universities and research centres
Goal 4.2	Provision of incentives to companies for innovation	
Goal 3.2	Creation of necessary conditions so that citizens make use of these rights	• Creation of public spaces with internet access for all citizens, in central spots in the city
Goal 6.2	Establishment of links and partnerships with other KCs	
Goal 7.2	Improvement of existing human capital's skill level	• Exploitation of results of 'Mindport' project • Reinforcement of municipality's public colleges
Goal 2.3	Improvement of ICT use in schools, houses and businesses	• Improvement of citizens' skill level regarding ICT
Goal 8.1	Improvement of immigrants' and minorities' living conditions	
Goal 5.1	Continuous review of the international environment, for the latest developments concerning the services that KCs offer	
Goal 5.2	Adaptation and integration of best practices to the policies, processes and services offered by the city	
Goal 1.4	Reinforcement of public libraries' network	• Reinforcement of municipality's library
Goal 3.1	Definition and reassurance of knowledge society rights (accessibility, information, education and training, participation) for all citizens	

Figure 9.5 Actions for String #1: Access to Knowledge

priority (the first goal is considered the most important), as resulting from the application of KnowCis.

A short description of the actions shown in Figure 9.5 is presented:

Goal 2.2 Development of WiFi and WiMax network: This action concerns the development of a complete network of Wi-Fi and WiMax antennas within the municipality's premises. The main objective is to provide free access to students or people with disabilities and low-cost access to other citizens. Municipality executives intend to seek co-operation with the private sector, so as to identify the appropriate business models to achieve this objective.

Goal 4.3 Development of Virtual Business Incubator: The main purpose is the creation of an internet community that will provide complete consulting support for the integrated development of business ideas and creation of companies. Indicative services to be provided are: submission of new and innovative business ideas; qualitative assessment of ideas; evaluation of their feasibility; practical support to further develop and establish the ideas that are considered to be feasible; support for the elaboration of a business plan; provision of alternatives for financing the business plan; access to knowledge related to common problems and best practice in similar cases; consulting support regarding the required steps for new company creation, and so on.

Goal 2.4 Full reconstruction of metropolitan web-site: The existing web-site will be fully redesigned so as to be more functional and, attractive and to better respond to the need of citizens to access knowledge in an efficient and effective way. The new web-site will follow all interoperability standards. It will offer advanced services to citizens and businesses and will incorporate a special section, where all knowledge regarding the KC initiative will be easily accessible and retrievable.

Goal 1.2 Creation of City's Forum in the metropolitan web-page: A discussion forum will be created inside the municipality's web-site. This forum will be accessible by all citizens and will act as a public space where they can discuss anything and exchange knowledge concerning the municipality they live in. Moreover, citizens will be able to easily create their own blog page. Finally, a free e-mail account will be offered for everyone.

Reinforcement of Info-Centre addressed to young people: In the municipality, there is currently an Info-Centre addressed to young people which has as its main purpose to acquaint them with ICT, as well as to provide reliable and timely knowledge on a variety of issues: education, vocational training, free time, job finding, and so on. This action is intended to further enhance the operation of the Info-centre, by developing and improving its infrastructure and by introducing new added-value services.

Reinforcement of Citizens' Desk Office: The municipality currently operates the 'Citizens' Desk Office', to provide reliable information to citizens regarding services offered by the municipality, to gather reports from citizens regarding problems in the city, and so on. This action is intended to better exploit available ICTs for the enhancement of the role of this structure and for the provision of new services. An example is the creation of an integrated IT system for the systematic, fully automated recording of problems reported by citizens as well as for the monitoring of their resolution.

Goal 7.1 Creation of section in Municipality's web-site addressed to people recently moved to the city: A special section will be created in the website, addressed to persons that recently moved to the city. The typical target client will be a knowledge worker who settled in the city and is seeking a wider range of information than one who has been living there longer. Beyond ongoing training activities, for example, this information may include: entertainment calendar, trends in local high-tech industries, information about income taxes, cultural and recreational activities, working visas, business opportunities and so on.

Goal 8.2 Initiatives for the better promotion of cultural, entertaining, athletic activities taking place in the city: The purpose of this action is to design and implement various means for the enhancement of the promotion of the various cultural, entertainment and athletic activities taking place in the city, in order to increase citizens' participation.

Goal 1.3 Better knowledge flow from/to universities and research centers: The municipality's executives will investigate the possibility of creating an organization charged with the duty of facilitating the dissemination and flow of knowledge / research results, from universities and research centers to the private sector. The organization will also act as intermediary when a company needs research support. The following actors can participate in this organization: municipality technology company, private companies based on the municipality, universities, research centers, and so on.

Goal 3.2 Creation of public spaces with internet access for all citizens, in central spots in the city: This action concerns the creation of public spaces in specific spots in the municipality (such as the City Hall, the Library, etc.) where citizens will have free access to computers and internet.

Goal 7.2 Exploitation of results of 'Mindport' project: The municipality participated in the project 'MINDPORT', a modular collaborative e-learning architecture for life-long learning over broadband computer networks' which had as its purpose to develop an advanced e-learning platform, including innovative and fully adaptable features. This action concerns the exploitation of this project's results by the municipality's colleges: through the developed platform, colleges can offer online courses to citizens.

Reinforcement of municipality's public colleges: Currently, there is a series of colleges already operating in the municipality (such as the College of Informatics, College of Advanced Technologies & New Media, College of Business Management, etc.), offering the possibility to citizens to develop their skills and have access to life-long learning programmes. This action concerns the reinforcement of these colleges in order to: accept more students per year; improve the quality of provided courses; introduce new courses; decrease the level of tuition fees for young people; seek co-operation with other colleges, and so on.

Goal 2.3 Improvement of citizens' skill level regarding ICT: This action concerns a series of interventions to further improve the citizens' skills regarding ICT: reinforcement of the College of Advanced Technologies & New Media and of the College of Informatics, improvement of schools' IT infrastructures, implementation of workshops and seminars, collaboration with private schools, and so on. In addition, two special sections will be created in the municipality's web-site. One will provide updated information and comprehensive knowledge regarding the 'dangers' of the internet (viruses, spyware, spam e-mail, frauds, and so on). The other section will inform citizens and companies of the advantages of open-source software, such as the considerable cost savings and the free access to their source code.

Goal 1.4 Reinforcement of Municipality's library: The existing library must be significantly reinforced. Its current book collection is relatively limited, so the first step will be to enhance it. A web-site will also be created to offer a series of e-services: access to its collection information, electronic reservation of books, information on forthcoming books and editions, and so on. Moreover, ways of co-operation with other national and international libraries will be explored. Finally, the library can play the role of an urban innovation engine, for example through the organization of 'thematic soirées'.

In conclusion, the main outcomes from the application of KnowCis and KnowCis 2.0 to Maroussi, are:

- Identification of City's main strengths and weaknesses, based on the indicators assessment (indicators are used in KnowCis).
- Selection of strategic goals for the development of Maroussi as a KC (KnowCis)
- Prioritization of strategic goals (KnowCis)
- Selection and formulation of citizen-centered specific actions so as to achieve the strategic goals (KnowCis 2.0)

It should be noted that the implementation of some of these actions has already begun, while many other actions are scheduled to begin in the near future. Preliminary results and qualitative assessments indicate that the actions contribute to the attainment of the strategic goals.

CONCLUSION: LIMITATION AND FUTURE RESEARCH CHALLENGES

During the last few years, the theme of KC has been significantly evolved as a major topic of interest in the context of the KBD field. In this respect, and being multi-disciplinary by nature, the theme of KC attracts researchers from a wide variety of disciplines. It is only recently that researchers as well as local authorities' policy makers have started looking at the potential of formulating integrated strategies to bridge the knowledge divide and develop successful KC. However, the lack of integrated KC development strategies still exists and tends to become an important problem for local authorities and decision makers worldwide.

This problem has been identified by the authors in two ways: on the one side, by considering the factors that are important and affect the process of formulating development strategies for any city, which render the procedure particularly complex; on the other side, by conducting a comparative analysis of existing cities' approaches so as to formulate their KC development strategies. From the review of cities' cases, it can be concluded that each city's approach is different and that only in a few cases have integrated KC development strategies been formulated, using specific methodologies. In the majority of other cases, the KC strategy cannot be considered as integrated, since these cities were only based on ad hoc solutions and methods in order to define and formulate their strategies.

The main part of the chapter is devoted to the proposed KnowCis 2.0 methodology, which is based on KnowCis and further enhances it by adding new features. In this respect, the main characteristics of KnowCis are initially presented in brief, for the readers who are not acquainted with it. Then, the new features offered by KnowCis 2.0 are analyzed. KnowCis 2.0 has as its main objective to support local authorities in the process of designing citizen-centric interventions which consist of groups of actions, called 'strings of actions'. Each string of actions comprises more than one action and has a common goal which refers to the real, daily life of citizens and enterprises.

The proposed methodology has been successfully applied as a pilot at a Greek municipality, and a description of this pilot application is included in the chapter. The initial results from this pilot application are positive.

In addition, KnowCis 2.0 has the advantage that, by design, it can be easily adjusted and adapted so as to serve the needs of cities of different size and of different context, assets, problems and so on. This adaptability can be mainly achieved through the consideration of alternative strings of actions than the ones proposed by the authors.

It should be noted that the most important limitations of the KnowCis 2.0 methodology are the following:

- The concept of KC is particularly broad and covers many aspects of everyday life in a city. In this respect, one limitation of the proposed methodology is the fact that it incorporates only 10 strings of actions mainly related to citizens' needs. So, additional strings can be included in the methodology in order to cover additional aspects, such as business and entrepreneurship development, more efficient and effective operation of local authorities, and so on.
- An information system has been developed in order to support local authorities for the application of KnowCis methodology. However, such an information system does not exist for the support of KnowCis 2.0 application. Preferably, such systems should be appropriately interconnected. So, this limitation constitutes another field of future research.
- Another limitation, which also constitutes an important future research challenge, is to explore ways of synthesizing the knowledge, outcomes, results and lessons learnt from the application of the KnowCis 2.0 methodology to a series of cities. Such a synthesis (stored in a central database and accessed through a web portal) should be a very useful and valuable tool for local authorities as well as central governments all over the world, wishing to adopt and implement KBD approaches.

REFERENCES

Asia-Pacific Economic Cooperation (APEC) (2000), *Towards Knowledge-based Economies in APEC*, Economic Committee, APEC Secretariat, Singapore.

Carrillo, F.J. (2006), 'A taxonomy of urban capital', in J. Carrillo (ed.), *Knowledge Cities: Approaches, Experiences and Perspectives*, Oxford: Butterworth-Heinemann/Elsevier, pp. 43–58.

City of Melbourne (2005), *City Plan 2010: Towards a Thriving and Sustainable City*, Melbourne Council.

Dang, D. and K. Umemoto (2009), 'Modeling the development toward the knowledge economy: a national capability approach', *Journal of Knowledge Management,* **13** (5), 359–372.

Delft (2010), http://www.delft.nl/delften/Business/Knowledge/Delft_Knowledge_City, accessed 10 January.

Dublin Chamber of Commerce (2008), 'Developing a Knowledge City Region: A Ten Point Plan', http://www.dublinchamber.ie/uploads/Knowledge_City_Region.pdf, accessed 10 January 2011.

Ergazakis, K., K. Metaxiotis and J. Psarras (2004), 'Towards knowledge cities: conceptual analysis and success stories', *Journal of Knowledge Management*, **8** (5), 5–15.

Ergazakis, K., K. Metaxiotis and J. Psarras (2006a), 'A coherent framework for building successful KC in the context of the knowledge-based economy', *Knowledge Management Research & Practice*, **4** (1), 46–59.

Ergazakis, K., K. Metaxiotis and J. Psarras (2006b), 'A unified methodological approach for the development of knowledge cities', *Journal of Knowledge Management*, **10** (5), 65–78.

Ergazakis, K., K. Metaxiotis, J. Psarras and K. Grammatikos (2006c), 'Applying the KnowCis methodology to a Greek municipality: a case study', *Knowledge Management Research & Practice*, **4** (4), pp. 293–309.

Ergazakis, E., K. Ergazakis, K. Metaxiotis and D. Askounis (2007), 'An integrated decision support model for a knowledge city's strategy formulation', *Journal of Knowledge Management,* Annual Special Issue on Knowledge-Based Development 2007, **11** (5), 65–86.

Ergazakis, E., K. Ergazakis, K. Metaxiotis, E. Bellos and V. Leopoulos (2008), 'An AI-based decision support system for designing knowledge-based development strategies', *International Journal of Intelligent Systems Technologies and Applications,* **5** (1/2), 201–233.

Ergazakis, E., K. Ergazakis, K. Metaxiotis and Y. Charalabidis (2009), 'Rethinking the development of successful Knowledge Cities: an advanced framework', *Journal of Knowledge Management,* **13** (5), 214–227.

Ergazakis, E., K. Ergazakis and K. Metaxiotis (2010), 'Building successful knowledge cities in the knowledge-based economy: A Modern Strategic Framework', in K. Metaxiotis, F.J. Carrillo and T. Yigitcanlar (eds), *Knowledge-Based Development of Cities and Societies: An Integrated Multi-Level Approach*, IGI Global, pp. 17–41.

European Commission (2000), *Innovation Policy in a Knowledge-Based Economy*, Office for Official Publications of the European Communities, Brussels.

Henn, G., J.R. Noenning and S. Richter (2009), 'Dubai Crystal and Ecopolis: the structure of a knowledge creating city', paper presented at the 2nd Knowledge Cities Summit, 5–6 November, Shenzhen, China.

Martínez, S.D. (2006), 'A comparative framework for knowledge cities' in J. Carrillo (ed.), *Knowledge Cities: Approaches, Experiences and Perspectives*, Oxford: Butterworth-Heinemann/Elsevier, pp. 17–30.

Montréal (2010), http://www.Montréal2025.com/mot_du_maire.php?lang=en, accessed 10 January 2011.

Montréal Knowledge City Advisory Committee (2003), *Montréal, Knowledge City,* http://www.Montréalinternational.com/docs/MtlSavoir_En.pdf, accessed 10 January, 2011.

Munich (2005), *Munich – City of Knowledge*, Department of Labor and Economic Development, City of Munich, Munich.

OECD (2001), 'The new economy: beyond the hype', www.oecd.org/EN/home/0,,EN-home-33-nodirectorate-no-no-33,FF.html, accessed 10 January 2011.

OKC (2010), http://www.melbourne.vic.gov.au/okc/Pages/About.aspx, accessed 10 January 2011.

Palacios, T.B. and R.S. Galvan (2006), 'Intellectual capital within Iberian municipalities (network)', *Journal of Knowledge Cities*, **10** (5), 55–64.

Streit, A. (2005), 'Munich as a Knowledge City: key factors and political strategies', presented at Knowledge Economy and Creativity, Amsterdam, 14–17 September.

World Bank (1999), 'Knowledge for development', *World Development Report 1998–1999*, Washington, DC.

Yigitcanlar T., K. O'Connor and C. Westerman (2008), 'The making of knowledge cities: Melbourne's knowledge-based urban development experience', *Cities Journal*, **25**, 63–72.

10. Designing: combining design and high-tech industries in the knowledge city of Eindhoven

Ana María Fernández-Maldonado

INTRODUCTION

During the last decade, the academic debate on the most important factors influencing urban and regional economic growth and competitiveness has been very lively and animated. Traditional business-oriented approaches focused on the economic qualities of a place, stating that in order to generate growth cities should attract firms and institutions. But a different view challenged the traditional rationale for economic growth, claiming that cities should attract not merely firms, but human capital and talented people, the most important asset for competitiveness in the new economic context. Issues linked to the creative city and the creative class popularized by Charles Landry (2000) and Richard Florida (2002), respectively, have been widely studied, discussed and criticized in urban studies. Academics have begun to pay attention to the cultural, symbolic and socio-spatial qualities of a place as important issues in the knowledge-based economy. Urban managers, particularly of industrial centres in decay, have embraced this new perspective, attempting to rebrand their cities as creative places (Kunzmann, 2004).

Gradually, it has become clear that both firms and people are important, so knowledge-based urban development approaches should not neglect any of these aspects. Cities worldwide have a considerable experience in shaping a good business climate, but many of the requirements and conditions for creative environments are fuzzy and difficult to achieve or to measure in practice (Trip, 2009). In the Netherlands, a country where the urban creativity discourse was well received by urban managers, local policy documents generally hold creativity-oriented views, but they still tend to engage in the business-oriented perspective, easier to implement in practice (Kooijman and Romein, 2007).

The present chapter focuses on ways to combine business and people oriented perspectives in practice, presenting the case of Eindhoven, a city with a high-tech profile which is considered as the 'brainport' – the economic engine – of the Netherlands. Aware that the synergy between high-technology and creative sectors has become crucial in the international competitiveness of knowledge-based regions, Eindhoven has successfully incorporated the creative design sector into its traditional high-tech production sector. Its several successful initiatives can serve as inspiration for other cities with similar ambitions.

The chapter is organized in six sections. The next section addresses the main assumptions of the business-oriented, the people-oriented, and the comprehensive perspectives of urban growth and development. The third section will describe the problems of implementing the comprehensive approaches in practice. The main features of Eindhoven's urban and knowledge development are the focus of the following section. The fifth addresses the organizational and socio-spatial aspects of the design orientation of Eindhoven. The last section presents the main conclusions from the process of combining design and high-technology in Eindhoven.

THEORIES OF URBAN GROWTH IN THE KNOWLEDGE ERA

The identification of the driving forces for city growth and urban competitiveness has been a recurrent topic in urban and regional economics. The importance of knowledge, technology and innovation for the success of cities is widely acknowledged, but the theoretical discussion on the main factors influencing knowledge and innovation continues. Two main views can be distinguished, the business-oriented and the people-oriented perspectives, considering financial capital or human capital, respectively, as the main engine of growth of cities and regions.

Spatial strategies to promote technological innovation based on the scale advantages produced by agglomeration or clustering of economic activities – technopoles, high-tech spaces, industrial clusters, science parks – have been among the most common tools by which cities and regions attempt to improve their local economies within a business oriented approach. These stress the role of technological spillovers in generating economic growth.

Other scholars claim that interactive learning is the most important factor to promote knowledge and innovation. Successful interactions between producers of theoretical knowledge (research) and practical knowledge (industry) would depend upon relationships based on mutual trust, but also on face-to-face contacts, indispensable for the exchange of 'tacit' knowledge (Storper and Venables, 2004). The government may also promote innovation by gearing the cross-fertilization of theoretical knowledge and practical knowledge with policy instruments. Such processes – focused on research–industry–government – have been called a 'triple helix' interaction because they do not respond to a linear process but to interactions among the constitutive elements (Etzkowitz, 2003).

The role of institutions in promoting long-term economic growth has also attracted considerable academic attention (Glaeser et al., 2004). 'Institutional thickness' has been considered as the secret ingredient of competitive places (Amin and Thrift, 1995). Formal and informal institutions can indeed shape the local business climate to promote interactive learning and mutual trust, for example; they can improve labour force participation and effort levels; and they can seize new opportunities and adjust to changing technological and economic contexts (Storper, 2010).

On the other hand, the awareness of the growing importance of consumer markets and demand-driven activities, has increased the academic interest toward the symbolic and cultural aspects of economic development. This new focus was initiated by studies addressing the role of human capital as driver of urban growth in US metropolitan areas. Glaeser and Shapiro (2001) claimed that during the 1990s, cities with strong human capital grew faster than those without it. Glaeser and Saiz (2003) identified the presence of high-skilled workers, as the main predictor of competitiveness and productivity growth.

After Florida's (2002) book on the creative class became an international best seller, great attention has been paid to creativity issues and their impact on the growth of cities and regions. Florida, Landry (2000) and Clark (2004) state that cities should nurture their 'creative workers', the producers of economic value in the form of new ideas. A city's success is linked to the cross-fertilization of ideas and tacit knowledge arising from the effects of face-to-face contacts between creative workers (Storper and Venables, 2004).

These assumptions radically change the rationale for economic growth: instead of attracting firms, cities should attract creative/high skilled people. Cafés, pubs, terraces, cultural events and other 'third places' acquire a new dimension, while 'quality of place' is considered necessary for urban competitiveness. This people-orientation has led to a growing interest toward cultural, artistic, media-related, recreational, and leisure functions as boosters of local economies.

A combination of these two approaches is also possible. Storper (2010) claims that jobs follow people, who in turn search for the benefits of large urban (home) markets. At the same time, people follow jobs because firms concentrate at these large urban markets, which allows them to

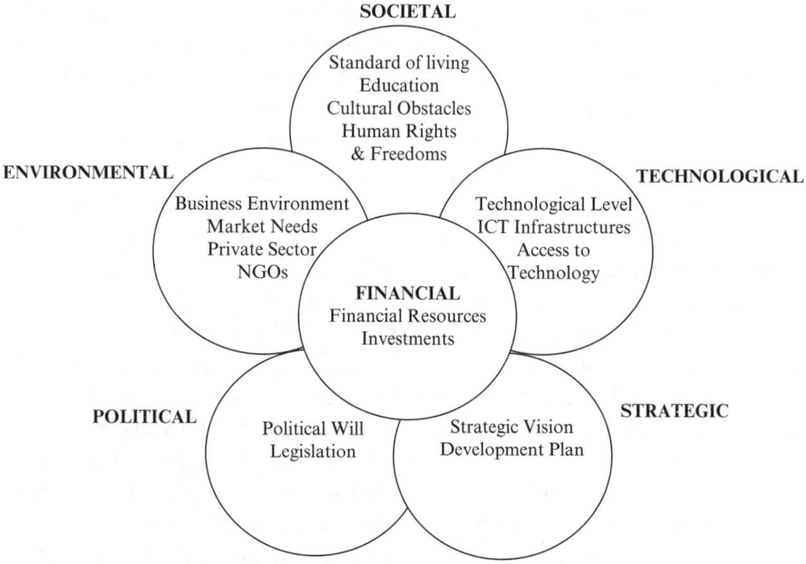

Source: Ergazakis et al., 2004.

Figure 10.1 Success factors related to the Knowledge City concept

produce more efficiently with economies of scale. This means that the direction of causality of urban growth may be 'fully simultaneously two-directional' (Storper, 2010: 2032). Consequently, concepts linked to the business orientation – as high-technology, agglomerations, clusters, entrepreneurship – and the people orientation – such as amenities, culture, high education – plus an environment characterized by organizational capacity, are all necessary for economic competition (Malecki, 2002).

Besides these considerations, new environmental and social challenges have made urban planners and designers aware for the need for a proper balance between the economy, the social and the environmental aspects of city growth. Knight (1995) was among the first to link knowledge-based development and sustainability issues, claiming that knowledge-based development – understood as the transformation of knowledge resources into local development – may be the best foundation for sustainable development. More recently, different studies have paid explicit attention to the criteria for successful knowledge cities, and they all include both business and people oriented criteria. For example, Ergazakis et al. (2004) have proposed six different categories: technological, strategic, political, environmental, societal and financial criteria (see Figure 10.1).

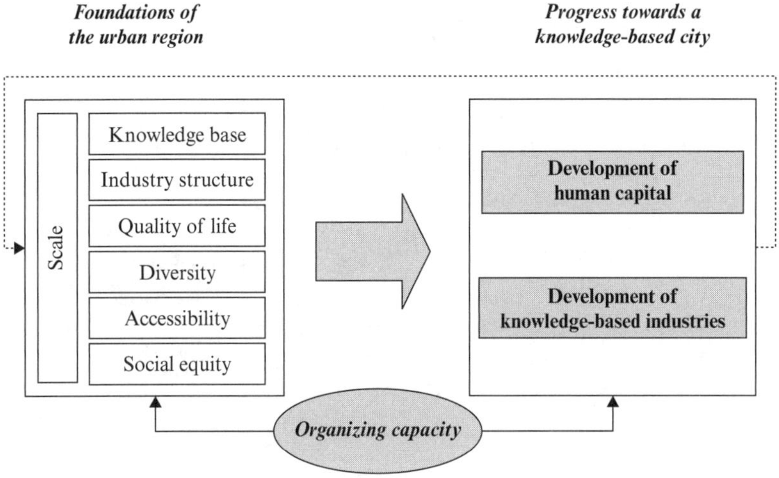

Source: van Winden et al., 2007.

Figure 10.2 Cities in the knowledge economy: a framework of analysis

A framework developed by EURICUR for European cities in the knowledge economy (van Winden et al., 2007) consists of seven criteria: knowledge base, industry structure, quality of life, diversity, accessibility, social equity and urban scale. These are considered the foundations to develop human capital and knowledge-based industries, which should be supported by local organizing capacities (see Figure 10.2).

Yigitcanlar (2009) narrowed down to three pillars for knowledge-based urban development: society (including quality of life, human and social development and intellectual capital), economy (competitive, creative, innovative and knowledge-based) and environment (sustainable urban development, triple bottom-line sustainability and unique identity) (see Figure 10.3).

Fernandez-Maldonado and Romein (2010) state economic, social and organizational qualities as the most important criteria to evaluate knowledge-based urban development processes (see Figure 10.4). A good level of quality in each of them should lead to producing prosperity, delivering projects for all people.

FROM THEORY TO PRACTICE

Putting such comprehensive frameworks into practice is not such an easy endeavour, however. Many former industrial centres have

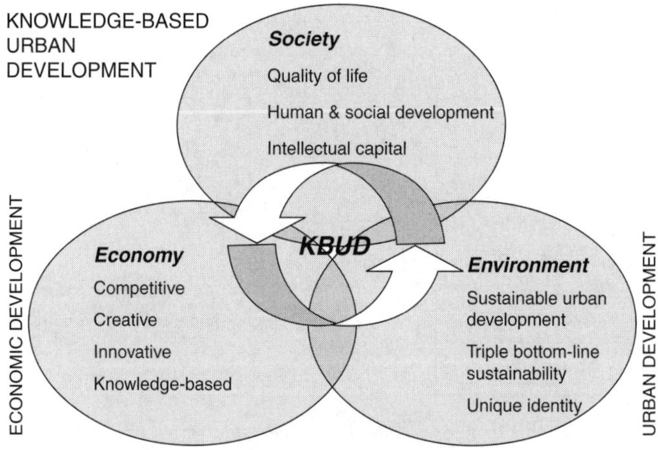

Source: Yigitcanlar, 2009.

Figure 10.3 The three pillars of knowledge-based urban development

embraced Knowledge City or Creative City initiatives as a way to deal with their problems of economic reconversion. But this requires much more than just re-branding themselves with fashionable slogans. The main issue at stake is to translate these new notions into feasible and effective policies.

At European level, the Lisbon Agenda does not specifically support creative city development: 'it strongly emphasizes knowledge and innovation, but not creativity as the link between' (Trip, 2009:14). At national and regional level, technological innovation is also the main concern in most economic policies.

At local level there is more attention to these issues, however. But even if cities may elaborate a comprehensive approach, with a proper balance between economic and social aspects, the implementation of this kind of strategy is generally based on business-oriented interventions. In the Netherlands, where Florida's message was particularly well received at local level, Kooijman and Romein (2007) examined the implementation of the creative city concept in local urban policy. They concluded that despite the growing awareness of the importance of cultural and creative aspects among city officials, 'the implementation of Florida's ideas has remained limited in the urban policy of the four largest Dutch cities. . . . Instead, the policy core lays most emphasis on giving explicit, direct support to businesses and creating a "business climate", as opposed to a "people-climate"' (2007: 32–33).

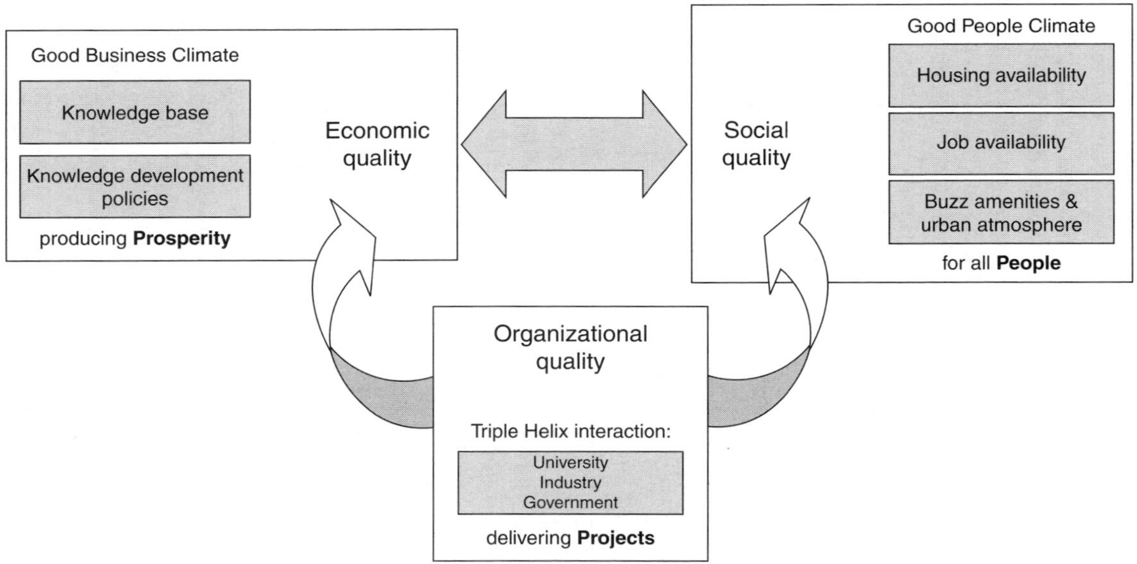

Source: Fernandez-Maldonado and Romein, 2010.

Figure 10.4 A conceptual framework for sustainable development for cities in the knowledge economy

This economic orientation occurs because the hard infrastructure (airports, digital links, high-tech spaces) can be established almost anywhere, but the establishment of the 'soft' infrastructure – an environment conducive to creativity – is a lengthy and slow process without guarantee of success (Baum et al., 2008). Many of the elements of creative cities remain imprecise and as such difficult to achieve in practice. How does one capture and measure the 'intangibles' associated to creative milieus such as tolerance, identity, authenticity, image, atmosphere, and so on? The main advocates of the creative city notion have not given a special emphasis on how to put their ideas into practice (Kooijman and Romein, 2007). While Florida (2002, 2005) tends to repeat the advice given in 1961 by Jane Jacobs, he does not really address how his ideas actually work in practice (Trip, 2009).

Besides the elusive nature of the elements linked to the creative city strategies, there are two other issues which pose specific problems for the urban practice, especially in those cities and regions which do not possess strong assets for knowledge-based development. These concern the proper urban scale, and path dependency.

Baum et al. (2008) have posed a relevant question regarding the possibilities of success of lower-tier cities in the knowledge economy. With evidence from Australian cities, they show that creative clusters settle in major metropolitan regions (Sydney, Melbourne and Canberra). Urban concentration is not only promoting the growth of the creative industries, but is also an important element promoting local specialization. 'Generally speaking, geographical concentration and local specialization are highly present in newer or more innovative activities, or those that depend on hard-to-imitate skills or knowledge' (Storper, 2010: 2028). In this context, smaller cities have greater difficulties.

Another thorny problem is for those cities without a strong tradition on industrial production or creative activities. Path dependency means that once local economies get a critical mass in a certain specialization, they get a self-reinforcing structural character. Evidence from industrial areas shows that their growth may also be driven by fortuitous events. But there is no clarity about how to get into this development path (Storper, 2010). This theoretical uncertainty also has important implications for the planning practice in less advantaged cities and regions.

The next sections show the case of Eindhoven, a Dutch city which has had a singular success reinventing itself as a knowledge node and by combining its technological base with the creative design sector.

THE REINVENTION OF EINDHOVEN AS A KNOWLEDGE CITY

The Netherlands belongs to the most economically advanced countries of the western hemisphere, and has strong assets in the transition toward the knowledge era. It has a very open economy, in which knowledge-intensive economic activities constitute a large and growing proportion. The Dutch population is highly urbanized and internationally oriented, and has a high education level. Its universities enjoy a good reputation at international level. The country also enjoys a well-developed ICT infrastructure and is among the best digitally connected countries of the world.

The Netherlands' largest concentration of high-technology firms is located in the Eindhoven region, in the province of North Brabant, close to the Dutch borders with Belgium and Germany. At approximately 100 km from the Randstad, Eindhoven is the fifth largest Dutch city (209 172 residents in 2007) and the biggest outside the 'heart of the Netherlands', the Randstad urban network, which includes the cities of Amsterdam, Rotterdam, The Hague and Utrecht (see Figure 10.5).

Thanks to an active regional partnership between companies, knowledge institutions and governments, and the presence of research labs – such as those of Philips, TNO (National Organization for Applied Scientific Research) and Eindhoven Technical University – Eindhoven

Figure 10.5 Location of Eindhoven and large cities of the Netherlands

has become the Netherlands' most important place for technology innovation. In 2004, the Dutch government appointed it as the national 'Brainport', the main location for the development of a regional innovation system, which provides it with additional public funds, granted with the objective to strengthen the Netherlands as a dynamic and competitive economy.

Industrial origin and evolution

By Dutch standards, Eindhoven is a relatively young city, which grew rapidly thanks to a process of industrial development driven by a local firm, Philips Electronics, which settled there in 1891. Although its economic base has expanded and diversified greatly, Philips is still a dominant firm, which is why Eindhoven is still considered Philips's company town. Eindhoven calls itself the 'City of Light' (Lichtstad) after Philips's initial business: a factory of light bulbs. With the hardware production sections and laboratories of Philips Electronics and other important electronic firms, Eindhoven scores the highest on high-tech industry employment and private R&D activities in the Netherlands.

After World War II, Eindhoven developed into the most important industrial centre of the Netherlands. Like many other industrial centres, it was affected by processes of de-industrialization since the 1980s, which caused job losses in the city and the whole region. Philips declared 6000 workers redundant, and DAF (vehicle manufacturer) 2500, while other firms closed, in a process that deeply affected the region's economic situation.

The process of restructuring of the regional economy was developed with the support of successive regional programmes. The first was the Stimulus programme (1993) for job creation and strengthening of the industrial fabric, partly funded by the European Union. To face the industrial downturn, a regional approach was sought, in which Eindhoven worked together with other municipalities in the region. 'The 34 municipalities in the Eindhoven region matched the European subsidies with a contribution of 11.50 Dutch guilders per inhabitant per year to create jobs in the area. Such a high municipal contribution to regional cooperation is unique in the Netherlands' (van der Veer, 1998: 42).

After Stimulus finished, the main regional stakeholders – in government, industry, and research and education – decided to cooperate closely with the objective to continue with the process of transition of Eindhoven's traditional industries toward a knowledge-based and high-tech centre. In 2001, the Horizon programme replaced Stimulus, focusing on industrial innovation, reduction of shortages of skilled labour, diversification of the knowledge industry, and international branding. These programmes produced a significant economic restructuring and economic recovery, upgrading the industrial structure to make it more high-tech and in line with its knowledge base.

The current structure of the regional economy consists of a few large firms – such as Philips, DAF and ASML (a joint venture of Philips and ASM International dedicated to electronics) – working closely with medium- and small-scale suppliers of specialized knowledge and design, and knowledge institutes. In Eindhoven only, the numbers of firms, institutes and jobs increased by one-third to a half between 1995 and 2000, and has increased a bit further in more recent years.

One of the best assets of Eindhoven is its organizational capacity, embodied in the high synergy between business, university and local government (Fernandez-Maldonado and Romein, 2010). The so-called triple helix is a very positive feature of this city-region, in which 'personal and institutional networks are very dense; there is a shared feeling of local pride and identity' (van Winden et al., 2007: 542). The collaboration between the main regional stakeholders has been institutionalized in the Foundation Brainport (Stichting Brainport). This has elaborated an ambitious and comprehensive programme, 'Brainport Navigator 2013' (Stichting Brainport, 2005), whose mission is to promote economic and social development toward a high quality of life for people in the region and, through this, to achieve a sustainable and globally competitive region.

The Brainport programme has replaced Horizon, and aims at the development and completion of the value chains of spearhead sectors. These are life-tech (life sciences, medical technology), high-tech systems (ICT, micro-electronics, nanotechnology, automotive and mechatronics) and creative industries.

Eindhoven's position in the knowledge economy

Two contrasting features characterize Eindhoven's development. On the one hand, it has great assets, due to the high quality of its industrial, economic, and knowledge base. It has the highest innovation index among the Dutch provinces. Its city-region is where most of the private R&D expenditures of the Netherlands is located (45 per cent of the national R&D expenditures). Further, the level of synergy between high-level education and high-tech local firms is remarkable. An examination of university–industry co-authored research publications among the 350 largest research universities worldwide concluded that the Eindhoven Technical University (TU/e) had the largest percentage of co-authorship with industry (Tijssen et al., 2009). Moreover,

> The technical university is considered highly important by local high-tech firms as a partner for contract research and as a supplier of new staff and trainees. Also, it is the cradle of new businesses and start-ups. The environment for these new firms is favourable, as the urban region has a rich pool of potential clients, suppliers and dedicated service providers. Several well-functioning business support networks are in place, with active participation of the local technology sector and academic institutions. (van Winden et al., 2007: 538)

On the other hand, Eindhoven has evident problems related to its modest urban scale and its location outside of the Randstad. Eindhoven does not possess the advantages of agglomeration required for attracting creative sectors. Furthermore, in the Netherlands, Eindhoven has the image of a provincial city, due to its relatively recent urban development from several villages. Its city centre lacks the historic architectural heritage that characterizes most Dutch cities, which constitutes an additional constraint to attract creative workers.

THE MARRIAGE OF TECHNOLOGY AND DESIGN IN EINDHOVEN

The decision to combine design and high-tech in the Eindhoven city-region developed from the stakeholders' gradual awareness of the current economic imperatives – the need to incorporate cultural knowledge and design distinctiveness into products and services – and, on the other hand, the strengths and weaknesses of their region. A significant gesture illustrates the new strategy: in 2004, Philips Electronics changed its motto 'Let's make things better' – which referred to technical innovation – into 'Sense and Simplicity', which refers to improved design. The regional consensus for the design orientation is remarkable: 'Policy makers, business sector, the Technical University, TNO Industry, the Design Academy, everybody in Eindhoven invests in the design dance' (van de Sande, 2005: 3), a fact which has facilitated the changes required at the level of institutions.

Eindhoven attempts to combine technology and design on different fronts, departing from the artistic, institutional, urban planning, or technology sectors. The concept of design in Eindhoven is then a comprehensive notion that includes industrial design, artistic design, urban design, as well as the design of innovative ways to tackle their own development problems. This design orientation has not been the fruit of fashionable urban trends, but a necessity coming from its endogenous economic development, and as such it has a certain tradition.

Eindhoven has solid foundations for its design orientation. It is the home of the Design Academy Eindhoven (DAE), the former design school of Philips, considered as one of the three institutions of 'international excellence' in the Netherlands. The design department of Philips Electronics, Philips Design, is one of the largest and longest-established design organizations in the world, counting more than 400 workers who work not only for Philips but also for other prestigious brands such as Nike, Levi's, Orange and Securitas (van de Sande, 2005). Besides, Eindhoven university has two faculties educating designers with a strong technical orientation: architecture and industrial design.

Organizational changes

Eindhoven does not attempt to improve its international design image to attract artists exclusively by a good quality of place, but by showing the other side of design: designers, processes, links with technology and innovative materials, and good communication. The largest design-related projects are coordinated by Design Connection Brainport (www.designconnectionbrainport.nl), an agency of the Brainport Foundation. The business sector, the creative industry and knowledge institutes work together in this agency for the implementation of the programme 'Design in Brainport 2005 – 2010'. Its mission is to reinforce the position of Eindhoven's city-region in the field of design in combination with technology, working in three main areas:

- get connected – aimed at giving designers, firms, technology institutes, and market partners the opportunity to meet and develop new ideas for innovative products;
- get noticed – aimed at showing the design strengths of the region at international level; and
- get support – aimed at assisting design starters on their way to entrepreneurship.

Design Connection Brainport organizes the Dutch Design Week (DDW), an annual nine-day event to show Dutch design and Eindhoven design to the world, which attracts a growing international audience. The DDW hosts lectures, workshops, fashion shows, seminars, and design exhibitions. These include the graduation projects of the Design Academy Eindhoven, and the award ceremony of the Dutch Design Week (DDW, 2010).

Foundation ALICE, a local lobby group for the creative and cultural industries is another important supporter of technology-design synergy in Eindhoven. ALICE provides information – mainly through electronic media – about the many design and creative initiatives as well as about design education, clusters, festivals, organizations, subsidies and support, and European art spaces. A 2003 study on the creative sector in the Eindhoven region commanded by ALICE found that the creative industries provided employment for at least 30 000 people (8 per cent total regional employment), the construction sector employed 7 per cent, while the education and ICT sectors provided 5.5 per cent of jobs each (Stichting ALICE, 2011).

The Eindhoven Council, on the other hand, has also developed a cultural policy, 'Total culture' (Cultuur totaal), launched in 2008. 'Total culture encourages the contribution of culture to the top position of the city, accommodates talent and brings broad social groups in contact with art and culture' (Commissie Cultuur Totaal, 2010: 3). The council decided that art, music, design and urban activities would be the spearheads of the cultural policy.

Socio-spatial transformations

Eindhoven also wants to attract creative people and visitors by offering a good quality of place. But the centre still struggles with its provincial image and the lack of architectural heritage. To change this image, the city formulated the policy 'Eindhoven as a city with an attractive heart', one of the four spearheads of the city's vision for its future development. Eindhoven may not have a rich medieval past, but it has a rich industrial past, which can be a valuable asset for quality of place. Therefore, the spatial strategy has been to redevelop the city centre, reusing Philips's obsolete factory buildings and compounds for residential and cultural purposes. These interventions will deliver the 'urban atmosphere' that Eindhoven needs.

The spatial transformation of Eindhoven has been developed in three phases, beginning with the redevelopment of the Stadhuis (Municipality) and its surroundings. The second phase consisted of the renovation of the White Lady (Witte Dame), a large building of the 1920s, which became empty in the 1980s. With its 'Light Tower' dominating Eindhoven's urban landscape, the White Lady is an emblematic building for local residents, as it accommodated Philips's initial factory of light bulbs. The building was saved from demolition by a group of artists and designers who made a redevelopment plan stating that the main functions should be related to design, ICT or culture. The most important design icons of Eindhoven, the Design Academy and Philips Design were later accommodated in the renovated White Lady (see Figure 10.6).

The third phase began in 2004 and is the most spectacular. It concerns the reuse of Strijp-S, an industrial area of 27 hectares close to the city centre, which was the largest compound of the Philips industrial complex.

Figure 10.6 The White Lady and its Light Tower

This spatial intervention – fruit of cooperation between private and public partners – is turning Strijp-S into a mixed-use complex of residential (approximately 3000 dwellings), 5000 jobs, and 30 000 m^2 of commercial, cultural and leisure facilities (see Figure 10.7). As the former Strijp-S was the breeding ground of many important innovations from Philips, the new Strijp-S aspires to continue as a place for innovation, to become a unique environment, a 'living laboratory', an 'experience community'.

One of the most ambitious initiatives within Strijp-S is Light-S, linked to Eindhoven's identity as the 'City of Light', whose mission is to show visitors and residents the role of public lighting and the latest innovations in the field. The new lighting solutions will create experiences that are related to the individual characteristics of the area. Light-S is a collaboration of Park Management Strijp, NRE Network and the City of Eindhoven, in which Philips Design designs the lighting (Strijp-S, 2010).

The first phase of the transformation of Strijp-S involved its most symbolic building, the Clock Building, transformed into a 'culture factory' which currently accommodates more than a hundred creative businesses. The construction of dwellings began in June 2010, and housing corporations are currently (March 2011) offering apartments and 'industrial lofts'. Furthermore, Strijp-S has become a place for events, concerts and

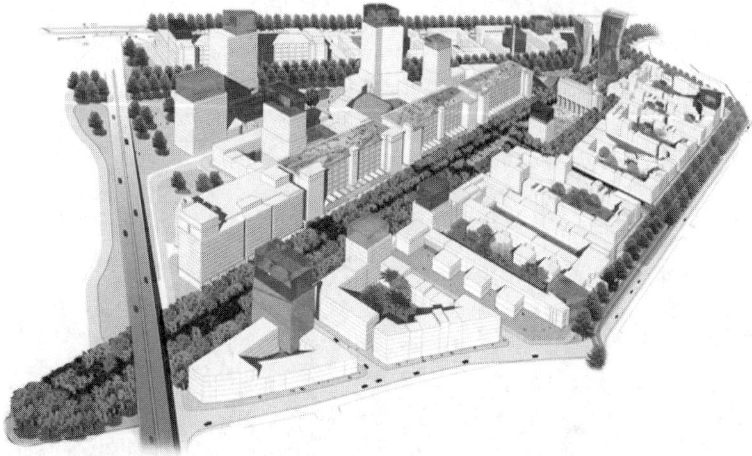

Source: Strijp-S, 2010.

Figure 10.7 Strijp-S, Master Plan of the former Philips complex

festivals. It is an important place for the Dutch Design week, but also for Flux/S, an annual international art festival, and STRP, an annual festival linking art and technology.

Besides these three significant steps towards the improvement of the quality of place of Eindhoven, the municipal department of art and culture has developed the concept 'Eindhoven laboratory city'. Among the different initiatives, it includes efforts to acquire empty buildings and to make these available for starting businesses in the creative and cultural sector (Gemeente Eindhoven, 2004).

But private initiatives are also providing accommodation and work space for artists and students. In December 2008, another vacant building (property of Philips) was occupied by a group of young artists and transformed into a cultural stronghold. After a strict selection procedure the 360 rooms (11 000 m^2) were allocated to 120 users – students of the Design Academy, of the Technical University, artists of different disciplines and a few families – who pay a low monthly fee for maintenance (de Graaf, 2009).

CONCLUSION

In the last years, knowledge-based urban development strategies have attempted to implement policies which give attention to both economic and socio-spatial aspects of city growth and development. However, some of the elements related to the socio-spatial aspects are difficult to implement in practice. To change and improve the 'urban atmosphere' of a city in order to make it attractive to creative workers is not only a matter of improving the commercial and entertainment functions of the city and branding it as creative. The practice shows that this should be a matter of a long-term strategy supported by all sectors of society.

This is precisely the case of Eindhoven, whose efforts in that direction are highly commendable. Eindhoven's strategy and corresponding projects and initiatives to make the city a design capital are not the fruit of top-down decisions, but are firmly embedded in dense and close networks among stakeholders from the different elements of the local Triple Helix. Eindhoven has experience in overcoming its own problems, and was able to reinvent itself as a high-technology region after de-industrialization processes deeply affected its economy in the 1980s and 1990s. In 2011, Eindhoven was selected for the third consecutive year as one of the seven most 'intelligent communities' of the world by the Intelligent Community Forum. As such, it should function as a role model in the current global economic context, for best practice in creating competitive local economies and pro-active societies (Intelligent Community Forum, 2011). The global recognition of Eindhoven's success story has given stakeholders and residents the necessary confidence in their experience to undertake new endeavours, such as the orientation to the creative sectors.

Despite their natural modesty, residents and stakeholders of Eindhoven exhibit a regional pride that motivates them to cooperate towards their clear and common objective to make Eindhoven a 'top-technology and design region'. Interviews with the different stakeholders revealed their clear awareness of the region's strengths and weaknesses in the new economic context. Design is widely considered as the instrument to improve the local knowledge-based development. There is a clear consensus about the position and ambitions of Eindhoven within this new context, a fact which has facilitated the orientation toward design.

Eindhoven has put an enormous amount of energy to implement urban projects that are gradually improving its attractiveness and 'urban atmosphere' by mixing residential, work and cultural functions. At the same time, the agencies and organizations in charge of putting Eindhoven on the map of design at national and international level and of linking the creative sector with high technology have done a good job, implementing many successful projects.

Thanks to the multiple public and private efforts, Eindhoven is gradually becoming an international attraction point in the field of design. It has a dense network of associations and organization dedicated to link technology and design. Local stakeholders note that students of the Design Academy do not immediately leave the city as in the past (van de Sande, 2005). The share of workforce in the creative sector in Eindhoven has increased, being among the highest in the ranking of Dutch cities (Marlet and van Woerkers, 2007). This suggests that, despite the long-term character and high level of difficulty of the process, the strategic orientation towards design has already achieved an own development dynamic in Eindhoven.

The organizational and socio-spatial initiatives of Eindhoven can serve as inspiration for other cities and regions with similar ambitions and aspirations. But to implement the lessons learned from the Eindhoven case in other situations, however, special attention should be given to other indispensable elements of Eindhoven's success story, such as the strong regional identity and the organizational qualities of the region.

REFERENCES

Amin, Ash and Nigel Thrift (1995), 'Globalisation, institutional "Thickness" and the local economy', in Patsy Healy, Stuart Cameron, Simin Davoudi, Stephen Graham and Ali Madani-Pour (eds), *Managing Cities: The New Urban Context*, London: Wiley, pp. 91–108.

Baum, Scott, Tan Yigitcanlar and Kevin O'Connor (2008), 'Creative industries and the urban hierarchy: the position of lower tier cities in the knowledge economy', in Tan Yigitcanlar, Koray Velibeyoglu and Scott Baum (eds), *Knowledge-Based Urban Development: Planning and Applications in the Information Era*, Hershey, PA: Information Science Reference, pp. 42–57.

Clark, Terry Nichols (ed.) (2004), *The City as an Entertainment Machine*, Amsterdam: Elsevier.

Commissie Cultuur Totaal (2010), Overwegingen van de Commissie Cultuur Totaal Eindhoven, www.creativeconnectioneindhoven.com/upload/pdf/Eindadvies_Commissie_Cultuurtotaal pdf, accessed 27 August 2010.

DDW (Dutch Design Week) (2010), 'About DDW', http://www.ddw.nl/content.php?lang=en&id=16, accessed 13 October 2010.

De Graaf, Peter (2009), 'Gekraakt voor de kunst: 360 kamers', *De Volkskrant*, 19 March p. 2.

Ergazakis, K., K. Metaxiotis and J. Psarras (2004), 'Towards knowledge cities: conceptual analysis and success stories', *Journal of Knowledge Management*, **8** (5), 5–15.

Etzkowitz, H. (2003), 'Innovation in innovation: the triple helix of university-industry-government relations', *Social Science Information*, **42** (3), 293–337.

Fernández-Maldonado, A.M. and A. Romein (2010), 'The role of organizational capacity and knowledge-based development: the reinvention of Eindhoven', *International Journal of Knowledge-Based Development*, **1** (1), 79–96.

Florida, Richard (2002), *The Rise of the Creative Class and How it is Transforming Work, Leisure, Community and Everyday Life,* New York: Basic Books.

Florida, Richard (2005), *The Flight of the Creative Class: The New Global Competition for Talent,* New York: Harper Collins.

Gemeente Eindhoven (2004), *Visie op Kunst en Cultuur. Eindhoven innovatieve cultuurstad,* Eindhoven.

Glaeser, E.L. and A. Saiz (2003), 'The rise of the skilled city', Harvard Institute of Economic Research, Discussion Paper number 2025.

Glaeser, E.L. and J.M. Shapiro (2001), 'Is there a new urbanism? The growth of US cities in the 1990s', *NBER Working Paper No. W8357*, http://ssrn.com/abstract=275431, accessed 2 March 2011.

Glaeser, E.L., R. La Porta, F. Lopez-de-Silanes and A. Shleifer (2004), 'Do institutions cause growth?', *Journal of Economic Growth*, **9** (3), 271–303.

Intelligent Community Forum (2011) 'Top Seven By Year', https://www.intelligentcommunity.org/index.php?src=gendocs&ref=Top7_by_Year&category=Events, accessed 8 April 2011.

Knight, R.V. (1995), 'Knowledge-based development: policy and planning implications for cities', *Urban Studies*, **32** (2), 225–260.

Kooijman, D. and A. Romein (2007), 'The limited potential of the creative city concept: policy practices in four Dutch cities', Presented at the Conference Regions in Focus, Lisbon.

Kunzmann, Klaus R. (2004), 'Culture, creativity and spatial planning', *Town Planning Review*, **75** (4), 383–404.

Landry, Charles (2000), *The Creative City: A Toolkit for Urban Innovators*, London: Earthscan.

Malecki, E.J. (2002), 'Hard and soft networks for urban competitiveness', *Urban Studies*, **39** (5–6), 929–945.

Marlet, Gerard and Clemens van Woerkens (2007), *Atlas voor Gemeenten*, Utrecht: Stichting Atlas voor Gemeenten.

Stichting ALICE (2011) 'Over ALICE', http://www.alice-eindhoven.nl/alice/over-alice-2/, accessed 4 April 2011.

Stichting Brainport (2005), *Brainport Navigator 2013. Lissabon voorbij!* Eindhoven: Stichting Brainport.

Storper, M. (2010), 'Why does a city grow? Specialization, human capital or institutions?' *Urban Studies*, **47** (10), 2027–2050.

Storper, M. and A.J. Venables (2004), 'Buzz: face-to-face contact and the urban economy', *Journal of Economic Geography*, **4** (4), 351–370.

Strijp-S (2010), 'Strijp-S, new dynamisch bruisend stadsdeel Eindhoven' www.strijp-s.nl/, accessed 24 August 2010.

Tijssen, R.J., T.N. van Leeuwen and E. van Wijk (2009), 'Benchmarking university-industry research cooperation worldwide: performance measurements and indicators based on co-authorship data for the world's largest universities', *Research Evaluation*, **18** (1), 13–24.

Trip, J.J. (2009), 'Creative city development in the Lisbon strategy: evidence from Dutch ERDF allocation', Paper Presented at the City Futures Conference, Madrid, 4–6 June.

van de Sande, E. (2005), '05: Redesigning Eindhoven', *Bright.nl. Vol van vernieuwing*, www.bright.nl/05-redesigning-eindhoven, accessed 17 August 2010.

van der Veer, J. (1998), 'Metropolitan government in Amsterdam and Eindhoven:

a tale of two cities', *Environment and Planning C: Government and Policy*, **16** (1), 25–50.

van Winden, W., L. van den Berg and P. Pol (2007), 'European cities in the knowledge economy: towards a typology', *Urban Studies*, **44** (3), 525–549.

Yigitcanlar, T. (2009), 'Planning for knowledge-based urban development: global perspectives', *Journal of Knowledge Management*, **13** (5), 228–242.

11. Clustering: concentration of the knowledge-based economy in Sydney

Richard Hu

INTRODUCTION

Sydney is Australia's top global city positioned in a global urban hierarchy as measured and ranked in an increasing number of global city literatures (Beaverstock et al., 1999; Friedmann, 1986, 1995; GaWC, 1998, 2009; Godfrey and Zhou, 1999; MasterCard Worldwide, 2008; etc.). Saskia Sassen, the author of the term 'global city', defines a global city's status from the perspective of its capacity to provide such 'producer services' as financing, banking, accounting, advertising, marketing and management consultancy and attests that these complexes of knowledge-based economy activities are usually located in central business districts (CBDs) of a few global cities (Sassen, 1995, 2001). This theorization of the global city and the clustering of the knowledge-based economy in the central city area is supposed to be applicable to Sydney too given the scholarly consensus on Sydney's status as a global city. A group of researchers have testified the argument of Sydney's status as a global city and the clustering of advanced producer services or the 'financialization' of workers in Central Sydney (Baum, 1997; Daly and Pritchard, 2000; O'Connor and Stimson, 1995; O'Neill and McGuirk, 2003; Searle, 1996, 1998b, 2008). However, an empirical study of how the knowledge-based economy has been concentrated in Central Sydney compared to Metropolitan Sydney in a systematic manner, and how this concentration has shifted temporally, will contribute to the literature and help testify the theories.

This chapter aims to make an empirical contribution to understanding the clustering of the knowledge-based economy in Central Sydney. In order to measure to what extent the knowledge-based economy is concentrated in Central Sydney and how this concentration has changed over time, I used the Location Quotient (LQ) tool to compare the employment by industries in Central Sydney with Metropolitan Sydney in 1996–2006.

The data of employment by industries were based on place of work and collected from Australian censuses in 1996 and 2006. The results indicate which industries are concentrated in Central Sydney, which industries with concentration fall into the category of the knowledge-based economy, and how the concentration patterns have shifted in a time series. Through systematically and temporally measuring the employment by industries in Central Sydney with reference to Metropolitan Sydney, the findings provide a holistic understanding of the concentration of the knowledge-based economy in Sydney, and testify and support the theories on the clustering of the knowledge-based economy in the central city areas.

CLUSTERING AND THE KNOWLEDGE-BASED ECONOMY

The term 'knowledge-based economy' is not new. A full genealogy of it could trace back to the 1960–1970s when buzzwords like 'knowledge society' or 'information economy' were invented (Godin, 2006, p. 18). Its resurgence in the 1990s was a result of the advancement of new information and communication technology (ICT) and its popularity was largely attributed to the dissemination of the Organisation for Economic Co-operation and Development (OECD). In 1996, the OECD stated that 'knowledge is now recognized as the driver of productivity and economic growth', and defined the knowledge-based economies as 'economies which are directly based on the production, distribution and use of knowledge and information' (OECD, 1996, p. 3). A shift to knowledge-based growth has been characterized by falling costs and rising efficiency in the transmission, retrieval, and analysis of information. According to the OECD (1996), the most distinguishing feature of a knowledge-based economy is the pervasive presence of knowledge as an input and an output throughout the economy. Thus, in a knowledge-based economy, the ability to create wealth is increasingly dependent on the effective management of knowledge, that is, 'the organizational capability to create, acquire, accumulate, disseminate, and exploit information and knowledge' (Gera and Mang, 1998, p. 150). The industries which fit the definition of the knowledge-based economy include: high- to medium-tech manufacturing; high-tech services; business services; financial services; health and education services; cultural and recreational services; and international transport services (Brinkley, 2008).

The knowledge-based economies indicate more tendencies towards geographical concentration or clustering than traditional less or low knowledge-based economies, suggesting enhanced association between agglomeration and productivity performance (Gabe and Abel, 2010; Sonn and Park, 2010). There have been numerous scholarly literatures on the geographical clustering of business activities and industry production. However, not many offer explanations specifically in relation to the context of the knowledge-based economies, especially to the concentrations of such industries as advanced producer services occurring in particular regions and in particular parts of cities, like the central cities. The basic clustering theories of the localization externalities, including a large pool of specialized labour, a large number of specialized local providers of intermediate inputs and services, and the positive technological spill-over (Krugman, 1991; Marshall, 1927), help explain the new knowledge-based economies too. The advantages of geographical proximity, such as traditional external economies of scale out of shared physical infrastructure and reduced transaction costs, and enhanced circulation of knowledge as well as inter-firm collaboration and networking (Porter, 1998), makes no differentiation of applicability between traditional manufacturing industries and new knowledge-based industries. However, they are far from sufficient to explain the clustering of the knowledge-based economy with the fullest plausibility.

The knowledge-based economy has witnessed significant cost reduction and efficiency improvement in transmitting and transacting knowledge and knowledge-related products and services through the mediation of the ICT. Nonetheless, the predicted 'death of distance' or 'death of cities' did not occur in a digital age, and has not indicated any sign of taking place in the foreseeable future either. Conversely, agglomeration of the knowledge-based economy persists and is becoming even denser. Two strands of theories specific to the context of the knowledge-based economy have been posited to explain this seemingly counter-intuitive phenomenon. Both strands of theories are centred on the characteristics and behaviours of the knowledge workers, the actors of the knowledge-based economy, to justify the non market-based externalities of the clustering of the knowledge-based economy.

One strand of theories is related to the indispensability of the face-to-face contact in today's knowledge production process. Storper and Venables (2004) suggest that the face-to-face contact is an important mechanism for co-ordinating economic activities, particularly those embedded in tacit knowledge and creativity in which people learn by doing and being around others. This important role of the face-to-face contact in the knowledge-based economy is attributed to the unique behavioural and communicational properties which give the face-to-face contact specific advantages as a technology of communication, coordination, and motivation. The major properties of the face-to-face contact include: it is an efficient communication technology; it allows actors to align commitments and thereby reduces incentive problems; it allows screening of agents; and it motivates effort (Storper and Venables, 2004, pp. 353–357). This kind of human capital externalities differs by particular types of workers. The knowledge acquisition required to drive innovation nowadays implies ever more frequent interactions between agents in order to share knowledge (McCann, 2007). In contrast to the knowledge-based activities which often require direct and instant contact to solve unforeseeable uncertainties, the knowledge spill-over facilitated by the face-to-face contact is of less importance to low-skilled labourers and personal service providers (Gabe and Abel, 2010).

The other strand of theories is related to diversity and the necessary density to generate diversity, which contribute to the productivity of the knowledge workers, or creative talents. Diversity in cultures and expertises leads to a high degree of knowledge production and diffusion, and diversity promotes tolerance to new ideas (Florida, 2002a; Jacobs, 1969). Urban areas with density offer a higher degree of diversity of specializations, and more favourable environments of innovation and knowledge production. An expert can easily contact people with similar or different specialties to exchange ideas and generate knowledge in large cities, especially the central city areas. Workers of the knowledge-based economy, who are mostly college educated and have particular creative talents, tend to congregate to capitalize from the benefits of clustering (Florida, 2002a, 2008).

METHODOLOGY

I used the LQ analysis to measure the clustering of the knowledge-based economy in Central Sydney in relation to Metropolitan Sydney in 1996–2006. The LQ analysis is widely used 'to identify the concentration of an industrial sector in a local economy relative to a larger reference economy' (Blakely and Bradshaw, 2002, p. 122). Employment is the most used variable in the LQ analysis which defines a ratio of employment shares: the local industry's share of total local employment compared with the industry's employment share in a wider reference region (regional, national, or even international) (Klosterman, 1990). An LQ > 1 indicates a higher than average degree of specialization in that sector locally compared with the reference region, and is interpreted as an indicator of concentration and competitive advantage (Spencer et al., 2010).

Geographically Central Sydney and Metropolitan Sydney are respectively represented by Sydney Local Government Area (LGA) and

Sydney Statistical Division (SD) in the Australian Statistical Geography Standards (ASGS) 2006 classified by the Australian Bureau of Statistics (ABS) for census data purposes.[1] The geographies and comparisons of Sydney LGA and Sydney SD in area, population and employment are shown in Figure 11.1 and Table 11.1.

The implementation of the research includes the following steps:

1. I collected the 1996 and 2006 census data on industry of employment for Sydney LGA and Sydney SD from the ABS. The census data was based on the place of work and collected by two digit industry subdivisions in the Australian and New Zealand Standard Industrial Classification (ANZSIC) 1993.
2. I calculated the LQs for all the industry subdivisions in Sydney LGA in 1996 and 2006 by the equation: $LQ_i = e_i/e_T \div E_i/E_T$ (e_i = employment in industry subdivision i in Sydney LGA, e_T = total employment in Sydney LGA, E_i = employment in industry subdivision i in Sydney SD, E_T = total employment in Sydney SD).
3. I selected the industry subdivisions with LQ>1 and employment share (that is e_i/e_T)>1 per cent in Central Sydney in 2006,[2] and calculated the selected industry subdivisions' employment changes and LQ changes in 1996–2006 respectively.
4. I displayed the results in three modes to interpret clustering: to what extent the knowledge-based economy was concentrated in Central Sydney, and how the concentration shifted over the period 1996–2006.
   - Mode 1: All concentrated industries of employment (with LQ>1 in 2006) are listed according to their LQs in 2006 from the highest to the lowest (displayed in Table 11.2);
   - Mode 2: All concentrated industries of employment (with LQ>1 in 2006) are plotted in the Growth Share Matrix diagram measuring employment shares, LQs and employment changes developed by Information Design Associates with ICF Kaiser International (1997) and ICF Consulting (2000). The Growth Share Matrix diagram simultaneously conveys information about the sizes of employment (in 2006), the employment changes (in 1996–2006), and the LQs of employment (in 2006) for concentrated industry subdivisions (LQ>1 in 2006) in Central Sydney by aligning employment changes along the horizontal axis, aligning LQs along the vertical axis, and plotting individual industries with 'bubbles' proportional to the numbers of their employment shares (displayed in Figure 11.2);

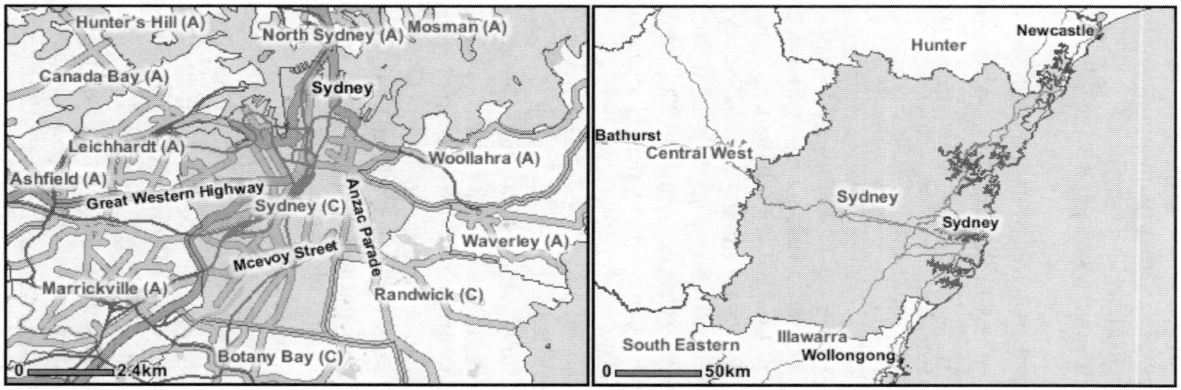

Source: Australian Bureau of Statistics.

Figure 11.1 Maps of Sydney LGA and Sydney SD

Table 11.1 Specifications of Sydney LGA and Sydney SD

Locality	Area	Population (2006)	Employment (2006)
Sydney LGA	29 km^2	180474	357767
Sydney SD	12428 km^2	4148570	1736824
LGA's Share in SD (%)	0.23	4.35	20.6

Source: Australian Bureau of Statistics.

- Mode 3: All concentrated industries of employment (with LQ>1 in 2006) are plotted in the Relative Share Matrix diagram measuring employment shares, LQs and LQ changes developed by Hu (2009). The Relative Share Matrix diagram simultaneously conveys information about the sizes of employment (in 2006), the LQ changes (in 1996–2006), and the LQs of employment (in 2006) for concentrated industry subdivisions (LQ>1 in 2006) in Central Sydney by aligning LQ changes along the horizontal axis, aligning LQs along the vertical axis, and plotting individual industries with 'bubbles' proportional to the numbers of their employment shares (displayed in Figure 11.3).

5. I interpreted the displayed data results to summarize to what extent the knowledge-based economy was concentrated in Central Sydney in different modes, and how the concentration patterns had shifted in 1996–2006.

RESULTS

Of the total 69 industry subdivisions by the ANZSIC 1993, 16 industry subdivisions had LQs more than 1 and employment share more than 1 per cent in 2006 in Sydney LGA. That is to say, these 16 industries were concentrated in Central Sydney compared to Metropolitan Sydney as measured by employment. The analysis and interpretation is thus focused on these 16 industry subdivisions.

The 16 subdivided industries are mostly services industries and can be categorized into three broad groups according to the nature of the services: commercial services; cultural and media services; and public and amenity services (see Table 11.2). The commercial services refer to the highly specialized services for business activities (finance, insurance, business, and property services). The cultural and media services are those services

Table 11.2 *Measuring employments of industry subdivisions and their LQs in 1996 and 2006*

Industry subdivisions (ANZSIC93)	Sydney LGA employment 1996	Sydney SD employment 1996	Sydney LGA employment share 1996 (%)	Sydney LGA LQ 1996	Sydney LGA employment 2006	Sydney SD employment 2006	Sydney LGA employment share 2006 (%)	Sydney LGA LQ 2006	Sydney LGA LQ change 1996–2006 (%)	Sydney LGA employment change 1996–2006 (%)
■ 75 Services to Finance & insurance	12453	19429	4.06	3.22	24528	38292	6.86	3.11	−3	97
■ 74 Insurance	10120	20304	3.30	2.50	13070	22659	3.65	2.80	12	29
■ 73 Finance	29675	58508	9.68	2.55	29815	55898	8.33	2.59	2	0
• 92 Libraries, museums & the arts	4818	11472	1.57	2.11	4711	10340	1.32	2.21	5	−2
♦ 62 Rail transport	2996	8547	0.98	1.76	4966	11046	1.39	2.18	24	66
• 91 Motion picture, radio & television services	3319	12652	1.08	1.32	5635	13964	1.58	1.96	49	70
♦ 82 Defence	3186	11961	1.04	1.34	4447	11262	1.24	1.92	43	40
■ 78 Business services	53668	174253	17.51	1.55	74085	211570	20.71	1.70	10	38
♦ 66 Services to transport	7472	18986	2.44	1.98	7184	20966	2.01	1.66	−16	−4

● 24 Printing, publishing & recorded media	9006	32284	2.94	1.40	10022	30526	2.80	1.59	14	11
◆ 81 Government administration	19590	49435	6.39	1.99	21011	66326	5.87	1.54	−23	7
◆ 71 Communication services	11145	36849	3.64	1.52	9935	33227	2.78	1.45	−4	−11
◆ 57 Accommodation, cafes & restaurants	18580	71304	6.06	1.31	21377	81233	5.98	1.28	−2	15
◆ 96 Other services	9831	30302	3.21	1.63	8083	35141	2.26	1.12	−31	−18
● 93 Sport & recreation	3826	16813	1.25	1.14	4368	20289	1.22	1.05	−9	14
■ 77 Property services	5511	24610	1.80	1.12	6597	31306	1.84	1.02	−9	20
. . .										
Total employment in the studies areas	306469	1539593	100.00	1.00	357767	1736824	100.00	1.00	0	17

Note: Commercial services ■; Cultural and media services ●; Public and amenity services ◆.

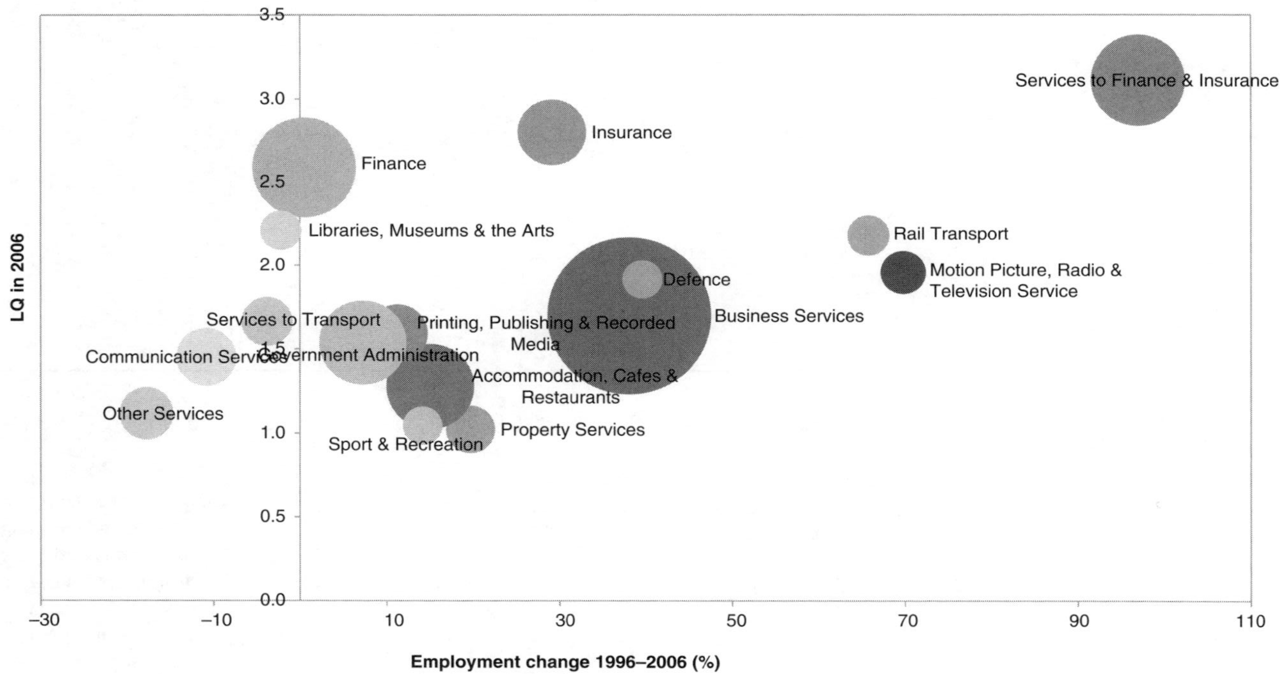

Figure 11.2 Measuring employment shares of industry subdivisions, LQs and employment changes

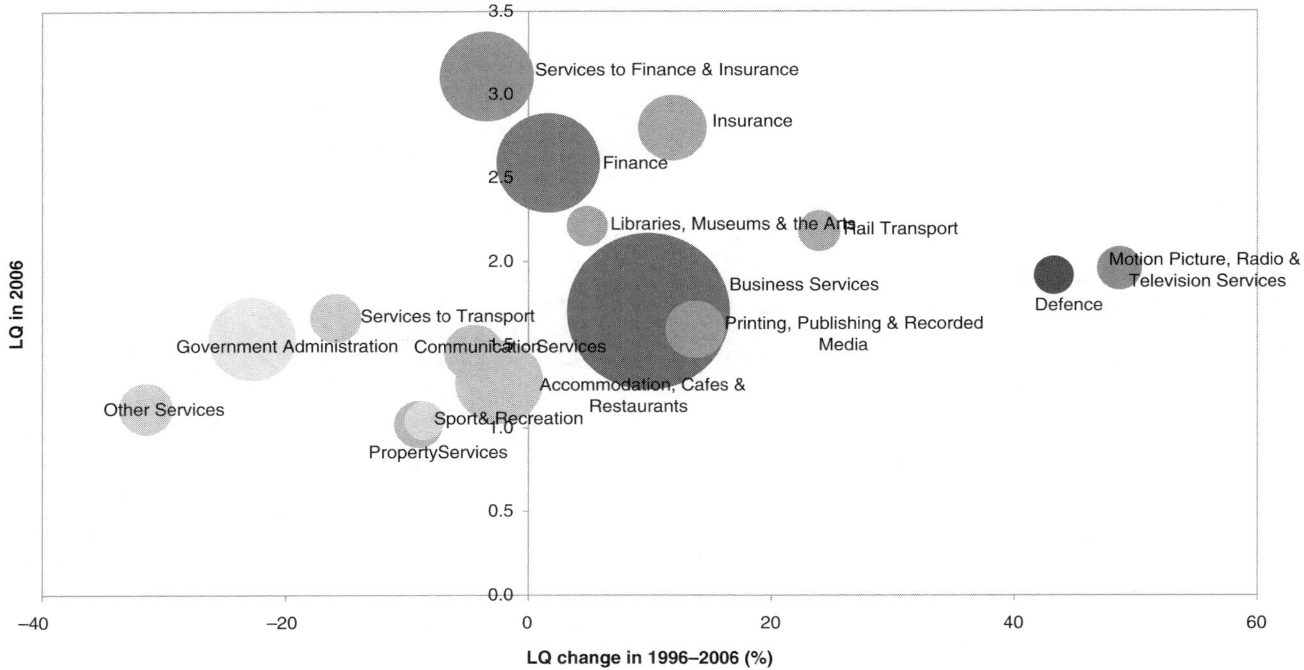

Figure 11.3   Measuring employment shares of industry subdivisions, LQs and LQ changes

which are informing, educating and entertaining people. The public and amenity services refer to the government administration, infrastructure and amenity services such as transport, communication and urban amenities (accommodation, cafes and restaurants). Judged by the nature of products and services of the three industry groups, industries in both the commercial services group and the cultural and media services group well fit the definition of the knowledge-based economy. The commercial services group, the cultural and media services group, and the public and amenity services group respectively accounted for 42 per cent, 7 per cent, and 22 per cent of total employment in Central Sydney in 2006. In total the three concentrated industry groups accounted for around 71 per cent of Central Sydney's total employment, among which the knowledge-based economy accounted for almost 50 per cent of the total employment and almost 70 per cent of the concentrated employments of industries in Central Sydney in 2006.

Table 11.2 lists the concentrated industry subdivisions by the sequence of their LQs in 2006 from the highest to the lowest. Industry subdivisions in the commercial services are the most concentrated in Central Sydney, especially in finance and insurance services. Though the industry subdivision Business Services in the commercial services group does not have a high LQ value (1.7), its employment share of 20.71 per cent guarantees its strong position as a clustered industry in Central Sydney. Some industry subdivisions from the other two services groups indicate quite high LQs in 2006, however, their rather small employment shares (Libraries, Museums and the Arts, 1.32 per cent; Rail Transport, 1.39 per cent; Motion Picture, Radio and Television Services, 1.58 per cent; Defence, 1.24 per cent) impact their bases as being industries with clustering.

Figure 11.2 and Figure 11.3 visually display the results in Table 11.2. Both Figure 11.2 and Figure 11.3 provide information of the LQs, employment shares of the clustered industry subdivisions, but respectively display their employment changes and LQ changes in 1996–2006. The two diagrams better illustrate how these clustered industries are compared with each other and had changed over the one decade period 1996–2006. Measured by sheer employment shares, top industries in Central Sydney are business services (21 per cent), finance (8 per cent), services to finance and insurance (7 per cent), and accommodation, cafes and restaurants (6 per cent) in contrast to the top industries measured by LQs, which are services to finance and insurance (3.11), insurance (2.80), finance (2.59), and libraries, museums and the arts (2.21). Figure 11.2 indicates that the majority of the clustered industries in Central Sydney had employment growth in 1996 and 2006 except for two industries which lost employment numbers modestly. Figure 11.3 indicates that half of the 16 concentrated industries in Central Sydney increased their degree of clustering with positive LQ changes while the other half of the industries decreased their degree of clustering with negative LQ changes in 1996–2006. The different patterns of employment changes and LQ changes of the clustered industries occur because the LQ changes depend on the employment numbers of the industries in Metropolitan Sydney region too. Figure 11.3 also indicates that, overall, industries with higher LQs tended to have positive LQ changes in 1996–2006, denoting an increasing trend of clustering of their employments. This increasing trend of clustering happened to established commercial services industries such as Finance, Insurance, and Business Services, as well as new creative cultural and media services such as Motion Picture, Radio and Television Services, and Libraries, Museums and the Arts, all of which are categorized as the knowledge-based economy.

DISCUSSION

The results of the data analysis show that the knowledge-based economy was on a trend of increasing clustering in Central Sydney in 1996–2006 in two broad groups of industry subdivisions: commercial services, and cultural and media services.

Sydney has been Australia's urban leader for its capacity of providing advanced commercial services since the 1980s. Sydney was the main urban beneficiary of Australia's increasingly globalized commodity and financial markets (Searle, 2008) as the central locus of international corporate headquarters and financial offices. By 1988, Sydney had 150 head offices of international institutions (43 in Melbourne) and 155 of the 185 Australian head offices of foreign banks (Daly and Stimson, 1992). In 1997 and 1998, some 61 multinational corporations set up Asia Pacific regional headquarters in Sydney, more than four times the total for any other Australian or New Zealand city (Daly and Pritchard, 2000). Comparing Sydney's employment structure with overseas cities indicates that Sydney's performance in finance and business services in the mid 1990s was approaching that of New York and London in the mid 1980s (Searle, 1996). A study done by the accountancy firm Price Waterhouse Coopers in 1998 compared Sydney with seven international cities (New York, London, Frankfurt, Singapore, Atlanta, Vancouver, and Kuala Lumpur) and concluded that Sydney was performing reasonably well across a wide range of measures (Price Waterhouse Coopers, 1998). Hall (1995) placed Sydney in the ranking of sub-global cities then, but other scholars including Searle (1996), O'Connor and Stimson (1995), Lepani et al. (1995), Newton (1995) and Baum (1997) argued that Sydney's economic characteristics of finance and producer services were indicative of its emergence as Australia's global city in the late 1980s and early 1990s. Geographically, these advanced commercial services indicating Sydney's growing status as a global city were concentrated in Central Sydney. The findings of this research reveal the continuing growth and clustering of these advanced commercial services of the knowledge-based economy in Central Sydney in the period 1996–2006.

Saskia Sassen defines a global city's status as its capacity to provide 'producer services' such as financing, banking, accounting, advertising, marketing and management consultancy and attests that these complexes of the knowledge-based economy are usually located in CBDs of a few global cities (Sassen, 1995, 2001). Searle (1998a) investigates changes in producer services location in Sydney based on an analysis of four industries of management consultancy, insurance, graphic design and data processing and concludes that 'globalization appears to have reinforced the traditional central city focus of Sydney's producer services sector' (Searle, 1998a, p. 237). Forrest (1996) examines the spatial clustering of the journey to work in Sydney and points out a decreasing dependence on the central city as a focus of employment other than those employed in the business, finance and information service sector. Research by O'Neill and McGuirk (2002) indicates that the surge of finance-based economic activities in Central Sydney helped sustain Australian economic prosperity in the late 1990s. The findings of these researches converge to point to the clustering of the advanced producer services in Central Sydney. This research has strengthened the literature by making a systematic analysis of the concentration of the knowledge-based economy in Central Sydney in 1996–2006, and supporting the argument for Sydney as a growing global city.

Apart from the increasing clustering of the commercial services, especially producer services as discussed above, Central Sydney's growing role as a knowledge-based economy centre is also seen in its increasing concentration of the cultural and media services in 1996–2006. This is indicative of some forms of urban functional transformations towards a hub of cultural and media services in Central Sydney. The clustering of the creative industries of cultural and media services in Central Sydney and Sydney's capacity of providing such services in a global context were attested by other researchers from different approaches too. Searle and Valence (2005) find an emerging inner Sydney multimedia cluster including graphic design, advertising and related media. They base their study on an empirical analysis of the multimedia firms' geographical locations in metropolitan Sydney area and observe the high concentration of the new information industry in Central Sydney as part of a shift towards an information economy (Searle and Valence, 2005). Set in a global context, Sydney's performance in the knowledge-based creative industries of cultural and media services was impressive too. In the index ranking global cities' capacity of providing producer services released by the Globalization and World Cities (GaWC) program at Loughborough University, Sydney ranked fifth in advertising performance of major global cities (Taylor, 2008, p. 56). Sydney's performance in other categories of producer services, such as accountancy, banking and financing, insurance, law, and management consultancy, was less impressive in a global context. Florida's (2002b, 2005) theory of creative class provides an explanatory framework for the increasing clustering of the creative cultural and media services in Central Sydney. The creative workers required by the new knowledge-based economy driven by information technology are the urban lifestyle class (Florida, 2002b) and they are globally mobile electronic migrants (Blakely, 2001; Florida, 2005). Sydney's cityscapes – built and natural lifestyle environment, and social tolerance and cultural diversity – are important assets of the city's competitiveness for a creative economy and creative city (Gibson, 2006; Throsby, 2006).

CONCLUSION

In this chapter I measured to what extent the knowledge-based economy was clustered in Central Sydney and how the clustering patterns of the knowledge-based economy had shifted in 1996–2006. Key findings include (1) the majority of the clustered industries in Central Sydney are knowledge-based services; (2) apart from the public and amenity services which support the local as well as the regional/national economy, the concentrated knowledge-based economy in Central Sydney basically falls into two broad groups – commercial services, and cultural and media services; (3) the clustering of commercial services and cultural and media services in Central Sydney was on a growing trend in 1996–2006. This chapter adds to the literature on the clustering of the knowledge-based economy in Sydney, and testifies Sydney's status as a growing global city as measured by its capacity of providing knowledge-based producer services and new creative industries with clustering in the central city area.

NOTES

1. Sydney LGA is the jurisdictional area of the local government City of Sydney which is very small in area (29 sq km) and population (180 474), and is generally regarded as Central Sydney encompassing the core CBD and its surrounding area. There is not

a metropolitan level of jurisdictional government in Greater Sydney. In practice, the geographical classification of Sydney Statistical Division (SD) defined by the Australian Bureau of Statistics (ABS) for census data collection purposes is used to refer to the metropolitan Sydney area which covers 43 LGAs in total.

2. One industry with LQ>1 in Central Sydney indicates its employment concentration in a relative sense, that is, relative to the industry's employment in the reference region of Metropolitan Sydney. However, one industry with LQ>1 does not necessarily indicate its employment concentration in an absolute sense. There are industries with very high LQs, but very small employment sizes. For example, the industry subdivision of Services to Mining had an extremely high LQ of 2.53 in Central Sydney in 2006, but its employment share was 0.09 per cent – too low an employment share to justify its concentration of employment. So only industry subdivisions with LQ>1 and employment share>1 per cent in Central Sydney in 2006 are regarded as industries with a certain degree of concentration of employment compared to Metropolitan Sydney.

REFERENCES

Baum, S. (1997), 'Sydney, Australia: a global city? Testing the social polarisation thesis', *Urban Studies,* **34** (11), 1881–1901.

Beaverstock, J.V., P.J. Taylor and R.G. Smith (1999), 'A roster of world cities', *Cities,* **16** (6), 445–458.

Blakely, E. (2001), 'Competitive advantage for the 21st-century city: can a place-based approach to economic development survive in a cyberspace age?', *APA Journal,* **67** (2), 133–144.

Blakely, E. and T. Bradshaw (2002), *Planning Local Economic Development: Theory and Practice* (3rd edn), Thousand Oaks, CA: Sage Publications.

Brinkley, I. (2008), *The Knowledge Economy: How Knowledge is Reshaping the Economic Life of Nations*, London: The Work Foundation.

Daly, M. and B. Pritchard (2000), 'Sydney: Australia's financial and corporate capital', in J. Connell (ed.), *Sydney: The Emergence of a World City*, Melbourne: Oxford University Press.

Daly, M. and R. Stimson (1992), 'Sydney: Australia's gateway and financial capital', in E. Blakely and R. Stimson (eds), *New Cities of the Pacific Rim*, Berkeley, CA: Institute of Urban and Regional Development, University of California, Berkeley.

Florida, R. (2002a), *The Rise of the Creative Cities*, New York: Basic Books.

Florida, R. (2002b), *The Rise of the Creative Class: And How It's Transforming Work, Leisure, Community and Everyday Life*, New York: Basic Books.

Florida, R. (2005), *The Flight of the Creative Class: The New Global Competition for Talent*, New York: Harper Business.

Florida, R. (2008), *Who's Your City?*, New York: Basic Books.

Forrest, J. (1996), 'Place of residence, place of work: the spatial clustering of the journey to work in Sydney', *Australian Planner,* **33** (3), 132–135.

Friedmann, J. (1986), 'The world city hypothesis', *Development and Change,* **17** (1), 69–84.

Friedmann, J. (1995), 'Where we stand: a decade of world city research', in P.L. Knox and P.J. Taylor (eds), *World Cities in a World System*, Cambridge: Cambridge University Press.

Gabe, T. and J.R. Abel (2010), 'Agglomeration of knowledge', *Urban Studies,* Online 10 September 2010, 1–19. doi:10.1177/0042098010371988.
GaWC (1998), 'The world according to GaWC 1998', http://www.lboro.ac.uk/gawc/citymap.html, accessed 7 November 2006.
GaWC (2009), 'The world according to GaWC', http://www.lboro.ac.uk/gawc/gawcworlds.html, accessed 20 March 2009.
Gera, S. and K. Mang (1998), 'The knowledge-based economy: shifts in industrial output', *Canadian Public Policy*, **24** (2), 149–184.
Gibson, C. (2006), 'Sydney's creative economy: social and spatial challenges', in R. Freestone, B. Randolph and C. Butler-Bowdon (eds), *Talking about Sydney: Population, Community and Culture in Contemporary Sydney*, Sydney: University of New South Wales Press.
Godfrey, B.J. and Y. Zhou (1999), 'Ranking world cities: multinational corporations and the global urban hierarchy', *Urban Geography*, **20** (3), 268–281.
Godin, B. (2006), 'The knowledge-based economy: conceptual framework or buzzword?', *Journal of Technology Transfer*, **31**, 17–30.
Hall, P. (1995), 'Towards a general urban theory', in J. Brotchie, M. Batty, E. Blakely, P. Hall and P. Newton (eds), *Cities in Competition: Productive and Sustainable Cities for the 21st Century*, Melbourne: Longman Australia.
Hu, R. (2009), *Transforming Sydney and San Francisco* (PhD thesis), Sydney: University of Sydney.
ICF Consulting (2000), *Toronto Competes: An Assessment of Toronto's Global Competitiveness*, Toronto: City of Toronto Economic Development Office.
Information Design Associates with ICF Kaiser International (1997), *Cluster-Based Economic Development: A Key to Regional Competitiveness*, Washington DC: Economic Development Administration, US Department of Commerce.
Jacobs, J. (1969), *The Economy of Cities*, New York: Vintage.
Klosterman, R.E. (1990), *Community Analysis and Planning Techniques*, Savage, Maryland: Rowman & Littlefield Publishers.
Krugman, P. (1991), *Geography and Trade*, Cambridge, MA: MIT Press.
Lepani, B., G. Freed, P. Murphy and A. McGillivray (1995), *The Economic Role of Cities: Australia in the Global Economy*, Canberra: Commonwealth Department of Housing and Regional Development.
Marshall, A. (1927) *Industry and Trade*, London: Macmillan.
MasterCard Worldwide (2008), *Worldwide Centers of Commerce Index 2008*, New York: MasterCard Worldwide.
McCann, P. (2007), 'Sketching out a model of innovation, face-to-face interaction and economic geography', *Spatial Economic Analysis*, **2**, 117–134.
Newton, P. (1995), 'Changing places? Households, firms and urban hierarchies in the information age', in J. Brotchie, M. Batty, E. Blakely, P. Hall and P. Newton (eds), *Cities in Competition: Productive and Sustainable Cities for the 21st Century*, Melbourne: Longman Australia.
O'Connor, K. and R. Stimson (1995), *The Economic Role of Cities: Economic Change and City Development, Australia, 1971–1991*, Canberra: Commonwealth Department of Housing and Regional Development.
O'Neill, P. and P. McGuirk (2002), 'Prosperity along Australia's eastern seaboard: Sydney and the geopolitics of urban and economic change', *Australian Geographer*, **33** (3), 241–261.
O'Neill, P. and P. McGuirk (2003), 'Reconfiguring the CBD: work and discourses of design in Sydney's office space', *Urban Studies*, **40** (9), 1751–1767.

OECD (1996), *The Knowledge-Based Economy*, Paris: Organization for Economic Co-operation and Development.

Porter, M. (1998), 'Clusters and competition: new agendas for companies, governments, and institutions' in M. Porter (ed.), *On Competition*, Cambridge, MA: Harvard Business Review Books.

Price Waterhouse Coopers (1998), *Sydney 2020: The City We Want (summary report)*, Sydney: Price Waterhouse Coopers.

Sassen, S. (1995), 'On concentration and centrality in the global city', in P. Knox and P. Taylor (eds), *Cities in Competition*, Cambridge: Cambridge University Press.

Sassen, S. (2001), *The Global City: New York, London, Tokyo*, New Jersey: Princeton University Press.

Searle, G. (1996), *Sydney as a Global City*, Sydney: Department of Urban Affairs and Planning.

Searle, G. (1998a), 'Changes in producer services location, Sydney: globalization, technology and labour', *Asia Pacific Viewpoint*, **39** (2), 237–255.

Searle, G. (1998b), 'Planning for global activities in Sydney', *Australian Planner*, **35** (1), 15–23.

Searle, G. (2008), 'The impacts of contemporary globalization on Australian cities', in B. Braun and A. Schuttemeyer (eds), *Australia Global: Australien im prozess der globalisierung*, Tubingen, Germany: Stauffenburg Verlag.

Searle, G. and G.D. Valence (2005), 'The urban emergence of a new information industry: Sydney's multimedia firms', *Geographical Research*, **43** (2), 238–253.

Sonn, J.W. and I.K. Park (2010), 'The increasing importance of agglomeration economies hidden behind convergence: geography of knowledge production', *Urban Studies*, online 25 November 2010, 1–15. doi:10.1177/0042098010382679.

Spencer, G.M., T. Vinodrai, M.S. Gertler and D.A. Wolfe (2010), 'Do clusters make a difference? Defining and assessing their economic performance', *Regional Studies*, **44** (6), 697–715.

Storper, M. and A.J. Venables (2004), 'Buzz: face-to-face contact and the urban economy', *Journal of Economic Geography*, **4** (4), 351–370.

Taylor, P. (2008), 'World city network', in C. Johnson and R. Hu (eds), *Connecting Cities: Networks*, Sydney: Metropolis Congress 2008.

Throsby, D. (2006), 'The economics of the creative city: iconic architecture and the urban experience', in R. Freestone, B. Randolph and C. Butler-Bowdon (eds), *Talking About Sydney: Population, Community and Culture in Contemporary Sydney*, Sydney: University of New South Wales Press.

12. Connecting: community supported universities for knowledge city transformation

Ana Cristina Fachinelli and Janaína Macke

INTRODUCTION

This study describes and analyses the elements that compose social capital, emphasizing the promotion of community transformation and the role of a regional university. Our study was made in the city of Caxias do Sul, located in the southern region of Brazil. The regional university is the University of Caxias do Sul (UCS), which is a community supported university (CSU) – as we will describe later on, it has a different concept from the community college idea in the USA.

In order to analyze the case of Caxias do Sul and its university, it is important to note that the model of the community supported university, and the knowledge city (KC) concept, have in their basis the idea of social capital as one of the essential elements for operational functioning. The social capital can be understood as the human capital that sets the structures forming the institutions of group cooperation. In fact, the social capital is a resource (Coleman, 1990) and is productive because it allows certain objectives to be reached that would not happen without it (Coleman, 1990). The effects expected can occur in two different ways: individual and collective. The individual social capital approach can be seen in social relations, in the form of trust and norms of reciprocity (Durston, 2000).

However, the collective social capital approach appears in complex institutions through collaboration and management. On the other hand, knowledge-based development does not exist in interpersonal relations, but in complex systems and in the common structures of management and sanction. For this reason, the classical definition of the community includes aspects such as activities coordinated with a certain common purpose, self-government, cultural superstructure and sense of identity (Durston, 2000). Some of these aspects can be observed in the case of the community supported university – University of Caxias do Sul – in southern Brazil.

The Brazilian model of community supported universities was developed mostly in the countryside of the states of Santa Catarina and Rio Grande do Sul, during the 1950s. However, its origin is dated as far back as the 19th century during the period of intense European immigration, when German and Italian immigrant communities were set up and established community schools, mainly for basic education.

From the beginning, the CSUs were treated by the same legal standards as the private and confessional universities. At the moment, there is an amendment under study in the National Congress known as Act 7639/2010, addressing the definition, qualification, prerogatives, and the purpose of the CSUs. The approval of the amendment will be the recognition of the social and historical function of these universities, in places in the countryside where traditional universities did not want to settle.

The CSUs are the result of the joint efforts of various social segments, emerging from local (municipal) authorities in a way to coordinate elements of the civic community. They were intended to raise the socioeconomic and cultural levels of the communities, in areas less supported by state and federal institutions. These local initiatives show advantages in comparison to the larger metropolitan and culturally urban areas, in the educational perspective (Machado, 2009).

Currently, the CSUs are joined in an association, the Brazilian Association of Community Supported Universities (*Associação Brasileira das Universidades Comunitárias* – ABRUC), which groups 54 nonprofit institutions of higher education. In the state of Rio Grande do Sul, the CSU form the Consortium of *Gaúcho* Community Supported Universities (COMUNG), in almost all municipalities in the countryside, providing education, science and technologies courses.

The COMUNG institutions account for more than 40 colleges, serve more than 380 municipalities and have more than 180000 undergraduate and graduate students. Today the CSUs represent the largest system of higher education in Rio Grande do Sul. These universities provide two major services: (a) higher education in communities where this was not available; and (b) stimulating the participation of the community educational system.

A community supported university is not subjected to corporate interest, its assets are not the property of any individual, cannot be given to anyone as inheritance, and have a net of relationships of common interests with the community. It acquires a public dimension, even though not a state or federal university (Frantz and Silva, 2002).

Therefore, this study aims to analyze the elements that compose social capital through a community supported university. Moreover, the deep understanding of how the relationships are established among social capital and the values of a knowledge city can be a central element for governance and for creation of public policies.

THE KNOWLEDGE CITY CONCEPT: A TRANSFORMATION FACTOR

In the last 30 years, one of the most important points in the global economy is the creation of the concept of value in a knowledge-based economy (Martinez, 2006). 'Basically, the so-called Knowledge Economy. . .is a transition from predominantly material-based value production systems to predominantly knowledge-based value-production systems' (Carrillo, 2006, p. 44).

In the context of regional development, the concept of 'value' has already been seen with the emergence of the knowledge city, 'where the political agenda is developing the context or structural capital from human capital growth to collective wealth' (Edvinsson, 2006, p. 63).

In spite of the many cities that have been proclaimed as KC and many others that aim to become KC, the 'common framework for the understanding and development of a KC' is still under construction (Carrillo, 2006, p. 43), but has already benefited from the success stories of KCs (Ergazakis et al., 2006). Thus, global communities are configured around an organization of values.

In a review of major publications in the field, Ron Dvir (2006) confirms that the concept of the knowledge city is in its beginning, but even so it generates a pertinent approximation of the concepts involved from the point of complementary perspectives such as capital systems (Carrillo, 2004), regional intellectual capital (Bounfour and Edvinson, 2005), information technology (Kominos, 2002), urban process (Landry, 2000), urban history (Kunstler, 2004), and desired characteristics for a city (Ergazakis et al., 2004).

The organization of values appears in capital systems that characterize and structure them. In this context, the structure of the capital systems is basically considered as an economic model once it treats knowledge-based values that allow the future development of a human system, in this case a city, through a new combination of existing values, traditional or knowledge-based. In other words, a knowledge city can emerge from the identification, evaluation and systematic and integrated development not only of its traditional capital but also of its knowledge capital (Carrillo, 2006).

In this chapter we concentrate on the perspective of the capital systems (Carrillo, 2004), but specifically on the aspect of essentialism.

> In recent years, we have also witnessed the birth of new concepts and paradigms that started to affect urbanization and ease the impacts of the above mentioned change and challenges. Carrillo (2004) categorized these new concepts and paradigms under four groups: dematerialisation (i.e. a lesser volume of material inputs and outputs); environmentalism (i.e. a greater concern with sustainability); experience upgrade (i.e. the capacity to attain the same results without the conventional means of space and time), and essentialism (i.e. the understanding and pursuit of ever more fundamental values). (Yigitcanlar, 2010)

The understanding and pursuit of more fundamental values – essentialism – can be one of the elements triggering the transformation of a city. In the case of community social capital, fundamentals such as reciprocity and interchange dynamism can be a base on which a KC can emerge. In other words, the central paradigm of social capital – reciprocity– could be the center of conversion of values of a city.

COMMUNITY SOCIAL CAPITAL AS A CONNECTING FACTOR IN CAXIAS DO SUL

The term 'social capital' appeared in the academic community with the intent to establish the importance of networks and relationships based on trust, co-operation, and collective action as a basis for the survival and functioning of neighborhoods in cities. The studies of Coleman (1988), Putnam (2002) and Fukuyama (2000) indicated the importance of this capital in the relationship among individuals as well as in nations, and it is considered as an inherent resource in extended family relationships, and social organizations.

This capital is represented by characteristics of the social organization that can improve the efficiency of the society, and facilitates the coordination of actions. Studies of this subject have identified a number of common elements for its creation, such as social networks, trust, reciprocity, civic participation and social norms (Nahapiet and Ghoshal, 1998; Onyx and Bullen, 2000).

Social networks are characterized by collective actions of individuals in the society (Onyx and Bullen, 2000). In order for a network to be formed, it is necessary to have spontaneity in social interactions, the capacity to form new associations and to cooperate within the established referential terms (Fukuyama, 2000).

A second element that is characteristic of social capital is trust. This is considered a fundamental element for the provision of inter and intra organizational depth (Smith et al., 1995). Currie and Stanley (2008) consider that trust is derived from the rules of reciprocity and of the systems of civic participation.

Regarding relationship building, trust between partners is considered a determinant factor for an efficient exchange of knowledge (Dirks and Ferrin, 2001; Nahapiet and Ghoshal, 1998; Tsai and Ghoshal, 1998; Li et al., 2007). Fukuyama (2000) considered trust as an existing expectation in the community: honesty and cooperation are part of regular behaviour, which is based on established norms accepted by all. Putnam (2002) use the example of the rotating credit associations that have united people, (friends and families) for the purpose of contributing financially on a monthly basis in order to establish a central fund to be applied for the benefit of the group members.

Another element of social capital is reciprocity. By reciprocity Onyx and Bullen (2000) understand an action that benefits others, in the sense of a future return.

Civic participation for Coleman (1988) is seen as an action in association of different types. Putnam (2002, p. 30) concluded that a civic community is characterized by 'acting citizen engaged and involved in the public spirit by egalitarian political relationships in a social structure strengthened by trust and cooperation'.

Characteristics of a civic community are: a group of citizens, which implies equal rights and obligations for all individuals, a unified community through horizontal relationships of reciprocity and cooperation (however the vertical relationships of authority and dependence are hardly present); the perception of responsibility among the leaders; the existence of wide participation by the citizens in government; the importance given to public spirit by the citizens in general; and trust among the members of that society (Putnam 2002).

In the study of social capital and its importance in the creation of intellectual capital, Nahapiet and Ghoshal (1998) propose three dimensions of social capital: structural, relational, and cognitive. For these authors, social capital can be understood as 'the sum of the actual and potential resources embedded within, available through and derived from the network of relationship possessed by an individual or social unit' (Nahapiet and Ghoshal, 1998, p. 243).

These dimensions of social capital have worked as a basis to advance the understanding of the concept in various researches (Macke et al., 2010). In the structural phase of social capital what is analyzed is: the presence, or lack, of ties between the members; a configuration of the morphology of the network, describing the patterns of the ties through the variables such as density, connectivity, and hierarchy; and the intentional content of the network – in other words, if it was created for one objective and is used for another.

The relational dimension describes the types of personal relationship, developed through a history of focused interactions that influence the components and behaviors, such as trust, respect and friendship, which will determine the level of socialization, acceptance and prestige.

The third dimension of social capital, which Nahapiet and Ghoshal (1998) call cognitive, refers to the resources that emanate shared views, interpretations and significance systems, primarily codes and narratives.

Considering the literature about knowledge cities, we can observe that the social capital permeates the different types of capital of knowledge. For this reason, social capital can be understood as a connecting element of the capital systems. This argumentation is especially valid in the analysis of the case of the emerging city that will be discussed further in this chapter.

A COMMUNITY SUPPORTED UNIVERSITY IN CAXIAS DO SUL

Italian Immigration

The expansion of capitalism, related to political transformation during the process of unification in Italy, created a surplus of workforce during the nineteenth century. The scenario brought many problems to the Italian population, such as hunger, misery and difficulties of access to land.

This resulted in the emigration of thousands of poor Italians, who crossed the Atlantic Ocean on board ships to Brazil. The majority of immigrants were poor and illiterate. To emigrate, they sold the little they had and left with the whole family for destinations mapped out by emigration agents working for the Brazilian government.

The occupation by Italian immigrants of the northeastern region of Rio Grande do Sul state (RS) started in 1875. A census conducted in December 1876 counted 2000 Italian immigrants living in this region. In 1886, the empire started to govern these nuclei. Today, with a population of 410 166 inhabitants, Caxias do Sul is the second most populous city of RS. The city is highly industrialized, is the second pole metal-mechanic in the country and one of the largest in Latin America with more than 6500 industries. Accounting for approximately 5.83 per cent of GDP of RS, Caxias do Sul is the fourth most developed city in the state and also the twelfth most developed city in Brazil, with a Human Development Index of 0.857. Brazil's HDI in 2009 was 0.813 (PNUD, 2010).

The CSU of Caxias do Sul

A major strength of community social capital is the central role of the moral dimension in the construction of a 'good society' (in the words of Putnam, a civic community). Moreover, there is an emphasis on citizen participation in collective affairs, the role of the family and schools in civic education, the quest for balance between rights and responsibilities and the recognition of cultural diversity, without compromising the identity of groups and communities (Etzioni, 2003; Schmidt, 2010).

Community social capital is an alternative path between excessive regulation of the state and the market; for communitarians, the values of solidarity, reciprocity and community ties will prevail, naturally, upon market forces and the logic of policy. In this sense, the virtues of responsibility for the collaboration norms of reciprocity and altruism may build a civic community.

However, from the perspective of essentialism, both the reciprocity and the dynamics of exchanges are essential elements of the paradigm of social capital and can be identified as a fundamental value for the region and for Caxias do Sul in previous studies, and also in the creation of the University of Caxias do Sul.

Two research studies about the evaluation of social capital levels in the south of Brazil – Monastério (2003) and Bandeira (2003) – mention the northeastern region of the RS as having one of the highest levels of social capital in the state. Morover, the reasons for this good performance in generating social capital are: (a) a greater participation in voluntary associations; (b) a more intense social life, evaluated in different practices, such as gathering friends, going out with colleagues, visiting relatives and friends, among others; (c) political participation, measured by the affiliation to political parties, enrollment to public jobs and participation in public manifestations and participative budgets (Bandeira, 2003). Monastério's (2003) study includes variables such as: (a) social and economic aspects, like the Gini index, average area of rural properties, area used by 50 per cent of the smallest properties, among others; (b) city management quality; and (c) social capital index built from more than twenty variables identified in literature and adapted for the state reality.

Further evidence of local values is the existence of the University of Caxias do Sul, which has some pre-conditions that characterize the community oriented element. In 1949, the city of Caxias do Sul created a High School of Arts; in 1958, the Diocesan Miter created the Economic Science School and in 1957 the Sisters of S. José Congregation created the Nursing School. In the year of 1960 the Law School was created and kept by the Hospital Society Nossa Senhora de Fátima. In the 1960s, the various community organizations began seriously working at creating a university. Three institutions of the community in Caxias took the initiative: the City Hall, the Diocesan Miter of Caxias do Sul and the Hospital Society of Nossa Senhora de Fátima, represented respectively by a Mayor, a bishop of the Catholic Church and a representative of the healthcare industry. The next thing that happened was the conception of the UCS, under the sign of plurality and respect for the differences among its people, as a university. The Presidential Decree number 60.200 of 10 February 1967 established the Caxias do Sul University which, as intended by its creators, would have a regional character. This ideal persisted, but in 1968 and the beginning of 1969, UCS created three university campuses: one in Bento Gonçalves, one in Lajeado in the Taquari Valley, and the third one in the region of Campos de Cima da Serra, in Vacaria, extending the university to these cities and preparing students for graduation in one of seven different degrees (Zorzi, 2009).

Nowadays, UCS is in the region that has the most diversity and dynamic economy of the Rio Grande do Sul state, where it keeps fulfilling its mission and contributes to the sustainable development of the region. In this sense, it develops its activities of teaching and researching while expanding to dozens of cities used in this study, without losing the perspective of a university.

UCS, in its totality, reaches a wide geographical area which includes 70 cities with more than one million inhabitants. UCS also has more than 35 000 students majoring in one of the 53 courses offered.

According to Frantz and Silva (2002) the community supported universities are distinct: (1) their creation was stimulated by a group of organizations of the civil society and, in some cases of public entities; (2) they do not have profits, and their financial results are reinvested in the university; (3) they are deeply inserted in the regional community; (4) the deliberative governing body includes representatives of the several segments of the academic community (professors, students, employers) and the regional community; (5) the management team (the Dean's office) are professors of the university, in many cases elected by the academic community and by the representatives of the regional community; (6) the universities abide by the laws that govern private institutions; (7) the administrative control and the financial management are done by the institution; in case of activities stopping, the assets are given to a similar institution.

Nowadays, the regional communities, to which regional universities report, are no longer the traditional communities of the past. They are permeated by contrasts, heterogeneity and contradictions, but they do maintain significant levels of social capital, which assure the capacity to cooperate in projects of collective interest. The message of community supported universities leans on the assumption that they can count on the recognition of the regional community (regional legitimacy) and that the institutional management is guided by the will of the united academic community (internal legitimacy).

Community institutions do not come from relations and interests of a limited group of people. They presuppose relations and interests extensively shared. The community institutions develop environments where even with conflicts, rivalry and competition, the sense of trust and reciprocity is preponderant and is catalyzed by aggregative and innovative leadership (Schmidt and Campis, 2009).

For this reason, it seems evident that a community supported university cannot have the social-level knowledge-based development as a prerequisite without strengthening the knowledge that the university generates, produces, distributes and shares.

Besides the importance of universities as drivers of knowledge cities, as well as anchors for knowledge workers (Garrett-Jones, 2007), the role of a community university extends beyond the production of human capital, towards the economic sense of the term, furthering the demands of the labor market and considering the demands linked to the development of the community it serves. In fact the Universidade de Caxias do Sul recognizes its role in society as being a fundamental element of the local culture. Therefore it endeavours to offer courses related to the regional needs.

SOCIAL COMMUNITY CAPITAL: THE BINDING ELEMENT FOR THE COMMUNITY AND FOR THE COMMUNITY SUPPORTED UNIVERSITY

The history of the CSUs in southern Brazil shows that they came into existence because of the combined efforts of various segments of society including local governing authorities as well as local civic organizations. This can be an indicator of a strong presence of social community capital. This concept has been developed by means of interventions and studies in communities in Latin America and the Caribbean, supported by the Economic Commission for Latin America and the Caribbean (CEPAL).

For Durston (1999), the community social capital is a specific version of social capital. The norms of cultural values and trust, as well as the interpersonal networks of reciprocity are precursors of more complex institutions oriented by norms pursuing the common wellbeing. The search for the common wellbeing defines not only the community social capital, but also emphasizes its precursor elements such as cultural values, trust levels, and the reciprocity present at the community level in the social system.

Community social capital, within the logic, is not an individual resource but a form of social institutionality of the community that pursues the common wellbeing as objective. Different from formal institutions of joint assets such as cooperatives and social institutions, community social capital refers to norms, practices, and interpersonal relationships that exist and are observed within a group that does not yet have an institutional status. It is an 'informal institutionality' in the interior and exterior of community organizations, or wider social systems (Durston, 1999).

In addition to being a precursor of complex institutions oriented by norms of common wellbeing, reciprocity is a central element in the paradigm of social capital. Therefore by observing the functioning of the systems of interchange between CSU and the community that supports it, it is possible to verify that social capital is the binding element that unites actors and social structures, establishing a feedback dynamic:

- When a university has strong ties with the community, this presupposes a strong presence of human capital, which in addition to being an attribute of a community, also manifests, by its own nature, the institutional complexity. In other words, universities are important as drivers of KCs and anchors for knowledge workers (Garrett-Jones, 2007), and the role of a community university extends beyond the production of human capital (towards the economic sense of the term) to the development of the community it serves.
- In addition, there is an added benefit from education toward the development of community social capital, due to community participation and the commitment of the citizens in school affairs. Studies indicate that the longer a person studies, the higher will be the probability that he or she will participate in community affairs. The school, through its implicit and explicit programs, educates the moral and cognitive capabilities that promote an attitude of cooperation and by doing so provides a favorable influence on social capital (Vogt 2009; Hall, 2003; Worms, 2003; Offe and Fuchs, 2003).

The development of CSUs can also be linked to the value of work in the local culture. Earlier researches about social capital in Caxias do Sul region showed that the variables associated with the working environment had the highest rates in evaluating social capital. The explanation also involves the issue of low proactivity and involvement in the community: a possible clue may be in the meaning of 'work'. A 'cult of work' predominates in the region which can be understood as a glorification for what is done for the cultural heritage of Italian immigrants who think that everything can be achieved through hard work. As demonstrated by Tesser (2003), obstinacy combined with entrepreneurialism became the unmistakable mark of immigrants chosen by their descendants.

When the levels of subsistence are exceeded, work becomes a way of social recognition. No matter if it has built a multinational or reached a higher position, work is important as a source of identity, status and dignity. This type of recognition cannot be achieved in isolation, it can happen only within a social context (Fukuyama, 1996).

Therefore, obstinacy and working together to search for recognition created networks of relationships sometimes, based on collaboration, since the immigrants needed to build – besides houses and churches – norms of reciprocity and systems of participation. However, due to cultural characteristics, this feeling of dedication and collaboration in the work environment can be spread through neighbors in the community.

These differences suggest that the community under study has a high level of bonding social capital, characterized by strong relations of mutual aid in the context of family or close circles, with other individuals or groups with common interests. This type of social capital is characterized among people in some way similar. Though not necessarily disregarding the 'different', the bonding social capital can exclude them from 'clubs' or 'circles of trust' (Neumann and Neumann, 2004). This kind of mutual support may be limited to those included in this group and might not extend to minority groups within and outside the local area.

Another type of social capital – less apparent in this case – grows in communities characterized by great tolerance and a high degree of personal initiative, creating weak ties and contributing to the establishment of bridging social capital. This type of social capital is developed among people of different groups, such as in race, generation, gender, religion or political preference; it arises when people go beyond the geographical, social and cultural borders (Neumann and Neumann, 2004).

Putnam (2002) also calls attention to this fact, stressing that strong ties (such as close kinship and friendship) are less important than weak links (such as knowledge and affiliation with associations) to support community cohesion and collective action.

The weak ties are more likely to unite members of small different groups than the strong ties, which tend to focus on certain groups. Horizontal extensive, but isolated, relations sustain cooperation within each group, but the systems of civic participation encompassing different social groups promote a broader cooperation (Putnam, 2002).

The fact that these two types of social capital exist, does not imply that the presence of one excludes the emergence of the other. Indeed, a truly civic community needs both of them (Coleman, 1990).

CONCLUSION

By its deep insertion in the regional community, the CSU can be a transforming element in knowledge-based development. In the concept of regional university, the 'regional' element is clear and situates itself in the axle of the forces of the knowledge society.

In addition universities are vectors of modernity in the societies where they function. They are places where people learn and where thoughts are developed into rational processes with a scientific spirit connected to modernity. But they do not limit themselves to a strictly instrumental view of rationality, and they try to control the flow of rationality by a contrasting set of ideas of an ethical nature, which allows the emergence of opinions.

It is true that factors of an economic, educational, and cultural nature pressuring our societies today could possibly contribute to the implementation, or reinforcement, of a fundamental definition of the actions that currently dominate our societies – what we call the instrumental rationality (Molitor, 2010), characterized by its pursuit of efficiency and a rationality unlinked from its cultural origins. This carries a considerable risk: the banalization, or cultural standardization of the university. If this tendency is not handled carefully a university might be very efficient, based on certain criteria and yet at the same time become widely 'banalized' having lost everything that gave it an identity, and what is worse its real function within the community that it serves (Molitor, 2010).

The challenge for universities is to openly define their cultural objectives (which express the sense) and their political objectives (which express the coherent solidarities) and apply them to their actions. In other words, to define and share a model that unites the search for efficiency (imposed by the environment) and responsibility (that is, our way of choosing, and defining our answers) (Molitor, 2010).

If universities are the places where people think about and discuss the various orientations of society, we must protect and stimulate this work positively. From this point of view, community supported universities can be a reference for a city that thinks about its future from the perspective of knowledge-based development.

In the case presented here, we see Caxias do Sul as an emerging Knowledge City owing to its communitarianism, which reflects the values and the potential in terms of social community capital. In short, a true community must be built together, from the culture of sharing and reciprocity. For sure, there is always much to advance in the trade-off between security and freedom – between the feeling of belonging and the risk of intolerance to diversity (since the inclusion of some means, concomitantly, the exclusion of others). Nevertheless, a sensible discussion of shared human values is a *sine qua non* condition for the balance of forces constituting a community.

REFERENCES

Bandeira, P.S. (2003), 'Algumas hipóteses sobre as causas das diferenças regionais quanto ao capital social no Rio Grande do Sul', in S.M.S. Correa (ed.), *Capital social e desenvolvimento regional*, Santa Cruz do Sul: EDUNISC, pp. 15–59.

Bounfour, A. and Edvinsson, L. (2005), *Intellectual Capital for Communities: Nations, Regions and Cities*, Boston: Butterworth-Heinemann.

Bourdieu, P. (1986), 'The forms of capital', in J.G. Richardson (eds), *The Handbook of Theory: Research for the Sociology of Education*, New York: Greenwood Press, pp. 241–258.

Carrillo, F.J. (2004), 'Capital cities: a taxonomy of capital accounts for knowledge cities', *Journal of Knowledge Management*, **8**(5), 28–46.

Carrillo, F.J. (2006), 'A taxonomy of urban capital', in F.J. Carrillo (ed.), *Knowledge Cities: Approaches, Experiences, and Perspectives*, Oxford: Elsevier.

Coleman, J.S. (1988), 'Social capital in the creation of human capital', *American Journal of Sociology*, 94, 95–120.

Coleman, J.S. (1990), *Foundations of Social Theory*, Cambridge: Harvard University Press.

Currie, G. and Stanley, J. (2008), 'Investigating links between social capital and public transport', *Transport Reviews*, **28**(4), 529–547.

Dirks, K.T. and Ferrin, D.L. (2001), 'The role of trust in organizational settings', *Organization Science*, **12**(4), 450–467.

Durston, J. (2000), *¿Qué es el capital social comunitario?*, Santiago de Chile: Naciones Unidas.

Durston, J. (1999), *Construyendo Capital Social Comunitario: una experiencia de empoderamiento rural en Guatemala*, Santiago de Chile: Naciones Unidas.

Dvir, R. (2006), 'Knowledge city, seen as a collage of human knowledge moments', in F.J. Carrillo (ed.), *Knowledge Cities: Approaches, Experiences, and Perspectives*, Oxford: Elsevier.

Edvinson, L. (2006), 'K-City and society entrepreneurship for intellectual capital growth', in F.J. Carrillo (ed.), *Knowledge Cities: Approaches, Experiences, and Perspectives*, Oxford: Elsevier.

Ergazakis, K., Metaxiotis, K. and Pasarras, J. (2004), 'Towards knowledge cities: conceptual analysis and success stories', *Journal of Knowledge Management*, **8**(5), 5–15.

Ergazakis, K., Metaxiotis, K. and Psarras, J. (2006), 'An emerging pattern of successful knowledge cities' main features', in F.J. Carrillo (ed.), *Knowledge Cities: Approaches, Experiences, and Perspectives*, Oxford: Elsevier.

Etzioni, A. (2003), 'Communitarianism', in K. Christensen and D. Levinson (eds), *Encyclopedia of Community: From the Village to the Virtual World*, Thousand Oaks, CA: Sage pp. 224–228.

Frantz, W. and Silva, E.W. (2002), *As funções sociais da universidade: o papel da extensão e a questão das comunitárias*, Ijuí: Ed. Unijuí.

Fukuyama, F. (1996), *Confiança: as virtudes sociais e a criação da prosperidade*, Rio de Janeiro: Rocco. (F. Fukuyama (1995), *Trust: The Social Creation Virtues and the Creation of Prosperity*, New York: Free Press.)

Fukuyama, F. (2000), *A grande ruptura: a natureza humana e a reconstituição da ordem social*, Rio de Janeiro: Rocco. (F. Fukuyama (1999), *The Great Disruption: Human Nature and the Reconstitution of Social Order*, London: Profile Book.)

Garrett-Jones, S. (2007), 'Knowledge and cooperation for regional development', *Prometheus*, **25**(1), 31–50.

Hall, P.E. (2003), 'El capital social en Gran Bretaña', in R. Putnam (ed.), *El declive del capital social: un estudio internacional sobre las sociedades y el sentidocomunitario*, Barcelona: Galaxia Gutenberg.

Kominos, N. (2002), *Intelligent Cities – Innovation, Knowledge, Systems and Digital Spaces*, New York: Spon Press.

Kunstler, B. (2004), *The Hothouse Effect*, New York: AMACON.

Landry, C. (2000), *The Creative City – A Toolkit for Urban Innovators*, London: Earthscan.

Li, L., Barner-Rasmussen, W. and Björkman, I. (2007), 'What difference does the location make?: A social capital perspective on transfer of knowledge from multinational corporation subsidiaries located in China and Finland, *Asia Pacific Business Review*, **13**(2), 233–249.

Machado, A.M.N. (2009), 'Universidades comunitárias: um modelo Brasileiro para interiorizar a educação superior', in J.P. Schmidt (ed.), *Instituições Comunitárias: instituições públicas não-estatais*, Santa Cruz do Sul: Edunisc.

Macke, J., Vallejos, R.V. and Toss, E.D. (2010), 'Building inter-organizational social capital instruments to evaluate collaborative networks', *iBusiness*, 2, 67–71. Retrieved 30 March 2010, doi: 10.4236/ib.2010.21007, from http://www.SciRP.org/journal/ib

Martínez, S.D. (2006), 'A comparative framework for knowledge cities', in F.J. Carrillo (ed.), *Knowledge Cities: Approaches, Experiences, and Perspectives*, Oxford: Elsevier.

Molitor, M. (2010), 'La Universidad en la Sociedad del Conocimiento', Simposio Inovación y Conocimiento, lecture notes, Guayaquil, Ecuador.

Monastério, L.M. (2003), 'Medindo o capital social: uma análise das regiões do Rio Grande do Sul', in S.M.S. Correa (ed.), *Capital social e desenvolvimento regional*, Santa Cruz do Sul: EDUNISC, pp. 61–84.

Nahapiet, J. and Ghoshal, S. (1998), 'Social capital, intellectual capital and the organizational advantage', *Academy of Management Review*, **23**(2), 242–266.

Neumann, L.T.V. and Neumann, R.A. (2004), *Desenvolvimento comunitário baseado em talentos e recursos locais*, São Paulo: Global/IDIS.

Offe, C. and Fuchs, S. (2003), 'Se halla en declive el capital social? El caso alemán', in R. Putnam (ed.), *El declive del capital social: un estudio internacional sobre las sociedades y el sentidocomunitario*, Barcelona: Galaxia Gutenberg.

Onyx, J. and Bullen, P. (2000), 'Measuring social capital in five communities', *Journal of Applied Behavioral Science*, **36** (1), 23–42.

PNUD (Programa das Nações Unidas para o Desenvolvimento) (2010), *RelatórioIDH*. Recovered in July 2010, http://www.pnud.org.br/pobreza_desigualdade/.

Putnam, R.D. (2002), *Comunidade e Democracia: a experiência da Itália moderna*, 3rd edn, Rio de Janeiro: FGV. (R.D. Putnam, R. Leonardi and R.Y. Nanetti

(1993), *Making Democracy Work: Civic Traditions in Modern Italy*, Princeton: Princeton University Press.)

Schmidt, J.P. (2010), 'O comunitário em tempos de público não estatal', *Avaliação*, **15** (1), 9–40.

Schmidt, J.P. and Campis, L.A.C. (2009), 'As instituições comunitárias e o novo marco jurídico do público não-estatal', in J.P. Schmidt (ed.), *Instituições Comunitárias: instituições públicas não-estatais*, Santa Cruz do Sul: Edunisc.

Smith, K.G., Carroll, S.J. and Ashford, S.J. (1995), Intra- and interorganizational cooperation: toward a research agenda', *Academy of Management Journal*, **38**(1), 7–23.

Tesser, N.A. (2003), 'Caxias do Sul: pérola do desenvolvimento', in P.L. Zugno and V.B.M. Herédia (ed.), *Seminário Internacional Vêneto: modelos de desenvolvimento comparados*, Caxias do Sul: Educs, pp. 87–95.

Tsai, W. and Ghoshal, S. (1998), 'Social capital and value creation: the role of intrafirm networks', *Academy of Management Journal*, 41, 464–478.

Vogt, O.P. (2009), 'Capital social e instituições comunitárias no sul do Brasil', in J.P. Schmidt (ed.), *Instituições Comunitárias: instituições públicas não-estatais*, Santa Cruz do Sul: Edunisc.

Worms, J.P. (2003), 'Viejos e nuevos vínculos cívicos en Francia. Se halla en declive el capital social? El caso alemán', in R. Putnam (ed.), *El declive del capital social: un estudio internacional sobre las sociedades y el sentidocomunitario*, Barcelona: Galaxia Gutenberg.

Yigitcanlar, Tan (2010), 'A comparative knowledge-based urban development analysis: Vancouver, Melbourne and Manchester vs. Boston', The Third Knowledge Cities World Summit: From Theory to Practice Proceedings, Melbourne, Australia, p. 112–126.

Zorzi, I. (2009), 'Universidade de Caxias do Sul: um exemplo do modelo de universidade Comunitária', in J.P. Schmidt (ed.), *Instituições Comunitárias: instituições públicas não-estatais*, Santa Cruz do Sul: Edunisc.

13. Promoting: programs for and challenges of the knowledge-based small business

Joan K. Imukuka, Bhishna Bajracharya, Linda Too and Greg Hearn

INTRODUCTION

Small businesses have long been recognized for their contributions to innovation, job creation and the overall health of most economies (Audretsch, 2004; North et al., 2001; Tilley and Tonge, 2003). Government policies in most countries, therefore, often include support measures and infrastructure to help nurture small businesses, particularly in relation to their innovation-related needs (North et al., 2001). Most recently, there has been growing interest in fostering the emergence of new and innovative small businesses, especially in the high-technology and knowledge-intensive sectors (Bridge et al., 2009). The 'high technology' and 'knowledge-intensive sectors' are those sectors of the economy that have significant levels of research and development expenditure, a high degree of human capital employed in science and technology-based activities and patent intensity. Typical examples include biotechnology, telecommunications, computer applications, energy, pharmaceutical, electronics, and materials technology sectors (Madsen et al., 2004). Within these sectors are emerging firms known as 'knowledge-intensive' or 'knowledge-based' businesses, which are seen as potential engines of economic growth (Davis and Botkin, 1994).

To stimulate the formation of knowledge-based businesses and increase their survival chances, an array of policy initiatives such as business incubators, innovation centres, knowledge precincts, and science and technology parks have been introduced across the globe. While such policy initiatives have proliferated since the 1980s, and are reported to have had success in some cases, potential challenges exist that could hinder them from achieving their intended goals. This chapter discusses the emergence of knowledge-based small businesses in Australia and the impending challenges facing policies aimed at promoting and protecting them. It begins by providing a brief overview of Australia's small business sector, followed by a discussion of what constitutes a small business, the characteristics of knowledge-based small businesses and their role in the economy. The chapter then discusses Australia's current policy initiatives and their challenges, and ends with a brief concluding summary.

OVERVIEW OF THE SMALL BUSINESS SECTOR IN AUSTRALIA

Small businesses have long dominated the Australian economy in terms of the number of businesses, share of employment and GDP (Landstrom, 2005). According to the Australian Bureau of Statistics (ABS) there were just over 2 million actively trading businesses in Australia as of June 2009 (Australian Bureau of Statistics, 2010a), of which 95.6 per cent are classified as small. Small businesses in Australia commonly operate in industries such as construction (16.7 per cent), professional, scientific and technical services (11.3 per cent), rental, hiring and real estate services (10.6 per cent) and agriculture, forestry and fishing (9.9 per cent) (Australian Bureau of Statistics, 2010b). Small businesses in Australia, as in other countries, are an important source of employment and contribute significantly to GDP. As of June 2009, Australian small businesses employed 4.8 million people, accounting for 48 per cent of the private sector employment. The share of employment in small businesses may have fluctuated slightly in response to the recent global financial crisis. Small businesses also contributed 34 per cent of private industry value added and exported goods worth A$1.2 billion in 2008–2009 (Australian Bureau of Statistics, 2010b). Although the majority of small businesses in Australia are non-employing, they nonetheless constitute a significant economic force that provides important products and services to the Australian economy. Table 13.1 depicts the current number of employing firms among Australian businesses.

DEFINING SMALL BUSINESSES

Before providing the definition of knowledge-based small businesses, it is important to first address the question of what constitutes a small business. While the pivotal role small businesses play in the economy is irrefutable, disagreements exist on what their definition should be. Across the globe the definition and concept of 'small business' varies widely depending on the perspectives and boundaries used. Definitions may be based on quantitative measures (employee numbers, financial turnover) or on

Table 13.1 Employing businesses in Australia as of June 2009

Firm size	Number of employing businesses and their share of employment
Micro (1–4 employees)	497 098 (60.6%)
Small (5–19 employees)	233 957 (28.5%)
Medium-sized (20–199 employees)	83 399 (10.1%)
Large (over 200 employees)	6 349 (< 0.8%)
Total	**820 823 (100%)**

Source: Australian Bureau of Statistics (2010a).

qualitative measures (independent management, operating capital mostly contributed by an individual/small group, small market share, owners are main decision makers) (Bridge et al., 2009; Curran and Blackburn, 2001; Schaper and Volery, 2007). Still within quantitative approaches there are differences, for instance, when using employee numbers, what constitutes a small business in one industry sector or country may be a large business in another. For example, in the USA any business employing fewer than 500 people is classified as small (Small Business Administration, 2010) whereas in Australia the limit is 19 people (Australian Bureau of Statistics, 2010a) and in the European Union it is fewer than 50 people (European Commission, 2001). The ABS defines businesses on the basis of employee numbers and further classifies them into micro (with fewer than 5 employees), small (with fewer than 20 employees), medium (with fewer than 200 employees) and large (with over 200 employees). The collective acronym 'SMEs' (small and medium-sized enterprises) is often used interchangeably with 'small businesses' and 'small firms' and includes micro, small and medium-sized businesses.

Because there is no such thing as an ideal definition, various definitions are in use today, which makes comparisons between countries and industry sectors complicated. Quantitative measures are often used by researchers and policy makers for practical reasons given that data is easily obtainable. Despite their pragmatism, quantitative measures are faced with the problem of their applicability to different industry sectors such as manufacturing and services. Manufacturing and services sectors are very distinct in their structural make up, therefore boundaries should be drawn when businesses are being defined to avoid uneven comparisons being made (Curran and Blackburn, 2001).

In contrast with quantitative approaches that are based on numbers, qualitative measures define businesses on the basis of non-quantitative characteristics such as market share, independence, decision making, control and ownership (Bridge et al., 2009; Schaper and Volery, 2007). The main problem facing qualitative approaches is that they are difficult to operationalize. For instance, in the UK Bolton Report of 1971, a small business was defined as 'one that has a relatively small share of the market, is independently managed by its owners or part-owners in a personalised way with no formal management structures, and is not part of a larger enterprise with decision making resting entirely on its owners without outside control' (Bridge et al., 2009). While qualitative approaches may assist in differentiating small businesses from large firms, differences within the small business cohort still exist. The management structures and internal operations of micro-businesses differ from those of medium-sized businesses. Further, small businesses are not confined to a particular industry and are often run by owners with diverse backgrounds. With such diversity, small businesses can be classified as 'home-based', 'ethnic', 'family-controlled', 'start-ups', or 'knowledge-based'.

DEFINITIONS AND CHARACTERISTICS OF KNOWLEDGE-BASED SMALL BUSINESSES

Having discussed the concept of small business, we now focus on an emerging type known as knowledge-based small businesses – which have captured the attention of policy makers in recent years. The notion that the world has shifted towards a knowledge-based economy has highlighted the importance of knowledge-based sectors and the firms operating within them. The Organisation for Economic Co-operation and Development (OECD) defines the knowledge-based economy as 'an economy in which the production, distribution and use of knowledge is the main driver of growth, wealth creation and employment across all industries' (OECD, 1996). It is argued that 'knowledge-based' sectors are now the engines of economic growth, replacing traditional sectors such as primary resources, manufacturing and construction (Beck, 1992; OECD, 1996). Not surprisingly, there has been growing scholarly interest in understanding the behaviours of 'knowledge-based' or 'knowledge-intensive' small businesses as they are sometimes called. Theoretically, there have been difficulties in explaining exactly what a knowledge-based small business is as different authors view them either from a products and services perspective or from an organizational characteristics perspective as shown in Table 13.2 overleaf.

Although these definitions provide some reasonable understanding of what knowledge-based businesses are, the various terms ('innovative',

Table 13.2 Definitions of knowledge-based businesses/knowledge-intensive business services

Authors	Definitions
Davis and Botkin, 1994	Businesses that provide 'smart' products
Miles et al., 1995	Businesses that provide services that involve economic activities which are intended to result in the creation, accumulation or dissemination of knowledge
Alvesson, 1995	Refers to firms that are undertaking complex operations of an intellectual nature where human capital is the dominant factor
Bettencourt et al., 2002	Enterprises whose primary value-added activities consist of the accumulation, creation, or dissemination of knowledge for the purpose of developing a customized service or product solution to satisfy the client's needs
Smedlund and Toivonen, 2007	Are expert companies that provide services to other companies and organizations

'technology-based', 'high employment-growth', 'value-adding', 'entrepreneurial high technology' etc.) commonly used to describe them make the concept vague. In explaining what knowledge-based businesses are, Miles et al. (1995) identified three main characteristics: they (a) rely heavily on professional knowledge; (b) are primary producers of information and knowledge or use knowledge to produce intermediate services for their users' production process; and (c) are of competitive significance and provide services mainly to businesses. Given that knowledge is their primary resource and source of differentiation (Dawson, 2000b), knowledge-based businesses are hugely intellectual capital dependent. Dawson (2000a) categorizes intellectual capital as (a) human capital which comprises the skills and capabilities of the individuals working within these firms, (b) structural capital which is the organizational infrastructure, e.g. technology and processes, and (c) relationship capital which refers to the relationships with clients, suppliers, distributors, partners, alliance members, academics, regulators and others as well as the organizational image and brand.

While there is no consensus on what constitutes a knowledge-based business, there is some general agreement that these firms are typically found in knowledge industry sectors such as computers and related activities, research and development and other business services (Muller and Doloreux, 2007). However, the knowledge industry is wider than initially thought. When Machlup (1962) first introduced the knowledge industry concept, the major sectors identified were education, information services, information technology, mass media and research and development. Nowadays other creative and cultural industries such as advertising, design, crafts, real estate, insurance, arts, media, business services, publishing etc. are also included in the definition.

From this discussion, there appear to be some observable characteristics associated with knowledge-based small businesses. First, they are not confined to science and technology, education and research and development, but also operate in a wide range of other cultural and creative industry sectors such as the arts, advertising, film and so forth. Second, knowledge (especially in tacit form) is the most strategic resource and is what sets them apart from other small businesses. Third, they are innovation-focused, growth-oriented and entrepreneurial, and that is what makes them key players in today's knowledge-based economy.

POLICY INITIATIVES SUPPORTING KNOWLEDGE-BASED SMALL BUSINESSES

In general, government policies supporting small businesses are based on the assumption that new jobs will be created and economic growth will be enhanced (Curran, 2000; Down, 2010; Shane, 2008). However Shane (2008) disagrees, claiming that not every business resulting from government intervention generates much employment or significantly enhances productivity. Regardless of the ongoing debate on whether or not governments should assist small businesses, every government, including free market economies, has some form of government intervention as a means of regulating its economy. Audretsch (2004) identified two main approaches towards small businesses: SME policy and entrepreneurship policy. SME policy primarily focuses on promoting existing small businesses while entrepreneurship policy is concerned with stimulating more entrepreneurial behaviour in a region or country. Depending on existing problems or opportunities emerging, policies towards small businesses may change. For instance, during the 1980s the UK Government was focused on increasing the quantity of small businesses, but by the 1990s the focus had shifted to improving the quality of small businesses (by supporting knowledge-based, high-tech, export oriented and value-adding), and after the 1990s the emphasis was on innovation (Bridge et al., 2009).

The economic significance of knowledge-based small businesses is widely acknowledged, as indicated by the growth in entrepreneurship policies as well as other innovation-related initiatives across the globe. Technology incubators, innovation centres and science parks represent some type of initiatives that have proliferated worldwide in recent years. The justification for these initiatives is that they provide an environment for knowledge-based small businesses to develop and grow; create opportunities for small businesses to exchange ideas with other closely located firms; enable small businesses to benefit from knowledge producers (universities or research institutions) and provide financial and other assistance to boost their innovative potential.

Australia has acknowledged the contributions knowledge-based small businesses make to employment and GDP. For example, the creative industries account for between 2 and 3 per cent of all employment and contribute approximately A$25 billion per annum to the Australian economy (Montgomery, 2007). Biotechnology companies, which are often spin-offs from research institutes, were estimated to contribute A$1.75 billion to the Australian economy in 2010–11, providing employment to just under 7300 people (Ellis, 2011). To support further growth of knowledge-based sectors and to boost their innovative potential, different levels of the Australian government have invested in both research and development and other direct support programs. For instance in the 2009–10 commonwealth budget, the Australian federal government set aside A$8.5 billion for science and innovation, an increase of 25 per cent from the previous budget (DIISR, 2009). The Australian federal government's Department of Innovation, Industry, Science and Research, through its AusIndustry division, offers various programs such as Commercializing Emerging Technologies (COMET), the Small Business Advisory Service and Enterprise Connect (OECD, 2010). At the state level, numerous assistance programs are also offered to small businesses. The Queensland Government, for example, has in the last decade been emphasizing the need to nurture creativity, knowledge and innovation to drive economic growth as part of its broader vision of transforming into a knowledge-based economy. Through its Smart State Strategy, the Queensland Government has provided financial support to start-up firms; innovation and commercialization advice; and skills development to knowledge-based small businesses (DEEDI, 2008). These services can be accessed through property-based developments such as the i.lab Technology Incubator, the Gold Coast Innovation Centre or the Innovation Centre Sunshine Coast.

Despite these huge investments, Australia still lags behind other advanced nations (e.g. Japan, Finland, South Korea, Sweden, Switzerland) in regards to research and development spending (DIISR, 2009) and this has undoubtedly impacted the number of Australian businesses engaging in innovative activities. In 2009, Australia received only 1550 patents compared to 95037 in the USA and 38066 recorded in Japan (Datamonitor, 2010). According to a published article in the *Business Review Weekly*, the success of Australian new and growing knowledge-based businesses could be adversely affected by the shift in government policies from innovation support programs to infrastructure spending (Walters, 2011). Government programs in support of innovation, the article claims, are being closed down, sold to the private sector or scaled down to certain limits. Examples include the Queensland based i.Lab Incubator, Triton Foundation and TeQstart, providing funding and other support services to knowledge-based small businesses, which were all sold to the private sector in 2009 (Walters, 2011). What this means is that funding for knowledge-based small businesses may become harder to access. In addition, Australian small businesses are hampered by innovation barriers such as lack of skilled staff, lack of access to additional funds, uncertain demand for new goods and/or services and lack of knowledge or technology to enable development or introduction/implementation (Australian Bureau of Statistics, 2010b).

CHALLENGES FACING INITIATIVES SUPPORTING KNOWLEDGE-BASED SMALL BUSINESSES

Because knowledge-based small businesses are heterogeneous, complex, and unique, designing and implementing effective policy initiatives necessary to meet their needs, can be challenging. The technologically complex environment, coupled with increased global competition and the ease with which information flows, makes knowledge-based businesses vulnerable. To survive in such a turbulent environment requires constant renewal of knowledge and the ability to apply it as well as the protection of intellectual capital. The success, and therefore effectiveness, of knowledge-based policy initiatives is dependent upon their impact on the small business sector and on the overall health of the economy. Critics of public policy tools for small businesses argue that without measured targets and specified timeframes in which they are to be achieved, it is difficult to determine their effectiveness (Storey, 1998). The following are seen as potential barriers that may prevent the policy initiatives from promoting knowledge-based small businesses:

Knowledge industry sector is wide Small firms operate in virtually all sectors of the economy, therefore deliberate efforts to provide assistance only to high-tech businesses or smart businesses will limit the potential of the knowledge industry sector. As pointed out earlier, the knowledge industry is not restricted to education, information technology, mass media and research and development, but also encompasses the creative and cultural industries as well as other business services. In light of this, policy makers are then faced with the challenge of identifying which sectors to target for assistance, what the specific needs are for the small businesses in these sectors and of designing appropriate programs for them. This is further complicated by the different development stages through which small businesses during their life cycle, as each requires different solutions.

Access to knowledge workers Small businesses are generally disadvantaged when it comes to accessing knowledge workers, that is, workers with 'high degrees of expertise, education, or experience, and whose primary job purpose involves the creation, distribution or application of knowledge' (Davenport, 2005). Knowledge workers spark innovation and growth in the organization, invent new products and services, design marketing products and create strategies (Davenport, 2005). Such workers tend to cluster around specific regions that can support and nurture their creativity; therefore proximity to knowledge assets is important. For small firms located in peripheral regions, the pressure is even more intense as these areas typically have difficulty in retaining knowledge workers. The issue for support programs is how to ensure that small firms regardless of their location can benefit from a pool of talented individuals.

Access to risk capital One of the problems that small firms in the knowledge-intensive sector face, particularly the high-tech businesses, is limited access to risk capital. Most financial institutions are reluctant to fund their ventures (Colombo and Delmastro, 2002) given their risky nature (Oakey, 1995; Storey, 1994). While public support programs are making efforts to provide financial assistance to small firms in the high-tech sector, alternative funding sources such as angel investors and venture capitalists are insufficient in most places. The challenge for public support programs is ensuring that funding is available to various small firms given their changing needs as they move from one development stage to another.

Technical expertise The increased importance of knowledge in today's global economy puts firms under pressure to acquire new knowledge, particularly small firms if they are to have a competitive edge. Managers of small businesses typically have limited training in technical and managerial skills, which can hinder them from thinking innovatively and strategically and can also prevent them from competing effectively in a global technology-based knowledge economy. Although business advisory and mentoring services are provided to small businesses owner/managers, some studies have shown that the uptake is generally low as most view them as irrelevant to their needs (North et al., 2001) This then raises the issue of how and in what ways the training programs should be designed and delivered.

Entrepreneurial orientation and managerial characteristics While policy makers have a key role to play in increasing the innovative capacity of small businesses, the level of, and extent to which, small businesses can engage in innovative activities also depends on the entrepreneurial orientation and managerial characteristics of the owner-manager (Mazzarol and Reboud, 2009). Small business owners have different motivations for starting a business, thus not all of them have the desire or visionary leadership to create an environment where innovation can flourish. Some small business owners are satisfied with the level of their business operations while others are interested in growth and increasing the quality of their products/services. The challenge for policy makers lies in identifying which businesses have innovation/growth potential or have the desire to engage in innovative activities.

Internationalization Vast opportunities exist for small businesses in the international arena, given the changing nature of the global economy. However, small firms may face both internal barriers (resource constraints, organizational capabilities and approach to exporting) and external barriers (tariff barriers, different customer habits, and foreign rules) which may hinder them from exploiting these opportunities (Leonidou, 2004). The main concern for policy makers is in ensuring that the right information on international trends and markets is provided to small businesses if they are to compete favourably in the international arena.

Liabilities of newness and smallness empirical studies have found that younger and smaller firms are less likely to survive than larger and older firms. Internal factors such as small size, lack of experience and organic structure, and external factors such as limited market and network resources, challenge the survival of young small firms. These characteristics contribute to the low levels of organizational legitimacy – a key resource that enables young firms to acquire additional resources necessary for their survival and growth. Given these and other pressing issues facing small firms, policy makers are then faced with the difficulties of providing the right infrastructure and other support services that can help small firms overcome these liabilities.

CONCLUSION

Knowledge-based small businesses are critical players in today's economy. They not only create employment but also add value to the economy through their innovative products and services. As such policy makers across the globe have introduced a range of policy initiatives designed to foster their development and growth. Like other governments, the Australian government has channelled significant financial and other resources towards building technology incubators, innovation centres and science parks as a mechanism for promoting such businesses. Despite these investments, Australia still lags behind other industrialized countries both in terms of the number of patents lodged by businesses and the levels of research and development expenditure. This limits the ability of businesses to engage in innovation related activities.

Given the heterogeneity, complexity and uniqueness of knowledge-based small businesses, designing policy initiatives is always going to be challenging. One important issue that needs to be addressed when designing policy initiatives is the need to focus on enhancing and protecting intellectual capital in knowledge-based small businesses – a critical resource on which their success depends. Intellectual capital is critical because it embodies the knowledge necessary for the operations of knowledge-based small businesses and also serves as a source of competitive advantage. Policy initiatives also need to move beyond the notion that knowledge-based businesses are predominantly found in high-tech sectors. Businesses operating within the creative industries, for example, also have the potential to create jobs and generate wealth in today's economy. However, it is essential that policy initiatives are targeted towards businesses that are likely to engage in innovative activities and those whose growth potential is clearly evident.

REFERENCES

Alvesson, M. (1995), *Management of Knowledge-Intensive Companies*, Berlin/New York: de Gruyter.

Audretsch, D.B. (2004), 'Sustaining innovation and growth: public policy support for entrepreneurship', *Industry and Innovation*, **11**(3), 167–191.

Australian Bureau of Statistics (2010a), *Counts of Australian Businesses, Including Entries and Exits, June 2007 to June 2009*, Canberra: Australian Bureau of Statistics.

Australian Bureau of Statistics (2010b), *Innovation in Australian Business, 2008–09*, Canberra: Australian Bureau of Statistics.

Beck, N. (1992), *Shifting Gears: Thriving in the New Economy*, Toronto: Harper Collins.

Bettencourt, L.A., Ostrom, A.L., Brown, S.W. and Roundtree, R.I. (2002), 'Client co-production in knowledge-intensive business services', *California Management Review*, 44, 100–128.

Bridge, S., O'Neill, K., and Martin, F. (2009), *Understanding Enterprise: Entrepreneurship and Small Business* (3rd edn.), Basingstoke: Palgrave Macmillan.

Colombo, M.G. and Delmastro, M. (2002), 'How effective are technology incubators? Evidence from Italy', *Research Policy*, 31, 1103–1122.

Curran, J. (2000), 'What is small business policy in the UK for? Evaluation and assessing small business policy', *International Small Business Journal*, **18**(3), 36–50.

Curran, J. and Blackburn, R. (2001), *Researching the Small Enterprise*, London: Sage.

Datamonitor (2010), *Country Analysis Report: Australia In-depth PESTLE Insights*, Sydney: Datamonitor Asia Pacific.

Davenport, T.H. (2005), 'Thinking for a living: how to get better performance and results from knowledge workers', available from http://books.google.com.au.

Davis, S. and Botkin, J. (1994), 'The coming of knowledge-based business', *Harvard Business Review*, **72**(5), 165–170.

Dawson, R. (2000a), *Developing Knowledge-Based Client Relationships: The Future of Professional Services*, Boston, MA: Butterworth-Heinemann.

Dawson, R. (2000b), 'Knowledge capabilities as the focus of organizational development', *Journal of Knowledge Management*, **4**(4), 320–327.

DEEDI (2008), *Smart State Strategy: Queensland's Smart Future 2008–2012*, City East: Department of Employment, Economic Development and Innovation.

DIISR (2009), *Powering Ideas: An Innovation Agenda for the 21st Century*, Canberra: Department of Innovation, Industry, Science and Research.

Down, S. (2010), *Enterprise, Entrepreneurship and Small Business*, Los Angeles: Sage.

Ellis, S. (2011), *Growing Potential: Industry Revenue Expands with the Return of Research Funding, IBISWorld Industry Report X0001 Biotechnology in Australia*, Melbourne: IBISWorld.

European Commission (2001), *Creating an Entrepreneurial Europe: The Activities of the European Union for Small and Medium-Sized Enterprises (SMEs)*, Final report from the Commission to the Council, The European Parliament, The Economic and Social Committee and The Committee of the Regions, Brussels: Final.

Landstrom, H. (2005), *Pioneers in Entrepreneurship and Small Business Research*, New York: Springer Science+Business Media, Inc.

Leonidou, L. (2004), 'An analysis of the barriers hindering small business export development', *Journal of Small Business Management*, **42**(3), 279–302.

Machlup, F. (1962), 'The production and distribution of knowledge in the United States', available from http://books.google.com.au

Madsen, H., Neergaard, H. and Ulhoi, J.P. (2004), Knowledge-intensive entrepreneurship and human capital', *Journal of Small Business and Enterprise Management*, **10**(4), 426–434.

Mazzarol, T., and Reboud, S. (2009), *The Strategy of Small Firms: Strategic Management and Innovation in the Small Firm*, Cheltenham, UK and Northampton, MA, USA: Edward Elgar.

Miles, N., Kastrinos, N., Flanagan, K., Bilderbeek, R. and Den Hertog, P.

(1995), *Knowledge-Intensive Business Services: Users, Carriers and Sources of Innovation*, Manchester: PREST.
Montgomery, J. (2007), 'Creative industry business incubators and managed workspaces: a review of best practice', *Planning, Practice and Research*, **22**(4), 601–617.
Muller, E. and Doloreux, D. (2007), 'The key dimensions of knowledge-intensive business services (KIBS) analysis: a decade of evolution', unpublished working paper, Fraunhofer Institute for Systems and Innovation Research (Fraunhofer ISI).
North, D., Smallbone, D. and Vickers, I. (2001), 'Public sector support for innovating SMEs', *Small Business Economics*, **16**(4), 303.
Oakey, R. (1995), *High Technology New Firms: Variable Barriers to Growth*, London: Chapman and Hall.
OECD (1996), *The Knowledge-based Economy*, Organisation for Economic Co-operation and Development, Paris.
OECD (2010), *OECD Studies on SMEs and Entrepreneurship: SMEs, Entrepreneurship and Innovation*, Paris: OECD Publications.
Schaper, M. and Volery, T. (2007), *Entrepreneurship and Small Business* (2nd Pacific Rim edn), Milton: John Wiley and Sons Australia.
Shane, S.A. (2008), *The Illusions of Entrepreneurship: The Costly Myths That Entrepreneurs, Investors, and Policy Makers Live By*, New Haven and London: Yale University Press.
Small Business Administration (2010), *The Small Business Economy: A Report to the President*, Washington: SBA Office of Advocacy.
Smedlund, A. and Toivonen, M. (2007), 'The role of KIBS in the IC development of regional clusters', *Journal of Intellectual Capital*, 8, 159–170.
Storey, D.J. (1994), *Understanding the Small Business Sector*, London: Routledge.
Storey, D.J. (1998), *Six Steps to Heaven: Evaluating the Impact of Public Policies to Support Small Businesses in Developed Economies*, unpublished manuscript.
Tilley, F. and Tonge, J. (2003), 'Competitive advantage in SMEs: introduction', in O. Jones and F. Tilley (eds), *Competitive Advantage in SMEs: Organising for Innovation and Change*, Chichester: John Wiley and Sons.
Walters, K. (2011), 'The end of innovation', retrieved 2 March 2011, from http://www.brw.com.au/p/sections/emerging_companies/the_end_of_innovation_9GjvKNlsLRQoSCibttsdbL

14. Enterprising: academics, knowledge capital and towards PASCAL universities

James A. Powell

INTRODUCTION

This chapter portrays an innovative approach from a consortium of universities that have developed new and highly effective ways of both knowledge sharing and active working with external colleagues from business, industry and civic society for the benefit of knowledge cities. In particular, these universities harness global imagination and unlock the talents of all partners to co-identify, co-create and co-produce flourishing futures projects and processes for real world impact. Even traditional academics in these universities are transforming themselves to become more enterprising, thus opening up deeper conversations with strategic partners so that all can flourish and add real value for their knowledge capitals.

Nearly a decade ago, Will Hutton, of the Work Foundation, proposed that Manchester, in the UK, had all the attributes to become an 'Ideopolis' – a 21st century knowledge city with sufficient capability, talent and facilities to enable it to flourish in the global knowledge economy. His idea was honed and developed into a working entity by a powerful team of senior Manchester leaders into what has become known as Manchester: Knowledge Capital – a name invented by the three CONTACT Universities of Greater Manchester and endorsed by the Deputy Prime Minister of the day, John Prescott (now Lord Prescott). The present author helped lead that development and hence write this chapter.

Key in this development, and in other knowledge capitals throughout the world, has been the role universities must play in driving necessary cultural change, leading to more relevant innovations fit-for-purpose, thus enabling sustainable and wealth creating modern futures. For in such knowledge cities, universities have begun to reach out to their partners more smartly than ever before, often in interesting and novel ways, in their attempts to play what each sees as its role in coping with today's global crises, major societal challenges and to help citizens. Most are becoming more enterprising and deeply engaging with their communities:

- Enterprising in the way they *develop leading edge opportunities*, with high academic values – becoming involved in solving real world issues and problems.
- Engaging with Strategic Partners who bring their own expertise and imagination to *co-create* with them – universities and their partners realize they cannot do it separately if they want to develop innovations fit for the knowledge economy.

As Garlick suggests (2010)

> there is no doubt that, after decades of indecisiveness in policy circles, there is a mood amongst Higher Education Institutions (HEIs) for an approach to knowledge creation and distributions that better reflects their purpose; this would be in the fashion that John Dewey, Ernest Boyer and others have aspired to for many years, but their views may now be more timely.

This perspective is very different to the dominant paradigm presently forced on academic institutions through neoliberal funding agencies. In many ways, 'the university of today' has unfortunately become a 'Taylorist factory' according to Garlick, who is also not sure that Burton Clarke's (1998) seminal work on the entrepreneurial university has helped things improve in terms of beneficial outreach by the way it seems to limit the university perspective. However, he does go on to propose that the approach suggested in the present chapter, in its earlier forms, truly

> enables a more enlightened and creative approach that connects Higher Education Institutions (HEIs) to the big issues of the planet, connecting them properly with their communities, in order to build meaningful and ethical partnerships.

For universities for a Modern Renaissance see their students and staff as a hugely valuable tool for concerted action beyond publication and the curriculum, and still remain as economically viable as it would be under other less connected approaches.

THE ROLE OF UNIVERSITIES

Not only are universities thinking differently about their role(s). Society increasingly expects the universities it funds to work with citizens and communities to enable them to flourish. Governments further believe this should occur through the creation of improvements in a knowledge economy that has huge economic, social and environmental problems; some see the universities as central to the development of all future forward looking and workable processes.

In the past, in order to understand the complexities, uncertainties and often 'wickedness' of difficult problems, academics were able to retreat to their 'ivory towers' and develop 'private frames of reference' to enable theory building and high level discussion. No longer: academics now need, and may even be demanded by governments, to use their deep and rigorously acquired understandings for the common good. And they must also now do this by developing new ways of working and knowledge sharing that enable them to make a real difference in the real world. They must do this by co-identifying worthy problems and co-designing solutions with external colleagues from business, industry, the civil and voluntary services and the community.

Nearly all universities now say they are reaching out to their local partners. However, sometimes this rhetoric doesn't translate into an actuality, implementations or real 'impact'. For, as a recent key Innovation and Productivity Report (Abrue et al., 2009) reveals, the objectives of industry and academia are still often distinctly different:

- What industry and the community want from academia are 'ideas and talent, rather than a cheap way of outsourcing R&D activities'. They want to meet the experts and to hear about what they are doing and then figure out how something that they learn may be of use to them. Firms value the direct assistance in problem solving, as well as access to skilled experts.
- Academics, on the other hand, still tend to pursue objectives from their own discipline with their studies 'underpinned by research-oriented rationales, rather than by the desire to commercialise technology', creating impact or developing improvements in the real world; their primary outputs are typically seen as knowledge, learning, trained minds, and some times as consultancy. For the most part, people in academic institutions seek to follow a career in academia.

Nevertheless, in an attempt to form better relationships with external partners, universities are beginning to engage in a diversity of ways which typically reflect local contexts and circumstances and the major academic thrusts each university holds dear. Furthermore, university 'reach-out' or outreach activity, as it is often called, is beginning to look different from traditional academic working, with the added contributions of partners combining their skills, so the sum of the parts is worth more than the parts taken individually.

THE GROWING DIVERSITY OF UNIVERSITY REACH-OUT IN KNOWLEDGE CITIES: EXAMPLE OF BEST PRACTICE ENGAGEMENT THROUGH THE WORLD

In terms of outreach to business and the community, the 'land grant' universities in the USA, through the way they were founded, have always had a strong relationship with local 'communities' in the richest sense of that word. For instance, universities such as Michigan State (MSU) now act as a beacon to the rest of the world of the kinds of best practices for developing, sharing and applying knowledge for the public good. So, since its inception in 1855, and then its renaming to Michigan State in 1964, MSU has increased its connections with south-eastern Michigan, putting major investment into community partnerships designed to help create the human and social capital necessary to ensure transformation of the region. By 2008, MSU's aim had become to be an exemplary 'engaged university', transforming and strengthening outreach partnerships to address key local state needs and developing broadly applicable models; with its academics' outreach activities, to external organizations and communities alike, being for 'reciprocal learning' which increased both the external partners' capacity to address issues, and the academic staff's capacity to produce scholarship that better reflects the realities outside the laboratory or library. Their recent *Handbook* (Fitzgerald et al., 2011) stands testimony to how much they have developed and shared workable and worthy ideas and processes – such guidance will undoubtedly improve the quality of all engagements by those university academics who wish to work actively with their local communities in knowledge cities.

Arizona State University (ASU) describes itself as being a new Model American University with eight design aspirations appearing in its guidebook as key transformations relating to:

- Leveraging our place
- Transforming society
- Valuing entrepreneurship
- Conducting use-inspired research
- Enabling student success
- Fusing intellectual disciplines

- Being socially embedded
- Engaging globally

ASU has lots to aspire to, but it is truly transformational in the way it is leading its own engagement change in the USA; universities in knowledge cities would learn much by adopting ASU's key transformational areas for themselves.

In Canada, the University of Victoria in British Columbia has also had a clear focus toward the social, cultural and economic advancement of the communities it serves close to home and around the world. It tries to build strong partnerships with community organizations, and actively engaging citizens from all walks of life is fundamental to its approach. Its community services are a key component in its type of external engagement; these take many forms, from joint research projects or educational programs that address community needs and supplying expert speakers to schools, seniors groups and community organizations, to partnering with businesses to explore the commercial potential of the latest campus discoveries and applying student knowledge and energy to organizational challenges.

In a similar, but more collective vein, the Association of Commonwealth Universities (Coldstream, 2001; Coldstream and Bjarnason, 2003) initiated a debate among its 500 members which led to a major conclusion that 'engagement should be a core value for all universities' (a phrase later expanded in other papers to read 'engagement with wider society as a core value. . .'). So even as recently as 2003, this was still 'juxtaposed to the stance of traditional universities as being "ivory towered, where aloofness was still defended" as a necessary condition both of undisturbed contemplation and of disinterested objectivity to enable better judgment'. Just one result of this, alongside growing interest in Australian outreach, was the setting up of AUCEA – the Australian Universities Community Engagement Alliance – with its strong endorsement from 34 Australian universities, of profound 'engagements', beyond the trivial, with external stakeholders outside academia, for mutual benefit.

Over the years AUCEA (Garlick and Langworthy, 2009) has developed powerful ways and means of engaged working with the community, benchmarking progress to ensure universities from this Australian consortium sensitively, caringly and effectively engage with communities to the greatest effect and for the highest impact. It defines the following principles as applying to the Engaged University:

- University community engagement is based upon a mutually beneficial exchange of knowledge and expertise between universities and communities;

- The university produces graduates who are ethical and engaged citizens;
- The university engages with its communities to create a more accessible, outward reaching and inclusive society;
- The university identifies its communities by acknowledging community values, culture, knowledge and skills, and works with those communities to develop a mutually beneficial agenda;
- Engaged research is designed, managed and disseminated as a partnership that addresses both academic and community priorities;
- Engaged learning and teaching programs respond to individual and community needs and opportunities and links to specific learning goals and experiences for students. Programs are designed and managed in partnership with communities, and are socially inclusive and globally and locally relevant;
- Community engagement is embedded in the governance, operations, budget, curricula, plans, policies and life of the university;
- Engaged universities articulate their mission, culture and values for the community, and regularly reflect on these in the context of community conditions and partnerships;
- The university and the community work together to monitor partnerships, measure impacts, evaluate outcomes, and make improvements to their shared activities.

Turning to a more business focused engagement, NESTA (the National Endowment for Science, Technology and the Arts – Stewart, 2008) uses the not dissimilar term 'connected university' for those British universities that are driving for innovative growth in the UK business economy. NESTA believes that such universities enable business, industry and the community to flourish, especially economically, by putting the following at the heart of their strategy:

- Recognition of the importance of building strategic partnerships with local firms, nurturing local clusters, creating national and international connections;
- The recruitment, development and promotion of intermediaries or 'boundary spanners' who build active and intelligent links between public and private sectors through a deep knowledge and experience of both partners;
- Monitoring of the benefits of university–business–industry interactions and using key performance measures to improve their effectiveness.

Continuing the discussion, but turning to a more business focus, Professor Tim Wilson (2009), the Vice Chancellor of University of Hertfordshire believes his university is in the vanguard of a new type of emerging university – those that are business-like and business-facing. As a leading 'business-facing university' in the UK, Hertfordshire is focused on developing new and creative approaches to learning, teaching and research with a commitment to adding value to employers, enterprise and regional, national and international economies. According to Wilson, 'it is an ambitious and entrepreneurial university with an international vision, putting students at the heart of what we do. The university encourages a constant interchange between businesses, academics and students. Many university staff members spend a proportion of their time working in industry, running their own businesses, keeping their knowledge up to date and help to develop students' business skills'. Hertfordshire has a wide range of facilities, services and skills available for industry and its proven expertise and commitment means that, whatever they are looking for, employers know it will deliver. For instance, it is the only university in the UK to have acquired its local business support agency – Exemplas. Exemplas is the primary mechanism for identifying and tapping into latent demand for our products and services, and works to provide personnel and skills solutions to business.

Moving the diversity discussion on, in another example of engagement, John Goddard (2009) argues more generally for 'all public-funded universities in the UK to have a civic duty to engage with wider society on the local, national and global' level. He is similarly keen for this to be done in a manner which 'links the social to the economic spheres'. He believes that in the context of the severe recession, global warming, aging populations and major social challenges right across the globe, we need to re-invent the 'civic university' that served us so well in its earlier manifestations. Indeed, citing his own university – Newcastle – as an exemplar, Goddard believes that 'globally competitive and locally engaged civic universities can contribute to attracting inward investing companies to specific locations, providing local business with world wide connections and attracting the mobile elite to an area, thereby adding to its cultural diversity and pool of entrepreneurial talent'.

Finland's new Aalto University goes further by developing a new forward looking 'community innovation agenda'. It aims to channel academic knowledge to create innovative solutions helping to tackle societal challenges. An international Aalto Camp for Societal Innovation (ACSI), arranged in the summer of 2010, piloted a concept that methodologically integrates research, education and innovation activities to solve concrete problems on social issues. The Camp served as a stepping stone for creating a global networking culture that links operators at the forefront of the development of innovative collaboration and operated in a multidisciplinary, communal and dialogue-oriented way. The participants collaborated in teams supported by a steering process and material aid to help promote their selected programs. They tackled six concrete community problems and challenges chosen from Helsinki and other nearby municipalities. Teams got to know these challenges on location during the Camp, building on their preparation process before they arrived and planning for the follow-through after the Camp. The solutions were showcased in an exhibition on the last day of the Camp and are now being transformed into real world developments. In order to keep in touch with progress on this exciting development, see www.ACSI2010.com.

Plymouth (Purcell, 2009) – another British university – aims to become *the* enterprise university. Like Hertfordshire, it is also truly 'business-engaging', delivering outstanding economic, social and cultural benefits from its intellectual capital to its region; like Newcastle it has 'reinvented the civic university' for the 21st century; like Aalto it has a strong societal innovation theme. However, it goes further than any of these by striving to be enterprising in everything it does. To Professor Wendy Purcell, its Vice Chancellor, Enterprise has a very clear definition, meaning a 'boldness or readiness in undertaking; adventurous spirit; ingenuity' and she is working to make her university

> pivotal in a city acknowledged as the enterprise capital of the south west of England. This is based on the firm belief that a university must be at the heart of its community and can drive economic, social and environmental change. A university does this through the creation of new knowledge, an innovative approach to partnership working and a group of staff and students that act as a power for positive change.

Plymouth has set up the policies to enable this vision to occur and is presently implementing university wide processes to enable the appropriate external impact.

Such an approach formed the basis for my own university's – Salford's – attempt at a more encompassing innovative engagement with business and the community in its third strand of all its activities. However, Salford has now gone even further, and not only engages as well as it can, it has also conceived of making 'academic enterprise' an overarching principle to all its outreach relationships – where teaching and learning, research and innovation and engagement, together seek to 'develop all academic opportunities beyond means currently employed with business and community to the highest academic standards and for the mutual benefit of the university and its external partners' (Powell, 2008, 2010, 2011; Powell and

Wainwright, 2009; Powell and Dayson 2012; Hall, 2009). It has also developed its own benchmarking tool, UPBEAT, which is now used by many other universities, to coach academics on the leadership and development of creative teams capable of successful collaborative partnerships with a range of external partners.

As a finale to this reach-out diversity discussion, I draw attention to Matthews et al.'s, (2009) proposal to develop an 'ecoversity' – one with a strong focus towards sustainability. These Australian authors' ideas build on earlier notions of engagement, connectiveness, academic enterprise, civic responsibility, business focus and enterprise, but go further in taking a more ethical stance and focusing their attention on using all these different externally facing academic skills to ensure the world meets its 'triple bottom line' obligations, with respect to social, environmental and economic issues.

What is perfectly clear from all these external engagement developments and aspirations, is that many universities, and especially those working in knowledge cities, now see themselves at the heart of their city region's growth and want to make a big difference in the real world, thereby having a strong impact and making real improvements for their citizens.

While this is not a complete list of the diversity that exists, it is hoped that it gives a flavor of what most global university reach-out aspires towards; most of the examples are presently from the western world, however, other examples of best practice would willingly be received by the author, especially as short cases to complete his understanding for later sharing with others.

TOWARDS A UNIFYING, WORKABLE AND CREATIVE ENGAGEMENT FIT-FOR-GLOBAL-PURPOSE: UNIVERSITIES FOR A MODERN RENAISSANCE

I applaud all the above mentioned approaches, especially the last one. For if we fail to achieve a truly sustainable world then we are all doomed. Universities have the capabilities, the skills, the facilities and the 'know how' to make the kind of changes necessary to achieve a truly sustainable difference. As Matthews et al. (2009) so rightly say, universities may be one of the few societal organizations that can provide the sort of

> unique innovation structure and relative independence for leading the way towards sustainable and creative futures based on engaged knowledge generation, ethical and moral principles and enterprising action. This is an

> increasingly rare capability in an 'institutionally thick', self-regulated, neoliberal economy and society where entity-based managerialism and risk aversion predominate and institutional discussion invariably centres on monetary cost and profit rather than wider social and environmental benefit.

However, for the future, and especially for successful and sustainable knowledge city collaborations, I would wish all existing university engagements to go further than this by taking a more proactive, interactive and highly integrating approach. This requires one last major component to the equation for success – how can universities engage with external partners in truly co-creating ways to ensure beauty, elegance and joy in socially inclusive and wealth creating ways? In other words, I believe universities should not do it *for* their citizens, businesses and communities, but rather *collectively with them* in 'co-creation' and 'co-production'. Fortunately, a new consortium of universities agree with this notion and have begun to strive for what they call a 'Modern Renaissance' – they are true collaborators, who use increasingly systemic explorations of world problems, leading to outputs and outcomes which create socially inclusive improvement of real impact.

The resulting idea of 'Universities for Modern Renaissance' (UMR) developed as a result of discussions by a European Universities Association (EUA) consortium, who tried to conceptualize their unique ways of working with local businesses and the communities in creative and constructive ways (EUA, 2006, Powell et al., 2006; Powell and Wainwright 2009). Based on their own case studies, undertaken to understand their own good UMR practices, the consortium realized it was the richness of their activities, the kind of foresight they used, their co-creation and co-production with partners and the resulting innovation that made the real difference. Other words previously used to describe universities like themselves – words mentioned in the earlier section of this chapter, such as engaged, civic or regeneration, or phrases like community enterprise – did not do justice to their creative, dynamic and co-creating activities. Rather, 'Universities for a Modern Renaissance' succinctly expressed the proactive, progressive, collaborative and developmental ways in which they engaged with business and the community; in their work this consortium sought to define what UMR meant (Powell and Wainwright, 2009).

The PASCAL International Observatory for place management, social capital and learning regions recognized the findings of this study and has recently taken up the idea, developed its own definition and adopted its future looking approach; its aim is to 'put new life, motivation and interest into its own developments for, and with, its own University members across the globe'. According to Bengtsson (2009), PASCAL's Chairman, the 'PASCAL Universities for a Modern Renaissance' (PUMR) program it has thus developed is 'something that has been missing in all outreach of engaged universities world wide and it is a concept which rightly points to something deep that is presently happening in our society'. PUMR clearly recognizes the needs and demands expressed by the aforementioned Coldstream, NESTA, Matthews, Garlick, Smith, Powell, Wilson, Purcell and Goddard, by encompassing all their underlying principles. However, it goes one step further, by seeking to work with others in society to

> co-identify real problems worthy of collective solution, the co-creation of solutions systemically fit-for-purpose in the global knowledge economy, the co-production of those solutions and their stage management into the real world, and further in ensuring the continuous improvement of all such solutions to reach more people with more constructive effect.

PUMR is a developmental program, now driven by PASCAL, which is attempting to empower a region, a city, a town or a village both to recognize the need for new knowledge and skills coming from its universities and also to provide citizens and communities with a higher 'buying power' to acquire the new and relevant knowledge and research at the leading edge. Through its developing academic support program, PASCAL provides access to different aspects and delivery from universities worldwide so that the regions could shop around to find the knowledge needed for different situations. In the common parlance for British universities this could lead to a real transfer of the 'third mission driver' from the university to the region, where the regions could define the kind of university they would like to have.

Summarized below are the key factors that PASCAL has borne in mind when developing the PUMR concept. These key success factors have been developed by PASCAL through a series of in-depth working discussions, both virtually and physically, at its regular meetings and with key interested universities and regions. The factors spell out the need, and perhaps even demand, for enterprise partnerships by those universities that want to work constructively and creatively with external partners in knowledge cities – from business, industry, the civil and voluntary services, the community and society at large – for mutual benefit and to create real impact. In short they demand:

- Forming meaningful, wealth creating, sustainable and socially inclusive partnerships between academia on the one hand and industry, business, the civil and voluntary services and the community on the other;

- Enabling the co-identification of 'real problems for solutions', increasingly fit for purpose for the knowledge economy from as broad a range of stakeholders as is possible;
- Searching for academic opportunities beyond means currently employed with business and community to the highest academic standards and for the mutual benefit of the university and its external partners;
- Unlocking the talents of all citizens working together with their university partners in co-creation, co-design and co-production;
- Developing beyond the traditional academic (critical, scholarly, research and science based) roles into 'action enabling' developments for the 'greater good' which deliver real world improvements;
- Requiring sharing of different kinds of knowledge and 'know-how', in mutually useful ways, by forming relevant strategic alliances;
- Making available professional and practice relevant education and problem based learning for future generations to ensure sustainability;
- Universities will adapt to not just giving information to the students in terms of 'tell and show', but will have to interact with them and act in other more conversational ways. The whole demography of lifelong learning will be different;
- Developing 'practical wisdom' through creative and 'virtuous knowledge sharing' with local businesses, social groups and all citizens for mutual benefit;
- Focusing key components of university activities on higher academic enterprise – sometimes called reach-out, outreach or 'third stream', not separated from normal academic activities, but an integral part of them;
- Harnessing the imagination, reason and daring from all city region talent, including the skills of the university itself, leading to improvements for all;
- Helping all society to cost effectively meet the 'triple bottom line' with respect to environmental, economic and social concerns, while also enabling them to flourish, grow and be creative – the essence of the human condition;
- Reaching out world-wide – to develop deeper conversations with relevant stakeholders to enable developments fit for purpose in the global knowledge economy;
- Helping build confidence and capability in all citizens (in business, industry, the civil and voluntary services, and the community) and developing a more appropriate work–life balance for the modern world.

PASCAL believes that any PUMR university must not just be involved in knowledge production and creation of IP, but open itself up to co-design and co-production to enable the knowledge city or region to cope with complexity, uncertainty and the challenges of all future problems.

The approach has clear and strong links with, and is underpinned by, system science, where academic researchers truly do try to relate their knowledge and 'know-how' to real problems, helping working businesses and communities who are unable to address difficult issues by themselves to do it better. The problems and issues they now have to consider are invariably complex, are often not easy to understand and may often be contextualized in a number of conflicting ways. As Erik Willan (2010) so rightly says, 'one of the key issues for PUMR type projects is that on the one hand "content is king", but on the other hand "context is kingdom".' Unfortunately, 'much of traditional university research is often only uni-disciplinary and context free'; it is general in outlook and tries to be applicable to any case. But, the sort of 'wicked problems' encountered in the real world (Rittel, 1972) and especially in knowledge cities, are multi-disciplinary in nature and require creative solution by trans-disciplinary teams. So, for instance, most regional problems are contextually founded and are richly systemic. As a result university projects in most regions must be true partnerships in both the selection of the problem to be explored and the way it is tackled. Unfortunately, while they really now want to help local businesses and communities, most universities do not have good organizational processes or the right collaborative mechanisms to engage in such issues in a deep and sustainable way. So, the PASCAL approach, with respect to PUMR, is to underpin the regional, and other constructive interactions, with real world issues, using a deeply systemic approach using the best principles of both systems and soft systems science. Furthermore, as in the Scottish Enlightenment, the nature of the PUMR engagements with all societies' problems will be dynamic, fast-acting, highly conversational and innovative in their systemic outlook, and universities would deliberately seek creative ways of co-creative team-working with business, industry, the civil and voluntary services and the community.

In short a cultural shift is needed in order that peoples' 'know how' banks – that which they remember to use in anger in their real world living – can be improved. Here, PUMR engagement will be a two way conversation, not a one way broadcast, and is both systematic and systemic. This improved conversation must be between all parties involved in developing an academic enterprise, including academics and their external partners. All must learn new ways of talking and listening, new modes of conversation, having quality conversation understandable by all in society, but informed by high academic values. The discussions must still be profound, but properly coordinated to enable an appropriate discourse. In the Modern Renaissance, PASCAL is looking to work towards setting up conversations where we can all work together to co-identify a worthy problem, understand the systemic nature of that problem, and then co-create and co-design solutions that are workable for those for whom the solutions are intended.

SHORT CASE EXAMPLES OF BEST PUMR PRACTICE

PASCAL has gained confidence in its PUMR approach from nearly 200 cases of best practice upon which it is based; these all show a common approach for successful university engagement with partners. All successful PUMR engagements seemed to be engendered from deep conversations with their partners in which team members need to step outside of their specific project and think reflectively about whether all their aims and objectives have been met. These cases are shown in some detail in www.upbeat.eu.com and in PASCAL's developing web-site www.pascalobservatory.org. The following short paragraphs show the essence and range of possible activities of those already striving to become PUMRs:

- the University of Victoria in British Columbia, Canada is engaging the 'Binners' of its city and also in Sao Paulo in powerful, cost effective and sustainable Waste Management Developments for the benefit of all;
- Using a sustainable 'Community Land Trust' development pioneered in the USA, Community Finance Solution, of Salford University, UK, has enabled a range of community groups to successfully develop and run a number of 'community-directed affordable housing schemes' for disadvantaged citizens in the UK;
- People's Voice Media, a social enterprise working closely with two Greater Manchester universities is coaching a thousand 'community reporters' in a constructive development known as 'Reuters for the Community'; using sensible, sensitive and cost-effective social media networking this project could enable the sort of 'media conversation' the BBC is looking to promote in the UK when it moves to Manchester;
- The University of British Columbia is working with local citizens to empower them to 'do-it-yourself' in retrofitting their homes to become carbon zero and highly sustainable.

- The UN Global Cities program, led by RMIT in Melbourne, Australia, works across the world to ensure smart city futures enabling citizens and communities to gain confidence to flourish in the global knowledge economy;
- The Aalto University's Camp for Social Innovation is using the skills of university expertise through the world to work with citizens in Helsinki to empower them to help solve six major local problems in their city; key in this is to use 'Flip-video' technology linked to powerful social media networks to continuously improve prospective solutions;
- 'Contraception: the Board Game' was developed by Barbara Asatorian-Hastings of Salford University, to effectively help young people learn about the correct use of contraception in a happy learning environment; this has cut down the number of unwanted pregnancies through the world and made its university inventor one of the top women inventors in Europe;
- Digital City is a concept developed by Janice Webster of Teesside University to put its city, Middlesbrough in the UK, at the centre of the modern knowledge economy revolution.

CONCLUSION

According to Garlick (2010), the knowledge economy has so far failed to deliver imaginative real outcomes in the form of sustainable enterprises and employment with the result that many regions outside the largest metropolitan centres are suffering a loss of human capital through unemployment, underemployment, 'brain drain' and retirement. Universities are often presently a part of this problem, having been party to such so-called knowledge transfer mechanisms as business clusters, science parks, 'creative milieus', social capital, etc. So, as John Tibbitt's (2009) explorations reveal, at the very least an 'engagement gap' exists between universities and true city-regional needs. It is PASCAL's belief that its PUMR approach, building on the best practice of other knowledge city engagements throughout the world, will make a real difference in enabling both PUMR universities and their related knowledge cities to flourish. It will do this by starting with the development of a better understanding of what 'knowledge city' and 'knowledge regional' expectations are, what they actually demand from their universities and what universities might do to help their regions creatively and constructively.

PUMR can lead to better ways of analyzing existing problems, especially holistically and from a trans-disciplinary perspective, and to better understanding of what the 'engagement gap' really is and how to coach traditional academics into enterprising ones who can make a real difference to academic enterprise partnerships. In discussing this issue further, Tibbitt (2009) was put in mind of

> much writing about social policy with attempts at trying to encourage collaboration between different services and the delivery of shared goals. So PUMR universities must attempt to codify what the collaborative relationship might be and to specify different kinds of relationship from the mere formal information sharing at one end of the spectrum, right through to a more sophisticated conversational process, to ultimately a merger between organizations – where people share their objectives, accountabilities and joint action.

And Tibbitt (2009) also wondered whether PASCAL's PUMR approach could 'develop the kind of successful thinking and engagement relationships there might be for sustainable success; we might also attempt to generate a better mapping of what could be the necessary improved engagements for all societal innovations'. I would personally support this stance, and go further, by agreeing with Garlick (2010) that the 'regional development agenda needs to go beyond knowledge generation and transmission, becoming "enterprising" *co-creation*'. Garlick uses the term 'enterprising' with the 'same characteristics of the key words of 'opportunity' and 'advantage' used by Sen (2009) with respect to the development of human capability'. Such an approach emphasizes individual 'ambition' and 'opportunity', rather than institutionally defined, competency-oriented, and path dependency learning to meet specified commodity objectives.

The PUMR is a global attempt to go beyond simply reaching out to society. It is proposing new ways of working and improved processes for the co-identification of problems felt worthy by society, and co-creation and co-design of sustainable solutions fit for the knowledge economy. Whatever it is called in future, society will increasingly demand university reach-out where:

- University partnerships are socially inclusive in order to achieve sustainable success, working for the 'common good'. This focuses member universities on engaging all the communities within their regions, and on all the communities within their own colleges and universities, to work collaboratively with them, in co-creation, to help them transform their own lives and enable all categories of citizen to flourish.
- Regional engagements built on value through co-creation. Value comes from working together with partners to co-identify problems,

co-design solutions, and then co-produce outcomes that address shared, important priority concerns.

- External engagement will co-create many different types of value. Even though today's political climate and economic circumstances may place greater emphasis on creating economic value, a truly modern regional renaissance needs to a more balanced approach based on co-producing many different types of value.
- The concept of 'eco-versity' is allowed to flourish and provide a more 'balanced scorecard' approach for assessing university engagements. This uses a 'triple bottom line' of environmental, economic and social sustainability, which is key to what PUMR members are currently seeking to do, but we need better metrics.
- Enterprising academics in them must be prepared to reach out, aggressively if need be, to add value because non-academic partners often find it hard to build sustainable relationships with higher academic institutions.
- Co-creating value with regional partners also co-creates opportunities for high quality research and learning for faculty and students because real solutions blend interdisciplinary points of view with the full complexity of social, cultural and economic settings.

Knowledge cities need universities that work in more inclusive, innovative and integrating ways with them. This requires a paradigm shift in the strategy of universities. However, as useful as they may well be, advanced notions such as PUMR will take at least a decade to embed, so we must be aware of this and the relevant time perspective; we must also be aware during the change process of the difficulties that will inevitably follow when we try to introduce PUMR to the traditional world of university life.

REFERENCES

Abrue, M., Grinevech V., Hughes, A., and Kitson, M. (2009), *Knowledge Exchange between Academics and Business, Public and the Third Sector*, UK-IRC, Imperial College and Cambridge University.

Bengtsson, J. (2009), private communication on PASCAL web-site www.pascalobservatory.org, resulting from 'Towards Universities for a Modern Renaissance', International Conference on the Future Directions of PASCAL, University of Glasgow, 14 December 2009.

Clarke, B.R. (1998), *Creating Entrepreneurial Universities – Organisational Pathways of Transformation*, IAU Press, Issues in Higher Education, Elsevier, p. 163.

Coldstream P. (2001), *Engagement as a Core Value for the University: A Consultation Document*, Association of Commonwealth Universities.
Coldstream P. and Bjarnason, Svava (2003), *The Idea of Engagement*, Association of Commonwealth Universities.
EUA (European Universities Association) (2006), 'Creativity in higher education – a Socrates project and briefing note', European Universities Association (EUA), http://www.eua.be/eua/jsp/upload/
Fitzgerald, H.E., Burack, C., and Seifer, S. (2011), *Handbook of Engaged Scholarship: Contemporary Landscapes, Future Directions. Vol. 1: Institutional Change*, East Lansing, MI, USA: Michigan State University Press.
Garlick S. (2010), private communication during PASCAL Conference on Universities for a Modern Renaissance, 12 December 2009 www.pascalobservatory.org
Garlick, S. and Langworthy, A. (2009), Benchmarking Workshop, the Association of University of Community Engagement in Australia, 30 April, AUCEA.
Goddard, J. (2009), *Reinventing the Civic University*, September, NESTA.
Hall, Martin (2009), University of Salford Strategic Plan 2009/10 to 2017/18, University of Salford, December.
Matthews, J.M., Garlick, S., and Smith, T. (2009), 'Ecoversity: towards a sustainable future', in *Journal of World University Forum*, World University Forum.
Powell, James (2008), 'Elaborating academic enterprise for the University of Salford', in K. Lane, P. van der Sijde, M. Lahdeniemi and J. Tarkkanen (eds), *Higher Education Institutions and Innovation in the Knowledge Economy*, ARENE Publishing, pp. 61–81
Powell, J.A. (2010) 'University knowledge through knowledge sharing – UPBEAT: university engagement through virtuous knowledge sharing and academic staff development', in H.E. Fitzgerald, C. Burack, and S. Seifer (eds), Handbook of Engaged Scholarship: Contemporary Landscapes, Future Directions. Vol. 1: Institutional Change, East Lansing, MI, USA: Michigan State University Press, pp. 1–29.
Powell, J.A. (2011) 'The university role in the innovative leadership of small to medium sized enterprises – towards "Universities for a Modern Renaissance" (UMR)', in the *International Journal for Entrepreneurial Behaviour and Research*.
Powell, J.A. and Dayson, K. (2012) 'Engagement and the idea of the civic university', in Paul Benneworth (ed.), *University Engagement with Socially Excluded Communities: Towards the Idea of 'The Engaged University'*, Vienna: Springer-Verlag.
Powell, J.A. and Wainwright, C. (2009), *Universities for a Modern Renaissance*, Institute of the Arts London and the University of Salford.
Powell, J.A., Druzhin, G., Khrykov, Y., Lawrence, K., Matei, L., Ozsoy, A., Reichert, S., Rzezuchowski, T., Saerheim, I., and Wainwright, C. (2006), 'Final report to the EUA in its Socrates funded Creativity in Higher Education Programme', Creative Universities for Creative City-Regions Thematic Network, European Universities Association.
Purcell, W. (2009) *Prospectus for the University of Plymouth*, Plymouth University.
Rittel, H. (1972) *Wicked Problems, Design Studies*, **2** (1).
Sen, A. (2009) 'Global citizens', lecture, UCL, London.
Stewart, F. (2008), *Breaking the Boundaries: Transformative Innovation for the Global Good,* NESTA.
Tibbitt, J. (2009), private communication on 'Towards universities for a modern

renaissance' International Conference on the Future Directions of PASCAL, – University of Glasgow, 14 December, www.pascalobservatory.org

Willan E. (2010), private communication, PASCAL conference 'Towards universities for a modern renaissance', 12 December 2009, www.pascalobservatory.org

Wilson T. (2009), *Prospectus for the University of Hertfordshire*, University of Hertfordshire.

15. Transforming: turning knowledge cities into a knowledge region

Caren Heidemann, Klaus R. Kunzmann and Klaus Wermker

INTRODUCTION: KNOWLEDGE SOCIETY, KNOWLEDGE CITIES, AND KNOWLEDGE REGIONS – MUCH RHETORIC, LITTLE ACTION?

In the 21st century knowledge has become a precious local and regional resource for post-industrial territories, which were severely affected by the economic and social implications of structural change. To compensate for the loss of industrial monopolistic power, and to remain competitive in a world economy, the new global division of labour forces cities and regions in Europe (and beyond) to develop knowledge as a local and regional resource. Consequently, preparing for a knowledge society has become the new political challenge. An abundant number of Anglo-American, German and French publications (for example, Meusburger 1998; Matthiesen 2004: Kunzmann 2008; Matthiesen and Mahnken, 2009, Roost 2010; Kaube 2009; Yigitcanlar 2010; Brake 2010; Kujath 2010) and special issues of journals (for example Hilpert 2006; Carrillo et al. 2010; Chapain et al. 2009; *Revue urbanisme* 2010; Matthiesen 2009) is covering the challenge.

To come from knowledge and awareness to action requires engagement at all tiers of governance (Kunzmann 2004a, 2004b; Stifterverband 2009; Ingallina 2010; Charles 2010). In Europe, where higher education is still a domain of the public sector, it depends on policies and strategies at four or even five tiers of government, from the local and regional, to the national and European tier. As a rule, policies at higher levels of planning and decision-making target knowledge institutions and their respective environments by promoting innovation and research. Thereby the spatial dimension of developing the knowledge environment is often neglected or remains weak. The European Union provides more funds for international research and means for innovative approaches to regional development, to remain competitive with North America and Asia. National governments, or state governments, as in the Federal Republic of Germany, gradually increase budgets for education and research to contribute their share to European knowledge strategies and to maintain their influence. Where regions have a role in knowledge development, they promote regional innovation, formulate regional strategies and implement policies from higher tiers. Finally, local governments shift their attention from industrial parks to knowledge environments. They aim to respond better to the spatial and social requirements of local knowledge institutions. Attracting talents, the best students, renowned scholars and innovative knowledge industries has become a prime concern of cities or regions wanting to remain competitive in the global economy.

Polycentric city regions, like the Ruhr in Germany, are facing particular problems, when pursuing knowledge strategies. As a rule they have to bring together self-assured local governments and to overcome traditional intra-regional jelousies. Thereby they have to rely to a large extent on external financial support from higher tiers of government. Worldwide there are very few examples where polycentric city regions were able to overcome the many impediments for joint knowledge strategies.

In this chapter, a recent initiative in the Ruhr Area in Germany, to turn an old industrial region into a knowledge region, will be sketched, changing the regional economy from coal mining and steel production to knowledge development. Suffering from multiple legacies of a glorious industrial past, the Ruhr in Germany is in a comparably weak position to compete with other metropolitan city regions in the country, such as Munich, Stuttgart, or Berlin.

The approach of the CampusRuhr Initiative, presented, is a unique strategic bottom-up process of spatial policy integration, involving major stakeholders of the regional knowledge society, picked individually from universities, other institutes of higher education, local economic development and urban development departments, research institutes, research foundations etc. The expected outcome of the CampusRuhr Initiative is a spatially and mentally integrated network of modern knowledge institutions in the former industrial region, which is a condition for the region to become an integrated knowledge environment. The efforts are still at the beginning, but it may be worthwhile to share the experience and encourage other city regions to undertake similar initiatives.

THE RUHR: FROM COAL AND STEEL TO KNOWLEDGE PRODUCTION

Until the early 1960s, the cities in the Ruhr, a powerful industrial region with a population of more than 5 million, had no university (Prossek et al. 2009). Nevertheless the polycentric region, which was dominated by coal and steel production, had a very skilled industrial labour force, and an excellent vocational training tradition. Academically qualified knowledge workers were not trained in the region. Engineers and managers were educated at state universities outside the region (primarily in Aachen, Cologne, Münster, Hannover, Clausthal-Zellerfeld or Braunschweig). Consequently academic knowledge milieus, profiling the region, were absent. Knowledge development was in the hands of the large and powerful coal and steel corporations. Hence a regional knowledge culture, beyond the regionally rooted iron and steel milieus, could not evolve. The local political elite grew almost exclusively from working class milieus and trade unions.

In 1960, things started to change. A far-sighted political initiative by the State of North Rhine-Westphalia launched a new vision for the region. During less than a decade the State Government (all major universities in Germany are state universities!) took action and established new state universities in Dortmund, Essen, Duisburg, and Bochum. However, it took more than forty years to root higher education in the traditional working class milieus and turn the industrial cities into emerging knowledge cities. Although coal mining and steel production have almost come to an end in the region, the cities still do not feel like gown towns, such as Heidelberg, Goettingen, Marburg or Tübingen. Given the social fabric of the cities, dominated by heavy industries, any effort to focus local development on the promotion of future oriented white knowledge industries is a challenge for the local political class. To respond to the challenges of structural change (and globalization), the cities in the region are competing rather than joining forces. Consequently, regional cooperation is rather the exception than the rule. And given the strong tradition of local self-government, the established regional authority is much too weak to set up a strong regional agenda for accelerated knowledge development. The State of North Rhine Westphalia, a strong political institution, which is quite independent from the Federal Government of Germany, cannot urge the region to review its local development priorities. The influence of the state is rather indirect by granting financial support for selected local projects. Given the explicit federalist structure of Germany, the Federal Government has only little power to intervene. Only via national industrial and labour policies has it a chance to influence and guide regional economic development policies. As all state universities are the responsibility of the independent states, the Federal Government can support universities and research centres only by launching generous research programmes.

The Ruhr in Germany is a polycentric city region with a population of more than 5 million and a few large cities, such as Essen, Dortmund, Duisburg, Bochum and Gelsenkirchen. The densely populated region is divided among three provincial authorities, which execute state policies and control local governments. The region has a unique institution, the Regionalverband Ruhrgebiet, a follow-up institution to the Siedlungsverband Ruhrkohlenbezirk, a regional authority established almost 100 years ago to guide regional spatial planning and development, much admired abroad for its innovative regional agenda. The Regionalverband Ruhrgebiet is not a top-down institution. It is governed by representatives of 11 municipal governments and 4 counties, surveying another 42 local governments, and by representatives of labour and corporate associations. The main objective of individual local governments in the regional Assembly is to take care that local interests are not sacrificed to regional concerns. Following the logics of the Association's charter and representative democracy, regional knowledge institutions do not have a voice in the regional assembly. Without much political legitimacy, and manoeuvring between a strong state and powerful local governments, this regional authority is very weak. It has no power over local governments, and is not legitimized to act in key policy fields such as transport, energy, housing or even education and research. What remains are, among others, regional marketing, waste management and forestry. Even regional intelligence is not a strong action area for the authority. To some extent, through its small agency for metropolitan development *metropoleruhr*, it can do some regional economic marketing and promote regional economic development by distributing state funds for special projects. Given this weak stance, aggravated by traditional intraregional jealousies between the major cities in the Ruhr, the regional authority is not in a position, and is not requested or encouraged by the local governments, to develop longer-term future oriented development strategies. Co-ordinating efforts of local governments and developing a regional knowledge profile is not a legitimized concern of the established regional authority in the Ruhr. Other regional institutions, such as the influential chambers of commerce, or the public-owned regional utility corporations for energy, water and sewage pursue their own corporate interests. The responsible managers are praised and rewarded for their corporate success, not for their contributions to regional development, and not for overcoming local parochialism.

THE RUHR 2010: AN IMPRESSIVE KNOWLEDGE LANDSCAPE . . .

Mapping the impressive success of half a century of efforts to restructure a powerful old industrial landscape into a modern knowledge environment reveals the magnitude of changes in the region (Kunzmann 2001, 2004a, 2004b; Tenfelde and Urban 2011; Engel et al. 2011; Kunzmann 2011). Up to the year 1960, coal mines and steelworks in the region dominated the regional economy and a huge labour market. Together with the related forward and backward linkages in logistics, chemicals and heavy machinery production, the majority of jobs were dependent on the industry, which dominated the regional economy. Today, just four mines are still exploiting coal, and, according to political decisions made in the beginning of the new millennium, for a number of reasons all coal mining will come to an end in the region by 2018. Coal on the world market is much cheaper than in the Ruhr, labour costs in the region are too high, the European Commission did not accept the high subsidies given to the coal industry by the German Government, and environmental concerns increased the costs for exploiting the coal deposits. As a consequence, the Ruhrkohle, the once powerful coal corporation, headquartered in Essen, has already changed its name into Evonik, a corporation involved in chemical and various non coal related production in the region and branches all around the world. Similarly steel production is decreasing in the region. Only one steel works in Duisburg is still producing raw steel in the Ruhr. Other steelworks have been demolished and replaced by shopping centres, as in Oberhausen or dismantled and transported to China, as the Westfalenhütte in Dortmund. Wherever local initiatives or new spatial pioneers succeeded in gaining access to derelict pits and production sites of the coal and steel corporations, protected as industrial heritage since more than a decade ago, they turned them into locations for culture, and related cultural and creative industries.

Knowledge industries, following the rationales of state ministries for education and research, economics and labour, as well as university boards, never grasped the chance to turn industrial brownfields into knowledge establishments. This is a legacy of the industrial past, where educational priorities were set on the qualification of a skilled blue-collar labour force, and the dual system of professional education in Germany. The fact that only 8.6 per cent of the labour force in the region had a university degree in 2005, and only 20 per cent of high school graduates were eligible for studying at a university shows that the region has to accelerate its efforts to remain competitive as a labour market with other city regions in Germany and beyond.

Nevertheless, looking at the state of knowledge industries in the Ruhr in

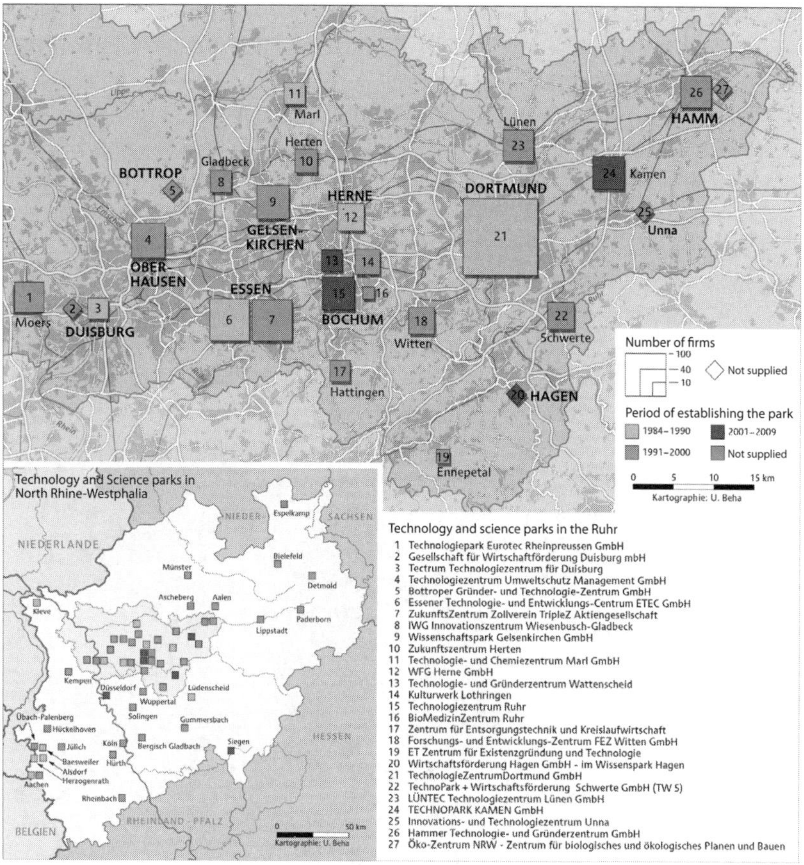

Figure 15.1 Technology and science parks in the Ruhr

2010, the changes are impressive (Müller-Bölling and Rohe 2011; Stiftung Mercator 2010). In 2010, 15 institutes of higher education are located in the Ruhr. Six universities (the Technical University in Dortmund, the universities in Duisburg/Essen and Bochum, the University of the Arts Essen, the small private university in Witten-Herdecke, and the Distance Learning Correspondence University (*Fernuniversität*) in Hagen) and nine colleges of applied arts and sciences (Fachhochschulen) are located in the polycentric region. With the exception of Oberhausen, all cities in the Ruhr with a population of more than 100 000 have their own local institute of higher education. They provide undergraduate and graduate education for around 165 000 students. sixty per cent of these students come from the region, only 13 per cent are students from foreign

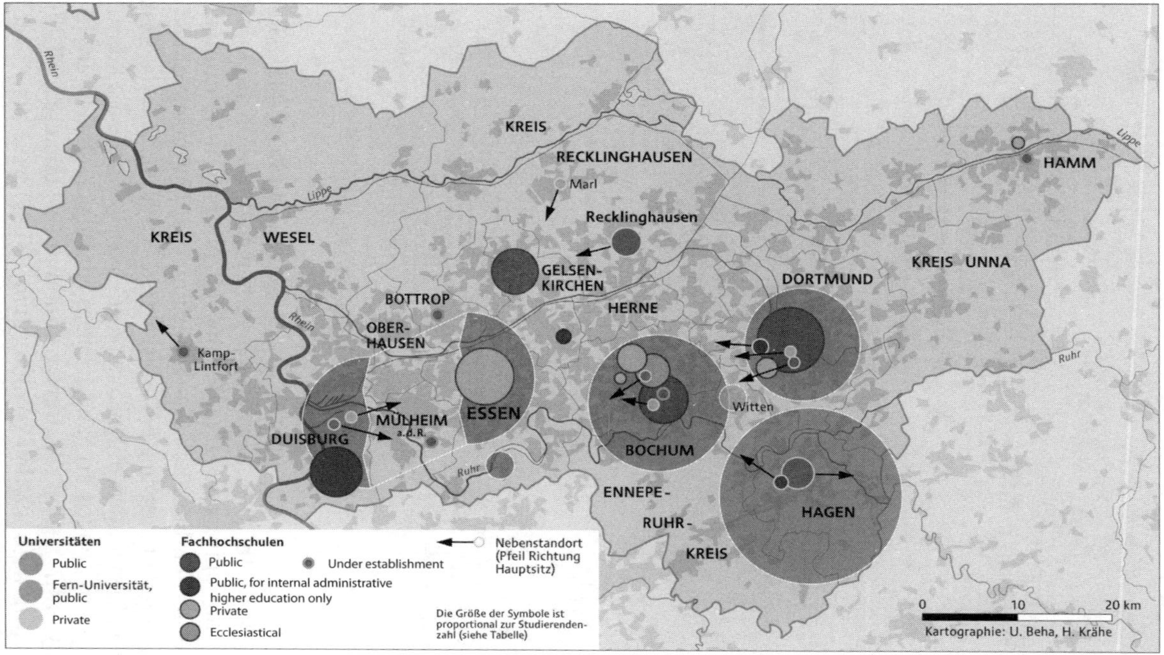

Figure 15.2 Institutes of higher education in the Ruhr

countries, mainly from China, South East Europe and the Middle East. Every year 20 000 students enrol in one of the regional institutions of higher education. More than 10 000 teaching staff and researchers are working at these knowledge institutions and in a multitude of public and semi-public research institutes and science centres which have been established all over the region during four decades of strategic regional restructuring. These institutes included four Fraunhofer, four Leibnitz and three Max Planck Institutes. Traditionally, however, a considerable share of basic and applied research activities are done outside institutes of higher education in Germany. Together they form impressive innovative knowledge cores in the former industrial region. In their neighbourhood more than 30 technology and science parks have been established. The biggest one is developed in the neighbourhood of the Technical University of Dortmund, and benefits from the availability of land at out-of-town locations. These new technology parks have become the cradles of innovation and future oriented technologies and the home of many new firms and enterprises. They add new fields of knowledge and expertise in nano-, plasma and bio-technologies, in environmental and life sciences or in communication and information sciences, to traditional areas of competence such as logistics and energy production. Additionally, the particular challenges of structural change in a region dominated for a century by heavy industries, have nurtured the evolution of expertise in basic and applied regional science, which is increasingly sought after beyond the Ruhr. All this forms a dense network of innovative knowledge institutions, which employ a new generation of regionally educated and trained knowledge workers and attract international talents from beyond the region. Thus, at the beginning of the 21st century the Ruhr does easily benchmark with the density of knowledge industries in other metropolitan regions in Germany (Kunzmann 2011).

The impressive transformation of the Ruhr from a traditional industrial knowledge region to a modern post-industrial knowledge region is still in progress. Given the gigantic task, a few more decades will be required to bring this transformation to an end, respectively to a new cycle of innovation (Kunzmann 2009a).

. . . THOUGH A KNOWLEDGE REGION WITH A FEW SHORTCOMINGS

When exploring the knowledge dimension of the transformation process in the region at the beginning of the new millennium, however, some shortcomings cannot be overlooked:

- When the first new universities were established by the state government in the 1960s and related research establishments followed, they could not be located at the inner city sites of the traditional industries. Like out-of-town shopping malls they had to be built as campus universities on virgin land at the outer fringes of the cities and far from built-up areas, though without the facilities and the spirit of traditional campus universities as known from the Anglo-American world of higher education. Following early criticism of the academic community in the region only the University of Essen was built on a former derelict site at the edge of the city centre. The power of the established regional industries, owning most of the land in the region, did not allow more forward-looking locational decisions. This, obviously, slowed down the integration of the new knowledge institutions into the cities of Bochum, Duisburg and Dortmund, spatially, economically and socially. Today the cities are confronted with two urban development challenges. They have to find new uses for abundant industrial brownfields in the inner city. And they have to overcome the locational disadvantages of the pragmatic decisions made a few decades ago, when appropriate sites for the new universities were selected.
- The international image of the region as an innovative science region is still weak. It reflects the low international profile of the young though economically strong state of North Rhine-Westphalia. This makes the region comparably less attractive for international elite students and scholars in comparison to more appealing cities such as Munich and Berlin, or to internationally renowned universities, such as Heidelberg, Karlsruhe or Aachen. This does not reflect a lower scientific quality of the regional institutions of higher education. It is rather the consequence of a traditionally much introverted nature of the region, the absence of hospitality and the dearth of cosmopolitan and media covered lifestyle milieus. After having successfully graduated from universities in the Ruhr, many international students proceed for further qualifying doctoral and post-doc studies to the United States or other more Anglophile countries, while only a few students from abroad are successfully attracted and encouraged to continue their research career in the region.
- The presence of the regional institutions of higher education in the cities is not visible. Mostly located at the outer fringe of the cities, the functional university buildings are not representative elements of the polycentric urban landscape, not palpable parts of everyday city life. Student milieus did not generate alluring student entertainment quarters in the precincts of the universities, attractive alike to stu-

dents and researchers, to citizens and tourists. Mainly for pragmatic and financial reasons derelict industrial buildings were not considered to be appropriate structures for modern knowledge institutions. Universities are not integrated into the urban landscape. They are seen as factories on knowledge islands producing degrees rather than as urban symbols of knowledge and civic pride. Though this deficit has been widely acknowledged, a recent decision to locate a new institute of higher education in Muelheim was once more taken against an inner city location (Ruhrbania 2009). Housing policies in the region, traditionally targeting miners, steelworkers and related working class communities, hardly provide the particular needs of housing for the new academic middle class. Consequently, no urban districts emerged satisfying the requirements of the new urbanites.

- Even after almost half a century, universities and knowledge institutions are still not an integral part of the regional society. Although much acclaimed in local and regional marketing brochures, they are not an essential target of urban and regional policies, nor a fully acknowledged element of strategic local development. Local political circles are still over-dominated by representatives of the traditional industrial complex. The generational change from miners and steelworkers to IT managers or eco-science knowledge workers is progressing very slowly. It seems there are still many mental cultural and ideological barriers to be removed. Only few representatives of the new knowledge class sit in local councils. Hence the interests and requirements of the new scientific community are not well articulated in local planning and decision-making processes. It reflects the fact that the managerial class of the regional industries and the academic class of the regional knowledge institutions are still two widely separated communities, with only few communication bridges. On both sides, external linkages are usually favoured over local and regional ones.
- Not surprisingly, a significant deficit in the region is the relative dearth of regional discourse milieus. In the absence of intellectually profiled regional media, and the lack of a strong regional identity, regional discourse hardly takes place. Though again and again single efforts have been undertaken to promote a joint regional identity, local parochialism dominates. Regional solidarity is expressed only if the Ruhr is being criticized for its proneness to asking for public subsidies for promoting structural change and for cushioning the severe social implications of the long transformation process. A joint regional vision of necessary action for regional structural change does not exist. As soon as suggestions for the necessary

> functional division of labour in the region are being made, resistance is being expressed from local stakeholders, killing any effort for concentrated action. In addition it is known that the state government of North Rhine-Westphalia, being afraid of losing regional balance, does not support a strong Ruhr, speaking with one voice and potentially challenging the leadership of the state government.

In the past, no major effort was undertaken, either by the state government, or by the established regional authority, to embark on a joint regional knowledge strategy. Only the three universities (Bochum, Essen and Dortmund) signed a contract to overcome their isolation and to cooperate in selected fields of concerted action. It seems, however, that the cooperation is rather symbolic than real. The fear of state government intervention and the worry of losing individual freedom prevented the institutions agreeing on a better division of labour and promotion of scientific cooperation. Hence there is still much to be done to profile the polycentric city region as a knowledge region, regionally, nationally and internationally.

CONCLUSION: CAMPUS RUHR – A MUNICIPAL GRASSROOTS STRATEGY

In 2010, on account of the increasing competition among German institutes of higher education, and realizing that the spatial integration of the universities was unsatisfactory, local governments in the Ruhr started an initiative to overcome municipal boundaries and turn the individual knowledge cities into an integrated knowledge region. Inspired and led by the urban development department of Essen, a small group of persons committed to the region, not to single cities, and aware of the need to support the knowledge transformation of the region, came together, to jointly explore ways and means for developing a regional knowledge strategy from below. From below means that the initiative, labelled CampusRuhr, was not triggered by the university rectors in the region and not set in place and financed by the state government. Supported politically by the major cities in the Ruhr, the heads of urban planning departments promoted the initiative and authorized the urban development departments of Essen and Bochum to take action. Persons invited to join the ambitious group came from institutions involved in knowledge development, held positions as stakeholders for furthering knowledge development in the region, or promoted regional development for innovation and knowledge advancement. The members of the kick-off group were invited as knowledgeable and influential individuals, committed to the field, deliberately not as representatives of knowledge regional institutions. This was done to avoid time-consuming representative action, which by regional experience rather slows down consensus-finding processes or even gridlocks decisions to change the status quo in the region.

After agreeing on the need for such an initiative, in a first round, a regional conference was organized to attract a larger regional audience and seek consensus for further strategic action. Most cities and many stakeholders of regional knowledge institutions attended the event, articulated their expectations and contributed their knowledge to the initiative. They agreed that a regional strategy to profile the whole region – not single cities – as a knowledge region, had to be developed and implemented (Kunzmann 2009b). The inviting initiators of the event and the participants were aware that there was a long way to go, to orchestrate cities and to win unanimous support from all the knowledge institutions and related knowledge industries in the region. Three concerns dominated the discussion. First, what were the explicit regional, and not local, dimensions of such a strategy? Second, how should a regional strategy, which bridges local governments with knowledge institutions, be elaborated and who should do it? Third, who would be willing to finance the development of such a strategy, given the stance that it should evolve from below and not as a strategy imposed from the state government, with all the implications for ideologically motivated political intervention? (Party politics and election periods play a significant role in Germany.) Given the innovative character of the strategy, it would be almost impossible to convince local governments in the region to share the costs. Their weak financial status in times of the financial crisis would not allow them to invest in activities that were not mandatory for local governments. Too many voices would be raised in discord. Obviously such concerns could not be pushed aside during this first event, though the participants were aware that adequate ways had to be explored to deal with such fears and the implications for individual cities and institutions. On the other hand it was much easier to consent on the nature of regional challenges and on necessary fields of action for a joint regional strategy. Major challenges to profile the Ruhr as an internationally competitive knowledge region were seen to be factors like the ones mentioned above, in particular:

- The low international image of the region as a knowledge region for a number of reasons, though mainly due to the absence of internationally renowned prestige universities (Kunzmann 2002), although single faculties of these universities have a high international reputation, such as medicine, logistics, geo-engineering or spatial planning;

- The lack of a powerful regional authority and the lack of visionary regionally legitimized leadership;
- The absence of explicit spatial strategies to develop attractive knowledge quarters in the region.

Similarly, essential fields of a strategic action agenda, identified in this first round of communication, easily found consensus. They were:

- Enhancing the cosmopolitan profile of the region;
- Improving the regional accessibility of dispersed knowledge locations;
- Paying more attention to the spatial dimension of knowledge development in the region;
- Raising visibility of the knowledge complex in the cities;
- Attracting international conventions and congresses to the region;
- Improving conviviality and international hospitality for knowledge workers;
- Marketing the region as a place for advanced studies and post doc research in areas where the regional knowledge complex has particular competence;
- Raising the interest of regional media in the knowledge dimension of regional development;
- Improving the communication among knowledge institutions in the region and between the knowledge complex and regional communities;
- Increasing the political representation of knowledge workers in local parliaments and in the regional assembly.

The CampusRuhr Initiative had a good start. It encouraged the small group of regional knowledge enthusiasts to further commit to and follow up the project, and to continue where windows of opportunities were open. They were aware that a municipal grassroots strategy in a polycentric city region, which is burdened with all the economic, social, environmental and political legacies of its industrial past, requires much communication, mutual understanding, tolerance and patience, and the willingness of the knowledge institutions to cooperate more closely with their local institutions, while pursuing their academic goals and objectives.

The CampusRuhr Initiative has already triggered a number of actions, which will be crucial for promoting the regional strategic vision. A first step toward implementing the vision of the initiative was the drafting of an intercommunal knowledge contract to be signed by the mayors of the participating cities in the Ruhr. This contract, a weak, though quite symbolic instrument to put knowledge development higher on the political agenda, follows a similar contract, signed in 2003 by 11 cities to strengthen their inter-communal co-operation. The purpose of the knowledge contract is to raise citizens' general awareness of knowledge development, to increase the efforts to strengthen the regional knowledge complex, to formulate principles of knowledge development, to identify pioneering knowledge development projects jointly, to improve the regional accessibility of the institutes of higher education, to jointly organize international knowledge conventions, and to promote the regional universities nationally and internationally. The contract, moreover, should lay the foundations for a better institutional cooperation among the local governments. Signing the contract will become a media covered occasion for mayors, demonstrating their commitment to the Initiative.

Another project to support the vision will be the institutionalization of a regional knowledge forum as an opportunity to bring together stakeholders and the community of knowledge workers. This forum is conceived as a moving event, wandering from city to city, to raise awareness and to strengthen knowledge identities in the region. A third project is drafted by an interdisciplinary team of planners and researchers from the universities in Dortmund, Bochum and Essen. It aims to elaborate the basics for a spatial knowledge master plan for the Ruhr.

Given the industrial legacy of the region, and its comparatively poor metropolitan qualities, all these good intentions and activities will not transform the Ruhr into a future oriented knowledge heaven. They cannot compensate for decades of negligence though they can contribute to a gradual transformation of a region dominated for more than a century by heavy industries into a modern highly urbanized region, where a mix of traditional and knowledge industries provides attractive jobs for a better educated and more cosmopolitan regional population. The path to regional modernization is long and costly, but it seems that the cities in the region are learning and willing to take the necessary political decisions to transform themselves into knowledge cities and develop a knowledge network region. They have learnt that, like in football (the traditional arena of regional identity building), they can only win as team.

REFERENCES

Brake, Klaus (2010), 'Typen begabter Räume. Über die kontextuellen Interdependenzen von Wissen und Stadt', in *Polis, Magazin für Urban Development*, 32–37.

Carrillo, Francisco Javier, Kostas Metaxiotis and Tan Yigitcanlar (eds) (2010),

'Knowledge based development', *Journal of Knowledge Management*, Special Issue, **14** (5).

Chapain, Caroline, Chris Collenge, Peter Lee and Sako Musterd (eds) (2009), 'Can we plan the creative knowledge city?', *Built Environment*, Special Issue, **35**, (2).

Charles, David (2010), 'Universités et développement territorial; strategie de convergance', *Revue Urbanisme*, **82**, 74–76.

Engel, Klaus, Jürgen Grossmann and Bodo Hombach (eds) (2011), *Phönix flieg. Das Ruhrgebiet entdeckt sich neu*, Essen: Klartext Verlag.

Hilpert, Ulrich (ed.) (2006), 'Knowledge in the region', *European Planning Studies*, Special Issue, **14**(5), June.

Ingallina, Patrizia (2010), 'Attractivité and compétitivité: le role des knowledge industries en Ile-de-France', *Revue urbanisme*, **82**, 61–64

Kaube, Jürgen (2009), *Die Illusion der Exzellenz. Lebenslügen der Wissenschaftspolitik*, Berlin: Wagenbach Verlag.

Kujath, Hans Joachim (2010), 'Der Wandel des Städtesystems in der Wissensökonomie', in Frank Roost (ed.), *Metropolregionen in der Wissensökonomie*, Detmold: Verlag Dorothea Rohn, pp. 19–42.

Kunzmann, Klaus R. (2001), 'The Ruhr in Germany: a laboratory for regional governance', in Louis Albrechts, J. Alden and A. da Rosa Pires (eds), *The Changing Institutional Landscape*, London, Aldershot: Ashgate, pp. 133–158.

Kunzmann, Klaus R. (2002), 'Zur Internationalisierung der Universitäten im Ruhrgebiet', in W. Grünzweig, M. Kleiner and W. Weber (eds), *Bürokratie und Subversion. Die Universität in der permanenten Reform auf dem Weg zu sich selbst*, Reihe Bildung und Innovation, Bd. 1, Münster: LIT Verlag, pp.193–208.

Kunzmann, Klaus R. (2004a), 'Wissensstädte: Neue Aufgaben für die Stadtpolitik', in U. Matthiesen (ed.), *Stadtregion und Wissen: Analysen und Plädoyers für eine wissensbasierte Stadtpolitik*, Wiesbaden: VS Verlag für Sozialwissenschaften.

Kunzmann, Klaus R. (2004b), 'Creative brownfield redevelopment: the experience of the IBA Emscher Park initiative in the Ruhr in Germany', in Rosalind Greenstein and Yesim Sungu-Eryilmaz (eds), *Recycling the City: The Use and Reuse of Urban Land*, Cambridge: Lincoln Institute of Land Policy, pp. 201–217.

Kunzmann, Klaus R. (2008), 'Afterword', in Tan Yigitcanlar, Koray Velibeyoglu and Scott Baum (eds), *Knowledge-Based Urban Development Planning and Applications in the Information Era,* Hershey/New York: Information Science Reference, pp. 296–300.

Kunzmann, Klaus R. (2009a) 'Welche Zukunft hat das Ruhrgebiet? Sechs Szenarien für 2035 und danach', in Achim Prossek, Helmut Schneider, Horst A. Wessel, Burkhard Wetterau and Dorothea Viktorin (eds) *Atlas der Metropole Ruhr: Vielfalt und Wandel des Ruhrgebiets im Kartenbild*, Köln. Emmons Verlag, pp. 2008–2011.

Kunzmann, Klaus R. (2009b), 'The strategic dimensions of knowledge industries', *Planning Review*, 177, 40–49.

Kunzmann, Klaus R. (2011), 'Wissenschaftsregion Metropole Ruhr', in *Metropole Ruhr Raum für Zukunft*, Verlag Kommunikaton & Wirtschaft Oldenburg, pp. 72–80.

Matthiesen, Ulf (ed.) (2004), *Stadtregion und Wissen: Analysen und Plädoyers für eine wissensbasierte Stadtpolitik*, Wiesbaden: VS Verlag für Sozialwissenschaften.

Matthiesen, Ulf (ed.) (2009), 'Complex affinities. Current spatial developments in the context of knowledge and network dynamics', *Planning Review*, Special Issue, ETH Zürich.

Matthiesen, Ulf and Gerhard Mahnken (eds) (2009), *Das Wissen der Städte. Neue stadtregionale Entwicklungsdynamiken im Kontext von Wissen, Milieus und Governance*, Wiesbaden: VS Verlag für Sozialwissenschaften.

Meusburger, Peter (1998), *Bildungsgeographie. Wiissen und Ausbildung in der räumlichen Diskussion*, Heidelberg: Spektrum Akademischer Verlag.

Müller-Böling, Detlef and Wolfgang Rohe (eds) (2011), *Erfolgsfaktoren wissenschaftlicher Metropolregionen: Analysen und Handlungsempfehlungen für das Ruhrgebiet*, Essen: Stiftung Mercator.

Prossek, Achim, Helmut Schneider, Horst A. Wessel, Burkhard Wetterau and Dorothea Wiktorin (eds) (2009), *Atlas der Metropole Ruhr*, Köln: Emons Verlag.

Revue urbanisme (2010), *Universités: Territoires, mutations*, defis.

Roost, Frank (ed.) (2010), *Metropolregionen in der Wissensökonomie*, Detmold: Verlag Dorothea Rohn.

Ruhrbania (ed.) (2009), Hochschulstandort Ruhrbania *aktuell 07*, Mülheim.

Stifterverband für die Deutsche Wissenschaft (2009), 'Wo wissen wirkt, Städte der Wissenschaft', *Wirtschaft und Wissenschaft*, Heft 2/2009, Essen.

Stiftung Mercator (2010), *Wissenschaftsatlas Metropole Ruhr*, Essen: Stiftung Mercator.

Tenfelde, Klaus, and Thomas Urban (2011), *Das Ruhrgebiet; Ein Historisches Lesebuch*, Essen: Klartext Verlag.

Yigitcanlar, Tan (2010), 'Making space and place for the knowledge economy', *European Planning Studies*, **18**(11), 769–786.

PART III

Metrics for building prosperous knowledge cities

16. Commuting: the geography of Melbourne's knowledge economy

Kevin Johnson

INTRODUCTION

In our day-to-day work we are often asked which specific policy interventions will improve the local area employment self-containment (ESC) ratio. That is, the proportion of the resident workforce who live and work in the same location. A high ESC ratio is considered an ideal social, economic and environmental goal. Unfortunately the urban economy does not always generate high ESC ratios of its own accord and so policy intervention is necessary. As policy should be informed by evidence, we apply a range of statistical and modeling techniques to analyze demographic, geographical and economic data to answer the question.

Fortunately for us, the Australian Bureau of Statistics (ABS) Census data can be used to map a workforce's employment and residential distribution at the geographical scale of the Statistical Local Area (SLA). These data can be categorized into subsets of the workforce by industry of employment, occupation and any number of demographic variables. Commuter patterns in the subsets can then be examined, albeit with some limits on spatial accuracy.[1] Taking the time to investigate these different permutations of the Knowledge Economy (KE) workforce reveals preferences for residential and work locations. In turn, this highlights ways to influence job distribution and transport use.

In this analysis we have applied the first (descriptive) step in our analytical and modeling process to explore the KE across the metropolitan area of Melbourne, Australia, using data from the 2006 ABS Census. While the findings are largely self-evident, this descriptive work is a necessary prelude to a greater understanding of the complex causal relationships between commuting habits and the locational choices of residents and enterprises.

The knowledge economy is a sector in which people live and work within a distinct set of spatial patterns, including outside of established employment nodes (e.g. by working at home). The more we understand what creates these patterns, the better positioned we are to shape their evolution. This has important implications for the way our cities' economies and transport systems function and, in Melbourne's case, this can help shift the city towards a more efficient form.

Who is a Knowledge Economy Worker?

There are two simple ways to define the KE using ABS data: industry of employment and occupation, each of which is defined by hierarchical classification systems. This study used the former, assessing the description for each of the 717 (highest level) industry classes, 79 of which were included in the KE.[2]

Arguably it is more accurate to define individuals by their occupation, rather than their industry of employment. However, this study explores the spatial distribution of the KE: that is, where enterprises engaged in KE activities are located. By using the most detailed industry class classification, we are reasonably assured of excluding employees of KE enterprises who are not, themselves, KE workers.

It is true that the two approaches generate different data compilations. In Victoria, using occupation, rather than industry of employment, to define the KE defines a workforce that is 4.5 per cent larger. However, most of the variation is in primary and secondary industries not located in metropolitan Melbourne (e.g. agricultural research being carried out on a farm). Moreover, as knowledge imbues most economic activities, the boundaries of the KE workforce are always going to be fuzzy. Nonetheless, the intention is to undertake follow up work to compare the spatial variation in distribution using occupational or industry of employment classification.

The Knowledge Economy Subsectors

Using the 2006 ABS Census data for industry of employment in Melbourne, a KE workforce of approximately 244 000 people has been extracted as follows.[3]

1. Telecommunications, IT and Media (around 31 000 jobs or 13 per cent)
2. Finance and Banking (111 000 or 45 per cent)
3. R&D/Higher education (71 000 or 29 per cent)
4. Design-related industries (e.g. architecture) (27 000 or 11 per cent)
5. Cultural industries (e.g. performing arts) (6000 or 2 per cent).

Using these categories we gain a clearer conception of how the KE functions within the urban setting. It highlights the important differences between sectors of the workforce and the spatial dimensions of their commute patterns. It is the essential first step towards an analysis of how residential and employment locations of workers in Melbourne impacts on ESC.

BACKGROUND

Census data (ABS, 2006) show Metropolitan Melbourne[4] to be an employment sink (Figure 16.1). While a little over 10 000 people leave the metropolitan area to work, more than 40 000 commute in to Melbourne. The result is that more people work in the metropolitan area than live there and the overall metropolitan ESC is 98 per cent. At the more commonly used scale (SLA level), we find that around 22 per cent of all workers in Metropolitan Melbourne live in the same SLA as they work (ABS, 2006). Aggregating back up, we find that most commuting occurs within several large intra-metropolitan regions made up of collections of SLAs (Figure 16.2) (O'Connor and Healy, 2002).

These intra-metropolitan economic regions bear some resemblance (physically, if not in economic function) to Hoyt's (1939) original sectoral

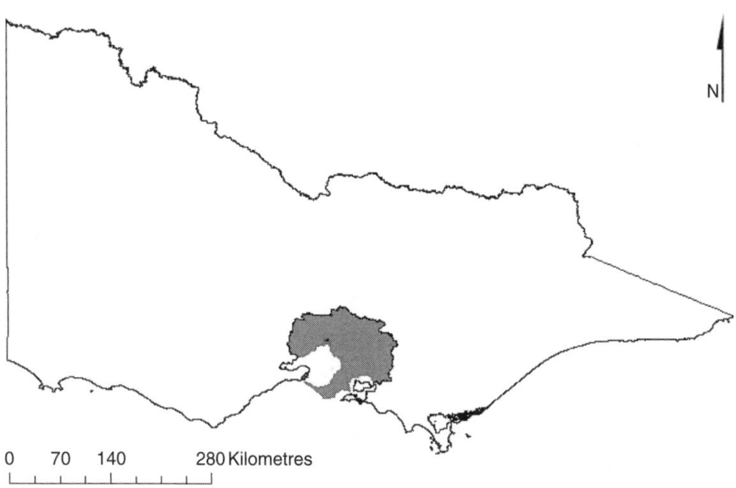

Source: ABS, 2006.

Figure 16.1 Melbourne Metropolitan Statistical Region

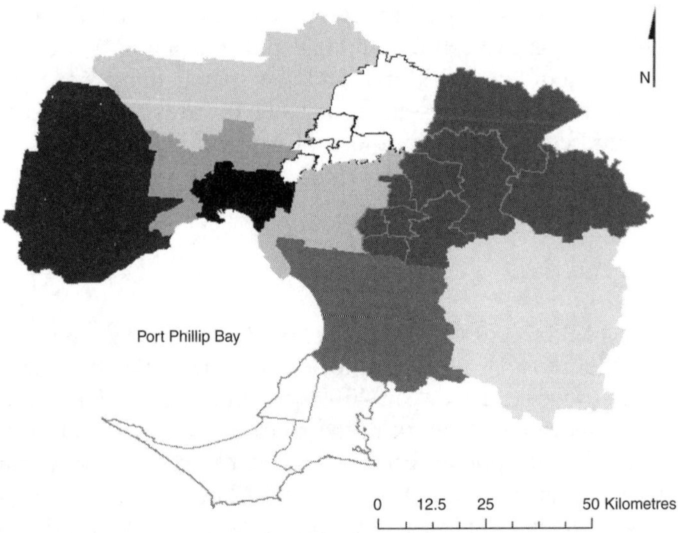

Source: ABS, 2006; O'Connor and Healy, 2002.

Figure 16.2 Melbourne's employment self-containment zones

model of city development, with commuting zones mostly radiating out from the inner urban area. The emergent pattern of ESC is one of most metropolitan residents living and working in a relatively spatially contiguous area, often 'stretched out' along transport corridors.

Understanding Employment Self-containment

The underlying concept in this analysis is employment self-containment. As a measure of local economic health, ESC has been extensively researched and is regularly used for economic planning (e.g. Trendle and Siu, 2007; Yigitcanlar et al., 2007; Coombes et al., 1986). For example, larger developers and local governments use it as a performance target for measuring the success of local employment generation strategies. The strategies usually aim to influence the location of jobs, rather than the place of residence of workers (i.e., they are local job creation strategies, rather than targeted workforce attraction strategies).

Unfortunately, while the research literature on ESC is quite strong, its application as a planning tool has not been as robust. In fact, local economic development planning is often based on a mix of simplistic metrics, anecdotal evidence, intuition, or the replication of ideas that are unsuited to local conditions. This and previous work on the link between ESC and geographical and demographic parameters of the workforce found numerous statistically significant relationships, and compounding, or feedback, effects between several variables.[5] Obviously commuting patterns and other locational factors evolve as the result of the complex interaction of many variables. Good local economic planning decisions will not be made until there is a better understanding of this.

To that end, the work described here is part of a larger research agenda to build a dynamic systems model of the geographical distribution of places of work and residence. The model will allow us to analyze the movement of people in a city and test policies designed to encourage preferred behavior and reduce unsustainable commuter patterns.

Influences on the Location of the Knowledge Economy

The assertion that there are measurable, and potentially manageable, influences on the spatial distribution of the KE has its theoretical roots in the literature on contemporary gentrification. There are two major schools of thought within this research. The first argues that inner urban gentrification is a result of consumer-led demand for different housing products (Zukin, 1982). The second claims that gentrification is driven by capital-led reinvestment in under-performing inner urban property (e.g. Smith, 1992). Both perspectives lend tacit support to the argument that there may be no endogenous economic reason for the KE to be tied to the inner urban area. Moreover, apart from a social shift towards a preference for living in the inner city, neither has the KE worker (i.e. the gentrification cohort) any functional need to live there. It may only have been the imperatives of property investment that led the KE workforce to its current locations.

This is not to say that KE jobs do not need to cluster, just that there is no unambiguous evidence that economic functionality dictates that they need to cluster in the inner urban areas. For example, Searle and Pritchard's (2005) study of Sydney's Information Technology and Telecommunications sector concludes that the sector's clustering is as much an effect of the entire city's economic functionality as it is the localization economies of the sector itself.

Equally, the literature supports the view that KE clustering is spatially linked to high amenity and housing, transport and services tailored to the characteristics of the KE worker (e.g. Baum et al., 2007; JVSVN, 2001). An examination of the concentration of KE jobs and workers (by place of residence) for each SLA in metropolitan Melbourne appears to confirm this. That is, we find a stronger association between the place of residence

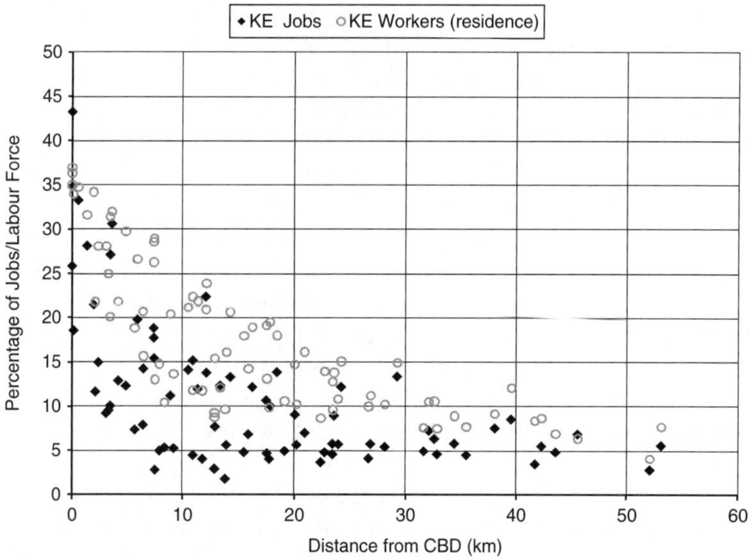

Source: ABS, 2006.

Figure 16.3 Proximity to CBD and knowledge economy place of residence and work

of KE workers and proximity to the CBD than exists between the place of work of KE workers and the CBD (Figure 16.3).

This visual confirmation of Baum et al.'s (2007) findings suggests it is reasonable to conclude that the KE is not necessarily spatially tied to the inner urban area. Instead, it is more likely associated with a set of conditions attractive to KE workers. These conditions – which most obviously include the presence of a university campus – are, more often than not, found in the central city.

Economic development strategies that target components of the KE may, therefore, have substantial scope to attract these jobs to other parts of the city if these conditions can be replicated. In fact, there are several small clusters of KE jobs in outer suburban areas of Melbourne, as will be explored later.

THE RESEARCH PREMISE

We began this work by assuming there would be distinctive spatial dimensions to the KE workforce and that these would vary between the sector's subsets. The expectations were that:

1. While overall employment self-containment for the KE is likely to be similar to that of the whole workforce, its characteristics will differ. Descriptive statistics confirm this.
2. Given the assumed link between KE jobs and specific parts of the CBD, as well as the range of other determining factors, the proportion of KE jobs in each SLA is not likely to be normally distributed across the 79 SLAs of metropolitan Melbourne. Geographical clustering, along with anomalous outliers, will result in a more complex distribution. In turn, factors such as clustering will be a response to influences such as historical precedent or the agglomeration of complementary skills (Glaeser, 2010; Johnson et al., 2006).
3. KE jobs will cluster in and around the CBD. This clustering will have an impact on ESC due to the limited availability of housing. To understand the commuting patterns, consideration will need to be given to residents in adjacent SLAs.
4. At the same time, given the relative affluence of parts of the KE workforce, many people will be willing to commute some distance. This assumption is based on job search theory (Trendle and Siu, 2007).
5. The Telecommunications, IT and Media sector will maintain proximity to the Finance sector, reflecting known (strong) inter-industry flows.
6. The Finance and Banking sector will be concentrated in the CBD and, therefore, its ESC will be lower than for other subsets of the KE due to relatively few dwellings in the CBD (see point 3).
7. Given that they also have a local area service role in the metropolitan economy, both Media and Finance jobs will be more widely distributed than R&D/Higher Education, Design and Cultural Industries jobs.
8. R&D/Higher Education jobs are likely to cluster near universities and established research/high technology areas. Conversely, job search and human capital theory suggests that these workers will live in a more widely distributed pattern.
9. Design and Cultural Industries will show signs of clustering together around, but not in, the CBD. Moreover, our previous research has also shown that Cultural Industries workers are more likely to live in proximity to their place of work.[6]

These expectations are based on interpretations of well-documented historical and cultural trends, for example the preference for the cultural industries workers to locate in vacated inner urban industrial areas. They are also based on Australian national accounts data, which demonstrates high inter-industry flows between IT/Media and Finance, contrasted with the self-contained nature of the Cultural Industries and R&D/Higher Education sectors (ABS, 2005).

Identifying Melbourne's Knowledge Economy Clusters

The first step in the analysis was to organize and evaluate the data to find *prima facie* evidence for continuing the study. When ABS data for employment by place of work and residence are disaggregated to extract KE workers, we found that the assumptions underlying the research premise (outlined above) generally hold, with some caveats. First, there is, in fact, a small difference between *overall* ESC ratios for the KE workforce (18.2 per cent) compared with the rest of the economy (22.6 per cent). This means that either more KE workers live further from their place of work or KE jobs cluster in concentrated employment nodes with little available housing. Further analysis revealed that the CBD-based Finance sector is the 'culprit'. After excluding the CBD-based Finance sector, overall ESC for KE is 21.9 per cent; not substantially different from the rest of the workforce. Moreover, looking at *average* SLA-level ESC for the non-Finance KE workforce, we find the ratio is 45.7 per cent, compared with 31.7 per cent for the rest of the workforce.[7] That is, non-Finance KE workers are far more likely to work close to where they live than other members of the labour force.

By looking at the ESC ratios for individual SLAs, we see many interesting variations. These suggest that KE jobs and the workforce cluster in a statistically significantly different way to the rest of the economy. In fact, as columns 1 and 2 of Table 16.1 show, most KE jobs are found in SLAs located in and around the CBD (Melbourne Inner) and the workers live near these jobs, concentrating in the eastern suburbs (e.g. Glen Eira Caulfield). When accounting for relative labour market size, we also see distinctive clusters of jobs by KE subsector (columns 3 and 4). For example, R&D/Higher Education jobs do, indeed, cluster around (but not in) the CBD and towards the south east around the Australian Synchrotron near Monash University.

From this, it was possible to identify five distinct geographical clusters: each a collection of contiguous SLAs (Figure 16.4). The key criterion was that the KE accounts for at least 20 per cent of the local jobs.[8] Anyone familiar with the economic geography of metropolitan Melbourne will not find the existence of these clusters surprising. They also are more-or-less aligned with seven of the ten Victorian State Government Specialized Activity Centres (Figure 16.5). The clusters are:

1. The 'Hoddle Grid'. This is the original CBD grid as defined by surveyor Robert Hoddle in the 1830s. Its KE activity is dominated by Finance sector workers.
2. 'The Edge'. Surrounding the CBD is a typical mix of former docks and working class suburbs now dominated by KE workers, par-

Table 16.1 Concentration of knowledge economy jobs in Metropolitan Melbourne

Industry of Employment	(1) Concentration of Jobs	(2) Number	(3) Local Concentration	(4) Percentage
Place of Work				
All KE workers	Melbourne (Inner)	66 378	Melbourne (Inner)	43.0
IT/Media	Melbourne (Inner)	5 323	Yarra (Richmond)	7.5
Finance	Melbourne (Inner)	48 119	Melbourne (Inner)	31.4
R&D/Higher education	Melbourne (Remainder)	14 267	Monash (South-West)	18.6
Design related	Melbourne (Inner)	3 688	Stonnington (Prahran)	5.9
Cultural industries	Melbourne (Southbank-Docklands)	1 017	Melbourne (Southbank-Docklands)	2.7
Place of Residence				
All KE workers	Glen Eira (Caulfield)	9 484	Melbourne (Inner)	36.9
IT/Media	Port Phillip (St Kilda)	1 628	Port Phillip (St Kilda)	5.9
Finance	Manningham (West)	3 616	Melbourne (Southbank-Docklands)	16.0
R&D/Higher education	Glen Eira (Caulfield)	2 691	Melbourne (Inner)	10.8
Design related	Yarra (North)	984	Yarra (North)	4.2
Cultural industries	Yarra (North)	426	Yarra (North)	1.8

Source: ABS, Census 2006.

ticularly Creative Industry workers in places such as Fitzroy, South and North Melbourne. 'The Edge' also incorporates the Parkville Bioscience Precinct – including the University of Melbourne's main campus – and the Alfred Hospital. It is an area that, presumably, once enjoyed very high ESC ratios.

3. 'The Knowledge Corner'. To the east of the CBD, the suburbs of Prahran, Richmond and Hawthorn is a mix of high (and some low) income households and businesses with a diverse range of KE activities, particularly IT/Media and Design.

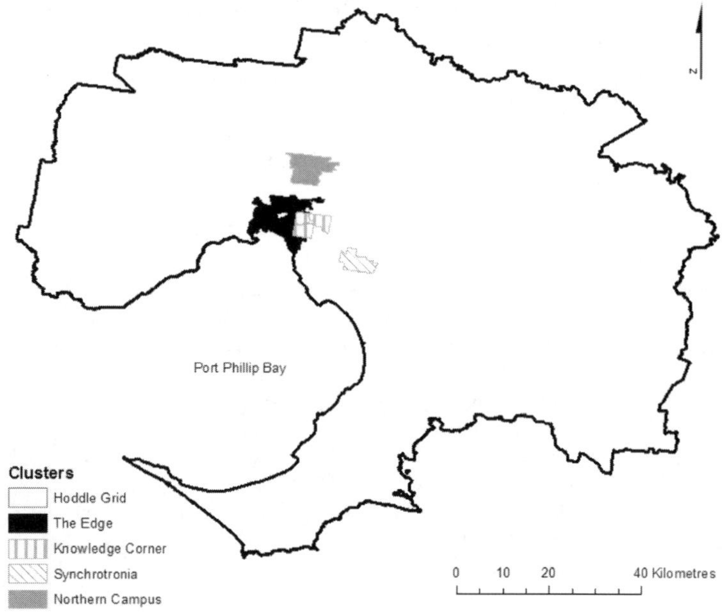

Source: ABS, 2006.

Figure 16.4 Location of Melbourne's knowledge economy clusters

4. 'Synchrotronia'. Centred on the Australian Synchrotron and Monash University's Clayton campus is a R&D/Higher Education cluster 20 kilometres to the southeast of the CBD.
5. 'Northern Campus'. La Trobe University's Bundoora campus and several health-related commercial/research precincts are at the centre of a growing R&D/Higher Education cluster around 14 kilometres to the north of the CBD. Although the SLA for this area does not quite meet the '20 per cent' criterion, it was included on the basis that it defines an important emergent R&D hub.[9]

Further analysis of the manner in which these clusters formed could be carried out, taking as a starting point Baum et al.'s (2007) categorization of four spatial forms. For example, 'The Edge' could be associated with Baum's 'Production District'. However, for the purposes of this chapter, the basic classifications outlined here are sufficient.

These five clusters account for around 34 per cent of all jobs in the metropolitan area and over two-thirds of all KE jobs; all of this in under 2 per cent of the total land area of the Melbourne Statistical Region (Table 16.2).

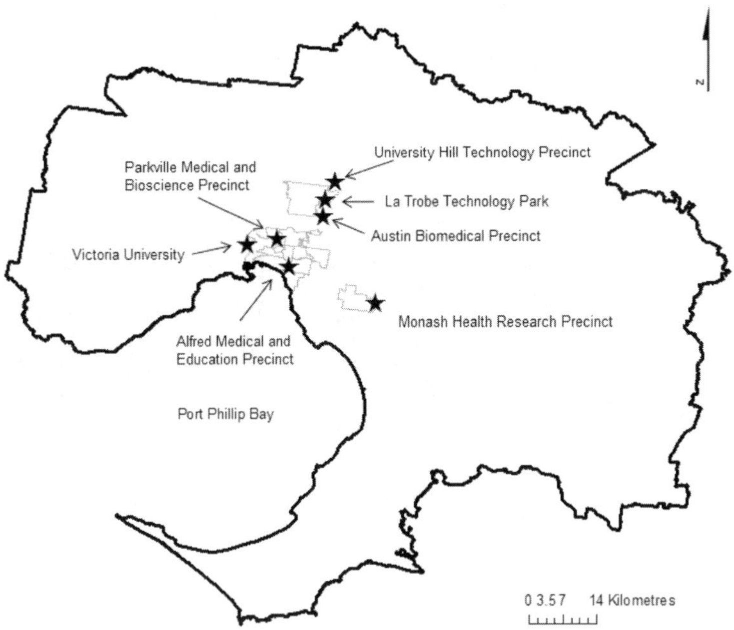

Note: Seven of the ten Specialized Activity Centres identified by the State Government as high technology research and commercial precincts are adjacent to the KE clusters used in this analysis.

Data source: ABS, 2006, DPCD, 2010.

Figure 16.5 Knowledge economy clusters and Specialized Activity Centres

Table 16.2 Knowledge economy clusters

Knowledge Economy Clusters	Total Jobs	KE Jobs	IT/ Media	Finance	R&D/ Higher Ed	Design	Cultural Indus-tries
Hoddle Grid	153395	66378	5323	48119	8915	3688	333
The Edge	243389	68330	10147	23187	24994	7272	2730
Knowledge Corner	70511	18127	3398	7401	3860	3108	360
Synchrotronia	33965	7604	412	601	6310	239	42
Northern Campus	28828	4098	244	827	2744	220	63
Rest of Metropolitan Area	1014970	80448	11259	30398	24443	12151	2197
Total	1545058	244985	30783	110533	71266	26678	5725

Source: ABS, Census 2006.

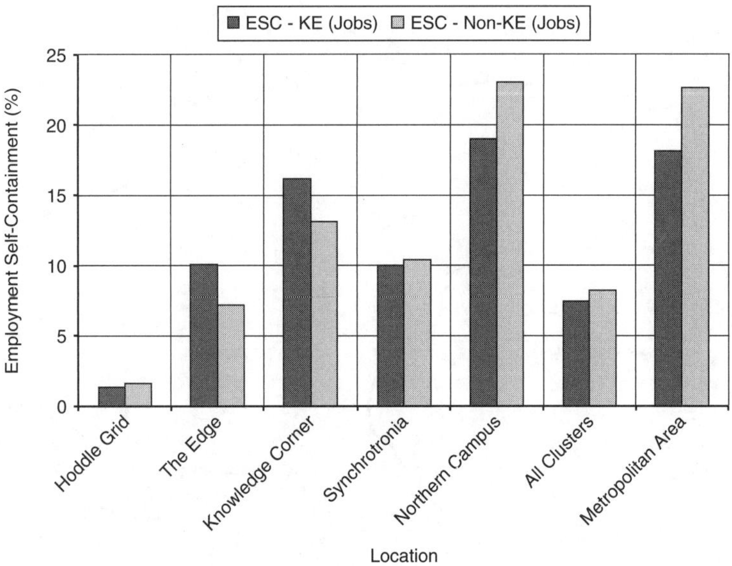

Source: ABS, Census 2006.

Figure 16.6 Employment self-containment by cluster – jobs (2006)

Employment Self-containment and Knowledge Economy Clusters

The next step was to compare ESC ratios for both KE jobs and non-KE jobs (Figure 16.6) and for KE and non-KE residents (Figure 16.7).[10] There are several notable patterns in these data, including the concentration of KE workers living and working in the inner urban area.

Although the KE has a slightly lower overall ESC ratio across the metropolitan area, this conceals the markedly higher ratios in the key KE clusters. Additionally, there are statistically significant differences between the ESCs for the KE and non-KE workforces with high correlations to proximity to the CBD. This would be worth further analysis at some point.

Commuting Patterns of Knowledge Economy Workers

Figures 16.8 to 16.13 show the commuter zones for the five clusters, separately and combined. In this case, 'commuter zone' is used to refer to the place of residence for 80 per cent of the KE workforce.

Again, the key point is the overall high concentration of the workforce in the inner urban area. Figures 16.10 to 16.12 clearly show divergent

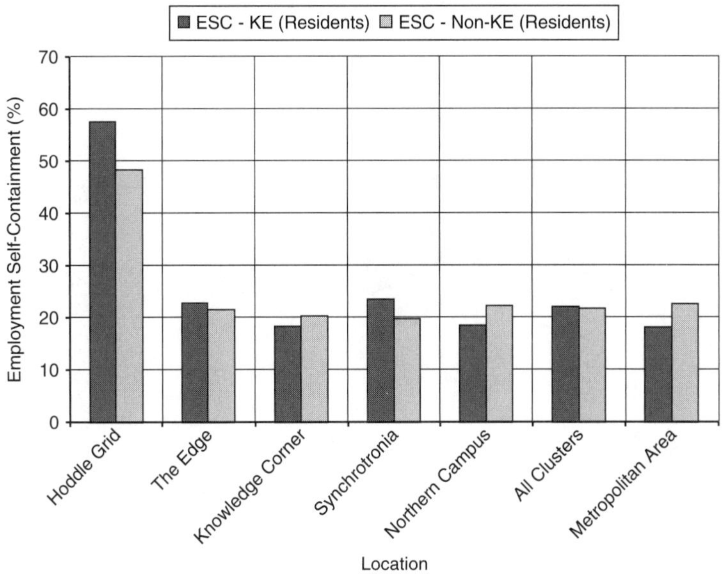

Source: ABS, Census 2006.

Figure 16.7 Employment self-containment by cluster – residents (2006)

patterns as the residential commuter zones focus around the respective clusters. As would be expected, on balance, people will tend to live close to where they work. This pattern is strongly influenced by the economic dominance of the Melbourne CBD.

The Knowledge Economy Clusters, CADs and Melbourne's Polycentric Urban Form

Descriptive analysis of Melbourne's ESC patterns goes back some years, most usefully, the work of O'Connor and Healy (2002), which defines the city as a collection of interconnected, but relatively self-contained, employment zones. Recent Australia-wide analysis by Mitchell and Watts (2010) showed that all Australian metropolitan areas can be broken up in this way. An interesting study of commuting patterns in the UK also confirmed that London is a 'polycentric structure composed of simple flow patterns organized around a limited number of activity centres arranged in a hierarchical way' (Roth et al., 2010: 1).

Cities are not smooth landscapes. For example, the dominance of the CBD must be considered, as should the concentration of certain indus-

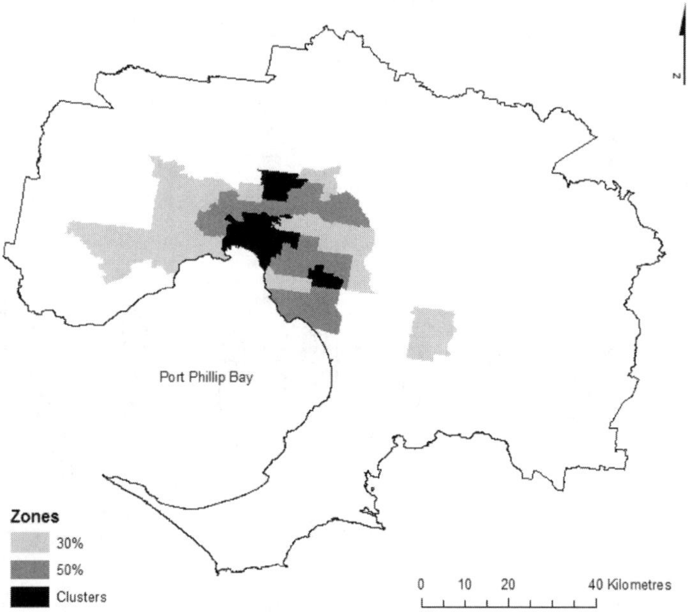

Note: All five clusters are shaded in black. The grey areas represent the place of residence of 80 per cent of the KE workforce for these clusters. For all Figures 16.8 to 16.13, darker grey represents areas where higher absolute numbers of commuters live (totaling 50% of the KE workforce). Lighter grey accounts for the next 30% of workers.

Data source: ABS, Census 2006.

Figure 16.8 Knowledge economy commuter zones

tries in purpose-built locations (e.g. industrial and office parks), historical antecedents, existing transport infrastructure and metropolitan-wide planning policies. Many parameters influence this structure and each can have an impact on the other, reinforcing or dampening effects. All of this points to the need for a systems-based model to understand it. As noted earlier, the ultimate objective of this work is to build a dynamic systems model based on a more detailed examination of financial, employment, land use and demographic data. This will account for the self-reinforcing and countervailing relationships and decision-making processes that lead to locational outcomes for enterprises and residences. There is certainly sufficient information to do this; it is just a case of continuing to build and calibrating a sufficiently robust model. This, though, is a topic for another occasion. For now, as Figures 16.9 to 16.13 show, it is clear that the sub-regional nature of metropolitan areas also applies to the KE. What

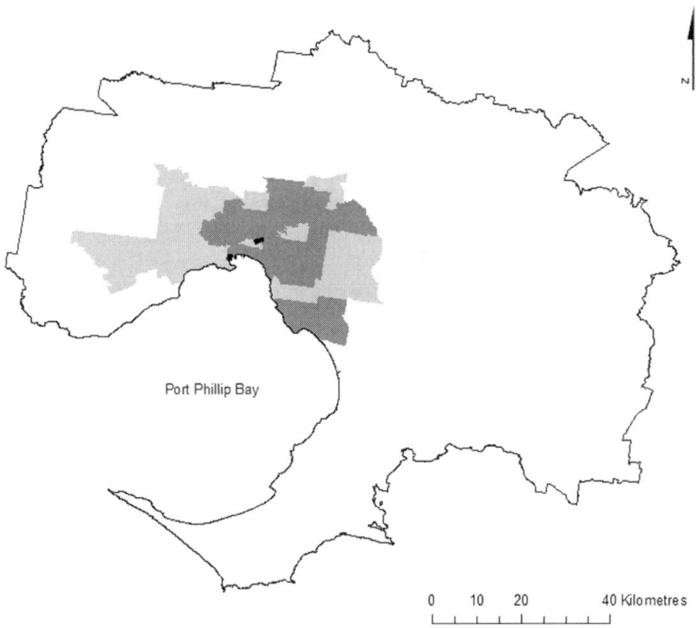

Figure 16.9 Hoddle Grid commuters

remains to be seen is whether there are significant differences between subsets of the KE.

Employment Self-containment, Commuting Zones and Knowledge Economy Subsectors

Examining the KE as five subsets disentangles the overwhelming effect of location on ESC and shows how the ratios change according to industry of employment. From this we can eventually comment on the merit of industry-specific planning policies designed to encourage ESC. The data are provided in full in Tables 16.3 to 16.10 (Note: Table 16.8 is an aggregation of all five clusters and Tables 16.9 and 16.10 summarize elements of the preceding tables).

Some general observations of these data are:

Cluster employment profiles

1. Three clusters have very clear KE characteristics:
    a. The Hoddle Grid is predominantly Finance.

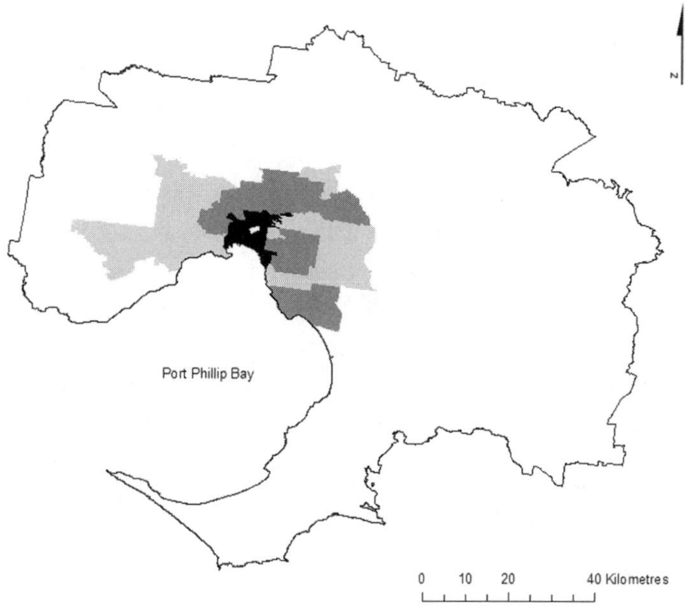

Figure 16.10 The Edge commuters

   b. Synchrotronia has a R&D/Higher Education focus.
   c. Although not a major employer, the Northern Campus is also a R&D/Higher Education Cluster.
2. As would be expected in inner urban areas, The Edge and Knowledge Corner have a mix of KE employment by industry subsector. If we control for actual industry size, however, we can see that Edge is the dominant Cultural Industries cluster and that Knowledge Corner is the dominant IT/Media and Design-related cluster.

Core area employment self-containment

1. All five clusters have an overall (residential) ESC ratio of around 19 per cent for the KE workforce (Figure 16.14).
2. Residents in the Hoddle Grid (the CBD) are more than twice as likely to be working in their residential SLA as those living and working in the other four clusters – not surprising given the job opportunities present in the CBD.
3. Similarly, local residents make up a far smaller proportion of total KE jobs found in the Hoddle Grid. By this measure, the Northern Campus cluster has the highest proportion of jobs filled by locals.

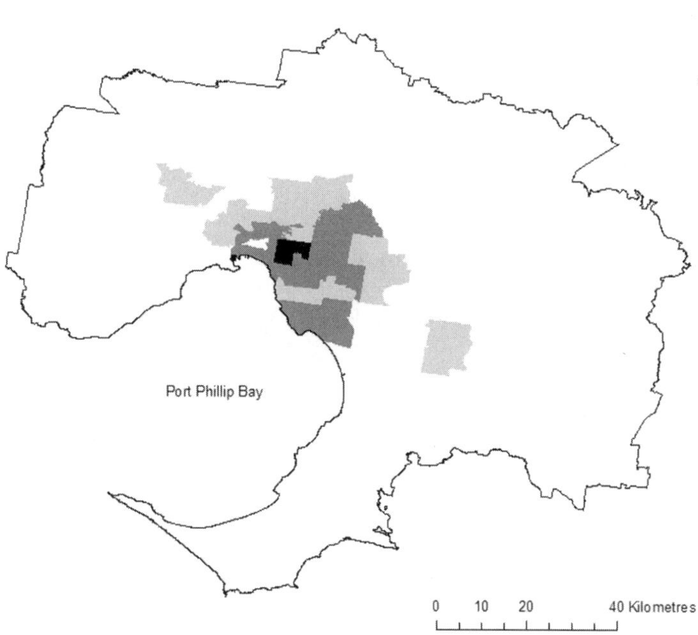

Figure 16.11 Knowledge Corner commuters

4. Partial correlations of place of residence and work (controlling for distance from the central city and local labour market size) confirm that the R&D/Higher Education workforce is the most likely to live and work in the same SLA.

Core and/or adjacent area employment self-containment

1. The Edge has the highest proportion of workers commuting in from adjacent SLAs.
2. By combining the core and all adjacent SLAs[11], we find that The Edge and the Hoddle Grid have the greatest (residential) ESC ratios for the KE. Again, a much smaller proportion of available jobs is taken up by locals (Figure 16.15).
3. By contrast, a far higher proportion of KE jobs is filled by locals in the clusters further afield. Most people living adjacent to Synchrotronia and Northern Campus, however, do not work in these sectors.
4. It is reasonable to conclude that Design-related or Cultural Industries workers will either live and work in the same SLA, or

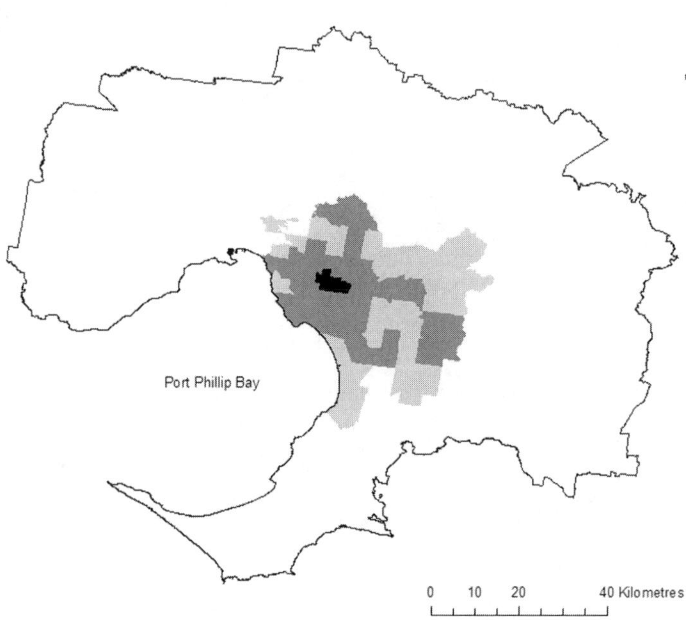

Figure 16.12 Synchrotronia commuters

commute some distance to work (i.e., not from adjacent SLAs). For R&D/Higher Education workers, a similar picture emerges: they will live and work quite locally, or commute from elsewhere in the metropolitan area.

The Relationship Between Industry of Employment and Self-containment

The next step was to look more closely at whether there was any discernible relationship between industry subset and its ESC ratio. Figure 16.16 shows average ESC by industry subset for the five clusters combined. The striking feature is the high proportion of Cultural Industries and Design-related jobs that are taken up by locals, contrasted with the relatively consistent ratio of residents working locally for all industries. This pattern is the same for all clusters (Figure 16.17), and strongest within the core SLAs of each. That is, Design-related and Cultural Industry workers are very likely to live in the same SLA as they work, but much less likely to live in adjoining SLAs. This is in contrast to the other three subsets, where the reverse is generally the case.

Reasons for this are likely to relate to housing and transport costs. On

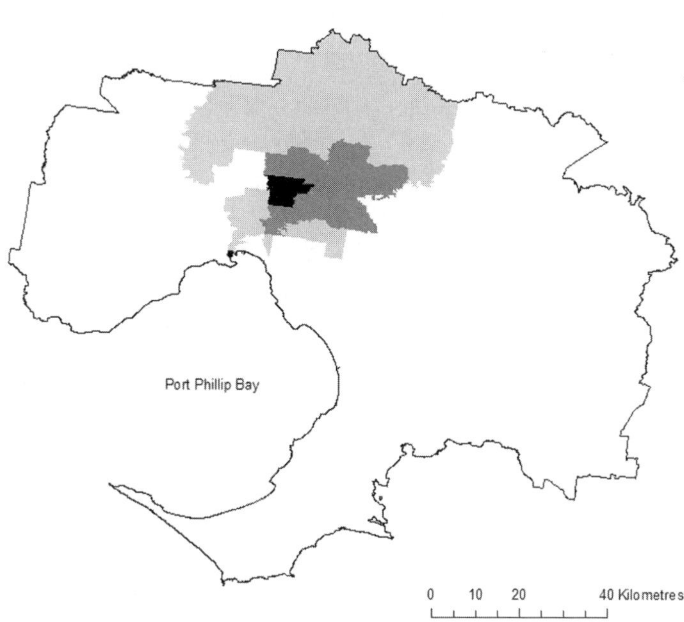

Figure 16.13 Northern Campus commuters

Table 16.3 ESC Hoddle Grid and surrounds (2006) (%)

Hoddle Grid	ESC Residents (Core SLAs)	ESC Local Jobs (Core SLAs)	ESC Residents (Adjacent SLAs)	ESC Local Jobs (Adjacent SLAs)
Total K Economy	57.6	1.3	35.1	13.8
IT/Media	50.3	1.5	22.5	15.6
Finance	72.9	1.0	58.3	13.1
R&D/Higher education	44.6	2.6	16.9	14.1
Design related	46.9	2.3	22.6	18.9
Cultural industries	50.0	6.3	8.0	24.9

Source: ABS, Census 2006.

average, Design and Cultural industries workers have lower incomes, which undoubtedly has implications for willingness to commute (Trendle and Siu, 2007) and the capacity to secure housing (many of the jobs are located in or near areas with high cost housing). Having said that,

Table 16.4 ESC The Edge and surrounds (2006) (%)

The Edge	ESC Residents (Core SLAs)	ESC Local Jobs (Core SLAs)	ESC Residents (Adjacent SLAs)	ESC Local Jobs (Adjacent SLAs)
Total K Economy	22.7	10.1	35.6	24.8
IT/Media	22.2	10.2	42.6	29.8
Finance	14.3	7.5	24.6	21.1
R&D/Higher education	27.6	9.6	45.0	24.5
Design related	31.0	15.3	36.7	26.7
Cultural industries	46.7	22.1	53.9	35.5

Source: ABS, Census 2006.

Table 16.5 ESC Knowledge Corner and surrounds (2006) (%)

Knowledge Corner	ESC Residents (Core SLAs)	ESC Local Jobs (Core SLAs)	ESC Residents (Adjacent SLAs)	ESC Local Jobs (Adjacent SLAs)
Total K Economy	18.2	16.2	8.2	24.4
IT/Media	19.0	13.1	13.5	28.0
Finance	13.9	14.0	6.9	21.2
R&D/Higher education	17.1	17.5	6.2	25.4
Design related	31.5	18.9	13.4	26.8
Cultural industries	39.2	52.5	5.1	24.4

Source: ABS, Census 2006.

however, our previous research controlled for income and still found these subsets have high levels of ESC. That is, these workers are far more likely to live in immediate proximity to their place of work, wherever that may be (Geografia, 2009).

As a word of caution, it should be noted that in analyzing the Cultural Industries we are dealing with relatively few jobs and these conclusions should be treated as exploratory. When we take into account adjacent SLAs, it is R&D/Higher Education workers who are more likely to live and work locally. Given that they make up almost one third of the KE workforce (compared with 2 per cent and 13 per cent for Cultural Industries and Design respectively), or over 71 000 jobs, they can have a substantial impact on commuting.

Table 16.6 ESC Synchrotronia and surrounds (2006) (%)

Synchrotronia	ESC Residents (Core SLAs)	ESC Local Jobs (Core SLAs)	ESC Residents (Adjacent SLAs)	ESC Local Jobs (Adjacent SLAs)
Total K Economy	23.4	10.0	5.4	20.5
IT/Media	13.0	10.9	2.3	18.2
Finance	8.0	16.5	0.8	16.1
R&D/Higher education	40.9	8.6	14.7	21.4
Design related	18.4	23.0	1.0	13.0
Cultural industries	52.8	45.2	1.0	14.3

Source: ABS, Census 2006.

Table 16.7 ESC Northern Campus and surrounds (2006) (%)

Northern Campus	ESC Residents (Core SLAs)	ESC Local Jobs (Core SLAs)	ESC Residents (Adjacent SLAs)	ESC Local Jobs (Adjacent SLAs)
Total K Economy	18.5	19.0	5.6	39.3
IT/Media	14.9	32.0	1.8	25.4
Finance	10.1	23.2	2.6	38.5
R&D/Higher education	29.1	14.2	12.4	42.5
Design related	22.6	36.4	2.1	27.3
Cultural industries	38.4	60.3	0.7	9.5

Source: ABS, Census 2006.

Looking at the data in this format also shows that most locally resident KE workers will work in the locally specific subsector, but still account for a fairly low proportion of the jobs available. For example, the Hoddle Grid has a very high proportion of residents who work in the local Finance sector (73 per cent, which is 42 times the job-related ESC). Equally, Synchrotronia's residents who work in the KE, mostly do so in R&D/Higher Education (41 per cent, which is almost five times the job-related ESC).

Figures 16.18 and 16.19 illustrate this point for the Knowledge Corner (a Design-related cluster) and Synchrotronia (R&D/Higher Education). They show the difference between how many residents work in the primary KE subsector and how many jobs they account for. All this is

Table 16.8 ESC All clusters and surrounds (2006) (%)

All Clusters	ESC Residents (Core SLAs)	ESC Local Jobs (Core SLAs)	ESC Residents (Adjacent SLAs)	ESC Local Jobs (Adjacent SLAs)
Total K Economy	22.1	7.4	26.8	20.5
IT/Media	20.9	8.6	30.2	25.3
Finance	15.2	4.4	24.1	16.4
R&D/Higher education	26.8	9.0	29.1	23.2
Design related	30.5	13.2	26.1	24.5
Cultural industries	44.6	24.6	30.5	32.7

Source: ABS, Census 2006.

Table 16.9 ESC core and adjacent residents (2006) (%)

Industry	Hoddle Grid	The Edge	Knowledge Corner	Synchro-tronia	Northern Campus	All Clusters
Total K Economy	36.4	30.6	10.5	7.2	7.2	19.1
IT/Media	23.6	34.5	14.8	3.3	3.5	20.3
Finance	59.2	20.7	8.6	1.4	3.6	16.4
R&D/Higher education	18.6	38.2	8.4	18.0	14.4	21.2
Design related	23.9	34.4	17.6	2.6	4.3	20.5
Cultural industries	9.6	50.9	12.5	4.0	4.8	25.6

Source: ABS, Census 2006.

Table 16.10 ESC core and adjacent local jobs (2006) (%)

Industry	Hoddle Grid	The Edge	Knowledge Corner	Synchro-tronia	Northern Campus	All Clusters
Total K Economy	15.1	34.8	40.6	30.5	58.3	27.9
IT/Media	17.1	40.0	41.1	29.1	57.4	33.9
Finance	14.1	28.5	35.3	32.6	61.7	20.8
R&D/Higher education	16.7	34.0	42.8	30.0	56.7	32.2
Design related	21.2	42.1	45.7	36.0	63.6	37.8
Cultural industries	31.2	57.6	76.9	59.5	69.8	57.3

Source: ABS, Census 2006.

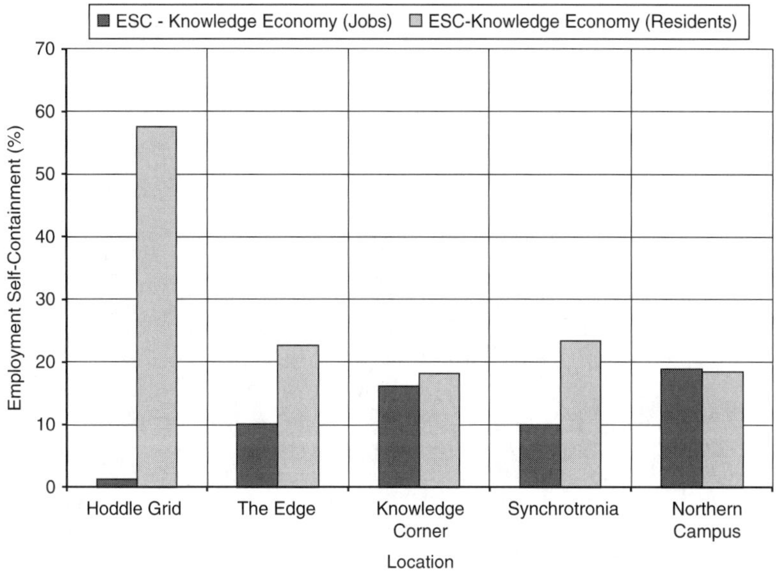

Source: ABS, Census 2006.

Figure 16.14 ESC by cluster – core SLA only (2006)

saying is that the economic characteristics of a job cluster attract people to live in the area accordingly. However, it also indicates that there is scope to increase this, given how few of these jobs are taken up by local residents.

How Do They Commute?

This research is just a descriptive first step and there are many ways in which the data can be organized and investigated. For example, one subgroup of the people living and working locally comprises those who work from home. This is of particular relevance to the KE given the presumed ease with which many can work out of home offices or studios, or run mobile businesses. While Census data show overall work-from-home proportions in Australia have declined (ABS, 2001; ABS, 2006)[12] it is still high for the KE. In fact, a person is almost twice as likely to work from home if they are part of the KE. For some subsectors, this figure is even higher (Table 16.11). Further analysis of this is part of the future research agenda for the modeling project.

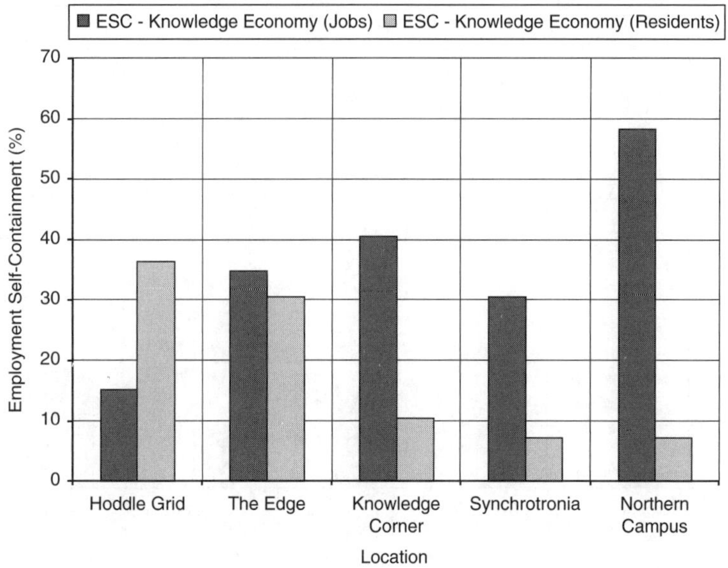

Source: ABS, Census 2006.

Figure 16.15 ESC by cluster – core and adjacent SLAs (2006)

CONCLUSION

At the outset, several assumptions were made about the geographical distribution of KE jobs and workers. For the most part these assumptions have been confirmed. The KE workforce generally reflects the overall sub-regional structure of the metropolitan economy, but with distinctive nuances. There is clearly merit in building a model of the decision-making processes that lead to the KE locational outcomes. A model in this form will be a useful decision-support tool for developing better policies to stimulate KE activity in employment nodes around the metropolitan area (for example in Melbourne's CADs).

Additionally, within the KE there are distinctive distribution and commuting patterns, as well as assumptions that can be drawn from the analysis. These include:

- There is an obvious concentration of Finance workers in the CBD;
- As the inter-industry flow data suggest, IT/Media and Finance tend to group, in this case, in the inner city clusters;

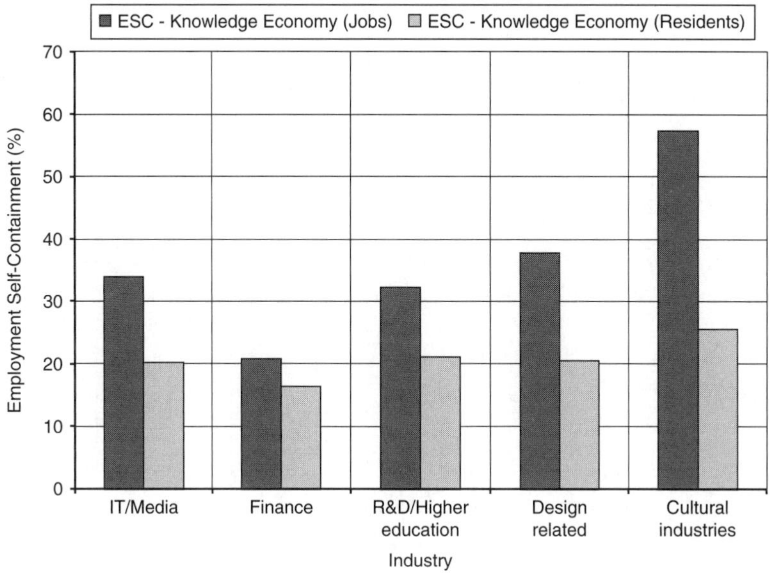

Source: ABS, Census 2006.

Figure 16.16 ESC by industry subsector (2006)

- The limited geographical association between R&D/Higher Education jobs and other KE jobs;
- In the two outlying clusters (Synchrotronia and Northern Campus) a high proportion of available KE jobs are taken up by people living in (and to a lesser extent around) the relevant SLAs. There are, however, significantly more KE workers living near (or mostly in) these clusters but working elsewhere. The converse is true for the three inner urban clusters. This is perhaps the most interesting finding given it reveals the potential for increasing the ESC ratios;
- Design-related, Cultural or R&D/Higher Education workers live and work in the *same* SLA more so than other KE workers. However, for as yet unexamined reasons, they are also less likely to live in SLAs *adjacent* to their place of work than the other two industry subsets;
- It appears that the preference of KE workers to live closer to the central city may be a stronger driver of the geography of the KE than the economic necessity for KE jobs to be thus located. Earlier research appears to confirm this (e.g. Searle and Pritchard, 2005), as

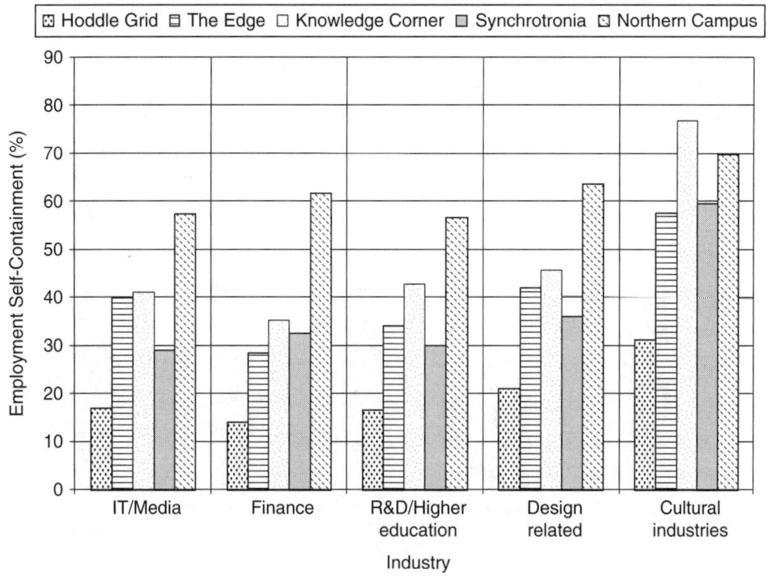

Source: ABS, Census 2006.

Figure 16.17 ESC by subsector and cluster (2006)

do the relative concentrations of workers by job location and place of residence as shown in Figure 16.2; and

- After examining one element of the commuting patterns in a little more detail, it was found that KE workers are more than twice as likely to work from home as other workers. When looking only at Design-related or Cultural Industries, this disparity increases ten-fold.

These different patterns mean that off-the-shelf local economic development plans with blanket ESC targets are effectively a high risk proposition. There is far less likelihood of success without a more thorough analysis of what is driving (directly or indirectly) specific locational outcomes.

Any analysis must start with the basics, and this research has revealed some interesting features, many of which will be examined in future work. The most promising is in looking at the underlying reasons explaining why R&D/Higher Education workers live in the same SLA as their place of work, but not in adjacent SLAs (this finding holds even when decomposing the clusters into their constituent SLAs). It is likely to be a conse-

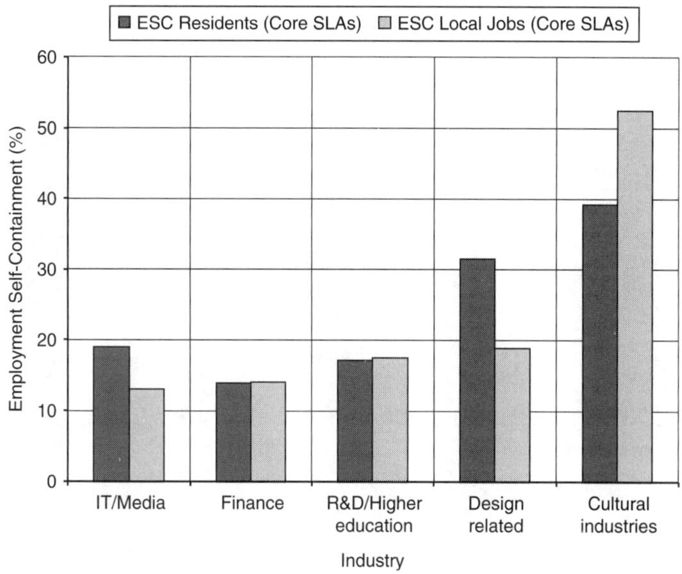

Source: ABS, Census 2006.

Figure 16.18 Knowledge Corner ESC residents and jobs (2006)

quence of job availability, development timing, local amenity and other historical factors. Quantifying these effects may lead to an improvement in the effectiveness of employment generation strategies designed to increase localized ESC around the two outer clusters.

To understand the dynamic nature of commuter patterns and the most powerful levers to influence them calls for more analysis and the application of sophisticated modeling techniques. This has already been done in relation to the functionality of the KE. (e.g. Etzkowitz and Leydesdorff, 2000). In our case, we have commenced investigating the demographic and economic influences on the geography of the sector. Our aim is to develop a truly systemic understanding of the factors that influence work, residential and commuting decisions. By being able to reliably model the impact of proposed planning and policy interventions on these decision-making systems, we hope to highlight more effective strategies to improve local economic development planning and raise ESC ratios. The ultimate goal is to contribute to the evolution of a metropolis that can be more efficient, more equitable and more sustainable.

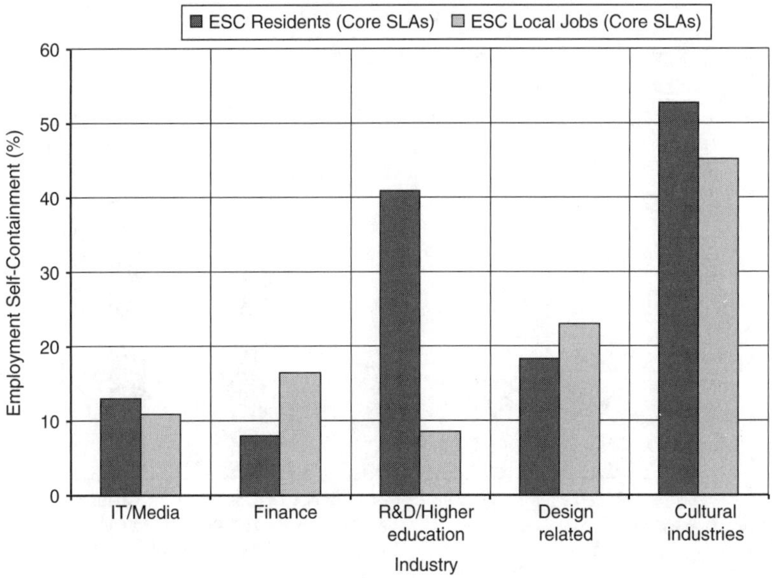

Source: ABS, Census 2006.

Figure 16.19 Synchrotronia ESC residents and jobs (2006)

Table 16.11 Working from home by knowledge economy subsector (2006)

Industry	Total Number	Working from Home(%)
IT/Media	2249	6.8
Finance	6226	5.4
R&D/Higher education	5961	7.9
Design related	3605	12.9
Cultural industries	1567	23.3
Other industries	42027	2.9
All industries	61635	3.7

Source: ABS, Census 2006.

NOTES

1. The scale at which place of work data is available does place some restrictions on the analysis. SLA boundaries do not necessarily conform to areas that are meaningful in an economic sense.

2. A more detailed paper, including appendices outlining the statistical tests applied to the research, was presented at the Global Knowledge Cities Conference in Melbourne in November 2010.
3. A sixth, health, was excluded in this preliminary research due to time constraints. This means that, for example, while health researchers are included (under R&D), surgeons are not.
4. Defined here using the ABS Metropolitan Statistical Region. It covers an area of around 7600 square kilometres in an arc around Port Phillip Bay.
5. Work on the entire Australian labor force found positive correlations between ESC and several locational parameters; length of residency; income band; educational backgrounds; occupation (by industry of employment) and selected industries of employment. So, for example, small business owners are more likely to live and work locally, as are 15–19 year olds; architecture graduates (more so than working architects); those who live some distance from a train station; and creative artists.
6. Unpublished research for various clients found that, with the exception of farmers, cultural industry workers were more likely to live and work in the same SLA than any other sector of the workforce (Geografia, 2009).
7. This analysis found several features unique to the finance sector, most probably due to a combination of the job characteristics and demographic characteristics of the workforce. Determining to what extent this sector should be treated separately will be one element in future modelling work.
8. This cut off was selected simply because the KE accounts for around 20 per cent of all employment in the metropolitan area.
9. Although the SLA for this area does not quite meet the '20 per cent' criterion, it was included on the basis that it defines an important emergent R&D hub.
10. 'Job' employment self-containment refers to the proportion of jobs filled by people living in the same SLA as the job is located. 'Resident' employment self-containment is the more familiar ratio and refers to the proportion of residents working in the same SLA as they live.
11. This is done on the basis that, in many cases, SLA boundaries do not create a useful or consistently comparable area of analysis.
12. One plausible but untested reason for this may be changing female workforce participation. It should also be noted that the figures for working from home refer to where a person worked on the day of the Census. It's a useful proxy, but not definitive, measure for working from home.

REFERENCES

ABS (2001), *Census 2001*, Canberra: Australian Bureau of Statistics.

ABS (2005), *Australian National Accounts: Input-Output Tables 2004–05*, Catalogue No. 5209.0.55.001, Canberra: Australian Bureau of Statistics.

ABS (2006), *Census 2006*, Canberra: Australian Bureau of Statistics.

Baum, S., T. Yigitcanlar, S. Horton, K. Velibeyoglu and B. Gleeson (2007), 'The role of community and lifestyle in the making of a knowledge city', Urban Research Program Policy and Practice Paper 2, Brisbane: Griffith University.

Coombes, M.G., A. Green and S. Openshaw (1986), 'An efficient algorithm to generate official statistical reporting areas: the case of the 1984 travel-to-work areas revision in Britain', *Journal of The Operational Research Society,* **37** (10), 943–953.

DPCD (2010), 'Central activities districts and transit cities', www.dpcd.vic.gov.au, accessed 20 October 2010.

Etzkowitz, J. and L. Leydesdorff (2000), 'The dynamics of innovation: from national systems and "Mode 2" to a triple helix of university-industry-government relations', *Research Policy*, **29**, 109–123.

Geografia (2009), Unpublished research, Melbourne: Geografia.

Glaeser, E. (2010), *Cities, Agglomeration and Spatial Equilibrium*, Oxford: Oxford University Press.

Hoyt, H. (1939), *The Structure and Growth of Residential Neighborhoods in American Cities*, Washington: Federal Housing Administration.

Johnson, S., L. Wrenn, M. Fry, R. Read, D. Bennet and B. Dean (2006), *Research Parks and the Biomedical Life Sciences*, Report to Piedmont Triad Research Park, Winston Salem.

JVSVN (2001), 'Next Silicon Valley: Riding the Waves of Innovation', Joint Venture Silicon Valley Network Working Paper, San Jose.

Mitchell, W. and M. Watts (2010), 'Identifying functional regions in Australia using hierarchical aggregation techniques', *Geographical Research,* **48** (1), 24–41.

O'Connor, K. and E. Healy (2002), 'The links between labour markets and housing markets in Melbourne', Australian Housing and Urban Research Institute Final Report Number 10.

Roth, C., S. Moon Kang, M. Batty and M. Barthelemy (2010), 'Commuting in a polycentric city', *Physics and Society*, arXiv:1001.4915v2*,* 1–9.

Searle, G. and B. Pritchard (2005), 'Industry clusters and Sydney's ITT sector: Northern Sydney as "Australia's Silicon Valley"?', *Australian Geographer*, **36** (2), 145–169.

Smith, N. (1992), 'Gentrification and uneven development', *Economic Geography,* 58, 139–155.

Trendle, B. and J. Siu (2007), 'Commuting patterns of Sunshine Coast residents and the impact of education', *Australasian Journal of Regional Studies*, **13** (2), 221–230.

Yigitcanlar, T., J. Dodson, B. Gleeson and N. Sipe (2007), 'Travel self-containment in master planned estates: analysis of recent Australian trends', *Urban Policy and Research*, **25** (1), 129–149.

Zukin, S. (1982), *Loft Living: Culture and Capital in Urban Change*, Baltimore: Johns Hopkins University Press.

17. Measuring: knowledge-based development metrics, evolution and perspectives

Francisco Javier Carrillo and Ricardo Emmanuel Flores

INTRODUCTION

Public discourse, media and overall global cultural expressions consistently refer to knowledge society and the knowledge economy as signs of our times. At the more specialized and professional level, knowledge-based development (KBD) has been established as an institutional field of research and practice. However, the nature, dimensions, processes and therefore measurement methods for knowledge-based phenomena are still preliminary.

The field of knowledge management is a relatively young one in the scope of economics and management science. In this field, to develop operational definitions and working metrics has been an ever-present goal. Furthermore, the complexities of social-scale knowledge processes and the practical and methodological issues concerning valid, comparable and accessible indicators present huge challenges to analysts and policy-makers. It is thus this chapter's purpose to present an overview of current approaches, and to provide a more consolidated vaulting block for future research and attempts at defining measurements for knowledge-based economies at different levels of analysis.

In looking at the evolution of KBD measurement methods, four major levels of knowledge-based metrics can be found: Organizational, Urban-Regional, National and Global. Measurement methods have been developed by researchers and agencies at each level. Often, these levels may overlap. For the purpose of this work, the categorization criterion is the broadest level at which the analyses are conducted in each method. In this chapter, organization-level methods are excluded as these have been more extensively studied and convey a distinctive problematic.

At the social levels (urban-regional, national, global) 23 separate methods are reviewed. An overview of these is presented in Table 17.1

Table 17.1 Breadth vs. degree of reductionism in a series of KBD metric methods

	Global	National	Regional / Urban
More systemic	World Capital Institute's Capital Systems Framework		Most Admired Knowledge City Awards
	Center for Bhutan Studies' Gross Domestic Happiness Study	Lin and Levinsson's Intellectual Capital Model	
	New Economic Foundation's Happy Planet Index	Intellectual Capital of the State of Israel	
	United Nations' Human Development Report		
	International Data Consulting's Information Society Index	Mercer's Human Resource Consulting Global Quality of Living	
	Australian Bureau of Statistics' Knowledge Based Economy	Cities Ranked and Rated	World Knowledge Competitive Index
	Organisation for Economic Co-operation and Development's The Knowledge Based Economy		
	Sussex University INEXSK Method	Progressive Policy Institute's State New Economy Index	Peru's Regional Competitiveness Index
	World Bank Knowledge Assessment Methodology	Este País' Knowledge Based Economy Index	Chile's Index of Regional Competitiveness
More reduc-tionistic	PRO INNO's European Innovation Scoreboard and Global Innovation Scoreboard	Center for Strategic Studies' Knowledge Based Economy	Urban Competitive Index

along two axes, first by breadth (i.e. from global to regional) and then by degree of reductionism. Reductionism is considered as the extent to which distinctive knowledge-based factors (education, human capital, R&D, social cohesion, connectedness, identity, etc.) are reducible to a single, often economic performance index rather than being considered distinctive elements in a multidimensional systems framework.

Comparative sheets for each method can be consulted in an earlier and lengthier monograph (Carrillo et al., 2010). Each method sheet includes ID elements such as name, authors and/or organization, year and cases of application, followed by descriptive elements such as structure, numerical algorithm for data processing, scope and constraints, a visualization example and method references.

Following the review, results are presented. First, the methods corresponding to the global, national and regional level are illustrated with a number of examples. Figure 17.1 contains an example of the comparative method sheets on which this account is based. Secondly, a discussion on current practices and methodological issues is presented with special reference to the landmark European Union KEI study. Finally, some general considerations and an emerging research agenda are discussed.

REGIONAL AND URBAN METRICS

The urban/regional metrics identified were fewer, and closer to the reductionist side of the scale than not. América Economía Intelligence's Urban Competitiveness Index was identified as one of the least intellectual capital-intensive metrics (América Economía, 2009). This method seeks to identify the best region for a company to do business in. Based on World Bank data, it includes over 50 different variables across two major dimensions: context and differential.

Chile's Ministry of Urban Planning generated a slightly different metric for evaluating regional competitiveness, the results of which are presented in their Index of Regional Competitiveness. This metric looks specifically towards factors for competitiveness in each region, primarily economic yield, population, number of companies, innovation, science and technology, infrastructure, government, and natural resources. Taking in 73 separate indicators, data is collected, quantified and normalized to thus glean the regional strengths and areas of opportunity (Ministerio de Planificación de Chile, 2009).

Peru's National Competitiveness Council's Regional Competitiveness Index is another regional metric that looks at regional comparison in a similar fashion to Chile's metric (Consejo Nacional de Competitividad,

State New Economy Index			
Authors:	Progressive Policy Institute / The Information Technology & Innovation Foundation	**Years implemented:**	1999, 2002, 2007, 2008, 2010
Description			
The purpose of the State New Economy Index is to measure the economic structure of states in the US and the degree to which that structure matches the ideal structure of the New Economy. The number of indicators used to calculate the index has varied for each edition of the index. The latest edition, published in 2010, utilized 26 indicators while previous used 28 in 2008, 26 in 2007, 21 in 2002 and 17 in 1999. The indicators are divided into five categories that, according to the authors of the Index, best capture what is new about the New Economy. These categories are: (1) knowledge jobs, (2) globalization, (3) economic dynamism, (4) transformation to a digital economy, and (5) technological innovation capacity. The names of the categories and the indicators contained in them have differed slightly through the different editions of the index. Scores in each indicator are calculated as follows: To measure the magnitude of the differences between the states instead of just their ranks from one to fifty, raw scores are based on standard deviations from the mean. Therefore, on average for most indicators, approximately half the states initially have negative scores (below the national mean) and approximately half have positive scores. The scores are equally adjusted (ten is added to each of the five indicator category totals) to ensure that all are positive. The overall scores are calculated by adding the states' adjusted scores in each of the five indicator categories and then dividing that total by the sum of the highest score achieved by any state in each category. Thus, each state's final score is a percentage of the total score a state would have achieved if it had finished first in every category.			
Scope and Constraints			
The application of this method offers insight as to the level of their efforts in implementation and consolidation of New Economy initiatives per state or region. It provides areas of opportunity, strengths, and weaknesses, which are useful for policy design directed to better focusing of states' economic and technological efforts. Its application is limited to United States of America and it has not been calculated on a yearly basis. Additionally, due to methodological variations and data discrepancies between the different publications of the Index, ranking comparisons among them are not exact.			
References and Sources			
Progressive Policy Institute (1999), 'The State New Economy Index', http://www.research.fsu.edu/techtransfer/documents/snei.pdf, accessed 21 February 2011. Innovation Technology & Innovation Foundation (2007), 'The 2007 State New Economy Index', http://www.kauffman.org/uploadedfiles/2007_State_Index.pdf, accessed 21 February 2011. Innovation Technology & Innovation Foundation (2008), 'The 2008 State New Economy Index', http://www.itif.org/files/2008_State_New_Economy_Index.pdf, accessed 21 February 2011. Innovation Technology & Innovation Foundation (2010), 'The 2010 State New Economy Index', http://www.itif.org/files/2010-state-new-economy-index.pdf, accessed 21 February 2011.			

Figure 17.1 Individual method sheet example. Progressive Policy Institute's State New Economy Index

2008). However, they include education and health to gauge competitiveness in the economy, as well as human and intellectual capital.

More KBD intensive, the World Knowledge Competitiveness Index, developed by Robert Huggins Associates, seeks to measure not only knowledge generation, but rather the degree to which knowledge is converted into economic value and how much of that wealth is transferred to citizens of a particular region (Huggins et al., 2005). Looking at the degree of competitiveness of each region's economies and factoring in the expenditure in research and development and education, as well as unemployment rates and ICT infrastructure, productivity levels, and citizens' access to private capital and knowledge-based employment, this metric gauges the efficiency of regional knowledge-based economies and identifies the returns of those economies to the region's citizens.

On the broader goal to capture a city/region systemic value structure as the integrated and not merely monetary profile, the MAKCi Study has been conducted since 2007 as the basis to the annual Most Admired Knowledge City Awards (Garcia and Carrillo, 2010). The study, based on a Delphi consultation of an international panel of experts, attempts to identify significant achievements in the overall knowledge base of a city as a result of deliberate development policies. The awards are presented to winners and runners-up in two categories: Knowledge City Region and Knowledge Metropolis. Capital dimensions are regarded as a complete and consistent system of value categories, deliberately aiming at capturing the overall condition of a human system (see Global Metrics below). The MAKCi Awards are reportedly evolving towards a distinctive KBD-Capital composite index.

NATIONAL METRICS

Seven metrics were identified for national analysis. Designed to provide a nation with insight as to its internal operations or standings in regards to intellectual capital, these methods all have use for the analysis of single nations. Much like the previous group of methods, these will be presented from those most reductionist to those least so.

The Center for Strategic Studies' Knowledge Based Economy – The Condition of the Mexican States report looks at the level of development of each state, but rather than looking solely at the political and economic factors, this study looks to see what factors are needed for a knowledge-based economy to emerge and evaluates each state based on how far they are in attaining it (Molina et al., 2005). The report provides strengths, weaknesses, and opportunities of each state, but the recommendations lie more in the generation of intellectual capital.

The Knowledge Based Economy Index (KBEI) put forward by 'Este País' Foundation takes a very similar approach to the Center for Strategic Studies (Friedrich Naumann Foundation et al., 2005). The KBEI also seeks to quantify the potential of each of the Mexican states in regards to knowledge-based economies. Generating their index on five major components, this metric focuses on the economic output and infrastructure, but also quantifies and compares exterior orientation, innovation systems, and education levels and qualified human resources per region.

Further towards the non-reductionist end of the spectrum, the State New Economy Index (SNEI) put forward by the Progressive Policy Institute (see individual method sheet example in Figure 17.1) seeks to gauge how much each of the states of the USA has adapted and managed the New Economy (Atkinson and Andes, 2008). Using 29 indicators, the SNEI divides them into five major categories being: generation of jobs related to knowledge, globalization, economic dynamism, penetration of digital economy in economic activity, and the capacity to innovate. This index then allows each state to have an idea of its standing within the nation, and where areas of opportunity lie while providing the nation a better view on general trends for future policy making.

The last three metrics found are more inclusive of Intellectual Capital, and can be classified as systemic in their approach. The Cities Ranked and Rated metric (Sperling and Sander, 2004) looks to compare the major cities in the USA amongst each other as well as 27 major Canadian ones, on the grounds of image, character, and quality of life. The key categories for the generation of this metric are: economy and job market, cost of living, weather, education, health, crime, transport, art and culture, quality of life, and leisure and free time. This study is conducted at a national level, and provides a concept of where the 'best place to live' might be.

Similarly, Mercer's Global Quality of Living city ranking (Mercer Human Resource Consulting, 2009) helps companies determine optimal compensation packages for expatriates taking into account discrepancies in living standards between the city of origin and the destination. This metric is built on 39 factors across ten categories, which include socio-political climate, socio-cultural factors, schools and education, infrastructure, leisure, economic climate, and the environment.

As mentioned earlier, method categorization was based not only on the unit of analysis, but finally on the level at which analyses are conducted and conclusions reached. The two former studies are based at city level but taken to a national level. As a case of direct KBD metric at a national level, *The Intellectual Capital of The State of Israel* (Pasher and Shachar, 2007) includes a more comprehensive and dedicated intellectual capital report with earlier editions in 1998 and 2004.

Finally, the recent work by Lin and Edvinsson (2010) provides a dedicated look at intellectual capital at a national level. In looking at 40 countries, they compare national IC profiles across several major regions such as Nordic countries, Central Europe, Eastern and Southern Europe, North America, Latin America, Australasia, Asia Pacific, Southeast Asia and the BRIC countries.

GLOBAL METRICS

The most common metrics tracked down were those focused on global-scale comparisons. Within this category, eleven different methods for quantification or comparison of development were selected, most including some KBD element in their metrics.

The European Innovation Scoreboard (EIS), developed by PRO INNO Europe, focuses on innovation initiatives, indicators, and tendencies of all members of the European Union. Being focused on innovation as a complement to the economy, the EIS downplays intellectual capital, and thus is relatively more reductionist. Quantifying innovation input and outputs across 26 indicators, the PRO INNO metric provides a method for comparison of nations in the European Union. Expanding on this same metric, PRO INNO subsequently launched a global study, named the Global Innovation Scoreboard (Pro Inno Europe, 2009), bringing the number of indicators down to nine, but broadening the scope to innovation input and output and technological capacity.

The World Bank's Knowledge Assessment Methodology (KAM) seeks to evaluate a nation's strengths and weaknesses in knowledge-based economy (World Bank, 2008). Adding more indices related to intellectual and human capital, while still focusing on economic performance, the KAM metric falls closer to the middle in regards to reductionist vs. non-reductionist approach to intellectual capital. Looking at economic programs and infrastructure tied to intellectual capital, as well as metrics based on the human side of nations, it is positioned in a middle ground and consequently a widely used metric for comparison.

Even more focused on intellectual capital, Sussex University's INEXSK Method rates nations based on their infrastructure, experience, skills, and knowledge (Mansell and Wehn, 1998). The knowledge element of this metric is relatively theoretical, as it aims to quantify social vision and social appropriation of information and communication technologies.

The remaining six metrics are increasingly skewed towards comprehensive capital valuation. The Organisation for Economic Co-operation and Development (OECD) method seeks to quantify the output of knowledge-based economies (OECD, 1996a, 1996b). Focusing on knowledge aspects such as the generation of knowledge, number of personnel in investigation, intellectual property generation, and international transfer of knowledge, the OECD's metric provides the means for global comparison in terms of intellectual capital.

A similar method is proposed by the Australian Bureau of Statistics in the form of the knowledge-based economy method (ABS, 2004). Using data from the Asian-Pacific Economic Co-operation (APEC) and the OECD, they rate nations' intellectual capital output on five scales, namely: innovation and entrepreneurial spirit, human capital, ICTs, social impact, and economy.

International Data Consulting and World Times developed a metric focused on information societies, the Information Society Index (ISI). It evaluates nations on four sub-indices: the degree of access to ICTs, degree of absorption of ICTs, degree of utilization of ICTs, and the degree of insertion of ICTs into information societies (IDC, 2000).

The three final methods seek an even more integrated approach, relying heavily on knowledge capital, and encompassing the human dimension. The United Nations' Human Development Report (HDR) focuses on the condition of a nation's people. Creating a metric based on nations' poverty index, human development, and gender development, the HDR aims to position the population at the center of the development quantification (UNDP, 2004).

Similarly, the New Economic Foundation Happy Planet Index (HPI) looks not only at wealth and development, but at culture, gastronomy, life expectancy, and the ecological footprint of nations. Built on three major indicators, the HPI looks primarily at life expectancy, vital satisfaction expressed by each nation's citizens, and the ecological footprint each nation leaves in the pursuit of the required standard of living for the nation to feel content (New Economic Foundation, 2009).

Taking this approach even further, Bhutan's Gross Domestic Happiness Study stems from the argument that a nation's development is truly seen not in industry or economy, but in the happiness of its people. Thus, the government of Bhutan sought to codify happiness on four main elements: focus on sustainable and egalitarian socioeconomic development, preservation and promotion of cultural values, preservation of the environment, and good governing practices (Ura, 2008).

Finally, the Capital Systems Framework has deliberately sought to develop a method to determine a community's relative position in regards to advancement towards KBD (World Capital Institute, 2001). The core purpose of this method is to capture the systemic interdependence of all major value elements (both tangible and knowledge-based) in an integrated framework (Carrillo, 2002). Designed around eight capital categories aiming at constituting a complete and consistent set of capitals, it includes Identity and Intelligence Capitals, Relational and

Financial Capitals, Human Individual and Human Collective Capitals, and Instrumental Tangible as well as Instrumental Intangible Capitals.

THE KNOWLEDGE ECONOMY INDICATORS PROJECT

Anyone interested in KBD indicators is bound to come across the Knowledge Economy Indicators (KEI) Project, a landmark in the field of Knowledge Economy metrics. Surprisingly, this project is less well known within the KBD community than some of the above methods. However, KEI is arguably the most substantial effort aimed at understanding and leveraging the potential use of social-level knowledge indicators for purposes of policy design and assessment. The project is generously documented at the Universität Trier webpage: http://www.uni-trier.de/index.php?id=26661. This section is based on a CD tutorial produced in Spanish as an educational resource (López et al., 2010).

Started in 2004, the KEI project ('Knowledge Economy Indicators: Development of Innovative and Reliable Indicator Systems') objective, was 'to develop and improve indicators for the knowledge economy, including the analysis of aggregation issues and the use of composite indicators'. The project covered indicators from 25 EC and 5 other European countries plus 6 non-European countries.

The KEI project reviewed current concepts and definitions on the Knowledge-Based Economy (KBE) and used such themes to classify existing indicators and explore them in depth. Literature reviews allowed the identification of some unexplored topics, which in turn permitted identifying the way in which these could be tackled through innovative approaches better suited for KBE understanding and assessment. Composite indicators were carefully analysed through a number of both statistic and participatory approaches.

These included the use of multi-criteria techniques, aggregation and weighting techniques and decomposition methods. An evaluation of analytical and presentational techniques was also included. Even simulation methods were used to investigate indicator robustness, as well as their resulting conclusions. The study assessed the quality and accuracy of indicators and associated data.

Hence, the KEI project aimed at developing new indicators and improving existing ones, with the goal of providing tools for monitoring KBE progress. The project classified existing indicators prior to checking in detail the nature of data and other information quality issues. Composite indicators were developed subsequently and subject to statistical and participatory tests. Finally, the robustness of composite indicators, as well as the conclusions reached by these, were validated through simulations.

In all, the KEI project is a formidable effort aimed at better understanding and managing R&D activities from a European perspective. However, its inclusive approach, globalized perspective and innovative approach make it a major reference for all future work in KBD metrics. The KEI project has set the ground for future R&D work in the field, particularly that aimed at international policy making.

EMERGING ISSUES

The KEI project was conducted in response to policy formulation and assessment in the EC. Also, it focused on a specific view of the KBE, namely an instrumental multi-factor perspective of knowledge as leverage to economic growth. This view of the Knowledge Society and the Knowledge Economy has been typified as *transitional* insofaras increase in monetary mass remains as ultimate social goal, and a dualistic approach prevails between 'tangible capital' (traditional physical and financial) and 'intangible' (intellectual or knowledge-based capital) (Carrillo, 2006). As a consequence of this approach value dimensions become heterogeneous, making it difficult to build a complete and consistent set of value dimensions or capital system (see Carrillo 1998, 2002, 2004, 2006, 2010a, 2010b for a discussion of these constraints on the space of possibilities for the concept of Knowledge Society).

Such a transitional perspective permeates the KEI project and consequently European ideas and policies (and to be fair, received views worldwide) on the Knowledge Society and the Knowledge Economy. The instrumental character or resource-view of knowledge is explicit in statements such as:

> [This is the view expressed in the third European Report on Science & Technology indicators (EC, 2003b)] **Knowledge is viewed as *the key resource* for competition in a globalizing world**, with knowledge creation and diffusion both deemed key factors in the ability of Europe to face increasing competition from low-wage countries. This means that the knowledge economy is considered also a *goal* for public policy and something to be encouraged by public policy. (Lopez et al., p. 4, bold and italics original)

The epistemological assumptions underlying this view are critical, for these conceptually determine how knowledge and its role in development is understood, operationalized, measured and, above all, incorporated into public policy design, management and evaluation. A system of indicators ultimately expresses the limits, elements and rules in a formal system, thus determining the space of possibilities. An instrumental or transitional view of the knowledge economy substantially reduces the vision of knowledge societies to a quantitative catalyst of economic growth instead of the qualitative evolutionary paradigm of social design it might be. Instead of challenging the current rules of the economic game, the social innovation promise of intellectual capital consists in adding some external elements as facilitators of current production factors. Alternative transitional views differ only in the amount of production sectors involved in the accounts:

> The only notable difference between the 'knowledge economy' and the 'knowledge-based economy' is that the former focuses on knowledge-intensive sectors, while the latter extends the concepts to all sectors of economic activity. We view the knowledge economy as much broader than a focus on knowledge-intensive sectors and so we use the definition of the knowledge-based economy that considers changes taking place across all sectors. (Lopez et al., p. 2)

As an alternative interpretation of knowledge-based value systems (be it societies, cities, economies, etc.) a *radical* or systemic perspective has been advanced (Carrillo, 1998, 2006; Von Mutius, 2005; Allee, 2009). Allee has stressed the existence of a common underlying nature of all capital forms. This is empirically shown in capital convertibility along value network transactions:

> Participants in a value network, either individually or collectively, utilize their tangible and intangible asset base by assuming or creating roles that convert those assets into more negotiable forms of value that can be delivered to other roles through the execution of a transaction. In turn, the true value of deliverables received is realized by participants when they convert them into gains or improvements in tangible or intangible assets (Allee, 2009, p. 430)

Von Mutius (2005) in turn has looked at the deeper implications of integrated capital systems. By reflecting on the received dichotomy between traditional capital and intellectual capital, he advances the following position:

> The proposal . . . is to place the idea of IC in a *broader context*. Not to dilute it, but enhance its impact. This context is broadened in three respects.
>
> First, it appears to be of vital importance not to discuss the theme of IC in isolation from *social capital*, but to make the inseparable *interconnection* of these two forms of capital a focus of exploration from the start. Both intellectual and social capitals are *intangibles, human and immaterial values*. And, in practice, they can be generated and increased only in rather similar ways: by sharing knowledge in cross-border relationships.

> Secondly, I would like to recommend that we consciously establish a conceptual *relationship* between the apparent *soft* topic of intangible assets or values and the *hard* strategic topic of tangible assets or material (physical and financial) value. This argument proposes that immaterial and material assets should be regarded in the future as being of equal weight and needing to be balanced in new ways on all areas of leadership and management activity.
>
> Finally, this requires addressing the theme on a *different level*. It is to be viewed, not as a subordinate or partial function of management or administration, *but as a comprehensive and interdisciplinary leadership task*. (Von Mutius, 2005, pp. 152–153. Italics in the original.)

Informally, Von Mutius was setting the requirements for a formal capital system (a complete, consistent and homogeneous system of value categories). From this perspective, this is highly convergent with the Capital Systems approach, a comprehensive taxonomy of value categories where all capital forms are valuable by themselves, not just subsidiaries to financial capital, and all constitute together a cohesive system (e.g. Carrillo, 2002). This system has evolved in a flexible system of accounts, applicable as an endogenous capital strategy (e.g. Carrillo 2005).

As a conceptual paradigm, the Capital Systems approach challenges many of the received practices on KBD operationalization and measurement. In particular, it redefines the core issue of aggregation and composite indicators. More widely, it overcomes epistemological assumptions that pervaded the received view on IC and KBE such as inductivism, intrinsic dualism and reductionism. These implications are beginning to be examined (Carrillo, 2010b).

CONCLUSION: RESEARCH AGENDAS

The field of KBD metrics is far from static. Actually, if judged by increasing attention in specialized fora such as dedicated publications and conferences, the topic seems to be on the rise. This is understandable due to the low degree of technical development relative to instrumental and applied developments in the IC and KBD arenas. In this final section, some of the most visible agendas in KBD metrics are described.

As mentioned in the acknowledgements note, this chapter is a result of the Research Program on KBD Metrics sponsored by the World Capital Institute at Tecnológico de Monterrey, México. It started in 2009 aimed at developing a MAKCi Index as an alternative to the current Delphi-based annual consultation determining award winners. It moves along a number of tracks including,

1. State-of-the-art in KBD metrics (Carrillo et al., 2010). An extensive literature review and critical analysis of concepts, methods, practices and lessons learnt in KBD metrics and other related composite indicator areas such as sustainability, quality of living, happiness, etc.
2. Statistical analysis of MAKCi data (Leal and Garcia, 2010). A search for patterns in the first four MAKCi studies data from 2007 through 2010, that could help assess the significance and constraints of the current annual study and help design a purpose-fit index.
3. Methodological trade-offs in composite indices development. In practice, decision-makers, evaluators and practitioners are concerned with having the most informative system of indicators at the most reasonable cost. This track aims at developing a series of tools for helping practitioners make the best cost/benefit decisions in implementing KBD indicator systems (García, 2011). Benefit here refers to the attributes of outcome data from a metrics canon perspective. Cost refers to real-world implementation requirements of aggregation and composite secondary sources.
4. Alternatives to GDP. Building on all previous tracks, this is convergent with the World Capital Institute long-term goal of assessing global assets and liabilities from a KBD perspective. This track is closely monitoring those developments worldwide that may contribute to develop sound and comprehensive as well as practical assessments of value balance for major social systems.

Another example of current KBD metrics research initiatives is the AICTE Project on Developing a Framework for Flexible Knowledge Management Indices started in 2009 at the Institute of Management Technology in Ghaziabad, India. The scope of this project is both at firm and societal levels. Project details can be found at the webpage http://www.imt.edu/AICTEResearchProject/index.asp

According to this source, the project goal is:

> Establishing, testing and validating a framework for developing Regional Knowledge Management Indices, which would be used for evaluating the extent and effectiveness of the processes for creation and utilization of Knowledge in different regions. The purpose of such indices would be to evaluate how different regions compare on various parameters of knowledge creation as well as distribution and use of knowledge within and across regions for economic growth and for larger good of the society.

A collaboration is already ongoing between Monterrey's Research Program on KBD Metrics and Ghaziabad's AICTE Project on Developing a Framework for Flexible Knowledge Management Indices. Links with other related initiatives as well as individual researchers and practitioners on KBD metrics are being explored.

Besides the inner research purposes of these agendas, there are also some practical expectations driving them. The interest on building composite indicators is aimed at improving the MAKCi annual study. The interest in the methodological trade-offs of indicator systems is aimed at providing decision-makers with practical guidelines in developing local KBD measurement practices that provide the most informative picture with the available information resources and processing capacity.

As reported by Garcia (2011) the use of composite indicators requires a careful balance between cost and benefit, which has been partly summarized by Nardo et al. (2005). According to these authors, the following considerations are important in building composite indicators:

Theoretical framework Selection and combination of single indicators into a composite indicator under a fitness-for-purpose criterion, where experts and stakeholders play a critical role.

Data selection Single indicators should be selected on the basis of availability, measurability, analytical soundness, comparability, geographic coverage, and relevance. Proxy data may be used if data are unavailable.

Imputation of missing data Missing values or outliers require the application of imputation techniques in order to evaluate impact on the composite indicator.

Multivariate analysis This can be used to check the overall statistical structure of the dataset, assess its suitability, or suggest methodological choices.

Normalization of the dataset This is fundamental to allow comparison and may help to identify outliers and highly skewed data, and to make scale adjustments.

Weighting and aggregation These depend on the theoretical framework previously selected, in order to verify correlation and compensation between indicators.

Robustness and sensitivity Involves testing in terms of the inclusion or exclusion of single indicators, the normalization procedure, the imputation of missing data, the aggregation method, and the choice of weights, as well as alternative conceptual scenarios for the selection of indicators and sensitivity analysis to clarify what sources of uncertainty are more influential in the scores and/or ranks.

Back to data An index should be transparent or decomposable so as to allow for the identification of the main drivers of a system performance, to see if indicators are correlated, to look for causal relationships, and to identify the dominance by few indicators.

Links to other indicators The composite indicator or its constituent indicators should be correlated with indicators published elsewhere, and the linkages should be identified via regression analysis.

Visualization of results This is important since the way a composite indicator is presented or visualized may enhance its interpretation on the part of the targeted stakeholders (after Nardo et al., 2005, Garcia, 2011).

As mentioned in the introduction, while KBD reaches a wider presence in social discourse, as well as in public policies and development programs, the need to operationalize and assess current understanding of social knowledge capitalization is rapidly escalating. Unless technically sound and transparent measurement systems become the language of KBD policy-making and assessment, there is a risk of public and media alienation of the promise of knowledge for development. According to a survey by Böhringer and Jochem (2007) of eleven prominent sustainability indices (actually including other highly integrated indices such as well-being and urban development, some included in this study) most comprehensive international composite indices are highly arbitrary and meaningless with reference to three key steps of index construction: normalization, weighting and aggregation. This would render most current practices on allegedly measuring sustainability (and, by extension, other complex composite phenomena such as social progress, well-being, quality of life and KBD) scientifically untenable.

Hence, the increasing attention to KBD is paired with the responsibility of developing satisfactory measurement methods, indicator databases and collaborative R&D efforts. Altogether, learnings from recent literature, diverse practices worldwide and focused collaborative research agendas are converging in the generation of sound and usable KBD metrics that can be applied at different levels. While major international agencies, national governments and large metropoles can continue to expand the KBD metrics knowledge base, local communities can engage in practices that serve their policy design and assessment, thus widening the global wealth of comparable data and contributing to develop a (KBD) metrics culture.

REFERENCES

Allee, V. (2009), 'Value-creating networks: organizational issues and challenges', *The Learning Organization*, **16** (6), 427–442.

América Economía (2009), 'Metodología del ranking y cálculo del ICUR 2009', http://www.americaeconomia.com/261534-Metodologia-del-ranking-y-calculo-del-ICUR.note.aspx, accessed 15 October 2009.

Atkinson, R.D. and S. Andes (2008), 'The 2008 State New Economy Index, Progressive Policy Institute, 2008', http://www.itif.org/files/2008_State_New_Economy_Index.pdf, accessed 15 October 2009.

ABS (Australian Bureau of Statistics) (2004), 'Knowledge Based Economy and Society (KBE/S) framework and indicators', http://www.unescap.org/Stat/ict/ict2004/17.KnowledgeBased_Economy&Society_Indicators.pdf, accessed 20 November 2009.

Böhringer, C. and P. Jochem (2007), 'Measuring the immeasurable – a survey of sustainability indices', *Ecological Economics*, **63**, 1–8.

Carrillo, F.J. (1998), 'Managing knowledge-based value systems', *Journal of Knowledge Management*, **1** (4), 280–286.

Carrillo, F.J. (2002), 'Capital systems: implications for a global knowledge agenda', *Journal of Knowledge Management*, **6** (4), 379–399.

Carrillo, F.J. (2004), 'Capital cities: a taxonomy of capital accounts for knowledge cities', *Journal of Knowledge Management*, **8** (5), 28–46.

Carrillo, F.J. (2005), 'A taxonomy of urban capital', Chapter 4 in F.J. Carrillo (ed.), *Knowledge Cities*, Oxford, UK: Elsevier/Butterworth-Heinemann, pp. 43–58.

Carrillo, F.J. (2006), 'From transitional to radical knowledge-based development', *Journal of Knowledge Management*, **10** (5), 3–5.

Carrillo, F.J. (2010a), 'Knowledge-based value generation', in Kostas Metaxiotis, Francisco J. Carrillo and Tan Yigitcanlar (eds), *Knowledge-Based Development for Cities and Societies: Integrated Multi-Level Approaches*. Hershey, US: IGI Global, pp. 1–16.

Carrillo, F.J. (2010b), 'Trends in KBD metrics', *IC6 Conference – Intellectual Capital for Communities in the Knowledge Economy: Nations, Regions, Cities and Emerging Communities*, Paris: The World Bank, Université Paris-Sud, The New Club of Paris.

Carrillo, F.J., A. Marín and R.E. Flores (2010), 'KBD metrics: current issues and trends' Paper submitted to the 2010 Knowledge Cities World Summit, Melbourne, Australia.

Consejo Nacional de Competitividad (2009), 'El índice de competitividad regional de Perú Compite 2008', http://www.cies.org.pe/files/GT/ppt-descentralizacion-5ta-sesion.pdf, accessed 20 October 2009.

Friedrich Naumann Foundation and Fundación Este País (2005), 'México ante el reto de la economía del conocimiento', http://estepais.com/sita/?p=21047, accessed 3 November 2009.

García, C. (2011), 'Measuring knowledge-based development: an overview of models and methodological issues', *International Journal of Knowledge Based Development* (forthcoming).

Garcia, B. and F.J. Carrillo (2010), 'The 2010 Most Admired Knowledge City Report. World Capital Institute and Teleos', http://www.worldcapitalinstitute.org/makci/history, accessed 18 February 2011.

Huggins, R., H. Izushi and W. Devies (2005), 'World knowledge competitiveness index 2005', Wales: Robert Huggins Associates Ltd.

Innovation Technology and Innovation Foundation (2007), 'The 2007 State New Economy Index', http://www.kauffman.org/uploadedfiles/2007_State_Index.pdf, accessed 21 February 2011.

Innovation Technology and Innovation Foundation (2008), 'The 2008 State New Economy Index', http://www.itif.org/files/2008_State_New_Economy_Index.pdf, accessed 21 February 2011.

Innovation Technology and Innovation Foundation (2010), 'The 2010 State New Economy Index', http://www.itif.org/files/2010-state-new-economy-index.pdf, accessed 21 February 2011.

IDC (International Data Consulting) (2000), 'Information Society Index, Leading IT Indicators', http://www.idc.com/groups/isi/DOCS/factsheets.pdf, accessed 11 November 2009.

Leal, A. and B. García (2010), 'Making MAKCi: identifying key elements in Knowledge-Cities Benchmarking', Paper submitted to the 2010 Knowledge Cities World Summit, Melbourne, Australia.

Lin, C.Y. and L. Edvinsson (2010), *National Intellectual Capital. A Comparison of 40 Countries*, New York, US: Springer.

López, A., J.A. Menéndez, D. Morales and J. Sesma (2010), 'Introducción al Proyecto KEI', Introduction to Knowledge Management Course, Doctoral Program in Administration, Monterrey, México Technólogical de Monterrey, Center for Knowledge Systems (CD).

Mansell, R. and U. Wehn (1998), 'INK – Knowledge Societies Information Technology for Sustainable Development, University of Sussex', http://www.sussex.ac.uk/spru/1-4-9-1-1-2.html, accessed 10 November 2009.

Mercer Human Resource Consulting (2009), 'Quality of Living global city rankings 2009', http://www.mercer.com/qualityoflivingpr, accessed 09 December 2009.

Ministerio de Planificación de Chile (2009), 'Índice de Competitividad Regional-ICR', Gobierno de Chile, http://www.subdere.gov.cl/1510/articles-75995_archivo_fuente.pdf, accessed 20 October 2009.

Molina A., H. Robles and R. Fuentes (2005), *La Economía Basada en el Conocimiento, Las Condiciones de los Estados Mexicanos*, México: ITESM.

Nardo, M., M. Saisana, A. Saltelli, S. Tarantola, A. Hoffman and E. Giovannini (2005), 'Handbook on constructing composite indicators: methodology and user guide OECD Statistics Working Papers 2005/3', OECD Statistics Directorate.

New Economic Foundation (2009), 'The Happy Planet Index', http://www.neweconomics.org/sites/neweconomics.org/files/The_Happy_Planet_Index_1.pdf, accessed 4 December 2009.

Organisation for Economic Co-operation and Development (1996a), *The Knowledge-based Economy*, Paris: OECD.

Organisation for Economic Co-operation and Development (1996b), *Employment and Growth in the Knowledge-based Economy*, Paris: OECD.

Pasher, E. and S. Shachar (2007), *The Intellectual Capital of The State of Israel*, Jerusalem: Office of the Chief Scientists.

Pro Inno Europe (2009), 'European Innovation Scoreboard 2008', http://ictnet.es/system/files/EIS_2008_Final_report.pdf, accessed 8 November 2009.

Progressive Policy Institute (1999), 'The State New Economy Index' http://www.research.fsu.edu/techtransfer/documents/snei.pdf, accessed 21 February 2011.

Sperling, B. and J. Sander (2004), *Cities Ranked and Rated*, Wiley Publishing, Inc.

UNDP (United Nations Development Program) (2004), 'Human Development Report 2004', http://hdr.undp.org/en/reports/global/hdr2004/, accessed 9 November 2009.

Ura, K. (2008), 'Explanation of GNH Index. Centre for Bhutan Studies', http://www.grossnationalhappiness.com/gnhIndex/intruductionGNH.aspx, accessed 21 February 2011.

Von Mutius, B. (2005), 'Rethinking leadership in the Knowledge Society. Learning from Others: how to integrate intellectual and social capital and establish a new balance of value and values', in Ahmed Bounfour and Leif Edvinsson (eds), *Intellectual Capital for Communities – Nations, Regions and Cities*, Oxford, UK: Elsevier, pp. 151–164.

World Bank (2008), 'Knowledge Assessment Methodology', http://siteresources.worldbank.org/INTUNIKAM/Resources/KAM_v4.pdf, accessed 9 November 2009.

World Capital Institute (2001), 'The capital systems framework', http://www.worldcapitalinstitute.org/capital_sist.html, accessed 27 July 2010.

18. Comparing: knowledge-based urban development of Vancouver, Melbourne, Manchester and Boston

Tan Yigitcanlar

INTRODUCTION

In the 21st century, the demand for knowledge capability diminishes the significance of material factors, resulting in a new era dominated by knowledge. Particularly in this era of the knowledge economy, knowledge-related activities, including creativity as a tacit knowledge form, have become central to creating employment and wealth, sustaining economic growth, and place-making (Friedmann, 2010). In the global knowledge economy, knowledge-intensive industries and knowledge workers are extensively seen as the primary factors needed to improve the welfare and competitiveness of cities. To attract and retain such industries and workers, cities produce knowledge-based urban development (KBUD) strategies, and this strategizing has become an important development mechanism for cities and their economies. Beyond this, KBUD is also being seen as the development pathway of the emerging knowledge cities (Yigitcanlar et al., 2008b). The process of planning and implementing KBUD approaches is neither quick nor simple. This is already understood by the research community, which has begun to concentrate its efforts on developing appropriate frameworks, methodologies, tools, systems, and metrics in the last few years. Taking into account these developments in the field, this chapter discusses the critical connections between knowledge city foundations and integrated KBUD mechanisms.

In particular, the chapter develops a conceptual understanding of KBUD that supports knowledge city formation and generation, as well as attraction and retention of investment and talent. Following this, the chapter introduces a KBUD assessment framework developed to provide a clearer understanding of the local and regional policy frameworks, and relevant applications of KBUD for cities to become prosperous knowledge cities. The chapter, and the KBUD assessment framework, demonstrate a method for measuring knowledge-based development capacity of cities by scrutinizing their economic, socio-cultural, enviro-urban and institutional development mechanisms and capabilities. It also compares the KBUD characteristics of four knowledge cities: Boston, Vancouver, Melbourne, and Manchester.

The chapter is prepared in six sections, and the remainder of the chapter is structured as follows. The second section provides an overview and gives relevant background to the knowledge-based development of cities and their transformation into knowledge cities. The third section provides more detailed information on KBUD and its processes. The fourth section presents the KBUD assessment framework. The fifth section reveals the results and discusses the findings of the comparative study of Boston, Vancouver, Melbourne, and Manchester. The chapter concludes with a discussion on the role of KBUD in knowledge city formation and the benefits of using the assessment framework to evaluate and assist in the (re)formulation of local and regional knowledge-based development strategies.

BACKGROUND

Over the last several decades, we have witnessed major economic, technological, social and environmental changes that have significantly impacted the patterns of urbanization, human activities and lifestyles. During the past few years, the challenges of globalization, knowledge economy, climate change, network society, transportation technologies, information and communication technologies, global division of labour force, rapid urbanization, and shrinkage of cities have become important topics of discussion (Yigitcanlar, 2010a). Particularly, the need for new spatial arrangements for cities to better cope with these challenges, and the necessity of adjusting city structures in order to become more compatible with the knowledge economy are among the most popular issues, and have heavily occupied the agendas of scholars, decision-makers and practitioners (MacKinnon et al., 2002). These issues revealed the need for developing and adopting new urban planning, development and management mechanisms to foster the sustainability of cities and make them resilient to change (Yigitcanlar, 2010b).

In recent years, we have also witnessed the birth of new concepts and paradigms that started to affect urbanization and ease the impacts of the abovementioned changes and challenges. Carrillo (2004) categorized these new concepts and paradigms under four groups: dematerialization (i.e. a lesser volume of material inputs and outputs); environmentalism (i.e. a greater concern with sustainability); experience upgrade (i.e. the capacity to attain the same results without the conventional means of space and time), and essentialism (i.e. the understanding and pursuit of ever more fundamental values).

Up until recently urbanization has been viewed primarily from the perspective of urban planning with a focus on the physical form and built environment of cities (e.g. on land use zoning, building and infrastructure), and very little consideration has been given to the knowledge resources or the cultures that produce knowledge. Traditionally, the emphasis has been on attracting tangible forms of production (i.e. labour, land and capital), and knowledge as an intangible asset was often ignored (Knight, 2008). With the advent of these new challenges, concepts and paradigms, greater attention needs to be shown in the restructuring of cities, so that they are able to house more knowledge-based activities and knowledge becomes a major source for local development (Metaxiotis et al., 2010).

The types of environments which need to be developed for knowledge-based activities differ significantly from those developed by commodity-based activities, and thus call for different development strategies. The most immediate impact of the knowledge economy in relation to the urban environment is the reduction in displacements made possible by the telecommunication technologies (i.e. changing working, schooling and shopping patterns). According to Graham (2002), present configuration, organization and lifestyles within urban centres are more the inheritance of tribal, hierarchical and material production patterns than they are good examples of urban design with a strong culture fit for knowledge societies.

One of the crucial tasks for cities in the era of knowledge economy, which is characterized by globalization, is that cities need to create environments where knowledge resources are valued, conditions are conducive to their development, and knowledge resources are securely anchored (Yigitcanlar et al., 2008a). With this perspective, the key conditions that contribute to the development of knowledge cities are outlined by Knight (1995) as: the community is able to define, perceive and value knowledge as a form of wealth; the city acknowledges the importance and contribution of knowledge workers; the city is able to make the public understand the nature and role of knowledge; knowledge resources are located considering regional contexts; priority is given to improving knowledge infrastructure; all members of society have access to careers in knowledge-based activities; the city is promoted as a centre of excellence; incentives and mechanisms are offered favouring investment in local knowledge resources; the city has a forward-looking vision, which emphasizes knowledge and other immaterial factors; and civic leadership is developed.

The rationale for developing or transforming cities into 'cities of knowledge' or 'knowledge cities' is widely accepted by scholars, decision-makers, practitioners and developers (Carrillo, 2006; van Winden et al., 2007; Yigitcanlar et al., 2008b; Ergazakis et al., 2009). However, traditional urban planning and development approaches do not provide a clear picture of how to form new development strategies that are knowledge-based or how to use urban planning mechanisms effectively to realize the knowledge-based development of cities. These vital questions put urban planning under the microscope and question its compatibility with the new conditions of the era of knowledge economy.

The rise of the knowledge economy has become the new main driver of global and local economic development, and achieving sustainable development – by creating a strong urban core, harnessing its economic strength, addressing social exclusion, and avoiding physical and environmental dereliction – has been the aim of urban planning in the era of knowledge economy (Yigitcanlar, 2009). However, traditional normative urban planning lacks the vision and capacity to deliver a sustainable and knowledge-based development. To date, the structuring of most of the cities has proceeded organically, as a dependent and derivative effect of global market forces. Urban planning has either responded slowly or not responded at all to the challenges and the opportunities of the global knowledge city (Yigitcanlar et al., 2008c). A decade into the new century the economic success of knowledge-based development policies in a number of cities and nations have led urbanists to consider whether existing policies are applicable to the knowledge-based development of cities – in other words, whether or not knowledge-based development can be planned. In recent years, this has led urban planning to consolidate its interest in the paradigm of post-modern social production under the rubric of 'KBUD' (Yigitcanlar and Velibeyoglu, 2008; Velibeyoglu and Yigitcanlar, 2010). Today examples around the globe (Yigitcanlar, 2009) confirm that it is possible to develop cities as, or transform cities into, knowledge cities, as long as appropriate and tailored KBUD policies are developed and implemented successfully.

KNOWLEDGE-BASED URBAN DEVELOPMENT

KBUD is a new form of development in the era of knowledge that aims to bring economic prosperity and environmental sustainability with a just socio-spatial order to cities (Yigitcanlar, 2009). The goal of KBUD is to produce a city purposefully designed to encourage the production and circulation of abstract work – a knowledge city (Cheng et al., 2004; Yigitcanlar et al., 2008c). The promise of KBUD is a secure economy in a human setting, and it has four major purposes: economic, socio-cultural, enviro-urban and institutional development.

Economic development codifies technical knowledge for the innovation of products and services, market knowledge for understanding changes in consumer choices, financial knowledge to measure the inputs and outputs of production and development processes, and human knowledge in the form of skills and creativity, within an economic model (Lever, 2002; Laszlo and Laszlo, 2007). Particularly in the era of knowledge, success in economic development is highly correlated with a city's ability to adapt in the knowledge economy (Nguyen, 2010).

Socio-cultural development indicates the intention to increase the skills and knowledge of residents as a means for individual and community development (Gonzalez et al., 2005). Social and human capitals of a society are seen as highly interrelated with its high level achievements in socio-cultural development (Frane et al., 2005).

Enviro-urban development builds a strong spatial network relationship between urban development clusters while driving an urban development that is ecologically friendly. In this sense, sustainable urban development and quality of life, particularly in the knowledge community precincts, play a significant role in the spatial formation of the citywide sustainable KBUD strategies (Yigitcanlar et al., 2008d; Yigitcanlar, 2010c).

Institutional development is key to orchestrating the KBUD and bringing together all of the main actors and sources so that they are able to organize and facilitate necessary knowledge-intensive activities and plan strategically for knowledge city formation (Yigitcanlar, 2009). The literature indicates that governing the KBUD via institutional leadership makes a big difference in achieving the knowledge city status (Baum et al., 2007).

These four development areas form the key pillars of the KBUD: economy, society, environment, and management. Along with these four pillars, sustainability and organizational capacities are also crucial for successful knowledge-based development of cities and regions (Figure 18.1).

EVALUATING THE KNOWLEDGE-BASED DEVELOPMENT LEVELS OF CITIES

Accurate evaluation of KBUD is central to determining knowledge-based development performance and levels of cities and benchmarking their achievements in knowledge-based development against successful

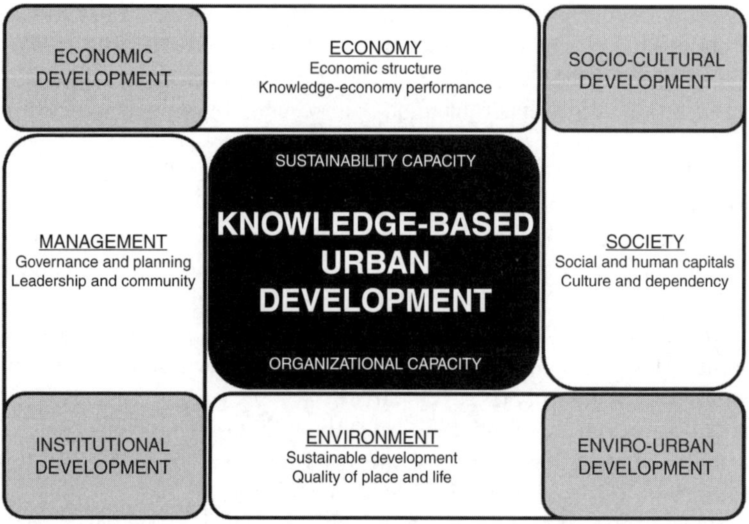

Figure 18.1 Pillars of knowledge-based urban development

knowledge cities. It is also central to informing policy-making as it points towards new strategic directions that will support realizing development that is more sustainable and knowledge-based.

Analysing and evaluating cities' knowledge-based development performances requires utilization of an accurate KBUD assessment framework. Although there are a number of frameworks developed for ranking cities considering their different characteristics by various institutions (i.e. Anholt, City Mayors, Foreign OECD, Policy, Mercer, UNDP, World Bank, World Capital Institute), currently there are not any knowledge-based development assessment frameworks available for a comprehensive KBUD evaluation. The research reported in this chapter develops a 'KBUD assessment framework' to specifically evaluate knowledge-based development performances of cities. Specifically tailored for the nature of the comparative KBUD assessment study presented in the following sections, the assessment framework contains two indicator sets for each of the four KBUD pillars, and four indicators for each of the eight indicator sets, totalling to 32 indicators (Table 18.1).

Following key literature's lead, each of the 32 indicators are selected on the basis of measurability, analytical soundness, comparability, geographic coverage, data availability, and relevance. In order to provide more accurate comparison, the use of proxy data for indicator values is avoided. All of the indicators are selected from a large indicator pool by using a multivariate analysis to determine the most suitable ones for each of the KBUD pillars. Multivariate analysis is also employed to see the correlations between indicators, look for causal relationships, and identify the dominance of any indicators.

Economic Development

The first domain or pillar of KBUD is economic development (see Figure 18.1). The literature indicates that in determining the economic development level of a city, in the era of knowledge economy, the key variables or indicators are mainly selected in relation to the city's 'economic structure' in general and its 'knowledge economy performance' in particular (Anand and Sen, 2000; New Zealand Government, 2007; World Bank, 2008).

In this KBUD framework, indicators related to 'economic structure' are selected as: gross domestic product; gross domestic product growth; foreign direct investment; and household disposable income (see Table 18.1).

Indicators related to 'knowledge economy performance' include: research and development expenditure; patents; knowledge workers, and knowledge-intensive services.

Socio-cultural Development

The second pillar of KBUD is socio-cultural development and, in line with the literature findings, the key indicators used in the evaluation of socio-cultural development are grouped under the 'social and human capitals' and 'culture and dependency' indicator sets (World Bank, 1996; OECD, 1998; Stone, 2001).

Indicators related to 'social and human capitals' consist of: educational attainment; tertiary education students; major university reputation, and access to broadband.

Indicators related to 'culture and dependency' are: workplace cultural diversity; societal cultural diversity; socio-economic dependency; and unemployment.

Enviro-urban Development

Enviro-urban development is the third pillar of KBUD, and a thorough literature review supports the key indicator sets – 'sustainable development' and 'quality of place and life' (Hemphill et al., 2004; Hezri, 2005; Singh et al., 2009).

Table 18.1 Knowledge-based urban development assessment framework

Pillars	Indicator Sets	Indicators	Definition
Economic development	Economic structure	Gross domestic product	Gross domestic product per capita
		Gross domestic product growth	Rate of real gross domestic product growth
		Foreign direct investment	International share in foreign direct investment
		Household disposable income	Growth rate of household disposable income
	Knowledge-economy performance	Research and development expenditure	National share in research and development expenditure
		Patents	Share in national patents
		Knowledge workers	Ratio of knowledge workers
		Knowledge-intensive services	Ratio of knowledge-intensive service employment
Socio-cultural development	Social and human capitals	Educational attainment	Educational attainment rate
		Tertiary education students	Ratio of tertiary education students to population
		Major university reputation	Global ranking of the major university
		Access to broadband	Access to broadband ratio
	Culture and dependency	Workplace cultural diversity	Cultural diversity ratio at workplace
		Societal cultural diversity	Ratio of overseas and interstate migrants
		Socio-economic dependency	Age-population ratio of those in and not in the labour force
		Unemployment	Unemployment rate

Enviro-urban development	Sustainable development	Eco-city status	International eco-city ranking
		Sustainable transport	Ratio of sustainable transport use
		Sustainable urban development	Statutory development plans emphasizing sustainability
		Climate change mitigation	Strategies in place for climate change adaptation or mitigation
	Quality of place and life	Housing affordability	Median house price ratio to median annual income
		Cost of living	International cost of living ranking
		Personal safety	International personal safety ranking
		Quality of life	International quality of life ranking
Institutional development	Governance and planning	Dedicated development authority	Knowledge-based urban development authority
		Strategic planning	Strategic planning for knowledge-based development
		Partnerships	Triple-helix and public-private partnerships
		e-Governance	International e-governance ranking
	Leadership and community	Local and regional leadership	Local and regional level leadership
		City branding	International city brand ranking
		Public participation	Public participation in decision making
		Income inequality	Income inequality level

Indicators selected for 'sustainable development' include: eco-city status; sustainable transport; sustainable urban development; and climate change mitigation.

Indicators related to 'quality of place and life' consist of: housing affordability; cost of living; personal safety; and quality of life.

Institutional Development

The final pillar of KBUD is institutional development. In light of the literature findings, the key indicators in the assessment of institutional development are clustered around two main indicator sets of 'governance and planning' and 'leadership and community' (Aron, 2000; Wilson and Beaton, 2003; Brinkerhoff and Morgan, 2010).

Indicators related to the 'governance and planning' indicator set include: dedicated development authority; strategic planning; partnerships; and e-governance.

Indicators of 'leadership and community' are: local and regional leadership; city branding; public participation; and income inequality.

A COMPARATIVE KNOWLEDGE-BASED DEVELOPMENT ANALYSIS

In order to demonstrate the utility of the KBUD assessment framework, this chapter reveals the results of applying the framework in a comparison of four successful city cases across the globe – Boston, MA, USA; Vancouver, BC, Canada; Melbourne, VIC, Australia; and Manchester, UK. The purpose of this comparative study is to demonstrate how the framework operates and provides a *raison d'être* for further in-depth analysis of KBUD of cities across the globe.

The first criterion for selecting these case studies was that the city was either considered for nomination, or nominated, or acknowledged by receiving a mention or an award at the World Capital Institute's Most Admired Knowledge Cities Awards (MAKCi – www.worldcapitalinstitute.org/makci.html – also see Garcia, 2009) within the last four years. The second criterion was cities within English speaking countries, so as to ease the comparison process – i.e. data availability in English and comparability of the governance systems.

The study area boundaries take into account metropolitan impacts, and therefore, rather than city boundaries, areas containing metropolitan urban centres and localities have been selected for the four cases (i.e. Greater Boston, Greater-Metro Vancouver, Metro Melbourne, and

Table 18.2 Salient characteristic of the case cities

		Boston	Vancouver	Melbourne	Manchester
Population	Local, 2007, people	4588680	2116581	3371888	2573500
Area	Local, 2007, km^2	7393	2422	6816	1281
Density	Local, 2007, people/km^2	620	874	495	2009
Median age	Local, 2008, age	34.50	34.60	36.10	35.00

Greater Manchester). Boston, Vancouver, Melbourne, and Manchester, when considered with their metropolitan regions, have a comparable population, area, density and median age. These salient features of the four case studies are listed in Table 18.2.

This empirical study's key comparison factors, the indicator pool, have been selected by considering the recently expanding literature on knowledge-based development. As explained in the previous section, a multivariate analysis was undertaken to refine the number of the indicators – eight for each of the KBUD pillars. In order to explore and evaluate the generic KBUD potentials of Boston, Vancouver, Melbourne and Manchester, the research focuses on the aforementioned 32 important features, or key indicators, of KBUD (see Table 18.1).

The methodology used in this analysis includes literature review, best practice analysis, government and international non-profit organization policy document content analysis, review of the city rankings conducted by non-profit and commercial surveying organizations, and statistical analyses of the fundamental data from governmental and non-governmental organizations that provide a comparison between the four knowledge cities.

The main datasets used for the statistical analysis are obtained from the following resources:

- World Bank, World Development Indicators Database
- United Nations, e-Government Survey
- OECD, Statistics Portal
- OECD, Composite Leading Indicators Database
- MERCER, Worldwide City Rankings
- Anholt City Brands Index
- QS, World University Rankings
- Internet World Statistics, World Internet Usage and Population Statistics

- USA Census Bureau, Census 2000 and 2006–2008 Community Survey
- Australian Bureau of Statistics, Census 2006 Community Profiles
- Statistics Canada, Census 2006 Community Profiles
- UK Office of National Statistics, Census 2001 Neighbourhood Statistics
- UK Office of National Statistics, 2008 Sub-national Population Projections
- Local economic development agency reports
- Local social and community development agency reports
- Local environmental protection agency reports
- Local urban planning and development agency reports
- Local institutional development agency reports
- Relevant literature and other (non-)government policy documents
- 2007–2009 Most Admired Knowledge Cities Award Reports
- Local media news and online sources

Once the datasets were collected, each indicator value was normalized in order to allow comparison between cases. Normalization of the datasets is particularly helpful for identifying outliers and highly skewed values, so that scale adjustments can be made when necessary.

Assigning an appropriate weighting for indicators is important and helps to verify correlation and compensation between indicators. However, for this comparative study, in the interest of simplifying the analysis, an equal weighting (3.125 per cent) was assigned to all indicators (see Appendix).

This empirical study has several limitations. The first limitation is that the indicators are equally weighted. Ideally, different weighting values need to be assigned to each indicator based on its importance. In this instance, the purpose of an equal weighting for all indicators is to simplify the assessment process.

For comparative studies of this kind, the robustness of the findings needs to be tested by focusing on the process of inclusion or exclusion of single indicators, normalization, the imputation of missing data, the aggregation method, and the choice of weights that might influence the scores and rankings. The second limitation of this study is that only a brief testing of the robustness and sensitivity of the findings, through the review of the literature on different KBUD aspects of the cities of comparison, has been done due to the complex nature of working in four different country contexts.

The last limitation of the study is that data was not available from the same period for all of the indicators. This is mainly due to the extensive limitation of data availability. In this comparative study, dates of the datasets fluctuate between a time span of 2005 and 2010, which is a relatively short limiting time frame.

Economic Development Analysis

The literature raises the importance of analysing various geographic levels to determine the economic development capacity of a metropolitan region (Agenor and Montiel, 2008; Pacione, 2009). Hence, in this empirical analysis, the macro (national and international) and meso (state or regional) geographic level economic performance indicators are measured along with the micro (local) geographic level economic indicators. In all case studies, out of eight economic development indicator values, three are collected in national, two in regional (state) and three in local levels.

The first indicator set in the economic development pillar of KBUD is the economic structure. While in the 'gross domestic product' and 'foreign direct investment' areas Boston was leading the other three cities with the figures of $81 499 and 17.54 per cent respectively, in the 'gross domestic product growth' Melbourne and in the 'household disposable income' area Vancouver took the lead with 2.29 per cent and 5.66 per cent respectively. The scores of these four indicators determined the overall economic structure, and assigned Boston the top ranking, followed by Melbourne, Vancouver and Manchester.

The second indicator set in this pillar is the knowledge-economy performance. In measuring the knowledge-economy engagement of the four case cities, Melbourne showed the best performance in the areas of 'research and development expenditure' and 'patents' with the figures of 29.31 per cent and 21.40 per cent. On two factors Vancouver and Boston easily outperformed the other cities: Vancouver with 47.51 per cent on the 'knowledge workers' and Boston with 50 per cent on 'knowledge-intensive services'. In the knowledge economy indicator set, Melbourne led, followed by Vancouver, Boston and then Manchester.

Not surprisingly in terms of overall economic development, Boston ranked best-performing city and receives the normalized top score of 100, while Melbourne becomes the first runner-up (94.23), Vancouver the second (76.26) and Manchester the third runner-up (53.88) (see Appendix and Table 18.3).

Socio-cultural Development Analysis

The research measures socio-cultural development at the local level by focusing on the critical social and cultural development aspects of the four study areas.

The first indicator set of the socio-cultural development pillar of KBUD is social and human capital. In this indicator set, Vancouver shows a higher performance than the other three cities, particularly in the areas of 'educational attainment' and 'access to broadband,' with 45.93 per cent and 42.60 per cent respectively. In the 'tertiary education students' variable, Melbourne, with 3.57 per cent and in the 'major university reputation' Boston, with Harvard University being the world's top ranked university, dominate the other cities. In the social and human capital indicator set Vancouver's lead is followed by Boston, Melbourne and then Manchester.

The second indicator set of the socio-cultural development analysis is culture and dependency, and in this area Boston and Vancouver show a clear dominancy over the other cities. For the indicators of 'workplace cultural diversity' and 'socio-economic dependency' Boston with 44.40 per cent and 0.76 respectively, and in the indicators of 'societal cultural diversity' and 'unemployment' Vancouver with 21.09 per cent and 4 per cent respectively are proved to be much stronger than the other competitors. In the culture and dependency indicator set Boston takes the first place and Vancouver, Manchester and Melbourne follow Boston's lead.

In the overall ranking of the cities in the socio-cultural development pillar of KBUD Vancouver (99.70) lags behind Boston (100) by a small margin, and Manchester (83.11) and Melbourne (78.41) take the third and fourth places.

Enviro-urban Development Analysis

The KBUD assessment framework evaluates enviro-urban development through two key indicator sets that measure the levels of sustainable urban development and the quality of life.

The first indicator set of this pillar is sustainable development. In three indicators of this set, 'sustainable transport' (45.3 per cent), 'sustainable urban development', and 'climate change mitigation', Boston receives the highest scores, but the other three cities each score very well and only a narrow margin behind. Among the four case studies, Vancouver ranks the best in moving towards achieving the 'eco-city status' (13th in 100 cities). The overall ranking for the sustainable development indicator set is, from the highest first, Boston, Melbourne, Vancouver and Manchester.

The second indicator set to define the levels of enviro-urban development is quality of place and life. Vancouver and Manchester dominate this category. Vancouver takes the first place in the international ranking of 'personal safety' and 'quality of life' (22nd and 4th in 100 cities). Manchester is ranked the best in the comparison in 'housing affordability' (4.57 per cent) and in the 'cost of living' (ranked 141st in 150 cities). This result marks Vancouver as the city with the highest quality of life and place. Manchester comes second, then Boston and Melbourne.

The overall ranking of enviro-urban development places Boston (100) at the top of the list, Vancouver (87.23) takes the second place, Melbourne (82.56) with a small margin the third and Manchester (72.25) the fourth place.

Institutional Development Analysis

The final pillar of KBUD is institutional development. The KBUD framework utilizes two indicator sets to evaluate institutional development: governance and planning, and leadership and community.

The first indicator set is governance and planning. In this set, Boston dominates other cities with achievements in 'partnership' and strong 'e-governance' systems and experience. Vancouver demonstrates outstanding 'strategic planning'. With the 'Manchester: Knowledge Capital' institution, Manchester shows world leadership in having a 'dedicated development authority' to oversee knowledge city formation and KBUD. Melbourne follows Manchester with the 'Office of Knowledge Capital' and 'Enterprise Melbourne' institutions. In this indicator set the ranking of the cities emerged as Manchester, Boston, Melbourne and Vancouver.

The second indicator set for the institutional development evaluation is leadership and community. In this indicator set, Boston and Melbourne strongly dominate the other cities. Boston leads the other three cities in establishing 'local and regional leadership' and 'public participation', whereas Melbourne is extremely successful in 'city branding' (8th in 100 cities) and in achieving relatively lower levels of 'income inequality' (0.30).

In the overall ranking of institutional development in comparing the four case studies, Boston (100) leads the other cities by only a small margin: Melbourne (98.53), Vancouver (97.20) and Manchester (91.37).

Knowledge-based Urban Development Analysis

The analysis has shown that in all four pillars of KBUD Boston overachieves when compared to the other three knowledge cities. Vancouver took the second place twice in the socio-cultural development and enviro-urban development pillars. Melbourne took second place in the other two KBUD pillars, economic development and institutional development. On the pillars where Melbourne ranked second, Vancouver ranked third. Melbourne ranked third in the socio-cultural development, and Manchester ranked third in the enviro-urban development. Overall, Manchester underachieved against Boston, Vancouver and Melbourne.

Table 18.3 Results of the comparative analysis

Pillars	Indicator Sets	BOSTON		VANCOUVER		MELBOURNE		MANCHESTER	
		Score	Normalized	Score	Normalized	Score	Normalized	Score	Normalized
Economic development	Economic structure	89.40	100.00	46.30	51.79	62.82	70.27	26.56	29.71
	Knowledge-economy performance	60.34	77.08	67.89	86.73	78.28	100.00	54.12	69.14
	Economic development total	74.87	100.00	57.10	76.26	70.55	94.23	40.34	53.88
Socio-cultural development	Social and human capitals	71.90	93.41	76.97	100.00	63.68	82.73	58.13	75.52
	Culture and dependency	82.80	100.00	77.26	93.31	57.62	69.59	70.44	85.07
	Socio-cultural development total	77.35	100.00	77.12	99.70	60.65	78.41	64.29	83.11
Enviro-urban development	Sustainable development	96.55	100.00	69.44	71.92	72.95	75.56	48.34	50.07
	Quality of place and life	65.42	91.06	71.84	100.00	60.77	84.59	68.69	95.62
	Enviro-urban development total	80.99	100.00	70.64	87.23	66.86	82.56	58.52	72.25
Institutional development	Governance and planning	82.81	94.79	81.18	92.93	82.20	94.09	87.36	100.00
	Leadership and community	94.49	100.00	91.15	96.47	92.50	97.89	74.64	78.99
	Institutional development total	88.65	100.00	86.17	97.20	87.35	98.53	81.00	91.37
Knowledge-based urban development	Knowledge-based urban development total	80.46	100.00	72.75	90.42	71.35	88.68	61.04	75.85

The overall ranking of the four case cities are formed by averaging and normalizing the scores they received from each pillar of KBUD. The analysis result has revealed that with the normalized top point of 100, as expected, Boston is the city with the highest capacity and achievements in KBUD. Boston is followed by Vancouver with a score of 90.42, Melbourne with 88.68 and lastly Manchester with a score of 75.85 (Table 18.3).

It is important to note that the ranking provided by the empirical research should not be interpreted to say that any of these cities is not performing well enough to sustain the knowledge city status. One of the purposes of using the KBUD assessment framework on highly successful knowledge cities is to show how the KBUD performance levels of the cities compare with the other benchmark cities. In this case, Boston (Greater Boston) was selected as a benchmark city to compare how Vancouver, Melbourne and Manchester perform in KBUD.

The analysis has shown that Vancouver is quite a competitive city, with opportunities in economic performance and institutional development, and in particular having a dedicated authority to oversee the KBUD of the city and the region.

Melbourne continues to rise in the Asia-Pacific region and is moving rather quickly to become the 'Boston of the Southern Hemisphere', with strong support from state and local governments, industry and businesses, university and research institutes and the unique 'Office of Knowledge Capital' and 'Enterprise Melbourne' Institutions. However, Melbourne still has a long way to go particularly in the socio-cultural and enviro-urban development areas in order to rival Boston's performance.

Manchester seems to be endeavouring diligently to regain the performance levels realized during the industrial revolution by fully adapting to the era of knowledge economy. The Manchester example also shows us that staying on top often proves a much harder and more daunting task than getting to the top. Particularly, for cities aspiring to hold knowledge city status, Manchester illustrates the importance of institutional development with its successful institution of 'Manchester: Knowledge Capital' and its achievements in a relatively short period of time.

CONCLUSION

In the knowledge era, cities need to adjust their local economies so as to be compatible with the global knowledge economy, and to develop strategies to become more competitive in order to succeed in the global competition for attracting investment and talent. However, just having a strong economy is not sufficient for cities to become competitive knowledge cities. Socio-cultural, enviro-urban and institutional developments are also important. Therefore, this chapter revealed that in the age of knowledge economy, in order to achieve prosperity, spatial restructuring of cities requires considering and responding to all four pillars of KBUD for a successful knowledge city formation.

Cities focused on the KBUD can adjust their local economies and spatial development policies so as to be compatible with the global knowledge economy. Also, by developing KBUD strategies to become more competitive, cities set the course that will enable them to gain the success they seek in global competition by providing socially just, ecologically sustainable, and organizationally strong city structures for attracting the right investment and talent. In the knowledge economy, urban areas can and should pursue knowledge-based development. Succeeding in such development will raise standards of living in the region and expand economic opportunity for residents.

The literature review and the comparative cities study provide some useful insights that other cities could consider while planning KBUD. These insights are grouped under five key points:

Firstly, a comprehensive approach is needed to develop knowledge cities. Solely focusing on economic means proved not to be successful. Therefore, cities should give enough and equal attention to all pillars of KBUD – economic, socio-cultural, enviro-urban and institutional development pillars. Beyond these pillars, the comprehensive KBUD approach should also embed a strong sustainability and organization capacity in its development process.

Secondly, KBUD is a daunting task, and therefore, policy makers need to be aware of the global economic, science and technology conditions operating in the world today. There is increasing competition from other regions to attract scientists and industry talent; knowledge carriers and whole teams are often targeted by other players to move institutions and knowledge bases. Therefore, planning and commercial strategies can certainly be structured directly to enhance the relevance of knowledge produced in a certain space but the conditions for high intensity of knowledge traffic are much more complicated than, for instance, the strategic use of land.

Thirdly, government policies, also at the local level, have a critical role to play in 'fostering the conditions' where intellectual vitality is made up of intensive collaboration networks that attract and retain knowledge carriers – i.e. agents, firms and workers. Partially this emphasis on the 'local' responds to the view that local institutions, businesses, organizations and academia are partners in fostering local development and are part of the local innovation system where they are embedded.

Fourthly, although learnings from other city experiences and exogenous assets are most valuable in strategizing KBUD, policy makers also need to build their niche and also unique development characteristics based on their endogenous assets. Only in this way can cities achieve a successful KBUD that will help them to become successful knowledge cities.

Lastly, benchmarking analysis, like the KBUD assessment framework presented in this chapter, would help cities to compare their potential and achievements and benchmark their progress against the high achiever knowledge cities such as Boston. It is the comparative analysis that makes possible the gap analysis which informs the specifics of KBUD strategies and how they could be (re)formulated to close the gap and move the city in the needed direction.

REFERENCES

Agenor P. and Montiel, P. (2008), *Development Macroeconomics*, 3rd edn, New Jersey: Princeton University Press.

Anand, S. and Sen, A. (2000), 'Human development and economic sustainability', *World Development*, **28**(12), 2029–2049.

Aron, J. (2000), 'Growth and institutions: a review of the evidence', *World Bank Research Observer*, **15**(1), 99–135.

Baum, S., Yigitcanlar, T., Horton, S., Velibeyoglu, K., and Gleeson, B. (2007), 'The role of community and lifestyle in the making of a knowledge city', Research Monograph, Griffith University, Urban Research Program, February, Brisbane, Australia.

Brinkerhoff, D. and Morgan, P. (2010), 'Capacity and capacity development: coping with complexity', *Public Administration and Development*, **30**(1), 2–10.

Carrillo, F.J. (2004), 'Capital cities: a taxonomy of capital accounts for knowledge cities', *Journal of Knowledge Management*, **8**(5), 28–46.

Carrillo, F.J. (2006), 'The century of knowledge cities', in F.J. Carrillo (ed.), *Knowledge Cities: Approaches, Experiences, and Perspectives*, New York: Butterworth–Heinemann, pp. xi–xv.

Cheng, P., Choi, C., Chen, S., Eldomiaty, T., and Millar, C. (2004), 'Knowledge repositories in knowledge cities', *Journal of Knowledge Management*, **8**(5), 96–106.

Ergazakis, E., Ergazakis, K., Metaxiotis, K., and Charalabidis, Y. (2009), 'Rethinking the development of successful knowledge cities: an advanced framework', *Journal of Knowledge Management*, **13**(5), 214–227.

Frane, A., Tomsic, M., Ronecevic, B., and Makarovic, M. (2005), *The Challenges of Sustained Development: The Role of Socio-cultural Factors in East-Central Europe*, Budapest: Central European University Press.

Friedmann, J. (2010), 'Place and place-making in cities: a global perspective', *Planning Theory and Practice*, **11**(2), 149–165.

Garcia, B. (2009), 'Making MAKCi: an emerging knowledge-generative network of practice in the Web 2.0', *VINE*, **40**(1), 39–61.

Gonzalez, M., Alvarado, J., and Martinez, S. (2005), 'A compilation of resources on knowledge cities and knowledge-based development', *Journal of Knowledge Management*, **8**(5), 107–127.

Graham, S. (2002), 'Bridging urban digital divides: urban polarisation and information and communications technologies', *Urban Studies*, **39**(1), 33–56.

Hemphill, L., Berry, J., and McGreal, S. (2004), 'An indicator-based approach to measuring sustainable urban regeneration performance', *Urban Studies*, **41**(1), 725–755.

Hezri, A. (2005), 'Utilization of sustainability indicators and impact through policy learning in the Malaysian policy process', *Journal of Environmental Assessment Policy and Management*, **7**(1), 575–595.

Knight, R. (1995), 'Knowledge-based development: policy and planning implications for cities', *Urban Studies*, **32**(2), 225–260.

Knight, R. (2008), 'Knowledge-based development: the challenge for cities', in T. Yigitcanlar, K. Velibeyoglu, and S. Baum (eds), *Knowledge-based Urban Development: Planning and Applications in the Information Era*, Hersey, PA: Information Science Reference, pp. xiii–xxv.

Laszlo, K. and Laszlo, A. (2007), 'Fostering a sustainable learning society through knowledge-based development', *Systems Research and Behavioral Science*, **24**(1), 493–503.

Lever, W. (2002), 'Correlating the knowledge-base of cities with economic growth', *Urban Studies*, **39**(5–6), 859–870.

MacKinnon, D., Cumbers, A., and Chapman, K. (2002), 'Learning, innovation and regional development: a critical appraisal of recent debates', *Progress in Human Geography*, **26**(3), 293–311.

Metaxiotis, K., Carrillo, F.J., and Yigitcanlar, T. (eds) (2010), *Knowledge-based Development of Cities and Societies: An Integrated Multi-level Approach*, Hersey, PA: Information Science Reference.

New Zealand Government (2007), 'Economic development indicators', Ministry of Economic Development, the Treasury and Statistics New Zealand.

Nguyen, T. (2010), *Knowledge Economy and Sustainable Economic Development: A Critical Review*, Munich: de Gruyter Saur.

OECD (1998), *Human Capital Investment: An International Comparison*, Paris: OECD.

Pacione, M. (2009), *Urban Geography: A Global Perspective*, London: Routledge.

Singh, R., Murty, H., Gupta, S., and Dikshit, A. (2009), 'An overview of sustainability assessment methodologies', *Ecological Indicators*, **9**(1), 189–212.

Stone, W. (2001), 'Measuring social capital: towards a theoretically informed measurement framework for researching social capital in family and community life', Research Paper No. 24, Australian Institute of Family Studies, Commonwealth of Australia, February.

Velibeyoglu, K. and Yigitcanlar, T. (2010), 'An evaluation methodology for tangible and intangible assets of city-regions: the 6K1C framework', *International Journal of Services Technology and Management*, **14**(4), 343–359.

van Winden, W., van den Berg, L., and Pol, J. (2007), 'European cities in the knowledge economy: towards a typology', *Urban Studies*, **44**(3), 252–550.

Wilson, D. and Beaton, L. (2003), *Promoting Institutional and Organizational Development: A Source Book of Tools and Techniques*, London: UK Department for International Development.

World Bank (1996), *Social Indicators of Development*, London: Johns Hopkins University Press.

World Bank (2008), *World Development Indicators*, Washington: World Bank Publications.

Yigitcanlar, T. (2009), 'Planning for knowledge-based development: global perspectives', *Journal of Knowledge Management*, **13**(5), 228–242.

Yigitcanlar, T. (ed.) (2010a), *Sustainable Urban and Regional Infrastructure Development: Technologies, Applications and Management*, Hersey, PA: Information Science Reference.

Yigitcanlar, T. (ed.) (2010b), *Rethinking Sustainable Development: Urban Management, Engineering and Design*, Hersey, PA: Information Science Reference.

Yigitcanlar, T. (2010c), 'Making space and place for the knowledge economy: knowledge-based development of Australian cities', *European Planning Studies*, **18**(11), 1767–1784.

Yigitcanlar, T. and Velibeyoglu, K. (2008), 'Knowledge-based urban development: local economic development path of Brisbane, Australia', *Local Economy*, **23**(3), 197–209.

Yigitcanlar, T., Velibeyoglu, K., and Baum, S. (eds) (2008a), *Knowledge-based Urban Development: Planning and Applications in the Information Era*, Hersey, PA: Information Science Reference.

Yigitcanlar, T., Velibeyoglu, K., and Baum, S. (eds) (2008b), *Creative Urban Regions: Harnessing Urban Technologies to Support Knowledge City Initiatives*, Hersey, PA: Information Science Reference.

Yigitcanlar, T., O'Connor, K., and Westerman, C. (2008c), 'The making of knowledge cities: Melbourne's knowledge-based urban development experience', *Cities*, **25**(2), 63–72.

Yigitcanlar, T., Velibeyoglu, K., and Martinez-Fernandez, C. (2008d), 'Rising knowledge cities: the role of knowledge precincts', *Journal of Knowledge Management*, **12**(5), 8–20.

APPENDIX

Table 18A.1 Comparative knowledge-based urban development analysis

Pillars	Indicator Sets	Indicators	Definition	Parameters	Weightings
PROFILE	Basic profile	Population	Population	Local, 2007, people	n/a
		Area	Area	Local, 2007, km^2	n/a
		Density	Density	Local, 2007, people/km^2	n/a
		Median age	Median age	Local, 2008, age	n/a
Economic development	Economic structure	Gross domestic product	Gross domestic product per capita	Local, 2007, $	3.125
		Gross domestic product growth	Rate of real gross domestic product growth	National, 2008, %	3.125
		Foreign direct investment	International share in foreign direct investment	National, 2008, %	3.125
		Household disposable income	Growth rate of household disposable income	National, 2006, %	3.125
	Knowledge-economy performance	Research and development expenditure	National share in research and development expenditure	State, 2006-2008, %	3.125
		Patents	Share in national patents	Local, 2007, %	3.125
		Knowledge workers	Ratio of knowledge workers	Local, 2006-2008, %	3.125
		Knowledge-intensive services	Ratio knowledge-intensive service employment	State, 2006, %	3.125
Socio-cultural development	Social and human capital	Educational attainment	Educational attainment rate	Local, 2006-2008, %	3.125
		Tertiary education students	Ratio of tertiary education students to population	Local, 2006-2008, %	3.125
		Major university reputation	Global ranking of the major university	Local, 2009, rank	3.125
		Access to broadband	Access to broadband ratio	Local, 2008, %	3.125
	Culture and dependency	Workplace cultural diversity	Cultural diversity ratio at workplace	Local, 2006-2008%	3.125
		Societal cultural diversity	Ratio of overseas and interstate migrants	Local, 2006-2008%	3.125

BOSTON		VANCOUVER		MELBOURNE		MANCHESTER	
Value	Score	Value	Score	Value	Score	Value	Score
4588680	n/a	2116581	n/a	3371888	n/a	2573500	n/a
7,393	n/a	2,422	n/a	6,816	n/a	1,281	n/a
620	n/a	874	n/a	495	n/a	2,009	n/a
34.50	n/a	34.60	n/a	36.10	n/a	35.00	n/a
81499.00	100.00	43287.00	53.11	45345.00	55.64	39992.00	49.07
2.02	88.21	0.41	17.90	2.29	100.00	0.55	24.02
17.54	100.00	2.49	14.20	2.59	14.77	5.13	29.25
3.93	69.40	5.66	100.00	4.58	80.89	0.22	3.89
5.54	38.90	8.78	29.96	29.31	100.00	14.41	49.16
6.70	31.31	12.50	58.41	21.40	100.00	3.50	16.36
43.30	91.14	47.51	100.00	20.34	42.81	32.20	67.78
50.00	100.00	41.59	83.18	35.15	70.30	41.60	83.20
35.50	77.29	45.93	100.00	19.88	43.28	21.42	46.64
1.24	34.73	1.71	47.90	3.57	100.00	1.53	42.86
1.00	100.00	40.00	60.00	36.00	64.00	26.00	74.00
32.20	75.59	42.60	100.00	20.21	47.44	29.40	69.01
44.40	100.00	22.51	50.70	33.51	75.47	18.60	41.89
6.60	31.29	21.09	100.00	9.95	47.18	18.60	88.19

Table 18A.1 (continued)

Pillars	Indicator Sets	Indicators	Definition	Parameters	Weight-ings
		Socio-economic dependency	Age-population ratio of those in and not in the labour force	Local, 2006-2008, value	3.125
		Unemployment	Unemployment rate	Local, 2007, %	3.125
Enviro-urban develop-ment	Sustain-able deve-lopment	Eco-city status	Eco-city ranking	Local, 2010, rank	3.125
		Sustainable transport	Ratio of sustainable transport use	Local, 2006–2008, %	3.125
		Sustainable urban development	Statutory development plans emphasizing sustainability	Local, 2010, value	3.125
		Climate change mitigation	Strategies in place for climate change adaptation or mitigation	Local, 2010, value	3.125
	Quality of place and life	Housing affordability	Median house price ratio to median annual income	Local, 2006–2008, %	3.125
		Cost of living	Cost of living raking	Local, 2008, rank	3.125
		Personal safety	Personal safety ranking	Local, 2008, % rank	3.125
		Quality of life	Quality of life ranking	Local, 2010, rank	3.125
Institu-tional develop-ment	Govern-ance and planning	Dedicated development authority	Knowledge-based urban development authority	Local, 2010, value	3.125
		Strategic planning	Strategic planning for knowledge-based development	Local, 2010, value	3.125
		Partnerships	Triple-helix and public-private partnerships	Local, 2010, value	3.125
		e-Governance	e-governance ranking	National, 2008, rank	3.125
	Leader-ship and comm-unity	Local and regional leadership	Local and regional level leadership	Local, 2010, value	3.125
		City branding	City brand ranking	Local, 2006, rank	3.125
		Public participation	Public participation in decision making	Local, 2010, value	3.125
		Income inequality	Income inequality level	National, 2005, gini coeffiency	3.125
Knowledge-based urban development				Normalized values	100.000

BOSTON		VANCOUVER		MELBOURNE		MANCHESTER	
Value	Score	Value	Score	Value	Score	Value	Score
0.76	100.00	0.86	58.33	0.98	8.33	0.87	54.17
4.10	99.90	4.00	100.00	4.50	99.48	6.40	97.50
25.00	86.21	13.00	100.00	25.00	86.21	99.00	1.15
45.30	100.00	24.47	54.02	15.00	33.11	20.82	45.96
4.00	100.00	3.95	98.75	3.90	97.50	3.85	96.25
4.00	100.00	1.00	25.00	3.00	75.00	2.00	50.00
5.97	74.22	7.72	41.99	8.04	35.10	4.57	100.00
99.00	70.21	64.00	45.39	36.00	25.53	141.00	100.00
99.00	39.84	22.00	100.00	29.00	91.03	99.00	39.84
37.00	77.40	4.00	100.00	18.00	90.41	99.00	34.93
2.75	68.75	2.50	62.50	3.50	87.50	4.00	100.00
2.50	62.50	4.00	100.00	3.50	87.50	3.00	75.00
4.00	100.00	2.75	68.75	2.50	62.50	3.50	87.50
4.00	100.00	7.00	93.48	8.00	91.30	10.00	86.96
4.00	100.00	3.20	80.00	3.30	82.50	3.10	77.50
23.00	89.44	16.00	94.37	8.00	100.00	99.00	35.92
4.00	100.00	3.70	92.50	3.50	87.50	3.60	90.00
0.38	88.50	0.32	97.73	0.30	100.00	0.34	95.14
80.46	100.00	71.35	90.42	72.76	88.68	61.04	75.85

19. Benchmarking: knowledge-based development metrics through the MAKCi exercise

Alicia Leal and Blanca C. Garcia

INTRODUCTION

Researchers and practitioners have agreed that one of the difficulties in creating and sustaining knowledge cities is the lack of benchmarks to identify those cities and regions that are generating knowledge-driven initiatives, thus triggering development and collective value for their regions (Chase, 2007). In such a challenging context, some key notions have emerged in recent years to characterize such benchmarks.

Following a knowledge-based development (KBD) perspective, this chapter will report on research findings obtained from statistical modelling applied to knowledge city benchmarking methodologies. The main objective is to put forward a knowledge-based taxonomy as a methodological tool to identify how tacit knowledge conversion generates quantitative intangible indicators by means of simulation and pattern modelling (Montgomery et al., 2006). For urban communities around the world, such research could provide valuable information to build their own knowledge-city quantitative taxonomy, and make comparative identifications of those key elements of knowledge-leveraging capabilities that greatly impact cities' knowledge capital.

Indeed, a parallel benchmarking difficulty is creating a city's systemic accountable base or taxonomy once the city's contextual benchmarks have been established. The first part of the chapter will thus depict how at this point in the benchmarking process, the Generic Capitals System (GCS) emerges as a value-based, knowledge management (KM) model that attempts a systemic, integrative perspective for city taxonomy building (Carrillo, 2002, 2004). It elicits a systematic assessment of a city's capital base (both tangible and intangible) and its capacity to recombine it in innovative ways. The taxonomy considers eight major capital categories, each one eliciting a number of subcategories according to the city it is attempting to characterize (Carrillo, 2004). The GCS categories adhere to the notion of knowledge as a social construction, in which the emergence of knowledge societies adopting knowledge-based frameworks is encouraged.

In this regard, a number of international authors have explored paths into monitoring and developing capital systems taxonomies with the GCS. It has been a point of departure or comparison in order to identify knowledge-leveraging as a core strategy in the landscape of emerging knowledge-based societies. The reset part of the chapter will thus expand on such research work and collaboration, elicited by the GCS taxonomy in recent years, and the metrical implications it has triggered (Garcia, 2010; 2008).

The chapter will then introduce a practical application of the GCS. It stems from recent research on knowledge city index pursuits, built on statistical probability. It will use logistic models to identify city benchmarking, and has used the Most Admired Knowledge Cities (MAKCi) consultation exercise as part of its input for statistical modelling. This chapter will thus advance some applications on how emerging models of knowledge-intensive networks such as MAKCi foster tacit knowledge-conversion and exploration of consensus patterns of knowledge city benchmarking.

A GENERIC CAPITALS SYSTEM

In considering different categories for potential knowledge cities in terms of size and nature, a parallel difficulty is creating a systemic accountable base once a specific benchmark has been established. A tool for knowledge city benchmarking is the value-based Generic Capitals System (GCS) taxonomy. It adheres to the notion of knowledge as a social construction, in which the emergence of knowledge societies adopting knowledge-based frameworks (third generation of knowledge management schemes) is encouraged. In this regard, a number of international bodies such as WB, UNO, OECD and the European Union have pointed out the path to monitoring and developing human capital (Carrillo, 2002: 379). It is believed that through knowledge-creation and learning schemes as core strategies in the landscape of emerging knowledge-based societies, development can actually flourish. Hence, the GCS emerges as a value-based third-generation KM model (Carrillo, 2006: 47) that attempts a systemic, global and comprehensive perspective that builds upon key points from successive generations of knowledge management frameworks. It elicits a systematic assessment of a city's capital base (both tangible and intangible) and its capacity to recombine it in innovative ways. The taxonomy considers eight major capital categories:

- C1. Identity capital
- C2. Intelligence capital
- C3. Financial capital
- C4. Relational capital
- C5. Human Individual capital
- C6. Human Collective capital
- C7. Instrumental-material capital
- C8. Instrumental-knowledge capital.

These eight GCS capital dimensions adhere to definitions of the knowledge city (KC) as a city 'purposefully designed to nurture knowledge' (Dvir and Pasher, 2004: 17). A knowledge city (KC) is 'a region that bases its ability to create wealth on its capacity to generate and leverage its knowledge capabilities through knowledge-based extended networks formed by enterprises and people' (Chatzkel, 2004: 62). In broader and also more concrete terms, a KC is one 'in which its citizenship undertakes a deliberate, systematic attempt to identify and develop its capital system, with a balanced and sustainable approach' (Carrillo, 2004: 34).

The underlying rationale for this taxonomy is to satisfy the formal requirements of value production as a complete, consistent and homogeneous system (Carrillo, 1998, 2002). The GCS builds upon other efforts to identify and value collective individual capital at either city or regional levels. This taxonomy identifies the basic capital elements of productive systems and its 'meta-capitals': those other forms of capital not productive in themselves but significantly leveraging the system's overall capacity. The GCS advances that a global orientation in measurement would 'advance accurate achievements, by means of a complete, consistent, systematic and inclusive capital system' (Carrillo, 2002). This is exemplified in the MAKCi nomination formats and general principles of the exercise. For these and other examples of practical capital taxonomy, please refer to the MAKCi reports and executive summaries, available for download from the World Capital Institute website, where each capital is given a practical dimension as each city displays its traits and components of intangible wealth.

MAKCi Impact within the KBD Community

The Most Admired Knowledge City (MAKCi) Awards have been established to create knowledge-based benchmarks. Over time, MAKCi foresees providing public sector officials, business and social leaders with the tools and indicators needed to improve knowledge creation, dissemination and re-use – ultimately resulting in an improved standard of living for all members of communities and regions (Chase, 2007). MAKCi study insights have indeed been relevant to the KBD community for a few reasons: it is clear that several cities and/or regions are in the process of forming a top tier of MAKCi winners. Likewise, another group of cities and regions is actively pursuing a knowledge-driven strategy, thus creating the possibility of entering MAKCi's top tier. On the other hand, there is growing evidence that most cities and regions have yet to understand the significant implications of not strategically managing societal knowledge creation, dissemination and re-use. Researchers from different regions around the world have understood such needs, and have regarded MAKCi as an innovative option amongst the existing KBD indexes and taxonomies.

Indeed, the knowledge-based development literature has long recognized the role that local city-regions may also play in the furtherance of the wellbeing agenda (Dvir and Pasher, 2004; Chatzkel, 2004). In that sense, Passerini identifies MAKCi as a useful multi-rater technique of eight capital dimensions (Passerini and Wu, 2008) in a conceptual discussion on how to identify the level of knowledge-creation and wellbeing of cities. Ergazakis (2009) on the other hand, uses MAKCi as a comparative tool for benchmarking research on K-Cities. On the practitioner side, Duekert et al. (2009), state how by generating an annual MAKCi nomination, the taxonomy has proved useful for city marketing and communication, while Batra (2008) uses the MAKCi taxonomy as a framework for developing Regional Knowledge Development Indices. Batra also found MAKCi can be used for evaluating the extent and effectiveness of the processes for acquisition, sharing and utilization of knowledge across regions. This applies to countries or cities, as well as to micro-level communities such as villages (Batra, 2008). Moreover, Chatzkel (2009) takes the MAKCi framework as a starting point in his journey into a thorough reviewing exercise and evaluates if MAKCi nominations are actually demonstrating a sound KC development effort. The assumption is that an improved 'MAKCi 2.0' version of the exercise could provide a more verifiable working model to evaluate if a city/region is galvanizing the necessary elements to achieve a sustainable knowledge-based environment (Chatzkel, 2009). Moreover, as Wang et al. (2008) put it in their own context, MAKCi as a knowledge city framework constitutes an inspirational model for urban construction in China from both theoretical and practical perspectives. These highlights exemplify how a knowledge-based taxonomy and index are intensely sought after in the universe of the knowledge societies, and how MAKCi can be relevant to a number of like-minded researchers around the globe.

A CONTEXTUAL CASE: THE MAKCi EXERCISE

Launched in November 2006, the Most Admired Knowledge City Awards (MAKCi Awards) is a consensus study that includes an annual consulting exercise established to identify and recognize those communities around the world that are successfully engaging in formal and systematic knowledge-based development processes under the flag of Knowledge Cities (WCI, 2007). The MAKCi consultation was first convened in early 2007, as a joint knowledge-based initiative of Teleos' Most Admired Knowledge Enterprises (MAKE) and the World Capital Institute (WCI). MAKCi merged the MAKE Awards methodology, with the WCI Generic Capitals System (GCS) taxonomy, resulting in the MAKCi Framework©, described earlier. Following these perspectives, the MAKCI Awards can be defined as a 'knowledge-based initiative whose contribution to innovation depends largely on human imagination and creativity and the knowledge assets available at a point in time and context' (Malhotra, 2000, in Goh, 2004). The MAKCi exercise, as a collaborative research study, represents a community space dedicated to build meaningful, collective knowledge that would contribute on an annual basis to the understanding of knowledge cities dynamics and transformations. Hence, the MAKCi exercise aims at structuring and mapping knowledge. It elicits tacit knowledge conversion through process-mapping and products (i.e. 2007 MAKCI Report). It also aims to develop knowledge databases – documenting best practices, expert directories, K-Cities intelligence etc., while also embedding knowledge within the MAKCi process.

A Delphi Iterative Cycle

The cornerstone of the MAKCi exercise is a consultation to a panel of experts, which is integrated on an annual basis by invitation only. A MAKCi executive committee invites the participation of researchers and practitioners with credentials in Intellectual Capital (IC), knowledge management (KM), knowledge-based development (KBD), and/or knowledge-based urban development (KBUD). As part of the emerging global network, experts are invited to interact on a virtual platform with fellow researchers and practitioners, all of them coming from diverse disciplines, regions, nationalities and ways of life. They converge in this consultation space to discuss and establish the relative future development capacities of worldwide urban communities by assessing their capital value base. In practice, the MAKCi Panel of Experts seemingly acts as a social knowledge network. Even further, as it conglomerates experts from a number of specific KBD regional CoPs, it fits the identified notion that characterizes it as a Network of Practice or NoP (Augier and Vandelo, 1999). In the MAKCi context, network membership seems to encompass knowledge-generating (learning) experiences tightly linked to the perceived belonging to the MAKCi network. Participants in the annual panel are offered access to first-instance information on knowledge-based development and knowledge city trends that could be of interest in their academic research activities, business-related ventures, research socialization and/or public sector activities (Garcia, 2010). Hence, their network membership motives could also include a sense of professional commitment to their local KBD community, a desire to increase and collaborate in the KBD emerging field and also a willingness to be part of the greater KBD community, especially where KM/KBD practitioner groups are limited or isolated in their local setting (Wasko and Faraj, 2008).

MAKCi Process and Methodology

The MAKCi consultation follows the Teleos adaptation of the Delphi technique used in the MAKE Awards, which has been replicated for MAKCi purposes. The Delphi Technique facilitates the identification of perceptual knowledge within a group of specialists involved in knowledge-intensive research. It therefore involves intensive and focused discussions, interactions and collective agreements that are supported by a virtual discussion platform during the three-stage duration of the MAKCi Exercise. Congregated around the annual MAKCi consulting exercise, the invited panel of experts selects nominee cities, finalist cities and winner cities in three successive voting rounds that actually reflect the profiles and dynamics of cities succeeding in the application of knowledge-based development initiatives, as follows:

MAKCi Round 1: Nominations

The first round of participation requires invited experts to nominate as many cities as they consider have the merits to be included as candidates and to provide reasons for each nomination. Nomination is based on the MAKCi Framework© and the MAKCi Nomination Form® as the tools to standardize the key elements of each nomination. Nomination information is made available at a discussion platform so as to allow the exchange of views on candidate cities on a permanent basis.

MAKCi round 2: selection of finalists

During this stage of the MAKCi process, and based on previous discussion on the MAKCi platform, participants choose their knowledge city finalists from the nominated cities, and send their votes on an automated survey platform for final count.

MAKCi round 3: selection of winners

During this final stage of the MAKCi process, participants choose their three favourite K-City winners amongst the finalists, and send their votes by the MAKCi automated survey which will count for the final voting results. Experts are encouraged to cast their vote over eight specific capital-based criteria stated in the MAKCi Framework, which is based on an assessment of a city's capital base (both tangible and intangible) and its capacity to recombine it in innovative ways. The major capital categories are derived from the Generic Capitals System, from which capitals criteria are emphasized. The MAKCi Framework, along with the MAKCi Nomination Form, are the key instruments to assist the panel of experts in determining which cities are worth the recognition and award status that the MAKCi exercise conveys.

MODELLING THE MAKCi CASE

In the first five years of the exercise, MAKCi was challenged first and foremost by a lack of accurate information at city level, that could standardize its nomination process. Such a lack was somewhat alleviated by expert participation and reliability. A well-informed panel was gathered and empowered to bring first-hand city information to the discussion forum. Hence, the information gap triggered quite a few research efforts into the path of purpose-built internationally known indexes (i.e. United Nations, 2010/2011; World Bank, 2010; OECD, 2009; European Commission, 2008; 2ThinkNow, 2010; GfK Group, 2009; GAWC, 2008; FDIMagazine, 2009/2010; Eurostat, 2010/2011; Cushman and Wakefield, 2010; Foreign Policy, 2010; Institute for Urban Strategies and The Mori Memorial Foundation, 2010; Mercer, 2010a; Mercer, 2010b; UBS, 2010; *Forum for the Future*, 2010 etc.: see Garcia, 2011; Gonzalez, 2011; Lin and Wen (2010) for reviews of these indexes). This supported comparisons between information availability and expert reliability for a sound KC benchmarking. Furthermore, some of this research yielded to the emergence of an algorithm to compare cities, information availability and expert reliability for an international cross-benchmarking standard that could complement collective MAKCi Index research (Gonzalez, 2011).

Further research was encouraged following cross-benchmarking efforts, using a statistical logistic model applied to the data from the MAKCi exercises 2007, 2008, and 2009. The research reported in this chapter was set out to develop a mixed logistic model, combining parts of both existing indicators and experts' opinions that could build statistical logistic scenes. A logistic model fed by existing capital dimensions indicators and experts' opinions on intangible capitals could thus elicit representative indicators. Thus, the present research first concentrated on an internal validation of the MAKCi exercise. As reported later in the chapter, the methodological steps used to build two possible statistical analysis scenarios were:

1. Definition of each capital applied to knowledge cities.
2. Formal definition of dimensions, variables and indicators for each capital.
3. Search for existing indicators concerning city level (for most cities).
4. Establish which capitals could be measured by indicators and which could be considered by opinion of experts.
5. Prepare the measuring instrument to collect data.
6. Activate the dynamics for data collection process.
7. Contact an expert participating sample.
8. Develop the exercise of data collection for selected cities.
9. Develop the statistical analysis.
10. Establish the model leading to the KC Index for the cities of interest.

The MAKCi exercise statistics, as described in previous sections of this chapter, provided the information considered in the present statistical modelling. Data available from experts voting during the third round of the exercise during three consecutive years (2007–2009) was the basis of the initial analysis, which is reported below. However, further factorial modelling scenarios fed by existing capital dimensions are beyond the scope of this chapter, and have been left for a future report on MAKCi metrical research.

Statistical Modelling for MAKCi

Regression analysis is a methodology that aims to establish a statistical relationship between two or more quantitative variables by means of a model, in order to predict the existence of a variable by the outcome of other interacting variables (Kutner et al., 2004). There are several types of regression models, but we shall focus attention on two particular models: the linear multiple regression model and the logistic regression model.

The linear multiple regression model is shown by the expression

$$y_i = \beta_0 + \beta_1 x_{1i} + \beta_2 x_{2i} + \ldots. + \beta_{p-1} x_{p-1i} + \xi_i$$

where: y_i represents the value of the variable of response (variable of interest) for the ' ith' observation; $\beta_0, \beta_1, \beta_2, \ldots, \beta_{p-1}$ represent the parameters of the model $x_{1i}, x_{2i}, \ldots, x_{p-1i}$ represent the values of the predicting variables (related variables) for the ' i ' observation, and ξ_i is the error term related to the ' ith' observation.

In this chapter, the model was adjusted using sample data by means of the minimum-chi-square (MCS) method. In order to be adopted, the method requires that the error standard deviation, considered itself a random variable, fulfils the following three conditions: it must be independent, with a normally distributed random variable with zero mean values and a constant variance.

Once parameters are obtained for the adjustment model it is preferable to perform an analysis of variance test (ANOVA) to verify that the opposing relation has scope at population level and that it is not only a matter of sampling behaviour. If the population relationships are verified to do forecasting, then the efficiency of the model is checked through a determination coefficient. If this measurement turns out to be satisfactory, tests should be performed to verify the adequacy of the model.

Researchers such as Box et al. (1978) emphasize the fact that a statistical relationship does not necessarily come from a causal relation, and could be only a behaviour relationship. It is the analyst's responsibility to decide on the causality of the variables. Hence, Montgomery et al. (2006) highlight that the relevance of this type of model remains determined by the context in which it is used, mostly in interpolations that remain endorsed by the sampling evidence.

Indeed, if the model is deemed suitable, the variable of interest must be considered as a randomly continuous variable that is normally distributed, which can impact in the forecasting and the interpretations derived from the use of the model.

Before a model was confirmed, research analysed other kinds of predictive models, in particular the logistic regression model:

$$\log\left(\frac{p_i}{1 - p_i}\right) = \beta_0 + \beta_1 x_{1i} + \beta_2 x_{2i} + \ldots. + \beta_{p-1} x_{p-1i} + \xi_i$$

where: p_i represents the probability of success in the 'ith' observation, $\beta_0, \beta_1, \beta_2, \ldots, \beta_{p-1}$ represent the parameters of the model, $x_{1i}, x_{2i}, \ldots, x_{p-1i}$ represent the value of the predictive variables (related variables) in the ' i ' observation, and ξ_i is the error term related to the ' ith' observation.

This model highlights that the explanatory variable increases the probability of the outcome. A large regression coefficient means that the risk factor strongly influences the probability of that outcome, while a near-zero regression coefficient means that the risk factor has little influence on the probability of that outcome. Logistic regression is a useful way of describing the relationship between one or more independent variables (e.g., age, sex) and a binary response variable, expressed as a probability, that has only two possible values, such as 'exists' or 'does not exist' (Christensen, 1997). Once the model is obtained, the scope, the efficiency and the adequacy of the model should be checked through statistical G2. Indeed, the analysis of regression is a very powerful and well founded statistical tool to forecast data behaviour. Therefore, the success of the analysis depends completely on the correct use of the tests and on making maximum use of the conclusions derived from such tests.

The eight capitals that compose the MAKCi framework were taken into account to perform the following statistical modelling, resulting in a MAKCi endogenous index.

By comparing the results of three successive editions of the MAKCi exercise, the possibility of establishing a model which could predict the relative position of the cities from the evaluation with its eight capital dimensions was explored. This had the aim of establishing an index with which each individual city could be identified, benchmarked and recognized as advancing initiatives of knowledge-based development. A first approach to the data was run with the information from the years 2007–09 by means of correlations between different capitals and inference from multiple regression models (see Tables 19.1 to 19.3).

In Table 19.1, highly similar correlations were observed between the different capitals, as well as with the order voters conferred to capital scores.

In contrast to the observed correlations in Table 19.1, in Table 19.2 some low correlations were observed between the eight capital dimensions and the variable 'place', while the capital correlations remain similar in both years.

In Table 19.3, higher correlations appear among the capitals, but not very high for the 'place' variable.

By analysing the difference between the correlations from one year to the next and comparing the results from Tables 19.1, 19.2 and 19.3, the Delphi method exercise in the MAKCi Awards changed somewhat. In 2007 the experts postulated the city that they considered to be the first, second and third place in every capital of the capital system, granting a score from 1 to 10 (where 10 is the highest). In the years 2008 and 2009, each expert proposed a city for the first place and then separately granted a score for the eight capitals, with the same procedure for the second and third places.

Table 19.1 Correlation coefficient of Pearson for the year 2007 data

r-Pearson 2007	Place	C1	C2	C3	C4	C5	C6	C7	C8
Place	1.00								
C1	−0.68	1.00							
C2	−0.67	0.77	1.00						
C3	−0.46	0.69	0.70	1.00					
C4	−0.61	0.71	0.70	0.71	1.00				
C5	−0.48	0.65	0.73	0.69	0.79	1.00			
C6	−0.57	0.76	0.83	0.63	0.71	0.76	1.00		
C7	−0.55	0.70	0.76	0.82	0.75	0.81	0.75	1.00	
C8	−0.59	0.61	0.76	0.62	0.76	0.78	0.71	0.77	1.00

Table 19.2 Correlation coefficient of Pearson for the year 2008 data

r-Pearson 2008	Place	C1	C2	C3	C4	C5	C6	C7	C8
Place	1.00								
C1	−0.33	1.00							
C2	−0.32	0.73	1.00						
C3	−0.24	0.60	0.60	1.00					
C4	−0.30	0.71	0.71	0.54	1.00				
C5	−0.34	0.63	0.64	0.48	0.51	1.00			
C6	−0.34	0.56	0.63	0.51	0.59	0.70	1.00		
C7	−0.33	0.70	0.63	0.68	0.64	0.50	0.58	1.00	
C8	−0.42	0.70	0.65	0.59	0.63	0.65	0.74	0.69	1.00

Table 19.3 Correlation coefficient of Pearson for the year 2009 data

r-Pearson 2009	Place	C1	C2	C3	C4	C5	C6	C7	C8
Place	1.00								
C1	0.36	1.00							
C2	0.25	0.81	1.00						
C3	0.36	0.72	0.71	1.00					
C4	0.38	0.81	0.81	0.71	1.00				
C5	0.32	0.80	0.77	0.68	0.81	1.00			
C6	0.38	0.77	0.77	0.76	0.80	0.84	1.00		
C7	0.29	0.72	0.76	0.76	0.72	0.70	0.70	1.00	
C8	0.42	0.77	0.77	0.72	0.80	0.77	0.84	0.78	1.00

Table 19.4 Model of multiple regression for place *of the cities*

Predictor	Coef	SE Coef	T	P	VIF
Constant	5.1805	0.3072	16.86	0.000	
C1	0.00514	0.05488	0.09	0.926	3.3
C2	0.10645	0.05474	1.94	0.053	3.2
C3	0.01486	0.04396	0.34	0.736	2.2
C4	0.00294	0.05109	0.06	0.954	3.1
C5	–0.02300	0.05210	–0.44	0.659	3.1
C6	–0.11646	0.05944	–1.96	0.052	3.5
C7	–0.02522	0.04951	–0.51	0.611	2.5
C8	–0.35251	0.06028	–5.85	0.000	3.4

S = 0.616867 R–Sq = 44.7% R–Sq(adj) = 42.2%

Analysis of Variance

Source	DF	SS	MS	F	P
Regression	8	55.3150	6.9144	18.17	0.000
Residual Error	180	68.4945	0.3805		
Total	188	123.8095			

Note: The regression equation is place = 5.18 + 0.0051 C1 + 0.106 C2 + 0.0149 C3 + 0.0029 C4 – 0.0230 C5 – 0.116 C6 – 0.0252 C7 – 0.353 C8

Due to the difference in the data collection for the year 2007 with regard to 2008 and 2009, it was determined to analyze only the information for the years 2008 and 2009 to avoid discrepancies. From observing the correlations, several models of multiple regression emerged. The place assigned by the experts was considered as the response variable and the capitals variable was considered as the predicting variable in the model. Once the atypical observations were eliminated the resulting models are as shown in Table 19.4.

Using the statistical software 'Minitab' to analyse obtained results, it is observed in Table 19.4 that it is possible to model the variable 'place' according to the eight capitals. The analysis of variance appears also with a lower p-value than 0.05, which leads us to conclude that there is a relation between the variable 'place' and the eight capital dimensions. Considering the variability value of 42 per cent in the variable 'place', looking at the capitals system we can imply that for the resulting model, such percentage should increase to improve the model.

Moreover, the adaptation of the model can be verified by observing Figure 19.1 with the residuals obtained in the 'Minitab'. In this graph it is shown that the assumptions are not fulfilled in the error structure established for the models of linear multiple regressions. Therefore, it was determined that this is not a suitable and reliable model to work with.

Despite the promising predictions, there are some considerations that must be taken into account for this benchmarking model:

1. The response variable for the regression model is a continuous variable, whereas in reality it represents an ordinal variable, which greatly impacts the interpretation of adjusted values.
2. Figure 19.1 of the fitted value against the residuals presents/displays a pattern that was highly expected due to the nature of the variables showing the lack of error in homoscedasticity and the assumption of a binomial behaviour.

Therefore a second approach to the data was considered but this time through logistic models. A different application of the logistic models (which predict the probability of occurrence of an event) was attempted for the purposes of this research. It advanced a statistical order for the cities stemming from experts' voting interventions that considered cities as Most Admired Knowledge Cities (MAKCi). The data were reorganized and the response variable was considered as a dichotomizing variable:

The city is considered as a Most Admired Knowledge City =1 or
The city is not considered as a Most Admired Knowledge City =0.

From this idea it is considered that positioning a city can be done by predicting the probability it has to be chosen as a Most Admired Knowledge City considering the allocation of the experts in the eight capital dimensions. Considering the data of two years 2008 and 2009 and after the exposition of a series of models from a constructivist perspective it is considered that the best modelling alternative is the use of a model of multiple logistic regression shown in Table 19.5.

Figure 19.2 (logistic regression) shows the considered values of the parameters of the model along with the associated p-values, but they will be interpreted with reserve due to the possible presence of multicollinearity (a relation that enters the assigned evaluations to the capital dimensions), in order to thoroughly review the complete model and the predictive power that each of the capitals can elicit.

For instance, seemingly both the levels of Human Collective capital and Instrumental-knowledge capital show an increase. This would have a significant effect on the probability of being considered as a Most

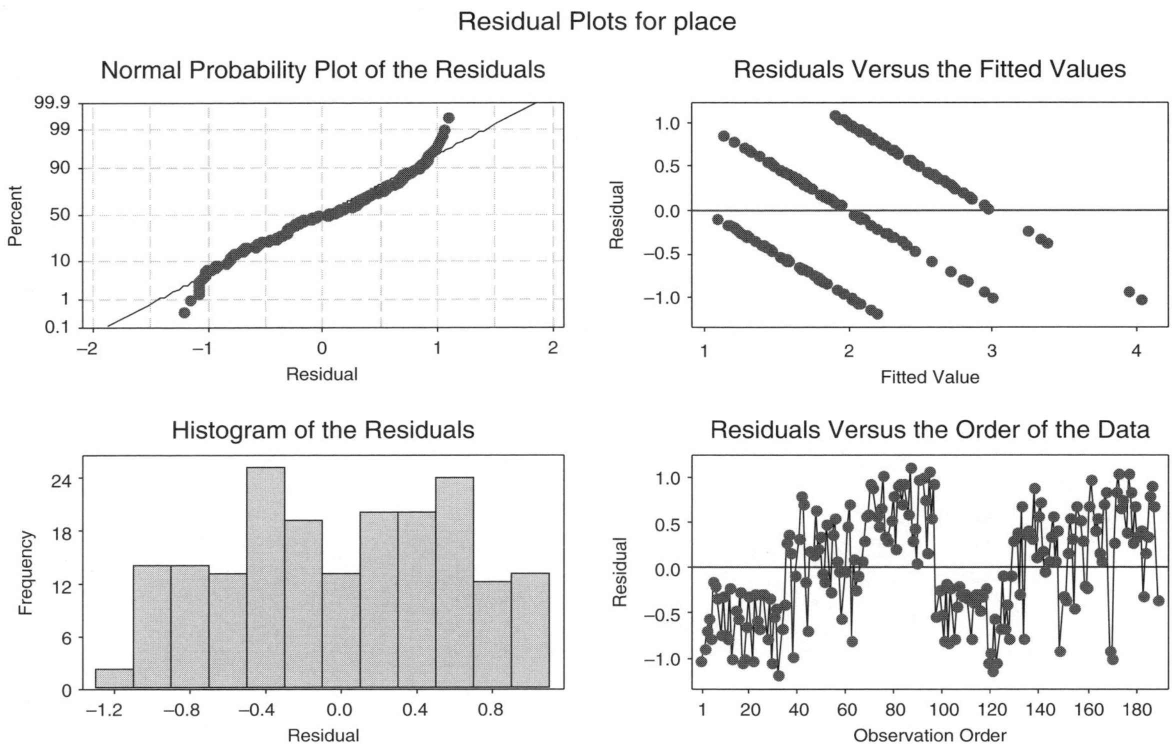

Figure 19.1 Residuals test for the model in Table 19.4.

Table 19.5 Model of logistic binary multiple regression for the variable 'place' for cities reviewed

Predictor	Coef	SE Coef	Z	P	Odds Ratio	95% Lower	CI Upper
Constant	–14.7250	2.21340	–6.65	0.000			
C1	0.177596	0.218180	0.81	0.416	1.19	0.78	1.83
C2	–0.143603	0.221756	–0.65	0.517	0.87	0.56	1.34
C3	0.0533521	0.184432	0.29	0.772	1.05	0.73	1.51
C4	0.0429494	0.210985	0.20	0.839	1.04	0.69	1.58
C5	0.0803247	0.209750	0.38	0.702	1.08	0.72	1.63
C6	0.412353	0.236410	1.74	0.081	1.51	0.95	2.40
C7	0.334628	0.213512	1.57	0.117	1.40	0.92	2.12
C8	0.671215	0.251246	2.67	0.008	1.96	1.20	3.20

Log-Likelihood = –100.801
Test that all slopes are zero: G = 95.093, DF = 8, p-value = 0.000

Goodness-of Fit Tests

Method	Chi-Square	DF	P
Pearson	172.722	183	0.696
Deviance	193.963	183	0.275
Hosmer-Lemeshow	18.963	8	0.015
Brown: General			
Alternative	2.350	2	0.309
Symmetric Alternative	1.915	1	0.166

Table of Observed and Expected Frequencies:
(See Hosmer-Lemeshow Test for the Pearson Chi-Square Statistic)

Value	Group 1	2	3	4	5	6	7	8	9	10	Total
1											
Obs	0	0	1	5	8	4	15	12	13	23	81
Exp	0.0	0.5	2.0	3.5	5.9	7.7	10.8	14.2	17.4	19.0	
0											
Obs	23	22	22	18	15	18	8	11	10	0	147
Exp	23.0	21.5	21.0	19.5	17.1	14.3	12.2	8.8	5.6	4.0	
Total	23	22	23	23	23	22	23	23	23	23	228

Measures of Association:
(Between the Response Variable and Predicted Probabilities)

Pairs	Number	Percent	Summary Measures	
Concordant	10210	85.7	Somers' D	0.72
Discordant	1679	14.1	Goodman-Kruskal Gamma	0.72
Ties	18	0.2	Kendall's Tau-a	0.33
Total	11907	100.0		

Link Function: Logit

Response Variable	Information Value	Count	
place	1	81	(Event)
	0	147	
	Total	228	

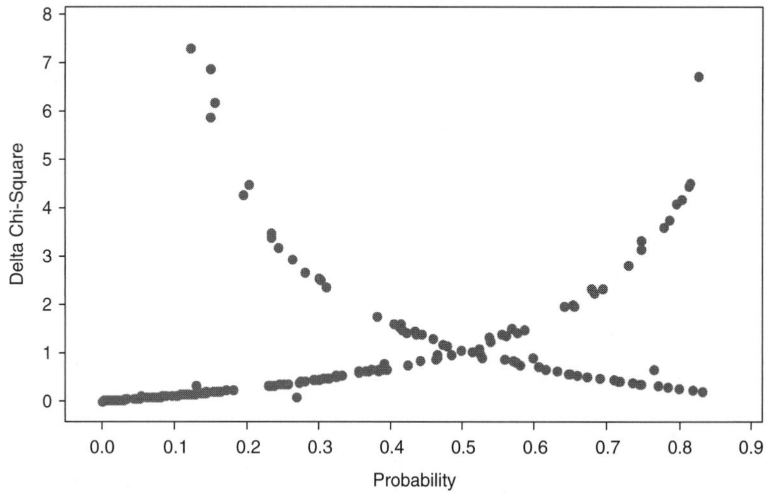

Figure 19.2 Test Delta Chi-Square vs. Probability

Admired Knowledge City to have an odds-ratio greater than the unit (>1). This means that those cities that count on greater values in these two capitals will have higher probabilities of being considered as 'most admired'.

As the statistical G is used to resist the hypothesis that all the coefficients in the model associated with the predicting variables are null, the associated p-value of 0,000 (see Figure 19.2) ratifies that at least one of the capitals explains the probability of the city to be considered as a Most Admired Knowledge City.

In the section of Goodness-of-Fit Test, in Figure 19.2, the associated p-values are the tests of Pearson, Deviance and Hosmer-Lemesshow and are greater than 0.05, so it is not possible to reject the model as it adjusts suitably to the observed data, as shown in Figure 19.2.

Finally, by observing Figure 19.2 we can remark that the majority of the observations are explained by the model itself, which helps to confirm that the model of logistic binary regression is adapted for the forecast of the probability that every city has to be considered the Most Admired Knowledge City.

Considering the information in Table 19.5, the logistic model of regression is established as follows:

$$\ln\left(\frac{p}{1-p}\right) = F(C_i)$$

where

$$F(C_i) = -14.725 + 0.17759\,C_1 - 0.1436\,C_2 + 0.05335\,C_3 + 0.04294\,C_4 + 0.08032\,C_5 + 0.41235\,C_6 + 0.33462\,C_7 + 0.67121\,C_8$$

It is deduced from here that the probability that a city has to be classified as the Most Admired Knowledge City is given for:

$$p = \frac{1}{1 + e^{-F(C_i)}}$$

so that any city that is evaluated using the capitals system will be able to be represented by such a probability.

CONCLUSION: GENERATING MAKCi BENCHMARKING TOOLS

Considering the average evaluation established by the experts in the different capitals for some cities assumed in a three-year period of MAKCi Awards, the information contained in Table 19.6 is obtained.

In Table 19.6, the column F(Ci) shows the prediction that the logistic model esteem for each city, the column *p* establishes the probability corresponding to each city to be considered as a Most Admired Knowledge City and the column MAKCi Index shows the square root of the probability as a form to attenuate the values of the probabilities.

From the full quantitative analysis displayed during these first research steps, it is advanced that the MAKCi index consists of the root of the probability associated with the logistic binary model to be considered as the Most Admired Knowledge City.

A MAKCi benchmarking, through city positioning, is therefore here advanced for the corresponding values obtained, which has been able to objectively determine a subjective panel of experts consensus. An advantage in establishing this model is that the index can be flexible/mobile by re-ordering the new annual information as it becomes available, consequently updating the valuable information at each edition of the exercise. It has therefore become apparent that the logistic models represent a valuable tool to establish the relation between these variables. Nevertheless, as of today the information obtained is limited. It is important to emphasize that from the statistical point of view, this MAKCi endogenous benchmarking model turns out to be very appropriate to explain the relation between the value in each one of the eight capital dimensions and the position as the Most Admired Knowledge City. For future MAKCi exercises,

Table 19.6 MAKCi Index for the cities nominated in the exercises MAKCi 2007, 2008 and 2009

Year	City	Generic Capital System										
		Identity C1	Intelligence C2	Financial C3	Relational C4	Human Ind C5	Human Col C6	Instr Tangible C7	Instr Intangible C8	$F(C_i)$	p	MAKCi Index
2007	Barcelona	9.2	9.0	7.0	9.4	8.8	9.0	9.7	8.4	−0.30	0.42	0.65
	Bilbao	9.2	8.3	8.3	9.0	8.5	8.8	8.5	8.7	−0.48	0.38	0.62
	Boston	8.0	8.7	8.9	8.8	8.5	8.0	9.5	9.2	−0.38	0.40	0.64
	Ottawa	8.3	9.0	8.0	9.5	9.3	9.3	8.0	9.5	−0.09	0.48	0.69
	Singapore	9.2	9.4	9.3	9.1	7.8	8.9	8.9	8.9	−0.32	0.42	0.65
2008	Bangalore	7.7	8.7	8.3	8.0	8.3	8.3	8.0	8.7	−1.21	0.23	0.48
	Manchester	8.9	8.7	8.0	8.4	8.1	8.3	8.9	9.0	−0.54	0.37	0.61
	Montreal	9.0	9.0	8.5	8.5	10.0	9.5	8.0	9.5	0.17	0.54	0.74
	Ottawa	8.7	8.4	8.4	8.4	9.0	8.7	9.3	9.1	−0.02	0.50	0.70
	Singapore	9.1	8.7	9.1	9.1	8.1	8.4	9.7	9.0	−0.09	0.48	0.69
	Valencia	10.0	9.8	8.6	9.4	9.8	9.6	9.2	9.6	0.77	0.68	0.83
2009	Barcelona	9.1	8.6	8.6	9.1	9.1	8.6	8.6	9.3	−0.10	0.48	0.69
	Boston	8.3	9.3	9.0	9.0	9.3	9.3	9.3	10.0	0.72	0.67	0.82
	Istanbul	9.0	9.0	9.0	8.0	8.0	8.0	10.0	8.0	−0.94	0.28	0.53
	Manchester	9.3	8.8	7.8	9.3	9.0	8.8	8.0	8.8	−0.65	0.34	0.59
	Melbourne	8.8	8.3	9.0	8.3	9.0	8.5	8.5	8.7	−0.63	0.35	0.59
	Montreal	9.8	9.3	8.8	9.5	9.5	9.8	8.3	9.3	0.31	0.58	0.76
	Shenzhen	8.7	7.3	9.7	8.0	7.3	8.7	9.3	9.7	0.39	0.60	0.77
	Valencia	10	9.8	9.6	9.6	9.8	9.6	9.6	9.8	1.10	0.75	0.87

such a model would expect that experts evaluate all finalist cities for a better appreciation of the information made available during the yearly exercise.

This chapter has attempted to explore statistical modelling capabilities in order to use the capitals that define the MAKCi taxonomy resulting in a MAKCi endogenous index. It is expected that a new path into research could be open to seek for other statistical exercises in order to better define a MAKCi index from a knowledge-based development perspective. Such research aspirations continue and a later report with new findings is expected at the end of the research project.

In the meantime, the MAKCi study aims to continuously provide new statistical data in order to enable planners, politicians, economists, and business and social leaders to create robust, viable strategies and approaches for enhanced urban design and development. The MAKCi exercise, in any case, is seemingly building a knowledge city observatory in which emerging urban development trends are evidenced. Indeed, MAKCi has firmly started a trailblazer journey as an authoritative resource for both the academic and practitioner communities. Designed to illustrate a practical knowledge-based development case, this piece of research work has thus explored how MAKCi can be a benchmarking tool collectively constructed, discussed and evaluated, making it relevant and useful to a number of like-minded researchers and practitioners around the globe.

REFERENCES

Augier, M. and M.T. Vandelo (1999), 'Networks, cognition and management of tacit knowledge', *Journal of Knowledge Management*, **3**(4), 252–261.

Batra, S. (2008), 'Developing regional knowledge development indices to support assessment of the global competitiveness of regions', Ghaziabad, India: Institute of Management Technology.

Box, G., W. Hunter, and J. Hunter (1978), *Statistics for Experimenters. An Introduction to Design, Data Analysis and Model Building*, New York: John Wiley & Sons.

Carrillo, F.J. (1998), 'Managing Knowledge-based value systems', *Journal of knowledge Management*, Special Issue on Knowledge-based Development II: Knowledge Cities, **8**(5), 61–72.

Carrillo, F.J. (2002), 'Capital systems: implications for a global knowledge agenda', *Journal of Knowledge Management*, Special Issue on Knowledge-based Development, **6**(4), 379–399.

Carrillo, F.J. (2004), 'Capital cities: a taxonomy of capital accounts for knowledge cities', *Journal of Knowledge Management*, Special Issue on Knowledge-based Development II: Knowledge Cities, **8**(5), 28–46.

Carrillo, F.J. (ed.) (2006), *Knowledge Cities: Approaches, Experiences and Perspectives*, Burlington, MA: Butterworth-Heinemann (Elsevier).

Chase, R. (2007), 'Foreword to the Most Admired Knowledge City (MAKCi) Report', *World Capital Institute and Teleos*, http://www.worldcapitalinstitute.org/makci, accessed 28 February 2011.

Chatzkel, J. (2004), 'Greater Phoenix as a knowledge capital', *Journal of Knowledge Management*, Special Issue on Knowledge-based Development II: Knowledge Cities, **8**(5), 61–72.

Chatzkel , J. (2009), 'A capabilities approach for building sustainable knowledge-based cities', 2nd Knowledge Cities World Summit, November, Shenzhen, China. Conference URL: http://kmrc.ise.polyu.edu.hk/kcsummit2009/eng/index.html

Christensen, R. (1997), *Log-Linear Models and Logistic Regression*, 2nd edn, Springer Texts in Statistics, New York: Springer.

Duekert, S., M. Hiegl, and J. Trinkwalter (2009), 'Regional knowledge management: the case of the metropolitan region Nuremberg (Germany)', *2nd Knowledge Cities World Summit*, November, Shenzhen, China. Conference URL: http://kmrc.ise.polyu.edu.hk/kcsummit2009/eng/index.html

Dvir, R. and E. Pasher (2004), 'Innovation engines for knowledge cities: an innovation ecology perspective', *Journal of Knowledge Management*, Special Issue on Knowledge-based Development II: Knowledge Cities, **8**(5), 16–27.

Ergazakis, K. (2009), 'Rethinking the development of successful knowledge cities: an advanced framework', *Journal of Knowledge Management*, Special Issue on Knowledge-based Development II: Knowledge Cities, **13**(5), 89–113.

Garcia, B. (2008), 'Global KBD community developments: the MAKCi experience', *Journal of Knowledge Management*, Special Issue on Knowledge-based Development II: Knowledge Cities, **12**(5), 129–141.

Garcia, B. (2010), 'Making MAKCi: an emerging knowledge-generative network of practice in the Web 2.0', *Journal of Information Systems and Knowledge Management,* Special Issue on Web 2.0 and the Evolution of KM, **40**(1), 125–136.

Garcia, C. (2011), 'Measuring Knowledge-based development: an overview of models and methodological issues', *International Journal of Knowledge-based Development* (Special issue on Knowledge-based Development metrics), in press.

Goh, A. (2004), 'Enhancing organizational performance through knowledge innovation: a proposed strategic management framework', *Journal of Knowledge Management Practice*, accessed 20 May 2007.

Gonzalez, O. (2011), 'Cities cross-benchmarking: MAKCi as a meta-ranking exercise', *International Journal of Knowledge-Based Organizations*, Special Issue on Knowledge-based Development, in press.

Kutner, J., A. Nachtsheim, and W. Neter (2004), *Applied Linear Regression Models*, 4th edn, Irwin: McGraw Hill.

Lin, C.Y. and Wen, C.T. (2010), 'Future centre in Taiwan: incubation process', Paper submitted to the 2010 Knowledge Cities World Summit, Melbourne, Australia.

Malhotra, Y. (2000), 'Knowledge assets in the global economy: assessment of national intellectual capital', *Journal of Global Information Management*, **8**(3), 5–15.

Montgomery, D., E. Peck, and G. Vining (2006), *Introduction to Linear Regression Analysis*, 4th Edn, New York: John Wiley & Sons.

Passerini, K. and D. Wu (2008), 'The new dimension of collaboration: mega and intelligent communities, ICT and well-being', *Journal of Knowledge Management*, Annual Special Issue on Knowledge Cities, **12**(5), 155–167.

Wang, D., Q. Wang, and J. Bie (2008), 'A review on theoretical progress of knowledge cities', Shenzhen, China: Shenzhen Graduate School, Harbin Institute of Technology.

Wasko, M. and S. Faraj (2008), 'The web of knowledge: an investigation of knowledge exchange in networks of practice', *Academy of Management Journal*, **33**(4), 258–272.

WCI (World Capital Institute) (2007), 'The Most Admired Knowledge City (MAKCi) Report', World Capital Institute and Teleos, http://www.worldcapitalinstitute.org/makci/history (accessed 28 June 2010).

20. Afterword

Concluding: directions for building prosperous knowledge cities

Joris van Wezemael

KNOWLEDGE-BASED (URBAN) DEVELOPMENT

The collection of chapters in this book witnesses both the vibrancy and the challenges of an engagement with the relations of knowledge, space and place. Making policies, plans and metrics for building prosperous knowledge cities meets a number of challenges. Challenges emerge from the intrinsic heterogeneity of the research field that has been coined as knowledge-based (urban) development (KB(U)D). It is heterogeneous because of the multi-disciplinarity of the field, which is nicely reflected by the contributing authors (see their biographical notes). The many facets of knowledge and their 'natural' strings to management, psychology, decision-making, planning policy-making or economics give a leverage to the KB(U)D debate.

However, the 'multiplicity' of the main headliner – 'knowledge' – complexifies simple notions of KB(U)D. Furthermore, the relation of 'knowledge' and 'development' is a fuzzy one. It is commonly acknowledged that much knowledge and learning is retrospective in nature (Weick 1995). Also, knowledge seems to be both an intimate friend and a complete stranger as it slips away when one tries to pin it down. This aspect reminds me of Wittgenstein's notion that the aspects of things that are most important for us are hidden because of their simplicity and familiarity.

'Development', on the other hand, may include diverse issues such as green development, land development, real estate, urban planning, economic development, human development (humanity), social development or sustainable development, to name but a few. Although most of the chapters in this book refer mainly to economic development (which is but one aspect of social change), this is neither necessary nor follows the knowledge capital idea in the sense the World Capital Institute and its main promotor Javier Carrillo (2004) define.

Given this rough outline the term 'knowledge' – excessively used these days – might run the risk of becoming an empty signifier that, as a prefix, adds but some gloss to more traditional debates. A precursor of such a faith is the term 'sustainability' in its historical adaptation (and abuse) through science, politics and various industries. Consequently, being given the honour of contributing with an afterword I would like to reflect on the question: how does (or could) our current 'knowledge' debate differ from other/older debates on cities? I will do so with an argument that includes four points:

- an invocation to feed off controversies, 'celebrate' uncertainties and address the uncertain relation of knowledge and action,
- an inquiry of how we can 'steer' with regard to 'self-organization' in KB(U)D,
- a notion on the deliberative potential of knowledge-based development, and
- the specificity of the 'U'(rban) with regard to KBD.

KNOWLEDGE: A MATTER OF FACT OR A MATTER OF CONCERN?

Firstly, I would like to introduce a productive uncertainty by highlighting the difficult and in many cases not so straightforward relations of knowledge and action. Certainly, I share the view that we must engage in an intense debate on knowledge. As von Hayek (quoted in Duguid, 2005) explains, division of labour implies a division of knowledge and the adding of knowledge to knowledge becomes the main driver of value creation (Drucker, 1993). This makes clear that the need for knowledge acting on knowledge is not generated by information and communication technologies (ICT) (as some debates seem to suggest) – rather, it is a twin of any form of social, spatial and economic organization that is based on the division of labour or that allows or generates a diversification of lifestyles, respectively. Therefore, as a matter of fact, an increasing division and diversification (that is partly enabled by ICT) fuels the need to recombine knowledge and let it act on itself.

However, as Kreiner (2011) states, 'knowledge society deserves its label not because of an abundance of knowledge, but because of a highly and consistently problematic stature of the link between knowledge and action.' This link – as a matter of concern (Latour, 2005) – is disputed in relevant contexts (be it in management studies or in business decision-making; in planning theory or in 'doing' stakeholder participation). I believe that the epistemic uncertainty between 'knowledge' and 'action' is one reason for the excessive use of terms such as 'creativity' in this context. Here I refer to epistemological uncertainty that refers to indeterminate knowledge of future consequences, a type of uncertainty typically related to the repercussions of cultural or social milieus, since the models representing such systems are so complex that predictions are unreliable. I suggest that a focus on the disputes may save our debates from a premature, ready-made notion of knowledge-based development: it lets the thing itself – knowledge – be deployed as a multiple and celebrates William James's notion of a 'Pluriverse'. I have explained elsewhere (van Wezemael, 2008b) that the complexifying nature of knowledge has been described in the analysis of project ecologies, geographies of knowledge-creation or in science and technology studies. Learning processes are fuelled by the connection of heterogeneous elements (practices which belong to different places or to different projects or organizations) and – given a learning environment – from the encounter with novel and unexpected processes. Pieces of data and information from previous work, elements of knowledgeability from different practices and sites, individual beliefs and experiences, collective narratives, guidelines from various organizations (e.g. in urban governance settings), meshworks of hardware (such as computer or traffic infrastructure) and also specific software and ICT network-designs form heterogeneous assemblages. Therefore, what a person, a project team, or an organization can do refers to its (collective) knowing. Collective knowing, again, emerges from the connections at one 'scale' (e.g. subjects in project teams) and therefore is an emergent property of the next larger scale (e.g. project teams). Therefore the components become part of the knowledge they produce. 'Knowing' thus 'cannot any longer be attributed to the knower, who participates in a further stage of becoming not reducible to his knowledge' (Phillips, 2006). Knowing always lies in between, in the connection.

Thus, as a first point I argue that we should feed off the controversies that we have towards 'knowledge' as a multitude instead of jumping to conceptions of knowledge as a link in simple means-to-ends relations.

STEERING, PLANNING AND STRATEGIZING

Secondly, on the basis of the uncertain relation of knowledge and action I would like to highlight the question of agency with regard to making policies and plans. Throughout the chapters there is a shared understanding among the authors that specificities of a knowledge-based development call for alternatives to top-down approaches and that we lack a single overview position. This highlights a second specificity of KB(U)D, as Franz in this book argues: '(A) "Knowledge City" development strategy hardly can be initiated by top-down command; it requires the voluntary involvement of a vast number of actors at different political levels.' In the same line Garner and Dornan, also in this book, argue that we can learn more from the 'how' than from the 'what' (and in a next step we should, I suggest, engage also more in the Deleuzian 'why'). They thus highlight a processual level and critically point at the limits of the transferability of so-called best practice. Here, the argument could receive some support from the Latourian notion that there can be no transport without transformation, and that any transport must pay its full costs of transaction (Latour 2005, p. 221). Furthermore, Garner and Dornan state that

> in the 'science' of knowledge-based economic development the ingredients are now well documented. However, ingredients can be combined into many recipes and those who are engaged in the process bring their own individual approach to that combination. . . . Cloned economic development strategies fail in the knowledge-based economy – where by definition, it is the unique combination of creativity and innovation that power success.

They thus argue for a truly relational approach, which, as I believe, must also be applied to knowledge itself (van Wezemael et al., 2011). Drawing on Garner and Dornans 'ingredients-and-recipe' metaphor I would like to point out some underlying ontological assumptions as they can become productive with regard to the question of agency, steering, and to the selection of epistemic strategies. If we, in this context, briefly reflect on the differences between simple, complicated and complex systems we can use Westley et al.'s (2006) analogies that relate a simple system to baking a cake, a complicated system to sending a rocket ship to the moon and a complex adaptive system to raising a child. The development of a city is more akin to a baby, exhibiting significant unpredictability within generally known (albeit very broad) patterns of overall development. Imagine a parent raising a child as though it was a linear system entirely subject to known specifications! These thoughts position KB(U)D in close proximity to complexity thinking, and they moot pressing questions of agency, multiple causation and self-organization (see for example the literature on planning and complexity).

Thus, in my reflection on agency (steering, planning, strategizing) in KB(U)D, notions of self-organization become paramount as no command-and-control architecture of governance can keep up with the openness of becoming and the multitude of agents and their actor-views.

I would like to argue that 'steering' in self-organized collectives (such as organizations, cities or city regions) is best understood as a trial-and-error exploration of possibility spaces (van Wezemael, 2010). This, in turn, calls for a failure-tolerant culture.

A NEOLIBERAL AGENDA?

If knowledge is viewed as a multiplicity (see above), then, and this is my third point, KB(U)D must reach beyond a neoliberal agenda. Whereas concepts such as knowledge capital offer a rich potential to seek for alternative urban becomings, there is also a strong attraction towards knowledge-and-development as an already-given, subjugating economic goals such as 'efficiency and growth'. However, we need to avoid this temptation in order to tap into the deliberative potential of 'knowledge' that is always disputed (see above), that cannot be 'owned', that is collective in nature, that only exists and only can become productive as it transgresses boundaries (of the individual, of peers, of teams, of organizations, of city regions etc; see Nonaka and Takeuchi, 1995).

The deliberative potential of 'knowledge' defines another bundle of specificities for KB(U)D. If 'knowledge' and 'value' are viewed and performed as unquestioned 'givens' that move along the 'molar lines', subjugating molecular voices (van Wezemael, 2008a), then they determine in advance what is noise and what are voices to be heard and to be debated. I argue in the line of Javier Carrillo (2004) and others when I stress the goal of admiring diverse sets of knowledge and ways of knowing that can be productive for all kinds of social innovation (Moulaert and Sekia, 2003) that is yet unknown and not limited from the start; this can also save 'knowledge' from becoming just another prefix to mainstream urban and regional policies.

Consequently, knowledge as a starting point for (urban) development urges us to engage in controversial questions that address what is the '(common) good', what makes a development 'right', and so on. Here emerges another aspect in the sense of a goal of what an engagement with KB(U)D is: 'Knowledge City' will not become just another buzzword for (merely) economically competitive cities; KB(U)D will not simply add to the past labels such as entrepreneurial and competitive cities and city regions. Or, more positively, using Powell's words (in this book), KB(U)D must aim at 'co-producing many different kinds of value'.

Another lesson with regard to the specificity of KB(U)D can be learnt with regard to 'making metrics'. As the now-classical criticism of Jane Jacobs highlights: just because a neighbourhood or a city does not score in the top rank of economic productivity does not mean that the quality of life, the density of social relations and place diversity are low! Authors do now consider that, given the multiplicity of knowledge, dimensions of KB(U)D withstand simple addition. Yigitcanlar in this book states that '(S)olely focusing on economic means proved not to be successful', and, 'although learnings from other city experiences and exogenous assets are most valuable in strategizing KBUD, policy makers also need to build their niche and also unique development characteristics based on their endogenous assets'.

However, I do not neglect that economic prosperity is important. Indeed, it is a pressing issue, and in many cases it is the starting point for getting stakeholders involved in novel strategies for a place. Accordingly, the vast majority of contributions in this book and the broader field aim for a kind of primary economic development. However, I point at the danger that sticking to an unbalanced discussion stratifies the debate and may not be the most productive deliverable from academic reflection (as economic development agencies and firms already advocate this point).

. . . AND THE CITY

My last point tackles the specificity of the 'urban' for KBD, starting from Massey's notion that space matters (2005). I will argue that we should handle the celebrated 'urban renaissance' with care as there are significant repercussions that appear on the horizon. A number of contributions in this book argue that 'leveraging urban form (does) optimize human interaction', as Martinus states, or that 'urban projects (. . .) are gradually improving its attractiveness and "urban atmosphere" by mixing residential, work and cultural functions' (Fernández-Maldonado in this book). However, although there is evidence that certain urban/spatial settings can increase KBD, there is certainly no guarantee that they always will do so, and, as has been argued above, any copy-paste strategy is very likely to fail as no strategy or technology ever works in total isolation.

Rather, the topological 'nature' of space leads to a complication of things. Heidegger famously explained that 'Dasein bringt schon die Sphäre möglicher Nachbarschaft mit sich; es ist von Hause aus schon Nachbar zu. . .' (1953, p. 138). Or, in the words of Thrift (1999),

> [W]e can easily say that space complicates because it immediately injects a notion of distribution. For the entire notion that we live in an infinite web of meaning, the fact is that this web is differentially distributed. Its elements do not crop up everywhere equally, however often deferred. Spatial distribution,

> by itself, can therefore begin to account for much of what happens in the world: from the start, the geographical world is a messy one, it does not cohere.

Space therefore means difference; it produces an order of concomitance with distinct and emerging properties.

KB(U)D, I would like to argue, stages knowledge cities as exceptionally dense intertwinings of physical, social, economic, mental and technological networks which, as a consequence, give rise to a relational notion of knowledge recombination and knowledge, thus, creation (van Wezemael, 2008b). It wants to tap into the potential for knowledge-creation that is related to the superimposition of a large number of relational networks. Here, Florida's shiny concept of a 'good people climate' has been influential. It is said to attract and retain creative and talented people who may fertilize the ground for a competitive business climate, and a good and competitive business climate (in turn brings about economic growth). This climate calls for high-quality housing, work empowerment, and a specialized consumption mix with whatever is already there. This very 'mix' generates topologies and neighbourhoods (see above). However, at least from a central European perspective, the celebrated renaissance of the (knowledge) city manifests itself in an increased density of buildings (not necessarily of people as the average floor space continues to increase), and altered forms of spatial organization (such as the juxtaposition of different groups with regard to social status or income as in 'gentrification' processes) call for an 'organization of disorder' (in the sense of Agamben's definition of security) in urban space. Urban renaissance and the (alleged) celebration of diversity may indeed erode the very substance of some knowledge-based development as the massive boom of security industries in city regions may indicate. This is because the rediscovered vibrancy of the urban coincides with a culture of fear and a neurotization of citizens (Isin, 2004). Such an urban society develops tendencies towards various forms of insularity (enclaves and exclaves of which gated communities are only one example). Thus, a reinforced attraction of so-called knowledge-workers should be aware of such repercussions that erode the very basis of the abovementioned 'good people climate'.

CONCLUDING REMARK

In this brief afterword, I made the claim that, in order to deliver an original contribution to urban development we should both recall and develop the specificities of KB(U)D. A relational view on knowledge and on space and place seems in line with empirical findings. But it also challenges key conceptions of scale such as the very relation of the 'local' and the 'global' that lose their essentialist modes of existence. Latour's strategy of 'localizing the global', 'redistributing the local' and 'connecting sites' may well be elaborated with regard to knowing and knowledge. As directions for building prosperous knowledge cities I suggested to harvest knowledge as a multiplicity, a deeper inquiry into knowledge and self-organization, an appreciation of the deliberative potential of knowledge and a careful handling of KBD with regard to place diversity.

REFERENCES

Carrillo, F.J. (2004), 'Capital cities: a taxonomy of capital accounts for knowledge cities', *Journal of Knowledge Management*, **8**(5), 28–46.

Drucker, P.F. (1993), *Post-Capitalist Society*, Oxford: Butterworth Heinemann.

Duguid, P. (2005), 'The art of knowing: social and tacit dimensions of knowledge and the limits of the community of practice', *Information Society*, **21**, 109–118.

Heidegger, Martin (1953), *Einführung in die Metaphysik*, Tübingen: Max Niemeyer Verlag.

Isin, Engin F. (2004), 'The neurotic citizen', *Citizenship Studies*, **8**(3), 217–235.

Kreiner, S. (2011), 'Dialogues and the problems of knowing: reinventing the architectural competition', *Scandinavian Journal of Management*, **27** (1), 160–166.

Latour, B. (2005), *Reassembling the Social*, New York: Oxford University Press.

Massey, D. (2005), *For Space*, London: SAGE.

Moulaert, F. and Sekia, F. (2003), 'Territorial innovation models: a critical survey', *Regional Studies*, **37**(3), 289–302.

Nonaka, I. and H. Takeuchi (1995), *The Knowledge Creating Company. How Japanese Companies Create the Dynamics of Innovation*, New York: Oxford University Press.

Phillips, J. (2006), 'Agencement/assemblage', *Theory, Culture & Society*, **23** (1–2), 108–109.

Thrift, N. (1999), 'The place of complexity', *Theory, Culture and Society*, **16** (3), 31–69.

van Wezemael, Joris (2008a), 'The contribution of assemblage theory and minor politics for democratic network governance', *Planning Theory*, **7** (2), 165–185.

van Wezemael, Joris (2008b), 'Knowledge creation in practice', in Scott Baum, Koray Velibeyoglu and Tan Yigitcanlar (eds), *Knowledge-based Urban Development*, Hershey: Idea, 1–20.

van Wezemael, Joris Ernest (2010), 'Modulation of singularities – a complexity approach to planning competitions', in Jean Hillier and Patsy Healey (eds) *The Ashgate Research Companion to Planning Theory. Conceptual Challenges for Planning Theory*, Aldershot: Ashgate.

van Wezemael, J.E., J. Silberberger and S. Paisiou (2011), 'Collective decision making in juries of urban design competitions', *Scandinavian Journal of Management*, **12** (1), 167–172.

Weick, K.E. (1995), 'Sensemaking in organizations', Thousand Oaks: Sage Publications.
Westley, F., B. Zimmerman and M.Q. Patton (2006), 'Getting to maybe: how the world is changed', Toronto: Vintage Canada.

Index